The Last Bur

The Last Bungalow

Writings on Allahabad

Edited by
Arvind Krishna Mehrotra

PENGUIN BOOKS

PENGUIN BOOKS
Published by the Penguin Group
Penguin Books India Pvt. Ltd, 7th Floor, Infinity Tower C, DLF Cyber City,
Gurgaon 122 002, Haryana, India
Penguin Group (USA) Inc., 375 Hudson Street, New York, New York 10014, USA
Penguin Group (Canada), 90 Eglinton Avenue East, Suite 700, Toronto, Ontario,
M4P 2Y3, Canada
Penguin Books Ltd, 80 Strand, London WC2R 0RL, England
Penguin Ireland, 25 St Stephen's Green, Dublin 2, Ireland (a division of Penguin
Books Ltd)
Penguin Group (Australia), 707 Collins Street, Melbourne, Victoria 3008, Australia
Penguin Group (NZ), 67 Apollo Drive, Rosedale, Auckland 0632, New Zealand
Penguin Books (South Africa) (Pty) Ltd, Block D, Rosebank Office Park, 181 Jan
Smuts Avenue, Parktown North, Johannesburg 2193, South Africa

Penguin Books Ltd, Registered Offices: 80 Strand, London WC2R 0RL, England

First published by Penguin Books India 2007

Typeset in Minion Regular by SÜRYA, New Delhi
Printed at Repro India Ltd., Navi Mumbai

A PENGUIN RANDOM HOUSE COMPANY

to the memory of Ravi Dayal
(1937–2006)
whose family appears inside

Contents

List of Illustrations

Fanny Parkes: 'The Ice Pits' and 'Temple of Bhawani and Suttees Alopi Bagh' from *Wanderings of a Pilgrim* (1850).

Matilda Spry: 'Rout of the Mutineers at Allahabad by Colonel Neill', 'The Judges' Court-House and Gallows at Allahabad', and 'Mess-House of the Officers of the 6th Bengal N.I., at Allahabad' from *Narrative of the Indian Revolt* (1858) by Sir Colin Campbell.

Rudyard Kipling: The Pioneer Press (2005); photo: Raghoo Sinha.

Edmonia Hill: 'Muir College Staff 1889' from *A History of the Muir Central College, 1872–1932* (1938) edited by Amaranatha Jha, and Advertisement from the *Pioneer* of 8 September 1888.

Amaranatha Jha: 'Group Photograph 1923' from *Sarojini Naidu: A Personal Homage* (n.d.) by Amaranatha Jha.

Sudhir Kumar Rudra: 'Cartoons of Allahabad University's Economics Department teachers by Saeed Jaffrey' from *Allahabad University Magazine*, Diamond Jubilee Number (1947).

Kate Chisholm: Advertisement from the *Pioneer* of 1 June 1888.

Kama Maclean: 'Contemporary Print of Tirtha Raj Prayag'.

Acknowledgements

I am grateful to the following for their advice and practical assistance during the preparation of this book: Rosinka Chaudhuri, Kate Chisholm, Ravi Dayal, Shamsur Rahman Faruqi, Indira Ghose, Lalit Joshi, Kama Maclean, Nandini Mehta, Hemendra Shankar Saxena, and Raghoo Sinha.

A Note on the Selection

First-hand accounts of pre-colonial Allahabad are few and far between. This selection, of necessity therefore, is focused mainly on the colonial city, from its rise, in roughly 1800, to its catastrophic end two hundred years later.

A Note on the Text

Most of the selections in this anthology are given without excisions. The few places where excisions became necessary are indicated by an ellipsis between paragraphs or between sentences in the text.

Descendants: An Introduction

'He was courteous to a fault and spoke beautiful English,' is how someone who was one of his students in the early 1970s described him.

'What did he teach?' I asked.

'Shakespeare.'

'What was he like as a teacher?'

'I can't say.'

'Why?'

'Because he seldom came to class. Well, he came a few times and then gave us a long list of things to read, Caroline Spurgeon, G. Wilson Knight, M.C. Bradbrook, you know what I mean. The next we heard he had left for Holland, to teach in a school there. He had a droll sense of humour.'

Arun Kumar Bhattacharya was a short, compact, neat-looking man. He had a bald head with a fringe of grey hair and a round, pleasant face. Occasionally, I would run into him in the English department of Allahabad University, where we both taught. He was twenty years older than me, but that was not why we did not have much to say to each other. There was something prickly about him, and I kept my distance. I always noticed, however, that Bhattacharya took great care over his appearance. His cotton shirts, even at the end of a hot day, looked freshly laundered, and his expensive leather sandals, it seemed, were dust-repellent. He lived in a yellow and white bungalow at the corner of Thornhill and Albert Road, and drove an Ambassador car, which, more so since he was often its only occupant, appeared to be too big for him, like an oversized jacket. He was a bachelor.

Although Bhattacharya had spent most of his life in Allahabad, he was not a native of the city. Unknown even perhaps to himself, he was part of a long migration that had brought increasing numbers of Bengalis, mainly, but other communities as well—Kashmiri Pandits, Gujarati Nagars, a few entrepreneurial Parsis—to Gangetic upcountry towns in the second half of the nineteenth century. What drew these people to places like Patna, Allahabad, and Cawnpore were the new opportunities in education and medicine, business and trade, the administration and the judiciary, opened up, ironically, by colonialism. The 'British Empire was the empire of Steam', Jan Morris has remarked, but though built as part of the infrastructure of colonialism and staffed chiefly by Anglo-Indians, the railways were crucial to this Indian migration.

∾

The colonial city of Allahabad, the area today known as Civil Lines, stands on the site of eight villages, which the British, to teach the natives a lesson, razed to the ground after the Mutiny of 1857. 'Helpless women, with suckling infants at their breasts, felt the weight of our vengeance no less than the vilest malefactors,' wrote a historian of the Mutiny of events in the city. And one British officer spoke of his day's work thus:

> One trip I enjoyed amazingly; we got on board a steamer with a gun, while the Sikhs and the fusiliers marched up to the city. We steamed up throwing shots right and left till we got up to the bad places, when we went on the shore and peppered away with our guns, my own old double-barrel bringing down several niggers.

In 1858, the year in which the governance of India passed from the East India Company to the Crown, the capital of the North-Western Provinces shifted from Agra to Allahabad. The changes to Allahabad which this brought about would have seemed dramatic to its inhabitants at the time. A significant rise in building construction followed the increase in the town's population, particularly around 1870. In the space of little more than a decade, centuries of isolation gave way to cosmopolitanism; village settlements to city roads and parks, tower clocks and spires, bandstands and covered markets, gymkhana clubs and newspaper offices, law courts and colleges, hospitals and libraries. To the rural sounds of belled cattle returning home was added the rattle of the latest printing machines of the Pioneer Press and the ping of the shuttlecock from a game of badminton in progress in the gardens of Belvedere House, described by a late nineteenth-century resident as 'a famous old bungalow which [had] been standing since the Mutiny days of 1857'. Belvedere House is where, in 1888, Rudyard Kipling wrote his short story 'Baa Baa, Black Sheep' and which, later, he recalled in 'Rikki-Tikki-Tavi'.

New service quarters *mohullas*—Allengunj near the university, Lukergunj near the railway station—came up to accommodate the growing population, and even today if one goes there one gets the feeling that one has come to a different part of the country. The shop signs are in Bengali and banner ads for 'Ranga-Java Deluxe Sindur' hang outside.

The Kashmiri Pandits had no *mohulla* of their own, but that is because many of them were vakils and made enough money on the High Court Bar to live more grandly. In the 1880s, Ajudhia Nath Kunzru was earning something like Rs 80,000 a year from his practice alone. Sir Tej Bahadur Sapru's palatial house on Albert Road has been torn down, and so has Kailash Nath Katju's on Edmonstone Road, but Motilal Nehru's Anand Bhavan still stands, a two-storey white building with a colonnaded verandah running round it. Judging by the standards of the time, it is not very large, nor is it ostentatious in the same way that contemporary Bania- or Punjabi-Gothic is. Motilal appears to have been a man of taste.

In Civil Lines, where initially only the British could occupy the bungalows, some of the best business establishments were Parsi-owned. Guzders was a bar and restaurant, T. Shaporjee & Sons was a general merchant's, C.D. Motishaw and Co., a car and motorcycle showroom, and J.M. Patell described itself as 'Photographers and Artists'. Opposite the High Court was Hotel Finaro. Owned by Rhoda Gandhi, it has been home to many generations of British and American researchers who have come to Allahabad to consult the regional archives after Independence or work in the record rooms of the High Court, the Commissioner's office or the Municipal Board.

∽

From the road, which was once Hastings Road and is now Nyaya Marg, the small six-room Hotel Finaro looks like someone's house. One of Allahabad's few remaining colonial bungalows, one part of it is still a private residence. Rhoda Gandhi's son Rustam now lives there. He runs the hotel, in addition to managing his manufacturing business.

A heavily built man in his mid-sixties, with a broad forehead and a lumbering walk, Rustam was wearing a bright chequered shirt and navy-blue trousers when I first met him. We sat in the verandah, where the only furniture was some straight-backed chairs, two of which we occupied. The ambience could not have been more unhotel-like.

Rustam said, 'If you want to know about Allahabad Parsis, you should go and see Meher Dhondy. She knows much more than I do. Moreover, she has many interesting things in her house. Her father was the photographer J.M. Patell, and she may even have some old photographs. We don't have anything like that in the Finaro, not even old hotel guest registers.'

I asked him if he remembered any of the guests who had stayed in the Finaro.

'I got to know Professor J.B. Harrison from the School of Oriental and African Studies in London quite well. He would be here for months at a time, working away in the municipality on the history of Allahabad's sanitation system. We have been in touch off and on. I also remember Gillian Buckee, who was working on the High Court. But I've no idea where she is now.'

∽

I had heard of Meher Dhondy. She used to teach in the Girls' High School and now gives English lessons at home. Her classes are much in demand. She was probably in her seventies but sounded youthful on the phone when I called her.

'Come at twelve-thirty,' she said, 'I should be through with my teaching by then. I have another batch of students coming later, so don't stay too long. I have sprained my right hand and am feeling a bit under the weather.'

I asked her how to get to her house.

'You know Rustam's workshop? We're right behind it, in the same compound. But don't take the first gate, which leads to Lokbharati Press. Take the second one, beside Gaytime. There's a PCO there and a bicycle repair shop. You'll see two neem trees when you reach the end of the compound. Our house is behind the big bungalow, opposite the trees. You can't miss it.'

The directions she gave me took me by surprise. Not only did I know the place, I had been going past it all my life. It had always looked to be uninhabited. The gates had disappeared long ago and only the gateposts remained, their plaster gone, revealing the bricks. The compound, though little more than a dusty field, was big enough to hold a football match. The bungalow stood at one end. It was a low, white building in surprisingly good repair, with a long verandah in front and castellation along the top. There was a cross sign on top of the portico, like a finial. Below the sign it said Pentecostal Church.

The beginnings of a footpath with wild shrubs on one side, where once there would have been a gravel drive lined with flowerbeds, appeared a little beyond the gatepost. I bicycled down the path, went past the bungalow, and immediately came to the neem trees. Opposite them, and hidden from the road, was a cottage with a tiled roof. The terracotta tiles looked freshly painted and gave the place a cheerful appearance. I arrived just when a class had ended and saw the students coming out, the boys wearing blue blazers and grey trousers and the girls in green cardigans and grey skirts.

Mrs Dhondy, a short, slender woman with the faintest of grey strands in her hair, greeted me in the verandah and took me inside. Her sitting room had a bare floor and though the furniture in it belonged to an earlier period, the photographs on the walls were contemporary. They showed smiling West Indian cricketers posing with a young man who, too, was smiling and looked like a business executive.

Mrs Dhondy saw me looking at the photographs and said, 'That's my son. He's passionate about cricket. Those pictures were taken in Sharjah.'

I began by asking her about her father.

'He was J.M. Patell. He spelt Patell with two l's, Pat-ell. Actually, it's the same as Patel, but he thought Patel was too common-sounding. He was a daylight photographer, one of the last of the breed. Unlike other photographers, my father did not use any form of artificial lighting in his studio. The glass panes in the roof let in natural light and he took his pictures in it. This limited the hours he could work. It was two hours in the morning and just one in the afternoon. If the results did not satisfy him, he asked the sitter to come back. In the end, the advances in technology drove him out of business. Photography had become cheaper, though the prints were not of the same quality as before. He closed down the business in the mid-1950s, preferring to do that than to change his way of working.'

'What happened to his cameras and other equipment?'

'You know how it is. People would come and say, "Mr Patell, we are setting up a studio. Your equipment is of no use to you now, why don't you give it to us." And he would hand it over to them.'

'Do you have any of his photographs?'

'Not really. But I'll look. Right now, I don't have the time. You see, my father was quite famous in Allahabad. He was more than a photographer; he was a photographer artist. People would bring him the picture of someone recently deceased, taken at the time of cremation or burial, or sometimes in the morgue, and ask him to show the person as he or she looked when still alive. My father would take a photograph of the picture and then set about transforming it, painting the eyes in, adding a bit of black to the hair, some pink to the lips. The customers would be delighted.'

I asked Mrs Dhondy how long her family had been settled in Allahabad.

'We've been here since the early 1900s. The bungalow used to be 18 Canning Road, but everyone knew it as Moti Sahib's *hatta*. Moti Sahib was C.D. Motishaw, my mother's father. In one part of the bungalow he had a motor showroom, the biggest motor showroom in the United Provinces. As a child, I remember sneaking into it to look at the gleaming new cars and motorcycles kept there. I do not recall any of the makes except one, a Packard. It was a big car, more like a picnic bus.

'My grandfather died in 1937 and 18 Canning Road passed to my grandmother, from whom I inherited it. Even in her time, we had a big rose garden. It was roses roses roses all the way to the front gate. In the middle of the garden was a circular platform, about twelve inches in height, where Mrs Benson's Anglo-Indian band played during my wedding reception. The band was nothing like the bands you see nowadays. It always included a pianist.'

Mrs Dhondy briefly interrupted her train of thought to ask if I'd like some coffee.

'Allahabad's Parsi community,' she resumed, 'which is now down to twenty members, was never very large. In my grandfather's time, it numbered around one hundred fifty. It was a matter of great pride with us that despite our small number the top man in every field, not just business, was often a Parsi. Your English department in the university had Dr P.E. Dustoor, the economics department had Dr J.K. Mehta, and among medical doctors there was Dr Hirji, the dentist. Rhoda Gandhi was his daughter. For many years after they left Allahabad, I kept up a correspondence with Dr and Mrs Dustoor. They would write to me from Kodaikanal and afterwards from Poona. I had preserved their letters, but at some point they got misplaced. I always say, if, God forbid, a thief were to break into our house, all he is going to find are photographs and papers, and more papers and more photographs.'

I asked again about the Patell photographs and she said that she was not certain where they were, or even if she had any. She then changed the subject.

She said, 'I do a bit of writing myself. I write poems mostly but also a little prose. I've written something on the Parsis that I'd like to show you. Like everything else, it is somewhere in this house, if I can only find it.

'Did you know, there's a lamp post outside All Saints Cathedral which says it was donated by C.D. Motishaw? It was one of four special lamp posts erected as part of the beautification of Civil Lines. Were the English ever to come back and see what we've done to this place, they'd look for the nearest well to jump into.

'The other day, there was a Toyota parked in front of our gate, leaving no space for my rickshaw to get out. I kept sitting in the rickshaw, glaring at the man whose car it was. He looked the *neta* type. But do you think he got the message? "My rickshaw does not have wings," I said to him, "so unless you move your car I cannot get out of the compound". To my rickshaw-walla I whispered, "Their ill-gotten money can buy these people cars, but no amount of money will buy them good breeding. Their fathers did not possess even a bicycle."'

Mrs Dhondy had switched to the local dialect, eastern Avadhi, which she spoke fluently, when she told me what she had said to the car owner and the rickshaw-walla.

She said, 'My husband keeps warning me that I'll get into trouble for the kinds of things I say. With Independence, we got freedom, but I don't think we got justice.'

The second 'we' referred to the Parsis. Mrs Dhondy said it with a note of bitterness, but it was so fleeting that I almost did not notice it. Outside, through the parted curtains, I saw students in the verandah, arriving for the next class. As I got up to leave, I asked her about the Pentecostal Church.

She said, 'They're our tenants. They're very quiet and are no trouble at all. They've been here a long time.'

∾

One of the earliest accounts to mention the Bengali presence in Allahabad was Bishop Heber's *Narrative of a Journey Through the Upper Provinces of India* (1828).[1] In it, Heber remarked that the 'Bengalees' who had come and settled in 'these provinces' when they were placed under British governors, were 'regarded by the Hindoostanees as no less foreigners than the English, and even more odious than Franks, from ancient prejudice, and from their national reputation of craft, covetousness, and cowardice'.

A later visitor, who travelled through some of the same places as Heber, was Bholanauth Chunder. He came to Allahabad in 1860, when the Mutiny was still fresh in everyone's minds. The size of the Bengali community had grown in the intervening decades, and it was this rather than the foreignness that caught Chunder's attention. 'Great numbers of Bengalees abound in Allahabad, some six thousand. Their errands are various—health, wealth, and pilgrimage,' he wrote in *The Travels of a Hindoo* (1869), a book which many at the time thought was written not by an Indian but by a European under a pseudonym.[2] Moreover, what to the 'Hindoostanees', in Heber's account, indicated the Bengali's

---

[1] For an excerpt, see pp. 38–45.
[2] For an excerpt, see pp. 78–90.

'covetousness', was to Chunder a sign of prosperity and generosity, some of which he partook of. He described his local host in the following terms, 'In the true spirit of a fast money-making and money-expending Kayust, Baboo N—is accustomed to keep an open house and table for all his friends passing on, and from, a tour of the Upper Provinces.'

By the turn of the nineteenth century, the Allahabad Bengalis were sufficiently large in number, and, perhaps more importantly, the print technology and rail and postal infrastructure were available, for someone to come up with the idea of launching a Bengali magazine from the city. This was Ramananda Chatterjee. Ramananda, who belonged to a poor Brahmin family from Bankura in Bengal, was educated at Calcutta University. At a comparatively young age, he was appointed principal of Kayastha Pathshala in Allahabad, where he lived from 1895 to 1908. Perhaps the greatest magazine editor India has known, he started *Prabasi* [Expatriate] in 1901, and a second magazine, *The Modern Review*, in 1907. The contributors to the inaugural issue of *The Modern Review* included Sister Nivedita ('The Function of Art in Shaping Nationality'), E.B. Havell ('The Indian Handloom Industry'), and Jadunath Sarkar ('Shivaji Letters'). It also carried reproductions of three Ravi Varma paintings, along with an editorial note on the artist, who had recently died. Ramananda said in the note, 'A foreign literature and foreign tongue, as English is, cannot serve as the medium through which we may know one another and interchange our deepest thoughts and feelings. The books, periodicals and newspapers which we write in English have their uses, but they do not either reveal or reach the heart of the nation.' The romantic idea that the heart of a nation can find expression only in the vernacular is still with us. Though today the idea seems a little out of date, a hundred years ago, in 1907, it would have sounded different: ardently nationalist, forward-looking, modern.

Differences with the college management over educational reforms made Ramananda resign from his Kayastha Pathshala job, and the following year, in 1908, he ran into trouble with the British over some of the views expressed in *The Modern Review*. For instance, to the stated British opinion that Indian nationalism was losing momentum, Ramananda wrote: 'Never in the history of the world has there been committed any aggression that did not end in raising up a greater force of resistance to overwhelm it.' Served with an order to close down the *Review* or leave Allahabad, he chose the latter option and returned to Calcutta, moving the editorial offices of the two magazines with him. By then he was also heavily in debt. Nirad C. Chaudhuri, who joined the editorial staff in 1928, wrote about the magazines in his autobiography *Thy Hand, Great Anarch!* (1987): 'The *Prabasi* stood for both nationalism and liberalism, and it was the magazine to which Tagore gave most of his new work. It also had the pick of the best work in fiction and poetry in the Bengali language. It was a great honour for any new writer to appear in it. . . . *The Modern Review* in English had an all-India circulation and was more weighty politically. It was read with interest and respect even by the British Governors.'

In Allahabad, both *Prabasi* and *The Modern Review* were printed at The Indian Press, founded by Chintamoni Ghosh. The Ghoshs came from Bally in Howrah district in Bengal. Chintamoni's father, Madhav Chandra, held an administrative job under the British, and in 1864 was posted to Benares. After two years in Benares, Madhav Chandra came to Allahabad on official work, but he was suddenly taken ill on the trip and died shortly afterwards. His mother, wife, and two children, Chintamoni, aged twelve, and an older daughter, all of whom had rushed from Benares when they heard of the illness, were with him when he died.

According to family legend, Chintamoni returned to Bally, then a week's journey from Allahabad, but did not stay there for long. His uncles, he discovered, were eyeing his share of the ancestral property and had hatched a plot to murder him. With few options open, Chintamoni decided that he must leave Bally at once and go back to Allahabad. It is difficult to imagine a boy his age taking this decision on his own, but Chintamoni's life, at least in the telling, with only family sources to go by, is like a fable.

In the beginning, things weren't easy for him. His mother and grandmother between them had a few gold ornaments, most of which they sold to clear off the debts accumulated during Madhav Chandra's illness and to make the journey to Bally. The rest they sold on their return to Allahabad, to meet expenses in their first months in the city. Chintamoni had attended school in Benares, where his teachers had found him to be a quick learner with an aptitude for maths. He now wanted to resume his education, but being the only male in the family he was forced to look for work instead.

His first job was with the *Pioneer* newspaper, where, at the salary of Rs 10 per month, he became a dispatch clerk. The large leather-bound registers in which he was supposed to make entries were, for a young boy, difficult to reach, and Chintamoni had them brought down and did the posting sitting on the floor. When his immediate Indian bosses saw that the lad was hard-working, they piled more work on him. But whenever he got the chance he spent time in the printing room. There he picked up the rudiments of the trade—typesetting, make-up, and imposition, all the while dreaming, as his biographer N.G. Bagchi writes, 'the far-fetched dream of owning a press someday!'

His father's death had interrupted his formal education, and he now did everything he could to make up for its lack. Luckily, his job at the *Pioneer* entitled him to a free copy of the paper. He read it every day, line by line, as though it were a textbook, and in this manner improved his English. He was with the newspaper for about seven years, and, when he left, it had to hire five men to do the work he had performed singlehanded.

Chintamoni's next job was with the Railway Mail Service, but he was there for a few days only. When a vacancy of head clerk arose at the meteorological department, he applied, and so impressed the English superintendent that though there were many applicants with better qualifications he was selected above them. It was during his years in the meteorological department that he got married and also discovered that he had an eye for business. He bought railway sleepers cheaply at an auction and after getting the wood chopped into small pieces, sold it as fuel at a modest profit. One day, he hit on the idea of converting some of the wood into cheap furniture and hired a carpenter to execute the plan. The profit from this new venture was considerable, and he was soon looking for a partner to expand the business.

The dream of being a printer, though, had not left him, and when a Crown hand press with accessories, belonging to a regimental unit, came up for sale, he saw his chance. Along with a friend who put up half the money, he bought the machine and had it installed in a room in his house. He could not afford to hire an assistant and did everything himself, including the printing, after coming back from his office in the meteorological department. There was, in an expanding city, no shortage of work and the press did extremely well, but before a year had passed his friend heard the call of God and, losing all interest in the business, decided to quit. Nevertheless, he was a decent sort and did not ask for anything more than what he had initially put in. Chintamoni, who knew a good deal when he saw one, immediately raised the funds to pay off his friend and on 4 June 1884 had the press registered as The Indian Press. He was thirty years old at the time.

During the early years of printing in India, as in Europe also, the roles of printer and publisher were combined in the same person. The first title published by Chintamoni from The Indian Press was a series of physical geography readers in 1887. The author was E.G. Hill, who later became professor of chemistry at the Muir Central College of Allahabad University. Hill had sold the copyright to Chintamoni against a one-time fee, so when the Department of Public Instruction approved them for school adoption it was the publisher and not Hill who reaped the benefits. The story goes that Hill once remarked to Chintamoni about how successful his books had been and Chintamoni, though not contractually bound to do so, immediately offered to share part of the profits with him; an offer that Hill, in keeping with such stories, graciously refused.

Two years later, in 1889, Chintamoni brought out a series of graded readers for Hindi, *Shikshavali*, that turned out to be even more successful. Compared with the books then available, which were printed in the Government Press on indifferent paper and had been prepared thirty years before, these readers broke new ground in language, content, layout, and typography. For generations of Indian children, they were their first experience of Hindi in the classroom, just as, later, the *Radiant Readers* were their first taste of English. Soon after *Shikshavali* was published Chintamoni decided to resign his job in the meteorological department and to devote all his time to running The Indian Press.

Chintamoni died in August 1928. The following month, the influential Hindi monthly *Saraswati*, which he had started in 1900, brought out a commemorative issue on him. It consisted of reminiscences and eulogies, some of the latter by Maithili Sharan Gupta and Mahabir Prasad Dwivedi, in poetic form. Dwivedi had been the editor of *Saraswati* from 1903 to 1920. During this period, he held perhaps the most important job in the Hindi literary world. For a writer to be published in *Saraswati* was a sign of national recognition. Dwivedi first came to

Chintamoni's notice when he saw a scathing review by him of a Hindi primer published by The Indian Press. The review so impressed Chintamoni that instead of being offended he offered Dwivedi the editorship of his magazine. The reminiscences in the commemorative issue were by Shyamsundar Das, who was the first editor of *Saraswati*, Ganganatha Jha, and C.Y. Chintamani, among others. On the last page were messages from abroad, including one from 21 Holland Street, Kensington, London, by E.G. Hill's widow.

The commemorative issue also carried a number of half-tone photographs. They showed Chintamoni's mother, his wife, or him with his grandchildren; others showed the Ghosh residences in Benares, Puri, and Allahabad. These were imposing buildings, colonial piles on a grand scale, but by themselves, without any sign of human activity in the foreground, the houses looked abandoned. The majority of the photographs, however, were about The Indian Press. These were pictures of typecasting machines and litho presses, cameras and photo-etching equipment, Linotype composing machines and offset printing machines. One picture, titled 'English Composing Room', showed rows of young men, their heads bent, seated behind wooden cases; others showed the stitching and binding rooms, the men, in them, working sitting on the floor. The pictures encapsulated the history of printing in the nineteenth and early twentieth centuries.

Perhaps the picture that best gives an idea of the scale of The Indian Press is of a bald man with a white handlebar moustache and wearing a dhoti and coat, sitting behind an office table that is placed in a doorway, blocking it. There are, on the table, some papers, a metal office tray, rubber stamps and an inkpad. A No Admissions sign is nailed on one of the door panels, on the other, a sign saying Post Office. The hundreds of book parcels that were dispatched every day from the Press, many by VPP to individual customers in remote villages, had led the postal department to set up a post office on the premises itself. In these parcels, in addition to school textbooks, went the copies of *Saraswati*; a Nawab Rai novel; the first illustrated title in Hindi for young adults; Mahabir Prasad Dwivedi's translations of Bhartrihari, Kalidasa, Jayadeva, Jagannath, and Herbert Spencer; Shyamsundar Das's annotated edition of *Ramcaritmanas*; the Valmiki Ramayana; scholarly editions of Vidyapati's poems and Tulsi Das's *Vinaya Patrika*; the first anthology of poems in Khari Boli; Edwin Greaves's Hindi grammar; Hindi translations of Fa Hian, Hsiuan Tsang, Alberuni, Shakespeare, Romesh Chunder Dutt, and Sharat Chandra; an early Hindi novel written specifically for women; and, in 1926, Sumitranandan Pant's *Pallavi*, a collection of poems which is generally said to contain his finest work.

Just as the Ghosh family bought houses in other cities, The Indian Press also expanded outside Allahabad. One of the photographs was of the company's Calcutta branch, its thirty-odd employees standing in a semicircle in front of it; another showed the Indian Publishing House building. Set up in 1908, Indian Publishing House was a subsidiary of The Indian Press and had its offices at 22 Cornwallis Street, Calcutta. It published books in Bengali and had brought out a history of the Bengali language, a life of Vidyasagar, and a two-volume Bengali dictionary. Rabindranath Tagore was one of their authors.

Tagore had first heard of Chintamoni Ghosh and The Indian Press through *Prabasi*, to which he was a regular contributor. It was unusual in the first decade of the last century for high-quality printing in Bengali to be done outside Calcutta, and Tagore had been struck by what a printer in Allahabad had achieved.

His own association with The Indian Press came about through the efforts of Charuchandra Bandhopadhyay, a Bengali writer who worked for *Prabasi* and had earlier worked for the Tagore family magazine *Bharati*, and of Nepal Chandra Roy, who was the retired headmaster of the Anglo-Bengali School in Allahabad. According to the deed of agreement registered in 1906 between Chintamoni and Tagore, The Indian Press became Tagore's main publishers. Apart from bringing out individual titles, *Gitanjali* (1910), *Gitali* (1914), and *Balaka* (1916) among them, they also published his collected poems in a ten-volume uniform edition, *Kavya Grantha* (1915-16).

Tagore's association with the Press ended in 1922 when he set up Visva-Bharati. He had donated to it the money from his Nobel Prize and all his earnings from royalties, but he still needed to raise more funds. He wrote to Chintamoni, asking him if he would surrender his rights to the Tagore titles so that Visva-Bharati could publish them and the profits could go to the university. Chintamoni agreed to do so, and though the loss of a best-selling author affected his balance sheet, he did not take a rupee in compensation. To his son Hari Keshab, to whom he would leave the responsibility of running The Indian Press after his death, he reportedly said, 'I have not merely given back the rights. I have made a permanent contribution to the nation.'

A glass-encased life-sized statue of Chintamoni Ghosh, his dates engraved on the pedestal, stands in the front hall, near the entrance, of The Indian Press. His right hand grips a walking stick; his left fist is clenched, to suggest determination. He has a full beard.

When I visited The Indian Press for the first time, a marigold garland, whose withered flowers were still a bright orange, gave a touch of colour to the statue. On one side of it, along a wall, were stacked reams of printing paper in white plastic wrapping. On the other was a row of wooden almirahs with glass fronts, the glass mostly missing or broken. The almirahs were padlocked and crammed with books, their titles illegible. On the wall was an oil portrait of a slender-looking elderly man in mortar board and gown. He was Shyamsundar Das.

I walked along the almirahs and came to a break in the row. Since there was no one around from whom I could ask for directions, I took a chance and turned into it, as into a doorway. I found myself in the midst of more almirahs, but arranged to form an office cabin. There was no electricity because of a power cut and it was dark inside the cabin, but once my eyes had adjusted to the darkness I could make out an office table and someone sitting behind it. He was Supratik Ghosh, Chintamoni's great-grandson.

Supratik, as I found out later, was in his mid-forties, but his square glasses, swept-back thinning hair and slightly sagging jaw made him look older. He seemed naturally reticent as well as suspicious of people he had not met before. To get him to talk about himself to a complete stranger was, initially, not easy.

Supratik said, 'After finishing school, I thought I would do mechanical engineering like my father, who had studied at Jadavpur. I spent a whole year cramming for the entrance exam, but could not make the grade. In the end I joined the university. I did a BSc and then took a master's degree in economics. After that, for many years, I worked for my father's company, Precision Tools. Essentially, we did work for two industrial units based in Naini, Hindustan Cables and

Triveni Engineering. But in the 1990s they were beset with labour problems and eventually closed down. We found it difficult to survive without them, and though we continued for a couple of years more we had to close down too. I have been with The Indian Press since then. You could say I am a late entrant.

'I tried my hand at publishing at first and brought out a set of six study guides, one on general knowledge, one on Indian history, one on political science, and so on, aimed at candidates taking the Provincial Civil Service exam. The guides sold well, especially in the shops on University Road. The snag came when I went to the booksellers to collect the money they owed me. They would never say they wouldn't pay, but all the same would fob me off with some excuse or other. Every few days I would make the rounds on my scooter and come away empty-handed. In the end, unable to recover a single paisa, I lost interest in the project. It's a dirty market.'

I asked him what he did now.

Supratik said, 'After the publishing thing failed, I bought a couple of second-hand Japanese offset machines and became a job-printer. It may come as a surprise to you, but 90 per cent of the work I get has to do with printing study guides similar to the ones I had brought out. There is these days a guide available for every competitive exam and university course. The demand for them is far greater than for textbooks. Occasionally, I get to do confidential work, like printing examination papers.

'I got out of publishing, but The Indian Press still has a small list. It consists of reprints of those of our old titles for which there is still a demand, like Meghnad Saha's *Treatise on Heat*. My uncle Satya Prasad, or Suttu Babu as everyone calls him, handles that side of the business. Some years ago, we did another reprint of Ishwari Prasad's *History of Medieval India*. I was never a student of English, but I doubt any Indian historian these days can match Ishwari Prasad's writing style.'

Our next meeting was again during a power cut, so I was surprised to find there was light in the cabin. It came from a solitary striplight suspended from the ceiling. In the background, I could hear the muffled sound of a genset. The ceiling, I noticed, was black with cobwebs and had wires stretched across it. Some of the wires led to a fan or to a light fixture, but often these were missing, leaving the wires hanging in the air.

Separating Supratik's cabin from the one adjoining it was a wooden partition with a door in the middle and glass panels on the sides. Unlike on my previous visit, the door, this time, was open. I could see, in the other cabin, a refrigerator that seemed to have been designed when Art Deco was all the rage; an office table heaped with papers that had turned yellow; a revolving office chair with torn upholstery; two empty drums of printing ink; and a metal typewriter cover, painted black, with Remington written on it. There was dust everywhere. It was as though, fifty or more years ago, the cabin's occupant had gone home one evening and not returned, and no one had entered the place since.

As soon as he saw me, Supratik pulled out a book from the bottom drawer of his table and gave it to me to look at. It was the second edition of Prasad's *Medieval India*, published in 1928.

Supratik said, 'I found it in one of the warehouses. It was the only copy left. I have rescued a few interesting things in this way. Or at least what to me has looked interesting.'

The book was heavier and thicker than I expected. Bound in boards, it showed the 'Pillar of Victory at Chittore' on the cover. Inside, the pages had generous margins, the printing was clean, the paper had not yet turned brittle, and the reproduction quality of the twenty-one black-and-white photographs, on art paper, was surprisingly good.

I asked Supratik if I could buy a copy of the reprint and he asked a peon to get it. The paperback reprint, as far as the production quality went, was no better than the dozens of cheap study guides displayed in the bookstalls on University Road. There was no half-title page, nor was there a 'history' of the book, giving the date of first publication, and dates of subsequent revised editions and reprints. Like the study guides, it was printed on cheap newsprint-like paper. The photographs were a washout.

I was in my mind still comparing the early edition with the recent reprint when Suttu Babu walked in. He was a delicate-looking man in his early seventies and had a small clutch bag tucked under his arm. Supratik introduced us.

Suttu Babu said, 'Ishwari Prasad was a regular visitor to The Indian Press. In his last years, when he could not move around much, I would go over to his house. He was at the time finishing a history of the French Revolution and a volume on the sources of Indian history. After his death, I asked his daughter about the manuscripts, but she pretended as though she had never heard of them. We were supposed to publish the books. I still have the contracts.'

I was hoping that Suttu Babu would sit down so I could ask him more about The Indian Press. His father, Hari Keshab, had been as much of an entrepreneur as Chintamoni. He continued with the printing and publishing businesses of The Indian Press, maintaining the same high standards, but he also diversified into other areas. He started a sugar mill in Bihar and, in Allahabad, built market complexes and residential units, which he rented out. When he died in 1953, *Saraswati* brought out a commemorative issue, just as it had done for Chintamoni, consisting of tributes, photographs, and messages. The opening tribute, in verse, was by Sumitranandan Pant. There was also a tribute by Ishwari Prasad, who wrote, 'I had enjoyed his friendship uninterruptedly for more than three decades, and sometimes half in jest and half in earnest, I used to say like Oliver Goldsmith, "My publishers are my patrons."'

Suttu Babu had lived through the decline of The Indian Press, but he did not give me a chance to put any questions to him. He did not sit down. His cabin was behind the one adjoining Supratik's, and taking his leave he scurried towards it.

After he had left, Supratik reached for the bottom drawer of his desk again and I thought he was going to show me another book. Instead, he brought out a manila envelope and very gently pulled out a folded sheet that came apart even as he was pulling it. Bits and pieces of the sheet lay scattered on the table, like the pieces of a jigsaw. I could make out, in the pieces, a printed diagram with words and dates written in Bengali. Some words were written in pencil. Supratik shrugged his shoulders and smiled.

Supratik said, 'I thought I'd show you our family tree, but I didn't realize the paper had become so brittle. There is a photocopy of it at home and if you're interested I could bring it next time we meet.' He then proceeded to return the jigsaw to its envelope.

∽

Ritu Rudra rose from her chair and, holding on to the furniture for support, taking one step at a time, asked me to follow her. At seventy-eight, she was naturally cautious in her movements, but her mental agility was of someone sixty years younger. She had recently had a cataract removed, and some years ago, operated on for breast cancer, but her suffering then, she said, was nothing compared to what she went through after the cataract, when she was unable to read or do the crossword for several weeks. She called it the worst period of her life.

We went through the kitchen and came to a large bright room at the back of the house. It seemed originally to have been a verandah and was scattered with books. I noticed a volume on Indian birds, books on philosophy and religion, paperback novels. Despite the layer of Gammexane powder that lay on them, termites had damaged the books and in some cases the holes were the size of a rupee-coin. She looked around the room and apologized for the mess.

She said, 'We had to demolish half the bungalow, as you know. The new owners are putting up a school there. The demolition was too much to bear and I shifted to a friend's place when it took place. I've just moved back and am still getting organized.'

Finally, in a pile on the floor, she found what she was looking for. It was a book called *Indian Christians: Biographical and Critical Sketches* published by 'G.A. Natesan & Co., Madras', 'Price Rs Three', and contained biographies of Krishna Mohan Banerjea, Lal Behari Day, Michael Madhusudan Dutt, W.T. Satthianadan, Pandita Ramabai, and Sushil Kumar Rudra, among others. Rudra was the first Indian principal of St Stephen's College, Delhi, and a close associate of C.F. Andrews and Mahatma Gandhi. When he died in 1925, Gandhi wrote in *Young India*,

> Ever since my return home in 1915, I had been his guest whenever I had occasion to go to Delhi. . . . He was the first Indian principal chosen in his college. I, therefore, felt that his intimate association with me and giving me shelter under his roof might compromise him and expose his college to unnecessary risk. I, therefore, offered to seek shelter elsewhere. His reply was characteristic: 'My religion is deeper than people may imagine. Some of my opinions are vital parts of my being. They are formed after deep and prolonged prayers. They are known to my English friends. I cannot possibly be misunderstood by keeping you under my roof as an honoured friend and guest. And

if ever I have to make a choice between losing what influence I may have among Englishman and losing you, I know what I would choose. You cannot leave me.'

Principal Rudra was Ritu's grandfather.

Ritu said, 'My great-grandfather, Pyari Mohan Rudra, came from a landowning family in Bengal and was baptised by the Scottish missionary Alexander Duff. The conversion caused a big outcry in his native village and he could not return to it for a while, for fear of harm. He was, though, an educated man, having gone to college in Calcutta, and had converted by choice. Later, he joined the clergy and was in charge of the Nadiya Mission, with many congregations under his care. I am told he wrote hymns in Bengali that are sung even today. We're not "rice Christians".'

We returned to the living room, which used to be her father's study, and sat down again. A maid emerged from the kitchen with two glasses of water on a tray. She said 'Good morning' to me, using the English phrase, which took me by surprise. She addressed Ritu as 'Ritu Baba' and they briefly discussed what the maid was going to cook for lunch.

The living room had a red stone floor. The stones were hexagonal and formed a honeycomb pattern. The false ceiling had rotted away and been dismantled, exposing the rafters and the undersides of the red roof tiles. The walls were a dark shade of blue, the coat of whitewash showing under the paintwork, and there were two skylights. Pushed against one of the walls was a large oval dining table, covered with a plastic sheet to protect the linen tablecloth. On a couple of smaller tables on the opposite wall were a Philips music system and stacks of cassettes and CDs. The music was Western classical, but not entirely. A corner table, near the entrance, was piled higgledy-piggledy with books and papers. The other furniture in the room consisted of an assortment of comfortable old chairs painted black, two old china closets with straight legs, and a teapoy. Above the music system were photographs of Ritu's parents. Her father's face was intense, narrow, reserved. He wore thick-rimmed glasses. Her mother's face suggested someone who might have laughed easily and was not easily ruffled. From what I could judge, Ritu, both in appearance and temperament, resembled her mother more than she did her father. It was her father, though, that she talked about, almost obsessively. He had died in a drowning accident in Kumaon in 1951. Listening to her speak about him, it could have been yesterday.

Ritu said, 'My father, Sudhir Kumar, was a student at Pembroke College, Cambridge, during the First World War. He used to tell us that, one by one, all the young men in his college enlisted and left, and though he continued to pursue his studies a time came when he was overcome with guilt and felt he too ought to enlist. Unable to get into the regular army, he served through the YMCA as a volunteer medical orderly in France. He was a stretcher-bearer, and his job was to rush the wounded from the battlefield to the hospital behind the lines. More than once, he told us, he had to hold a soldier's hand and comfort him while the doctor amputated the man's leg in an emergency operation.

'By the time my father finished his Tripos and returned to India in 1922, he was thirty-one years old but he still had no clear idea what he was going to do. C.F. Andrews suggested working with indentured labourers in Fiji, and he might have gone there had the possibility of an appointment at Allahabad University not opened up. My father had never taught before and the appointment was to a senior position, Reader in economics, but he applied all the same and got the job.

'Before he bought this house in 1932, we lived at 14 Muir Road, in a rented bungalow that had no electricity. When summer came, we hired a young boy, a punkah-coolie, to work the punkahs. He would sit in a corner of the room, pulling the cord, and occasionally dozing off. It wasn't a very effective way of staying cool.

'A Muir Road neighbour of ours was Bhagwat Dayal. He was in the English department, and we knew the family quite well. They had a fountain in the garden and I fell into it once. One minute my parents saw me playing near the edge of the fountain and the next minute they saw my legs sticking out of the water. This was in 1929, when I was two years old. It's almost my earliest memory.

'There was a performance of *The Monkey's Paw* in which Bhagwat Dayal played the old father. At one particularly poignant moment in the play he cried out, "O my son! O my son," sobbing loudly. And his young son, who was sitting in the audience, shouted, "Daddy, I'm here."'

I asked Ritu if she had any memories of Amaranatha Jha. Jha was only twenty in 1917 when the Muir College of Allahabad University made him professor of English, the first Indian to be so appointed; later, he served as the university's vice-chancellor for three terms, from 1938 to 1946. He was a big local figure, and since Allahabad was at the time an important city, he also made it on to the national news. I had come across a reference to Sudhir Kumar in Jha's diary and told Ritu about it. In the diary, a selection from which had appeared in the Jha memorial number of the *Allahabad University Magazine*, Jha mentioned a Book Tea held at Anand Bhavan on 20 April 1926 to celebrate Motilal Nehru's sixty-fourth birthday. At the Tea, Mrs Vijayalakshmi Pandit represented *Vanity Fair*, Shyam Kumari Nehru, 'A joy for ever', Mrs A.C. Banerji, *The Crescent Moon*, Mrs P.N. Sapru, *The Scarlet Letter*, Kailash Nath Katju, Sherlock Holmes, S.S. Nehru, *The Koran*, Kamala Nehru, *Arms and the Man*, P.N. Sapru, *The Light that Failed*, Amaranatha Jha, *The Mayor of Casterbridge*, and Sudhir Kumar Rudra, *A Student in Arms*. Motilal Nehru represented *The Light of Asia*.

Ritu said, 'My father and Amaranatha Jha were friends but they were never very close. Jha was an elitist out and out. He set great store by a student's family background, particularly when he was admitting one to Muir Hostel, of which he was warden. My father, who was an egalitarian, treated everyone the same. Jha's wife, though, was the opposite of her husband. She was a down-to-earth village woman from Bihar and did not know a word of English. I have a memory of her sitting in the courtyard of her house, chopping vegetables. She was very traditional. I never saw her wearing a blouse or appearing in public. Even when there was a dinner at the Jhas, she did not come out to meet the guests. It was as though Jha was embarrassed by her. On these formal occasions my mother went across to help with the arrangements and played the role of hostess.'

As we talked, a man dressed in a white shirt and white pyjamas came and stood in the front door. He said 'Salaam huzoor' and, shuffling off his chappals, sat down in the chair nearest the entrance. He sat on the edge of the chair, as though uncomfortable in it. The glasses he wore had thick lenses, behind which his eyes appeared to be of a grey colour. He had several teeth missing and looked very frail. After a while, Ritu asked him to go inside into the kitchen.

Ritu said, 'He's our tailor, Kadir Bux. He had a shop in Civil Lines, but the building was pulled down last year and a multiplex is coming up in its place. He now makes a round of his old customers and takes home whatever work he gets. My sisters and I try to give him something to mend or stitch whenever he comes. He also gets a cup of tea and a bit to eat. He usually turns up around lunchtime.'

Kadir Bux was not the only one who had visited Ritu that morning. Before him the milkman, the meatman, the fishmonger, the fruit and vegetable vendors, and the dhobi had been there. They had all come inside the living room, made their deliveries and left, and seemed well versed in the ways of the house. There were hardly any words exchanged between them and Ritu. The dhobi's family had worked for the Rudras for three generations. The grandfather, Sarju, Ritu recalled, always wore a pugree, a tight-fitting tunic, and a dhoti. He wore a gold earring in one ear and brought the week's washing on the back of a donkey.

On a subsequent visit, Ritu had mentioned her father's diary[3], adding that she did not know where it was and that it would be difficult to find. From time to time, I would remind her of it, and though she promised she would ask her sister Dipika to look, I was doubtful that it would ever turn up.

Dipika was the youngest of Sudhir Kumar's five daughters. Married to a Keralite, she had spent most of her time in south India, but returned to live in her father's house, the house in which she was born, after her husband's death. Ritu herself had never married. She had always lived in Allahabad and, before retirement, taught philosophy at Ewing Christian College. She had a doctorate from Claremont and had taught at Columbia University for a year. A third sister who stayed in the house was Pramila. She had retired from her teaching job at Lawrence School, Sanawar.

Then one day Dipika called to say that she had found the diary.

Since Jha and Rudra had been contemporaries, and both had taught at the same university and moved in the same circles, it had crossed my mind, when I first heard about it, that Rudra's diary may not be very different from Jha's. I could not have been more wrong.

Jha's diary had read like an engagement book. It enumerated, nearly always without comment, the names of the people he had met

---

[3]For an excerpt, see pp. 163–71.

('February 6, 1930: Called on Mrs Naidu at Anand Bhavan. Met Padmaja also'), the functions he'd attended ('February 5, 1921: Boy Scouts' Rally in honour of Lord Baden-Powell'), and the meetings he had chaired ('September 29, 1923: I presided over Professor Seshadri's lecture on 'Love Poetry in English'), with sometimes a glance at the day's political events ('March 11, 1922: Mr Gandhi has been arrested'). Rarely does Jha refer to anything personal and, when he does, he adopts the same dry, slightly gruff tone. On the day of his marriage, for instance, he wrote, 'June 22, 1922: I was married at Bettiah at midday to the youngest daughter of the late Pandit Harimohan Jha.' One of the few exceptions to this is when he was finally leaving the university, after being associated with it for thirty years, to become chairman of the Public Service Commission, Uttar Pradesh. On 31 March 1947 he confided to his diary, 'I wrote to Kewal Krishna and Ramji—and wept as I wrote, making over charge of the Muir Hostel to them. No one can realize what these boys have meant to a lonely man.'

After all the self-importance, all the honours—Fellow of the Royal Society of Literature, president of the All-India Lawn Tennis Association, and so on—this comes as a shock. The Jhas did not have any children of their own, which may explain the sense of loneliness he felt. He died in 1955. His enormous up-to-date library, consisting of several thousand titles, some of which, like Ezra Pound's *Quia Pauper Amavi* (Egoist Press, 1919), would today fetch good prices on the rare-books market, was bequeathed to the university, where, in the fitness of things, maggots reduced most of it to powder. His papers, which included a complete translation of the seventeenth-century Hindi poet Bihari, were either lost or destroyed.

Despite the reserve, Jha's diary was a window into the social and cultural world of Allahabad of the 1920s, 1930s, and 1940s; Rudra's, covering the same period, is centred on its domestic life. With an openness that is entirely beguiling and with a poet's eye for detail, he writes about the early years of his marriage and the rented Muir Road bungalow in which those years were spent; about the birth of his children and of two deaths; about making a sandpit and falling off a horse; about the purchase of a Fiat motor car and, in 1932, of 20 Albert Road, the very house in which, sitting in a black armchair, I had read the diary; and about the recruitment and dismissal of servants:

We have a cook, Abdul, who is a funny kind of bloke. I took him on when Mohini [Rudra's wife] was away in Lahore, expecting Bobby. He seemed to be a smart bearer and produced good chits. Mohini once got very angry with him and dismissed him. I am sorry I interfered and had him reinstated. Now he has hung around. He is jolly dirty, an absolute pig. I shudder to think he is our cook! I wish we could replace him. This summer, 1938, he nearly died of enteric.

Apart from the diary, 'The Rudra Book', as the family has always called the custom-made ruled notebook, contained the children's medical records and details of investments and expenses. These were in Mohini Rudra's hand. There were also, loosely kept between its pages, a few old receipts and letters, the latter still in the envelopes in which they were received. They were letters of condolence received by the family when Sudhir Kumar died.

Ritu had often talked about the family vacations in Ramgarh, Binsar, and Ranikhet in the Kumaon Hills. She remembered them mainly for the long walks, like the one from Binsar to Almora, a distance of fourteen miles. But on that occasion she had not walked and her father had had to carry her on his shoulders for most of the distance. Though a coolie had accompanied them, she refused to go to him, unable to bear his smell. Her mother, on these walks, would point out the wild flowers along the way and identify them for the children. When they returned to the cottage that had been hired for the season and was often set amidst an orchard, there would be a meal waiting for them, made by a cook who had travelled with them from Allahabad. The other servant who had travelled with them was the sweeper, whose hereditary job was to clean out the commodes.

But the Rudras took more than two servants with them when they went on vacation. Two pages in the diary gave a list of 'Vacation Requisites', itemized under seven headings, 'Bedding', 'Tiffin basket', 'Toilet', 'Bathroom', 'Bedroom', 'Drawing-room', and 'Dining-room'. The 'requisites', about a hundred-odd in number, included mosquito nets, plates, cups and saucers, a butter dish, toothpicks, tablecloths, a tin-opener, brandy, Listerine, carbolic soap, coat hangers, Bromo paper, buckets, soap dishes, face towels, phenol, curtains, vases, cushions, rugs, ashtrays, visiting cards, cigarettes, a cruet stand, mustard, forks, knives, spoons, tablecloths, soup plates, milk jugs, egg cups, serviettes, dishcloths and finger bowls. Nor was this all. Also forming part of the luggage, Pramila once told me, were a gramophone, gramophone records, a carom board, and a stack of storybooks from which Sudhir Kumar sometimes read aloud.

The bungalow may have had a fixed address, like, say, 20 Albert Road, but when the residents moved, it moved with them. The bungalow was a way of life, and while it lasted it was portable.

∞

Adjacent to the Rudra house, facing Thornhill Road, was the bungalow in which Arun Kumar Bhattacharya lived. The two bungalows were identical, and built around the same time, in the first decade of the twentieth century. A low brick wall, which any child could jump, separated the compounds. The bungalow was for a while occupied by an English family who were in the carpet business, and then by a down-at-heel Anglo-Indian who was a tenant. One morning, he turned up outside his neighbour Sudhir Kumar's gate, and after borrowing money from him disappeared without a trace. It later came out that he owed money all round, including rent to his landlord.

The next owner was a young Nepalese Rana, a man called Balendu Shah. He liked to live well, and had the means to do so. The first thing he did when he moved into the house was to order some high-quality European-style furniture for it. In local sporting circles, though, he was known less for his money than for his cricketing abilities. He was a fine bat. It was from him that in the late 1940s Khelat Chandra Bhattacharya purchased the bungalow, the furniture included. Khelat Chandra was Arun Kumar's uncle. He was a retired civil surgeon, but those who remembered him spoke of him in soldierly terms. They described him as a man of 'military bearing', as someone who stood 'ramrod straight'.

The Bhattacharyas were from Shantipur in West Bengal, and Arun Kumar's father may have been the first one in the family to leave the village in search of a new life. He came and settled in Benares, and got a job in a college there. Arun Kumar, who grew up in Benares, came to Allahabad in 1944, to do his BSc. He must have impressed Amaranatha

Jha, who admitted him to Muir Hostel, which in those days was the most anglicized of the university hostels and difficult to get into. (In the 1940s, Murian had the same ring that Stephanian has today.) He stayed there for two years and completed his degree. What he did next no one knows. As one of his closest friends said to me, 'There's a gap in the story.'

Arun Kumar returned to the university in 1950, to do his MA in English literature. This time, though, he did not seek admission to Muir Hostel but stayed with Khelat Chandra at 24 Thornhill Road. He stayed in one room in the rear of the house, but had his meals with the family. Since he had never married and felt no need to shift to a bigger place, he continued to live there, in that one room, even after he got a job and became a member of the English faculty of the university.

After Khelat Chandra's death, the responsibility of taking care of his old wife, and indeed of the house and the Ambassador car, the same one I would see him driving around in, fell largely on Arun Kumar. Though the Chandras had children of their own, a son and a daughter, they lived elsewhere, not in Allahabad. The son was in Calcutta, where he worked for Martin Burn, and he later settled in America. Arun Kumar, driving back from the university or from Civil Lines in his uncle's car, must have sometimes felt that he was returning not to his uncle's house but to his own.

'Batty did not have to buy a spoon in his life,' was a remark I often heard when I asked my older colleagues about him. Batty, as his friends called Arun Kumar, also had the reputation of being a miser. He certainly had the money, earned during stints of schoolteaching abroad, to back the reputation. When they went to the Coffee House, I was told, Batty was always the last in the company to reach for his wallet.

By the time he retired in 1985, Arun Kumar had bought his own place, a modest two-bedroom Allahabad Development Authority flat on the fourth floor, but he continued to live in the bungalow and to rent out the flat. At about this time, in the mid-1980s, he tried to sell off some of the Balendu Shah furniture: a mahogany gateleg dining table from C. Lazarus of Calcutta with eight chairs and a sideboard. He asked Rs 55,000 for them. Mrs Khelat Chandra had meanwhile died.

Ten years later, Arun Kumar was still living there, in the same corner bungalow on Thornhill Road he had first come to as a student.

He had been living in it for forty-five years and had grown used to the place. He was seventy years old and it would have seemed very unlikely to him that he was ever going to leave it and move into a flat. He got a good price for the flat and sold it off. As for the car, despite a few engine problems, it still enabled him to get around. He saw no call to change the car either.

Meanwhile, land prices in Allahabad had skyrocketed and the building mafia was eyeing Khelat Chandra's property. It was almost two acres of land, enough to build at least twenty independent houses. Arun Kumar's cousin, Khelat Chandra's son, was keen to sell too, and he even turned up in Allahabad one year with the intention of finalizing a deal, but with Arun Kumar refusing to move out, the sale fell through. On that occasion, to everyone's surprise, Arun Kumar produced Mrs Khelat Chandra's will (some say it was a letter written by her). It stated that the bungalow was to go to her son, but Arun Kumar could live in it for his lifetime. The only condition was that he had to maintain the bungalow and to pay the house and water taxes, a negligible sum of a few hundred rupees annually.

The episode had left Arun Kumar badly shaken. He confided to a friend that he felt unsafe; he said he felt under some sort of threat. He also had a heart condition, and he feared that there would be no one around to call out to should he need medical help at night. He looked more apprehensive, his friend said, than he had ever seen him.

Ritu remembers the date, 12 May 1995, even today. She had just finished watching *The World This Week* on TV, when she heard a banging on the door. Outside she found her servants standing in a huddle. Their quarters were close by, in a lane that ran along one side of her property, but since they were not usually awake at that hour she was surprised to see them.

The wedding season was on, and the servants had been waiting for the *barat* to arrive. A few people were waiting on the road, and had seen three men jump over her compound wall. One of the men had washed himself at the handpump outside the lane and gone off in the direction of the Anglo-Indian Colony. The other two had left on a scooter that was parked not far from her gate. They were in a hurry to get away. It all looked very suspicious and the servants had come out of concern, to check if everything was all right.

Ritu said, 'I double-checked all my doors and locks and finding everything was in order, went to bed. I heard about it only the next morning and immediately went across. He was lying on the floor, wearing blue jeans and a half-sleeve shirt, his hands not straight by his side but raised to about the level of his shoulders. There was a piece of electrical flex round his neck, the ends of the flex touching the palms. I recognized a journalist from the *Patrika* in the crowd and asked him what he knew. He gestured towards the men from the police station and said he had heard from them that Arun Kumar suffered from depression and had committed suicide. He tended to believe them. I said this was nonsense. I had known Arun Kumar all these years and he was just not the suicidal type. He was a fighter. In any case, it was impossible for a person to strangulate himself in this fashion, lying on the floor.

'But what happened subsequently is even more horrifying. Arun Kumar's closest surviving relative was his brother in Poona. He said that since it would take him two days at least to reach Allahabad, they should go ahead with the cremation.

'Unfortunately, the person who had contacted him misunderstood the message. He thought the brother had asked them to wait. In the forty-eight hours it took the brother to get here, the body had become so bloated and it stank so much that no one was prepared to go anywhere near it. In the end, they had to ply one of the sweepers with a lot of booze before he agreed to go inside and get the body out.'

Less than a month later, 24 Thornhill Road was demolished.

ॐ

When my father, a dentist, came to Allahabad from Dehra Dun in 1949, we first stayed with his elder brother at 20 Hastings Road. We did not live in the main bungalow but in a cottage at the back. It had a pitched roof, tiny rooms, a coal trough, a front verandah, and an oleander hedge. I call it a cottage because of its size and appearance, though at the time it was built it would have been the kitchen and pantry, which in the colonial bungalow were not attached to the main house but located a short distance from it. After two years of living in the cottage, we moved to Ghosh Building on Albert Road, in the heart of Civil Lines, where my father had set up his clinic. We would have been among the first people to live in a flat in Allahabad.

Ghosh Building was built in the same year that we came to Allahabad. It was a long, flat-roofed, modern-looking building, and lacked only chimneys to make it look like a factory. At street level, after a walkway that ran along the length of the building, was a row of about a dozen large shops with glass fronts. Upstairs were flats and insurance offices. Over the decades, the shops have changed hands and new businesses have opened in them. But some establishments, like Kohli Photo Service, which fifty years ago was just the sort of state-of-the-art photographer in town that J.M. Patell had found to be a threat, and Indian Medical Hall, a Bengali-owned rundown chemist that even today, even from a distance, smells like an old bandage, have been there since my childhood.

The clinic took up the front part of our flat, which meant that one entered the flat through the waiting room. Behind it was a drawing room and a dining area. The two bedrooms were to one side. Behind the dining area was a narrow balcony, at one end of which was a kitchen, whose inside was black with smoke from the *chulha*, and at the other a flush toilet, which was something of a novelty. The other novelty, for me, was our Electrolux refrigerator that ran on kerosene. Ghosh Building was one of several rental properties, spread across Allahabad, owned by The Indian Press.

In the last one hundred and fifty years, Allahabad has seen two migrations. The first began after the Mutiny of 1857 and ended a hundred years later, in the first decade after Independence. During it came the Ghoshs and the Chatterjees, the Nehrus and the Dhondys, and the Jhas and the Rudras. It made Allahabad what it was, and this anthology is a memorial to it. The second migration, which began in the 1980s, has largely been a local affair; from the Black Town to the White, from Chowk to Civil Lines, from Attarsuiya to Thornhill Road. It unmade the colonial city.

Like my parents, Arun Kumar had come to Allahabad towards the end of the first migration. He saw the second one coming but badly misjudged it. Instead of showing prudence and stepping out of its way, he dug in and paid the price. Allahabad has paid a price too. The second migration has dealt it a blow it is unlikely to recover from. The same forces of history that transformed it from a nondescript provincial town into one of the premier cities of the Raj have turned it into a provincial town once again, whose unchecked growth and collapsed civic amenities make it indistinguishable from dozens of other towns in north India. Seen in this way, Allahabad's is a terribly human story. It is a story of dust to dust, which may be one reason why some of us who live here love it so much.

ARVIND KRISHNA MEHROTRA

HSIUAN TSANG

Hsiuan Tsang (603–?665) was born in Chin-lu in the reign of Emperor Wen of the Sui dynasty. He was the youngest of four brothers. From an early age he showed remarkable learning abilities, and only had to hear a book once to comprehend it thoroughly. At the age of twenty he was ordained as a bhikshu and six years later, unhappy with the Chinese translations of the sacred books and inspired by Fa Hian's pilgrimage to the Buddhist Holy Land two hundred years earlier, he set out for India. He was in Kannauj during Harsha Vardhan's reign and has described the festival at Prayag, widely misunderstood to be a description of the Kumbh Mela, at which the king gave away alms to Buddhist monks. In Harsha's time, one tends to forget, Prayag was as much a Buddhist city as a Hindu one; it had stupas as well as 'Deva temples'. Hsiuan Tsang returned to China in 645, with enough Buddhist relics, statuary, and texts to load twenty-two horses. He spent the rest of his life poring over the texts, many of which he also translated.

∾

from *Buddhist Records of the Western World* (1884)

PO-LO-YE-KIA (PRAYÂGA)

This country is about 5000 li in circuit, and the capital, which lies between two branches of the river, is about 20 li round. The grain products are very abundant, and fruit-trees grow in great luxuriance. The climate is warm and agreeable; the people are gentle and compliant in their disposition. They love learning, and are very much given to heresy.

There are two *sanghârâmas* with a few followers, who belong to the Little Vehicle.

There are several Dêva temples; the number of heretics is very great.

To the south-west of the capital, in a Champaká (*Chen-po-kia*) grove, is a *stûpa* which was built by Aśôka-râja; although the foundations have sunk down, yet the walls are more than 100 feet high. Here it was in old days Tathâgata discomfited the heretics. By the side of it is a *stûpa* containing hair and nail relics, and also a place where (*the past Buddhas?*) sat and walked.

By the side of this last *stûpa* is an old *sanghârâma*; this is the place where Dêva Bôdhisattva composed the *śâstra* called *Kwang-pih* (*Śata śâstra vaipulyam*), refuted the principles of the Little Vehicle and silenced the heretics. At first Dêva came from south India to this *sanghârâma*. There was then in the town a Brâhman of high controversial renown and great dialectic skill. Following to its origin the meaning of names, and relying on the different applications of the same word, he was in the habit of questioning his adversary and silencing him. Knowing the subtle skill of Dêva, he desired to overthrow him and refute him in the use of words. He therefore said—

'Pray, what is your name?' Dêva said, 'They call me Dêva.' The heretic rejoined, 'Who is Dêva?' He answered, 'I am.' The heretic said, 'And "I", what is that?' Dêva answered, 'A dog.' The heretic said, 'And who is a dog?' Dêva said, 'You.' The heretic answered, 'And "you", what is that?' Dêva said, 'Dêva.' The heretic said, 'And who is Dêva?' He said, 'I.' The heretic said, 'And who is "I"?' Dêva said, 'A dog.' Again he asked, 'And who is a dog?' Dêva said, 'You.' The heretic said, 'And who is "you"?' Dêva answered, 'Dêva.' And so they went on till the heretic understood; from that time he greatly reverenced the brilliant reputation of Dêva.

In the city there is a Dêva temple beautifully ornamented and celebrated for its numerous miracles. According to their records, this place is a noted one (*śrî—fortunate ground*) for all living things to acquire religious merit.

If in this temple a man gives a single farthing, his merit is greater than if he gave a 1000 gold pieces elsewhere. Again, if in this temple a person is able to contemn life so as to put an end to himself, then he is born to eternal happiness in heaven.

Before the hall of the temple there is a great tree with spreading boughs and branches, and casting a deep shadow. There was a body-eating demon here, who, depending on this custom (*viz., of committing suicide*), made his abode here; accordingly on the left and right one sees heaps of bones. Hence, when a person comes to this temple, there is everything to persuade him to despise his life and give it up: he is encouraged thereto both by the promptings of the heretics and also by the seductions of the (*evil*) spirit. From very early days till now this false custom has been practised.

Lately there was a Brahman whose family name was *Tseu* (*putra*); he was a man of deep penetration and great learning, of lucid wit and high talent. This man coming to the temple, called to all the people and said, 'Sirs, ye are of crooked ways and perverse mind, difficult to lead and persuade.' Then he engaged in their sacrifices with them, with a view afterwards to convert them. Then he mounted the tree, and looking down on his friends he said, 'I am going to die. Formerly I said that their doctrine was false and wicked; now I say it is good and true. The heavenly Rîshis, with their music in the air, call me. From this fortunate spot will I cast down my poor body.' He was about to cast himself down when his friends, having failed by their expostulations to deter him, spread out their garments underneath the place where he was on the tree, and so when he fell he was preserved. When he recovered he said, 'I thought I saw in the air the Dêvas calling me to come, but now by the stratagem of this hateful (*heretical*) spirit (*viz., of the tree*), I have failed to obtain the heavenly joys.'

To the east of the capital, between the two confluents of the river, for the space of 10 li or so, the ground is pleasant and upland. The whole is covered with a fine sand. From old time till now, the kings and noble families, whenever they had occasion to distribute their gifts in charity, ever came to this place, and here gave away their goods; hence it is called *the great charity enclosure*. At the present time Śilâditya-râja, after the example of his ancestors, distributes here in one day the accumulated wealth of five years. Having collected in this space of the *charity enclosure* immense piles of wealth and jewels, on the first day he adorns in a very sumptuous way a statue of Buddha, and then offers to it the most costly jewels. Afterwards he offers his charity to the residentiary priests; afterwards to the priests (*from a distance*) who are present; afterwards to the men of distinguished talent; afterwards to the heretics who live in the place, following the ways of the world; and lastly, to the widows and bereaved, orphans and desolate, poor and mendicants.

Thus, according to this order, having exhausted his treasuries and given food in charity, he next gives away his head diadem and his jewelled necklaces. From the first to the last he shows no regret, and when he has finished he cries with joy, 'Well done! Now all that I have has entered into incorruptible and imperishable treasuries.'

After this the rulers of the different countries offer their jewels and robes to the king, so that his treasury is replenished.

To the east of the *enclosure of charity*, at the confluence of the two rivers, every day there are many hundreds of men who bathe themselves and die. The people of this country consider that whoever wishes to be born in heaven ought to fast to a grain of rice, and then drown himself in the waters. By bathing in this water (*they say*) all the pollution of sin is washed away and destroyed; therefore from various quarters and distant regions people come here together and rest. During seven days they abstain from food, and afterwards end their lives. And even the monkeys and mountain stags assemble here in the neighbourhood of the river, and some of them bathe and depart, others fast and die.

On one occasion when Śilâditya-râja distributed the alms in charity, there was a monkey who lived apart by the river-side under a tree. He also abstained from food in private, and after some days he died on that account from want.

The heretics who practise asceticism have raised a high column in the middle of the river; when the sun is about to go down they immediately climb up the pillar; then clinging on to the pillar with one hand and one foot, they wonderfully hold themselves out with one foot and one arm; and so they keep themselves stretched out in the air with their eyes fixed on the sun, and their heads turning with it to the right as it sets. When the evening has darkened, then they come down. There are many dozens of ascetics who practise this rite. They hope by these means to escape from birth and death, and many continue to practise this ordeal through several decades of years.

Going from this country south-west, we enter into a great forest infested with savage beasts and wild elephants, which congregate in numbers and molest travellers, so that unless in large numbers it is difficult (*dangerous*) to pass this way.

Going 500 li or so, we come to the country Kiau-shang-mi (Kauśâmbî).

Translated by Samuel Beal

RALPH FITCH

Ralph Fitch (?1550–1611) was a London merchant about whose early life practically nothing is known. He arrived in Goa, then a Portuguese colony, in 1583, 'in the company of M. John Newbery, merchant (which had been at Ormus once before), of William Leedes, jeweller and James Story, painter'. They were among the first Englishmen to set foot in India. While Story stayed back in Goa and married a half-caste woman, the others travelled through the domains of 'Zelabdim Echebar' (Jalaluddin Akbar), for whom they were carrying letters of introduction from Queen Elizabeth. Fitch's account does not say if the letters were ever presented to the emperor.

After a few weeks' stay in Fatehpur Sikri, the English party broke up. Newbery returned to England, by way of Lahore, Persia, 'and thence for Aleppo or Constantinople'. He never reached England, and nothing is known of what happened to him. Leedes stayed on in Fatehpur and found employment at court; nothing further is heard of him either. Before his departure, Newbery, as head of the mission, directed Fitch 'to go for Bengala and for Pegu', the capital of the ancient Mon kingdom in southern Myanmar.

Fitch did the first leg of that journey, from Agra to Allahabad, by joining a convoy 'of one hundred and fourscore boates laden with Salt, Opium, Hinge [asafoetida], Lead, Carpets and diverse other commodities' going 'downe the river Jemena'. He reached Allahabad sometime in November 1585, when work on Akbar's great fort was nearing completion.

Fitch returned to England in 1591, to take his place among the most remarkable of Elizabethan adventurers.

∽

from *Richard Hakluyt's Principal Navigations, Voiages, Traffiques and Discoveries of the English Nation* (1599)

From Agra I came to Prage [Prayāga, now Allahābād], where the river Jemena entreth into the mightie river Ganges, and Jemena looseth his name. Ganges commeth out of the northwest, and runneth east into the Gulfe of Bengala. In those parts there are many tigers and many partridges and turtle-doves, and much more foule. Here be many beggars in these countries which goe naked, and the people make great account of them; they call them Schesche. Here I saw, one which was a monster among the rest. He would have nothing upon him; his beard was very long; and with the haire of his head he covered his privities. The nailes of some of his fingers were two inches long, for he would cut nothing from him; neither would he speake. He was accompanied with eight or tenne, and they spake for him. When any man spake to him, he would lay his hand upon his brest and bowe himselfe, but would not speake. Hee would not speake to the king. We went from Prage downe Ganges, the which is here very broad. Here is great store of fish of sundry sorts, and of wild foule, as of swannes, geese, cranes, and many other things. The countrey is very fruitfull and populous. The men for the most part have their faces shaven, and their heads very long, except some which bee all shaven save the crowne; and some of them are as though a man should set a dish on their heads and shave them round, all but the crowne. In this river of Ganges are many ilands. His water is very sweete and pleasant, and the countrey adjoyning very fruitfull.

REGINALD HEBER

Reginald Heber (1783–1826) was born at Malpas, in Yorkshire, and educated at Brasenose College, Oxford, where he won the Newdigate Prize for Poetry. He was ordained in 1809, and presented to the living of Hodnet, in Shropshire. While at Hodnet, he was married and wrote the hymns he is best known for today.

Heber refused the Bishopric of Calcutta when he was first offered it. He did not want to endanger the future health of his wife and child, or sacrifice the brilliant prospects in England. But in the end of his strong missionary longings got the better of his judgement, and he agreed to go. He spent most of his three years in India travelling around the country, consecrating churches and graveyards, holding confirmations, founding schools, and solemnizing marriages. All this told severely on his health, and at Trichinopoly he was seized with an apoplectic fit when in his bath, and died.

Bishop Heber's journey up the Ganges to Allahabad was by a sixteen-oared boat with a covered-in portion for bedroom, sitting-room, and dining-room in the centre. He reached Allahabad in September 1824 and found it to be a 'desolate and ruinous' place. For different reasons, Mirza Ghalib, who came to Allahabad three years after Heber, was of the same view.

∽

from *Narrative of a Journey Through the Upper Provinces of India from Calcutta to Bombay, 1824–25* (1828)

Allahabad stands in perhaps the most favourable situation which India affords for a great city in a dry and healthy soil, on a triangle, at the junction of the two mighty streams, Gunga and Jumna, with an easy communication with Bombay and Madras, and capable of being fortified so as to become almost impregnable. But though occasionally the residence of royalty, though generally inhabited by one of the Shahzadehs, and still containing two or three fine ruins, it never appears to have been a great or magnificent city, and is now even more desolate and ruinous than Dacca, having obtained, among the natives, the name of 'Fakeerabad', 'beggar-abode'. It may, however, revive to some greater prosperity, from the increase of the civil establishment attached to it. It is now the permanent station (the *castrum Hybernum*) of the Sudder Mofussil commission, a body of judges whose office is the same with regard to these provinces as that of the Sudder Dewannee Udawlut for the eastern parts of the empire. The necessity for such a special court had become very great. The remoteness of the Sudder Dewannee had made appeals to it almost impossible, and very great extortion and oppression had been committed by the native agents of the inferior and local courts, sometimes with the connivance, but more often through the ignorance and inexperience of the junior magistrates and judges. They, when these provinces were placed under British governors, having been previously employed in Bengal and Bahar, naturally took their Bengalee followers with them, a race regarded by the Hindoostanees as no less foreigners than the English, and even more odious than Franks, from ancient prejudice, and from their national reputation of craft, covetousness, and cowardice. In fact, by one means or other, these Bengalees almost all acquired considerable landed property in a short time among them, and it has been the main business of the Sudder Mofussil Udawlut, to review the titles to all property acquired since the English Government entered the Dooab. In many instances they have succeeded in recovering all or part of extensive possessions to their rightful heirs, and the degree of confidence in the justice of their rulers, with which they have inspired the natives, is said to be very great. They make circuits during all the travelling months of the year, generally pitching their tents near towns, and holding their courts under trees, an arrangement so agreeable to Indian prejudices, that one of these judges said it was, in his opinion, one main source of their usefulness, inasmuch as an Indian of the humbler class is really always under constraint and fear in a house, particularly if furnished in the European manner, and can neither attend to what is told him, nor tell his own story so well as in the open air, and amidst those objects from which all his enjoyments are drawn. At Allahabad, however, where their permanent abodes are, these judges have a court house though a very humble one, thatched and inconvenient.

The only considerable buildings or ruins in Allahabad are the fort, the Jumna Musjeed, and the serai and garden of Sultan Khosroo. The first stands on the point of the triangle formed by the two rivers, and is strong both naturally and artificially. It has been a very noble castle, but has suffered in its external appearance as much as it has probably gained in strength, by the modernization which it has undergone from its present masters, its lofty towers being pruned down into bastions and cavaliers, and its high stone rampart topped with turf parapets, and obscured by a green sloping glacis. It is still, however, a striking place, and its principal gate, surmounted by a dome, with a wide hall beneath surrounded by arcades and galleries, and ornamented with rude but glowing paintings, is the noblest entrance I ever saw to a place of arms. This has been, I think, injudiciously modernized without, after the Grecian or Italian style, but within, the high gothic arches and Saracenic paintings remain. The barracks are very handsome and neat, something like those of Fort William, which the interior disposition of the fort a good deal resembles. On one side, however, is a large range of buildings, still in the oriental style, and containing some noble vaulted rooms, chiefly occupied as officers' quarters, and looking down from a considerable height on the rapid stream and craggy banks of the Jumna. The Jumna and Ganges are here pretty nearly of equal width; the former is the more rapid of the two, and its navigation more dangerous from the rocky character of its bed, and its want of depth in the dry season. At present both streams were equally turbid, but in another month, I am told, we should have found the water of the Jumna clear as crystal, and strangely contrasted with the turbid yellow wave of the more sacred stream, which is, however, when allowed some little time to clear itself, by far the most palatable of the two, and preferred by all the city, both native and European.

The Jumna Musjeed, or principal mosque, is still in good repair, but very little frequented. It stands on an advantageous situation on the banks of the Jumna, adjoining the city on one side, and on the other an esplanade before the fort glacis, planted with trees like that of Calcutta. It is a solid and stately building, but without much ornament. It had been, since the English conquest, fitted up first as a residence for the General of the station, then used as an assembly-room, till Mr Courtney Smith, apprehending this to be a insult to the religious feelings of the Mussulmans, persuaded the Government to restore it to its sacred character, and to repair its damages. The Mussulmans, however, are neither numerous nor zealous in Allahabad, and seemed to care a little about the matter. Nevertheless the original desecration was undoubtedly offensive and unjust, and the restitution a proper and popular measure.

The finest things in Allahabad, however, are Sultan Khosroo's serai and garden; the former is a noble quadrangle, with four fine gothic gateways, surrounded within an embattled wall by a range of cloisters for the accommodation of travellers. The whole is now much dilapidated, but was about to be repaired from the town duties, when unhappily the Birmese war arrested this excellent appropriation of an unpopular tax. Adjoining the serai is a neglected garden, planted with fine old mango trees, in which are three beautiful tombs raised over two princes and a princess of the imperial family. Each consists of a large terrace, with vaulted apartments beneath it, in the central one of which is a tomb like a stone coffin, richly carved. Above is a very lofty circular apartment, covered by a dome richly painted within, and without carved yet more beautifully. All these are very solemn and striking, rich, but not florid or gaudy, and completely giving the lie to the notion common in England, which regards all eastern architecture as in bad taste and 'barbarous'.

The houses of the civil servants of the Company are at some distance, both from the fort and the town, extending along a small rising ground, in a line from the Ganges to the Jumna. They are mere bungalows, and less both in size and ornament than at any station I have yet seen in these provinces. The situation is, however, pleasant and healthy. The city of Allahabad is small, with very poor houses, and narrow irregular streets, and confined to the banks of the Jumna.

I remained ten days at Allahabad, waiting the arrival of tents from Cawnpoor. During this time I had the pleasure of confirming twenty persons, two of them natives, and of preaching and administering the sacrament to seventy or eighty, of whom some were also natives, or at least in the native dress. The residents here are exceedingly anxious for a chaplain, but that one should be appointed at this time, I entertain but few hopes, though it is very sad that such a congregation should want one. For the present I hope to procure them one of the Church Missionaries.

Amid the other necessary preparations for my land journey, more numerous by far, and more various, than I had anticipated, I had to purchase a horse for my own riding, no elephant being either to be begged, bought, or borrowed in Allahabad, and no reasonable hope being held out of my procuring one in Cawnpoor. Indeed, most people tell me that a horse, during the greater part of the journey which I have before me, will be far preferable conveyance. To procure a tolerable one was not, however, an easy matter. Arabs are excessively scarce and dear, and one which was sent for me to look at, at a price of 800 rupees, was a skittish, cat-legged thing, not worth half the money. I went with Mr Bird, whose kindness and hospitality were unremitting during my whole stay, to look at a drove of up-country horses, just arrived from Lahore and Turkistan, and was exceedingly amused and interested by the picturesque groups of men and animals which met the eye in a crowded serai about nightfall, as well as with the fine forms of some of the colts offered for sale, and the singular appearance and manner of the grazier who owned the 'cofilah' or caravan, and his attendant saeeses. The former was an elderly man, six feet high, and more than proportionally corpulent, with a long, curling, black beard, spreading over his white peyrahoom. The latter were also large-limbed, tall men, with long hair in black strong ringlets hanging down their backs and over their ears, their little turbans set knowingly on one side, and neither they nor their master much darker than Europeans. Indeed, they exceedingly resembled some of the portraits of Italians by Titian; they rode well, and showed great strength; but what most amused me was the remarkable resemblance between horse-dealers all over the world, in turns of expression, in tricks of trade, nay, even in tone of voice and cast of countenance. I had fortunately an excellent judge in Mr Bird, but even he was perplexed for some time how to advise me. At length I fixed on a very handsome colt, too young, certainly, but strong, and very good-tempered, for which I gave 460 rupees. The old man went and came over and over again before he would take the price, but I was pertinacious; and at last, on Abdullah's suggesting that an additional present of something besides money would please him better, I gave him a piece of Dacca muslin, sufficient for a turban, and worth about eight sicca rupees, as well as a small phial of laudanum and brandy for an ear-ache, of which he bitterly complained. This satisfied him, and we parted very good friends, Mr Bird being of opinion that the price was really a fair one, and the horse extremely promising. It was also necessary to buy five tattoes for my servants to ride in turns, as there were no baggage-elephants to mount them on. This, however, was easily accomplished, and the animals, saddles, bridles, and all, were obtained, though very good ones of their kind, for sixteen rupees each. A long string of other necessaries followed, and I had the mortification to find that few of the things I had brought with me from Calcutta could be put on the backs of camels. It was with the greatest difficulty that a carpenter could be found in the whole city to drive a nail, or a blacksmith to make a horse-shoe; it being the festival of Rama and Seeta, all the world was employed in seeing the hero with his army of monkeys attack the giant Ravanu. Many other hinderances and disappointments occurred, but the delay they occasioned gave me an opportunity of seeing something of the Ramayuna festival, which consists in a sort of dramatic representation during many successive days, of Rama's history and adventures. The first evening I went with Mr Bird to the *show*, for as such it is now considered, and so entirely divested of every religious character, as to be attended even by Mussulmans without scruple. I found Rama, his brother Luchmun, and his betrothed wife Seeta, represented by three children of about twelve years old, seated in Durbar, under an awning in the principal street of the sepoy lines, with a great crowd round them, some fanning them, (of which, poor things, they had great need), some blowing horns and beating gongs and drums, and the rest shouting till the air rang again. The two heroes were very fine boys, and acted their parts admirably. Each had a gilt bow in his left hand, and a sabre in his right, their naked bodies were almost covered with gilt ornaments and tinsel, they had high tinsel crowns on their heads, their foreheads and bodies spotted with charcoal, chalk, and vermilion, and altogether perfectly resembled the statues of Hindoo deities,

'Except that of their eyes alone
The twinkle showed they were not stone.'

Poor little Seeta, wrapt up in a gorgeous veil of flimsy finery, and tired to death, had dropped her head on her breast, and seemed happily insensible to all which was going on. The brahmin sepoys who bore the principal part in the play, made room, with great solicitude, for us to see. I asked a good many questions, and obtained very ready answers in much the same way, and with no more appearance of reverence or devotion than one should receive from an English mob at a puppet show. 'I see Rama, Seeta and Luchmun, but where is Huniman?' (the famous monkey general.) 'Huniman,' was the answer, 'is not yet come; but that man,' pointing to a great stout soldier of singularly formidable exterior, 'is Huniman, and he will soon arrive.' The man began laughing as if half ashamed of his destination, but now took up the conversation, telling me that 'next day was to be a far prettier play than I now saw, for Seeta was to be stolen away by Ravanu and his attendant evil spirits, Rama and Luchmun were to go to the jungle in great sorrow to seek for her.'

('Rama, your Rama! to greenwood must hie!')

That, 'then (laughing again) I and my army shall come, and we shall fight bravely, bravely.' The evening following I was engaged, but the next day I repeated my visit; I was then too late for the best part of the show, which had consisted of a first and unsuccessful attack by Rama and his army on the fortress of the gigantic ravisher. That fortress, however, I saw, an enclosure of bamboos, covered with paper and painted with doors and windows, within which was a frightful paper giant, fifteen feet high, with ten or twelve arms, each grasping either a sword, an arrow, a bow, a battle-axe, or a spear. At his feet sate poor little Seeta as motionless as before, guarded by two figures to represent demons. The brothers, in a splendid palkee, were conducting the retreat of their army; the divine Huniman, as naked and almost as hairy as the animal whom he represented, was gamboling before them, with a long tail tied around his waist, a mask to represent the head of a baboon, and two great painted clubs in his hands. His army followed, a number of men with similar tails and masks, their bodies dyed with indigo, and also armed with clubs. I was never so forcibly struck with the identity of Rama and Bacchus. Here were before me Bacchus, his brother Ampelus, the Satyrs, (smeared with wine lees,) and the great Pan commanding them. The fable, however, can hardly have originated in India, and probably has been imported both by the Greeks and brahmins from Cashmere, or some other central country where the grape grows, unless we suppose that the grape has been merely an accidental appendage to Bacchus's character, arising from the fact that the festival occurs during the vintage. There yet remained two or three days of pageant, before Seeta's release, purification, and remarriage to her hero lover, but for this conclusion I did not remain in Allahabad. At Benaras, I am told, the show is on such occasions really splendid. The Raja attends in state with all the principal inhabitants of the place, he lends his finest elephants and jewels to the performers, who are children of the most eminent families, and trained up by long previous education. I saw enough, however, at Allahabad to satisfy my curiosity. The show is now a very innocent one, but there was a hideous and accursed practice in '*the good old times*', before the British police was established, at least if all which the Mussulmans and English say is to be believed, which shows the Hindoo superstition in all its horrors. The poor children who had been thus feasted, honoured, and made to contribute to the popular amusement, were, it is said, always poisoned in the sweetmeats given them the last day of the show, that it might be said their spirits were absorbed into the deities whom they had represented! Nothing of the sort can now be done. The children, instead of being bought for the purpose, from a distance, by the priests, are the children of neighbours, whose prior and subsequent history is known, and Rama and Seeta now grow old like other boys and girls.

GHALIB

Mirza Muhammad Asad-ullah Khan 'Ghalib' (1797–1869), nobleman, wit, letter writer, and poet, was born in Agra but spent his adult life in Delhi. He wrote in both Persian and Urdu. The letter below is addressed to Maulvi Muhammad Ali Khan, who was sadr-e amin or civil judge of Banda in the United Provinces. Ghalib passed through Allahabad in 1827 on his way to Calcutta, then the capital of British India. He undertook the journey, the longest he ever made, with the aim of vindicating his claim to a pension left him by his uncle, but in the end the journey turned out to be in vain and he had to return disappointed.

In Allahabad, Ghalib stayed in the Daryabad area, which is located along the banks of the Jamuna. In a second letter from Allahabad, not included here, Ghalib complained of being bitten by bedbugs at night and unable to sleep. This may explain why, in the present letter, he is so put out.

The letter forms part of a collection of thirty-four letters published in *Persian Letters of Ghalib* (1969), edited by S.A.I. Tirmizi. The translation is of the opening passages only.

∽

'A letter of grievance from my wanderings'

> This is a letter of grievance from my wanderings.
> This tale of the pain of partings will be told part by part.

Qibla of my life and wisdom and Ka'aba of my body and soul, greetings! I submit with my humblest greetings and prayer that if I have been away these last two days, then I now present myself on your account. May it suffice that in the mind's eye, I hold a perpetual place in your assembly. I have been most keen to speak with you and now turn helplessly to writing. I am at my wit's end: no matter what I say, I stand absolved. And I am sad: whatever I write I am pardoned. To put off poetry and speak plainly:

> Overcome by appalling creditors, sorrowful Ghalib
> lies lifeless, as if from weakness.

They say he's reached Benares alive.
Who'd have expected it of this limp weed?

The events up to Chillatara I have conveyed in two letters, one of which was sent by post and the other through a messenger I was not acquainted with. I would be happy to know that one of them has by good fortune reached you. In any event, I hired a boat from that point on, and travelling in it with a man and a pony, my guts all to-ing and fro-ing because of the strong wind, and my heart on fire from a strange fever, on the seventh day we entered a wilderness.

Oh Allahabad! May God damn that desolation where neither such medicine may be had as befits the ailing nor regard for those of rank. Its people are nowhere and its old and young are without charity and modesty. Its surroundings are the stuff of the world's notoriety and its ruins two leagues long. How unjust to call this fearful place a city, how shameful that men should reside in this trap for fiends. If one compares this land to the plain of hell, hell would burn in anger; and if one compares the icy winds of Zamharir to the winds that blow through this dank region, Zamharir would be insulted. How unhealthy! Since they say that the evil are forgiven by the good, it has cast itself with a thousand hopes—indeed with even more abjectness—by the side of Benares, and thrown the Ganga in between for intercession. Although it must weigh heavily on delicate Benares to have to gaze upon this misery, its heart finds comfort in the fact that the Ganga flows between them. By God, if my return from Calcutta takes me through Allahabad, I will renounce home and not return. All in all, a night and a day were spent in that hellish place without porters, as in a prison. The next day, when porters were found at the break of dawn, I travelled by water like the wind and pressed eagerly on to Benares. On the day I entered Benares, a relieving breeze blowing from the east fortified my soul and quickened my heart. The miracle of that gust of breeze cast up my dust like a flag of victory and did not fatigue me. Happy the city of Benares, that I, from an intensity of joy, should call it the world's heart-core; and excellent the environs of that city, that I, thrilling to its verdure, may properly see in it paradise on earth.

Translated by Prashant Keshavmurthy

BAHADUR SINGH BHATNAGAR

Bahadur Singh Bhatnagar (*fl.* early nineteenth century) was a resident of pargana Gondiwal in the province of Shahjahanabad. He moved to Lucknow in 1817, probably in search of employment, and lived there for the rest of his life. He commenced writing *Yadgar-i Bahaduri* in Lucknow and completed it on 1 Ramadan 1249 H (12 January 1834). The work is a storehouse of information about the political, social, cultural, and religious life of Muslims around the world, beginning from the birth of Islam. It also covers Hindu religion and Hindu religious ceremonies and has a brief history of the Hindu kings. Of particular interest is the account of European countries, and of European philosophers, explorers, and scientists. One chapter describes the establishment of British rule in India as well as its military, judicial, and revenue administration.

The excerpt below is from the section on Allahabad. Though it is doubtful that Bhatnagar ever visited the city, he is not alone in calling it 'desolate'. Mirza Ghalib, who was in Allahabad in 1827, wondered how 'this ghoulish place' could be called a city at all.

A copy of *Yadgar-i Bahaduri* is preserved in the Regional Archives, Allahabad.

∾

from *Yadgar-i Bahaduri* (1834)

Outside the gate of Khusrau Bagh is Karbala road. On the tenth day of Muharram, the ta'zias [replicas of the tomb of Imam Husain, the grandson of Prophet Muhammad, situated in Karbala, Iraq] are buried at Karbala. The following is a description of the ta'zia processions in Allahabad. On the night of [Husain's] martyrdom, the ta'zias of the rich as well as the poor of the city are carried to Chowk, which is brightly illuminated. A large crowd gathers at Chowk. Later, the people take the ta'zias to their residences and in the morning carry them along the road to Karbala, past the tomb of Sultan Khusrau, to bury them.

On the road near Karbala is the dwelling of a holy man. On the tenth day of Muharram, people belonging to the *Ithna 'Ashariyah* sect [the Twelver sect of Shi'ism], along with their flags, go there in large numbers and mourn. The reason for this is not known. Adjacent to the holy man's dwelling is an extensive garden. Its boundary wall is of masonry and it has a tall gate. Inside are buildings, along with many shady fruit-bearing trees. The wife of Daulat Rao Sindhia [a prominent Maratha chieftain] lives in this garden. It is said that during the reign of Emperor Akbar the populace of the city lived up to this point and all kinds of grains, fabrics, flowers, fruits and vegetables were available there. Towards the end of Akbar's reign the river Ganges became inundated and the strong dam that had been built there collapsed. A large number of buildings collapsed, killing many people. This news reached the ears of the Emperor and he had an even sturdier dam built. Therefore a large number of men have made their houses on the dam. Subsequently, Emperor Jahangir directed his attention to the settlement of this city and built many buildings there. In this way, all the monarchs of the house of Babur have been active in settling the above-mentioned city. They have laid gardens and constructed buildings as their memorials. At present, however, this city [Allahabad] is becoming desolate.

Translated from the Persian by N.R. Farooqi

FANNY PARKES

Fanny Parkes (1794–1875) was born at Conway in Wales, the daughter of Colonel William Archer and his wife Anne. Her father had served in the 16th Lancers and distinguished himself in the Revolutionary and Napoleonic wars.

From the moment she arrived in Calcutta as the wife of a Bengal Civil Service administrator in 1822, Fanny Parkes set about recording her impressions of the country—its people, its flora and fauna, and its customs and superstitions. So keen was she on the customs, she says, that her friends expected to see her some day 'at pooja in the river'. She also became something of a collector of Indian artifacts and, visiting England in 1839, claimed that her collection of 'Hindoo idols' was far superior to that of the British Museum. Though her husband, Charles Parkes, was a colonial administrator, Fanny herself, in what is unusual for a British woman of her time, was outspoken in her criticism of the East India Company's regime in India.

After four years in Calcutta, her husband was transferred to Allahabad as collector of customs. Except for short periods of travel and a stint at Cawnpore, Fanny Parkes lived in Allahabad from 1827 to 1838. From the ice-pits and the 'burra mela' to the Jumnapar goat ('an enormous fellow, with very broad, long, thin, and silky ears, soft as velvet'), there is hardly an aspect of 'the station' that Fanny Parkes does not touch upon in her monumental *Wanderings of a Pilgrim, in search of the Picturesque, during four-and-twenty years in the East, with Revelations of Life in the Zenana* (1850). She perhaps wrote more completely on Allahabad than anyone else except Harivansh Rai Bachchan,[1] a century later.

Fanny Parkes and her husband did not leave India until 1845, settling in St Leonard's on Sea. They did not want to leave but were forced to by Charles's ill health. He died in 1854. She lived on until she was eighty-one.

∽

from *Wanderings of a Pilgrim* (1850)

January 1827.—It is usual in India for those newly arrived to call upon the resident families of the station; the gentleman makes his call, which is returned by the resident and his family; after which, the lady returns the visit with her husband. An invitation is then received to a dinner-

[1]See pp. 133–47.

party given in honour of the strangers, the lady being always handed to dinner by the host, and made the queen of the day, whether or not entitled to it by rank.

Our debût in the Mufassil was at the house of the judge, where we met almost all the station, and were much pleased that destiny had brought us to Prāg. Prāg was named Allahabad when the old Hindoo city was conquered by the Mahomedans. We were very fortunate in bringing up our horses and baggage uninjured, and in not having been robbed *en route*. Lord Amherst has lost two horses, and his aide-de-camp three: guards are stationed around the Governor-general's horse-tents and baggage night and day, nevertheless native robbers have carried off those five animals. His lordship is at present at Lucnow.

We have spent the last three weeks most delightfully at Papamhow. Every sort of scientific amusement was going forward. Painting in oil and water colours, sketching from nature, turning, making curious articles in silver and brass, constructing Æolian harps, amusing ourselves with archery, trying the rockets on the sands of an evening, chemical experiments, botany, gardening; in fact, the day was never half long enough for our employment in the workshop and the grounds.

Papamhow is five miles from our own house, standing on higher ground and in a better situation, on the Ganges; when we can make holiday, we go up and stay at our country house, as our neighbours call it.

The old moonshee is cutting out my name in the Persian character, on the bottom of a Burmese idol, to answer as a seal. What an excellent picture the old man, with his long grey beard, would make! I have caught two beautiful little squirrels, with bushy tails and three white stripes on their backs; they run about the table, come to my shoulder, and feed from my hand.

∽

January 1828, Leap Year.—Tame buffaloes are numerous at Prāg. The milk is strong, and not generally used for making butter, but is made into ghee (clarified butter), useful for culinary purposes. Some most beautiful Barbary goats arrived with the cows; they were spotted brown and white or black and white, and almost as beautiful as deer. The

Bengālee goats yield a much larger portion of milk. I had also a Jumnapār goat, an enormous fellow, with very broad, long, thin, and silky ears, as soft as velvet. The Jumnapār are the best adapted for marching. Unless they can go into the jungle and browse, they become thin and lose their milk.

These goats, bred on the banks of the Jumna, thence called 'Jumnapār', are remarkably fine, and of a large size. We had a Doomba ram at Prag. The Doomba sheep are difficult to keep alive in this climate. Their enormous tails are reckoned delicacies; the lambs are particularly fine-flavoured.

Jan.—Our garden was now in good order; we had vegetables in abundance, marrowfat peas as fine as in England, and the water-cresses, planted close to the new well, were pearls beyond price. Allahabad is famous for the growth of the finest carrots in India. At this time of the year we gave our horses twelve seer each daily; it kept them in high health, and *French-polished* their coats. The geraniums grew luxuriantly during this delightful time; and I could be out in the garden all day, when protected by an enormous chatr, carried by a bearer. The upcountry chatr is a very large umbrella, in shape like a large flat mushroom, covered with doubled cloth, with a deep circle of fringe. Great people have them made of silk, and highly ornamented. The pole is very long, and it is full employment for one man to carry the chatr properly.

The oleander (kanér), the beautiful sweet-scented oleander, was in profusion—deep red, pure white, pink, and variegated, with single and double blossoms. I rooted up many clusters of this beautiful shrub in the grounds, fearing the horses and cows might eat the leaves, which are poisonous. Hindoo women, when tormented by jealousy, have recourse to this poison for self-destruction.

THE ICE PITS.

January 22nd.—My husband has the management of the ice concern this year. It is now in full work, the weather bitterly cold, and we are making ice by evaporation almost every night. I may here remark, the work continued until the 19th of February, when the pit was closed with 3,000 mann—a mann is about 80 lbs. weight. There are two ice-pits; over each a house is erected; the walls, built of mud, are low, thick, and circular; the roof is thickly thatched; there is only one entrance, by a small door, which, when closed, is defended from the sun and air by a jhamp, or frame-work of bamboo covered with straw.

The diameter of the pit, in the centre of the house, is large, but the depth not great, on account of the dampness of the ground. At the bottom is a small well, the top of which is covered over with bamboo; a channel unites it with a dry well on the outside, still deeper than itself, so constructed, that all the water collected in the pit may immediately run off through this duct, and be drawn up from the external well. This keeps the pit perfectly dry—a material point. The interior is lined, from top to bottom, with chātaīs (mats), three or four deep, which are neatly fastened by pegs round the inside; mats are also kept ready for covering in the top of the pit. Some ābdārs recommend a further lining of sulum (cotton-cloth), but it is unnecessary.

THE ICE PITS.

The Ice Pits

The ground belonging to the ice concern is divided into keeārees, or shallow beds, very like saltern-pans in England, about six feet square and a cubit in depth; between them are raised paths.

When the weather in December is cold enough to induce us to suppose water will freeze at night with artificial aid, the business of ice-making commences. At the bottom of the keeārees, the shallow square beds a black-looking straw is spread about a foot in depth, called 'pooāl' which is reckoned better for the purpose than wheat-straw. Some ābdārs think sugar-cane leaves the best thing to put under the pans in the ice-beds; next in estimation is the straw or grass of kodo (the *paspalum frumentaceum*) and then rice-straw, which is called 'puwāl', or 'pooāl', though the term 'pooal' is not applied exclusively to the straw of rice. The highest temperature at which ice was made in 1846, at Cawnpore, was 43° of Fahrenheit, or 11° above freezing point. At each of the four corners, on the pathway, is placed a thiliyā (an earthen jar), which is filled by a bihishtī with water.[2] The pooāl straw in the shallow beds must be kept perfectly dry, to produce evaporation and the freezing of the water in the little pans placed upon it; should rain fall, the straw must be taken up and thoroughly dried before it can again be used.

It is amusing to see the old ābdār who has charge of the ice concern, walking up and down of an evening, watching the weather, and calculating if there be a chance of making ice. This is a grand point to decide, as the expense of filling the pans is great, and not to be incurred without a fair prospect of a crop of barf (ice) the next morning. He looks in the wind's eye, and if the breeze be fresh, and likely to increase, the old man draws his warm garment around him, and returning to his own habitation—a hut close to the pits—resigns himself to fate and his hubble-bubble. But should there be a crisp frosty feeling in the air, he prepares for action about 6 or 7 P.M., by beating a tom-tom (a native handrum), a signal well known to the coolies in the bazaar, who hasten to the pits. By the aid of the little cup fastened to the long sticks, as shown in the sketch, they fill all the rukabees with the water from the jars in the pathway. Many hundred coolies, men, women, and children, are thus employed until every little pan is filled.

If the night be frosty, without wind, the ice will form perhaps an

[2]See the sketch of the Ice Pits, with this man and his mashk (water-bag)

inch and a half in thickness in the pans. If a breeze should blow, it will often prevent the freezing of the water, except in those parts of the grounds that are sheltered from the wind.

About 3 A.M., the ābdār, carefully muffled in some yards of English red or yellow broad cloth, would be seen emerging from his hut; and if the formation of ice was sufficiently thick, his tom-tom was heard, and the shivering coolies would collect, wrapped up in black bazār blankets, and shaking with cold. Sometimes it was extremely difficult to rouse them to their work, and the increased noise of the tom-toms—discordant native instruments—disturbed us and our neighbours with the pleasing notice of more ice for the pits. Each cooly, armed with a spud, knocked the ice out of the little pans into a basket, which having filled, he placed it on his head, ran with it to the ice-house, and threw it down the great pit.

When all the pans had been emptied, the people assembled around the old ābdār, who kept an account of the number at work on a roll of paper or a book. From a great bag full of pice (copper coins) and cowrie-shells, he paid each man his hire. About ten men were retained, on extra pay, to finish the work. Each man having been supplied with a blanket, shoes, and a heavy wooden mallet, four at a time descended into the pit by a ladder, and beat down the ice collected there into a hard flat mass; these men were constantly relieved by a fresh set, the cold being too great for them to remain long at the bottom of the pit.

When the ice was all firmly beaten down, it was covered in with mats, over which a quantity of straw was piled, and the door of the ice-house locked. The pits are usually opened on the 1st of May, but it is better to open them on the 1st of April. We had ice this year until the 20th of August. Each subscriber's allowance is twelve ser (24 lbs.) every other day. A bearer, or a cooly is sent with an ice-basket, a large bazār blanket, a cotton cloth, and a wooden mallet, at 4 A.M., to bring the ice from the pit. The ābdār, having weighed the ice, puts it into the cloth, and ties it up tightly with a string; the cooly then beats it all round into the smallest compass possible, ties it afresh, and, having placed it in the blanket within the ice-basket, he returns home. The gentleman's ābdār on his arrival at his master's house, re-weighs the ice, as the coolies often stop in the bazaars, and sell a quantity of it to natives, who are particularly fond of it, the man pretending it has melted away *en route*.

The natives make ice for themselves, and sell it at two annas a seer; they do not preserve it for the hot winds, but give a good price for the ice stolen from the sāhib loge.

As the ābdārs generally dislike rising early to weigh the ice, the cooly may generally steal it with impunity. The ice-baskets are made of strips of bamboo covered inside and out with numdā, a thick coarse woollen wadding. The interior is lined with dosootee (white cotton cloth), and the exterior covered with ghuwā kopra, a coarse red cloth that rots less than any other from moisture.

$\sim$

June 1st 1831.—Finding myself ill for want of exercise, I commenced rising early; dressing by candlelight, going out by moonlight, and mounting my horse at half-past 3 A.M.! What an unnatural life! The buggy is always sent forward to await my arrival at a certain spot. I never draw my horse's rein until I arrive at the place, the heat is so much greater when you walk your horse. I return in the buggy at 6 A.M., go to bed for a couple of hours, bathe, and appear at breakfast.

How often 'Chār vajr, barī fajr,' *i.e.* four o'clock in the early dawn, sleepy and unwilling to exert myself, have I thought of the proverb: 'Oh, thou who art so fond of sleep, why don't you die at once?'

Today the heat is dreadful; 89° even at the mouth of the thermantidote, and in the other parts of the house six degrees higher! After my early canter, I did not quit my chārpāi until 3 P.M., so completely was I exhausted by the heat.

Although by nature not inclined to the melting mood, I felt as if I should dissolve, such streams from my forehead, such thirst, and lassitude; I really 'thaw, and resolve myself into a dew.' The call all day is soda-water, soda-water.

To the 21st of June, this oppressive weather held its sway; our only consolation grapes, iced-water, and the thermantidote, which answers admirably, almost too well, as on the 22nd I was laid up with rheumatic fever and lumbago, occasioned, they tell me, by standing, or sleeping before it after coming in from a canter before sunrise.

22nd.—Heavy rain fell, the thermantidote was stopped, and the tattīs taken down; nor were they replaced, as the rain poured down almost night and day from that time until the end of the month.

30th.—We had a party at home: the thermometer during the day 88°; after dinner it rose to 91°, in consequence of the numerous lamps in the rooms, and the little multitude of servants in attendance.

A LIST OF SERVANTS IN A PRIVATE FAMILY

No. *Wages.*
Rupees per month.

1	A khānsāmān, or head man; a Musalman servant who purchases the provisions, makes the confectionary, and superintends the table	12
2	The ābdār, or water-cooler; cools the water, ices the wines, and attends with them at table	8
3	The head khidmatgār; he takes charge of the plate-chest, and waits at table	7
4	A second khidmatgār, who waits at table	6
5	A bāwarchī, or cook	12
6	Mate bāwarchī	4
7	Mashalchī; dish-washer and torch-bearer	4
8	Dhobee, or washerman	8
9	Istree wālā, washerman for ironing	8
10	A darzee, or tailor	8
11	A second tailor	6
12	An ayha, or lady's maid	10
13	An under woman	6
14	A doriya; a sweeper, who also attends to the dogs	4
15	Sirdar-bearer, an Hindoo servant, the head of the bearers, and the keeper of the sāhib's wardrobe; the keys of which are always carried in his kamarband, the folds of cloth around his waist	8
16	The mate-bearer; assists as valet, and attends to the lamps	6
22	Six bearers to pull the pankhās, and dust the furniture, &c.	24
23	A gwālā, or cowherd	4
24	A bher-i-wālā, or shepherd	5
25	A murgh-i-wālā, to take care of the fowls, wild-ducks, quail, rabbits, guinea-fowls, and pigeons	4
26	A mālee, or gardener	5

27	A mate, do.	3
28	Another mate, or a cooly	2
29	A gram-grinder, generally a woman who grinds the chanā for the horses	2
30	A coachman	10
38	Eight sā'īses, or (grooms), at five rupees each, for eight horses	40
46	Eight grass-cutters, at three rupees each, for the above	24
47	A bihishti, or water-carrier	5
48	A mate bihishti	4
49	A Barha'ī mistree, a carpenter	8
50	Another carpenter	7
52	Two coolies, to throw water on the tattis	4
54	Two chaukīdārs, or watchmen	8
55	A durwān, or gate-keeper	4
57	Two chaprāsīs, or running footmen, to carry notes, and be in attendance in the verandah	10

57	total.	Rupees per month *290*

During the hot winds, a number of extra coolies, twelve or fourteen, are necessary, if you have more than one thermantidote, or if you keep it going all night as well as during the day; these men, as well as an extra bihishti, are discharged when the rains set in.

We, as quiet people, find these servants necessary. Some gentlemen for state add an assa burdar, the bearer of a long silver staff; and a sonta burdar, or chob-dar, who carries a silver club, with a grim head on the top of it. The business of these people is to announce the arrival of company.

If many dogs are kept, an extra doriya will be required.

The above is a list of our own domesties, and the rate of their wages.

The heat of the climate, added to the customs and prejudices of the natives, oblige you to keep a number of servants; but you do not find them in food (*sic*) as in England. One man will not do the work of another, but says, 'I shall lose caste,' which caste, by the bye, may be regained by the expenditure which of a few rupees in a dinner to their friends and relatives. The Mohammadan servants pretend they shall lose caste; but, in fact, they have none: the term is only applicable to the Hindoos.

If your khānsāmān and sirdar-bearer are good and honest servants, you have little or no trouble with an Indian household; but, unless you are fortunate with your head servants, there is great trouble in keeping between fifty or sixty domestics in order.

∽

July 1831.—The crows are a pest; they will pounce upon meat carried on a plate, and bear it off: they infest the door of the Bawarchī Khānā (cook room), and annoy the servants, who retaliate on a poor kawwā, if they can catch one, by dressing it up in an officer's uniform, and letting it go to frighten the others. The poor bird looks so absurd hopping about. Sometimes they drill a hole through the beak, and passing a wire through it, string thereon five cowries; this bears the poor crow's head to the ground, and must torture it. Such cruelty I have forbidden. The crow is a bird of ill omen.

On a babūl-tree in the grounds are twelve or fifteen beautiful nests pendant from the extremity of slender twigs—the habitations of a little community of Byā birds. I took down three of the nests; they contained two, three, and four little white eggs; the parent birds made a sad lament when the nests were taken. If you take a nest with the young birds in it, the parent bird will follow and feed them. The natives consider it highly improper to shoot the Byā birds; they are sacred, and so tame. One of my servants has brought me a young bird, it flies to my hand when I call it. There is a pretty fable which says, 'The old put a fire-fly into their nests every night to act as a lamp.' Perhaps they sometimes feed their young on fire-flies, which may be the origin of the story. It is pleasing to imagine the sacred birds swinging in their pretty nests pendant from the extreme end of a branch, the interior lighted by a fire-fly lamp. The Byā bird is the Indian yellow-hammer; the nests I speak of are almost within reach of my hand, and close to the house. They are of grass beautifully woven together, and suspended by a long thin tapering end, the entrance hanging downwards. In the nests containing the young, there is no division, the swelling on the side is the part in which the young ones nestle together. Some of the nests appear as if they were cut short off: these are purposely built so, and contain two apartments, which are, I suppose, the places where the parent birds sit and confabulate on the aspect of affairs in general. The birds are very fond of hanging their nests from slender twigs, over a pool of water, the young birds thus being in greater safety.

The wood of the babūl (*Acacia arabica*) is extremely hard, and is used by the Brahmans to kindle their sacred fire, by rubbing two pieces of it together, when it is of a proper age, and sufficiently dried. It produces the Indian gum arabic. The gold earrings made in imitation of the flower of the babul, worn by Indian women, and by some men also, are beautiful.

My ayha is ill with cholera: there is no hope of her recovery. The disease came across the Jumna, about four miles higher up than our house, and is regularly marching across the country to the Ganges: as it proceeds no fresh cases occur in the villages it leaves behind.

The old peepul moans and rustles in the wind so much, that deceived by the sound, we have often gone into the verandah joyously exclaiming 'There is the rain!' To our sorrow it was only the leaves of the tree agitated by the wind.

In such a climate and during the hot winds, you cannot imagine how delightful the noise of the wind (like rain) in the old peepul appeared to us, or the lullaby it formed. It is a holy tree, every leaf being the seat of a god. They do not listen to the music of its rustling with greater pleasure than I experience ; indeed, my *penchant* for the tree is so great, I am half inclined to believe in its miraculous powers.

August 31st.—The ice has lasted four months and fifteen days, which we consider particularly fortunate. It was opened the 15th of April.

October.—We are collecting grass and making hay for use during the hot winds. The people cut the grass in the jungles, and bring it home on camels. We have one stack of hay just finished, and one of straw.

'Bring me the silver tankard.' 'I have it not, I know not where it is,' said the khidmatgār. The plate-chest was searched, it was gone.

It was the parting gift of a friend; we would not have lost it for fifty times its value. The servants held a panchayat, and examined the man who had charge of the plate. When it was over, he came to me, saying, 'I had charge of the tankard—it is gone—the keys were in my hands; allow me to remain in your service; cut four rupees a month from my pay, and let another silver cup be made.' The old man lived with us many years, and only quitted us when he thought his age entitled him to retire on the money he had earned honestly and fairly in service.

My tame squirrel has acquired a vile habit of getting up the windows and eating all the flies; if he would kill the musquitoes, it would be a very good employment, but he prefers the great fat flies— a little brute. The little squirrel is the only animal unaffected by the heat; he is as impudent as ever, and as cunning as possible.

October 24th.—A slight earthquake has just taken place—this instant. I did not know what the matter was; there was a rumbling noise for some time, as if a carriage were driving over the roof of the house. My chair shook under me, and the table on which I am writing shook also. I became very sick and giddy, so much so, that I fancied I had fallen ill suddenly. When the noise and trembling ceased, I found I was quite well, and the giddy sickness went off. I never felt the earth quake before. Every one in the house was sensible of it. At the Circuit bungalow, nearly three miles off, it was felt as much as on the banks of the Jumna.

In a native family, if a person be ill, one of the relations takes a small earthen pan, filled with water, flowers, and rice, and places it in the middle of the road or street, in front of the house of the sick person, believing that if any one *en passant* should touch the offering, either by chance or design, the illness would quit the sufferer and cleave to the person who had touched the flowers or the little pan containing the offering. A native carefully steps aside and avoids coming in contact with the flowers.

∽

1832, May.—Allahabad is now one of the gayest, and is, as it always has been, one of the prettiest stations in India. We have dinner-parties more than enough; balls occasionally; a book society; some five or six billiard-tables; a pack of dogs, some amongst them hounds, and (how could I have forgotten!) fourteen spinsters!

2nd.—Colonel Gardner has sent us twelve jars of the most delicious Lucnow chutnee, the very beau ideal of mixtures of sharp, bitter, sour, sweet, hot, and cold!

This station, which in former days was thought one of the least-to-be-coveted positions, has now become, what from the first we always pronounced it to be, one of the most desirable. We have a kind neighbourly society, as much, or even more of gaiety than we sober folks require, and, mirabile, no squabbling. I hope his lordship will not disturb our coterie by moving the Boards of Revenue and of Criminal and Civil Justice higher up the country, which some think not improbable. [. . .]

June 19th.—We drove into the Fort to call on a fair friend at 5 P.M. No sooner had I entered, the house, than we saw clouds of locusts in the air: immediately afterwards a heavy storm of rain fell, and the locusts were beaten down by it in great numbers to the ground. The native servants immediately ran out and caught them by handfuls, delighted to get them to make a curry; for which purpose they may, perhaps, be as delicate as prawns, which are most excellent. I took some to preserve with arsenical soap: they look like very large grasshoppers. I never saw a flight of locusts before; on our return home the air was full of them.

The food of St. John in the wilderness was locusts and wild honey: very luxurious fare, according to the natives, who say, either in a curry or fried in clarified butter, they are excellent. I believe they divest them of their wings, and dress them after the fashion of woodcocks.

Some assert that St. John did not live upon locusts, but upon the bean of a tree called by the Arabs Kharroub, the locust-tree of Scripture— a point too difficult to be decided by a poor haji in search of the picturesque.

◆

THE GREAT FAIR AT ALLAHABAD

Talking to a man who is in ecstacy (of a religious nature practised or feigned by fakirs) is like beating curds with a pestle.

1833, January.—The burā melā at Prāg, or the great fair at Allahabad, is held annually on the sands of the Ganges below the ramparts of the Fort, extending from the Mahratta Bund to the extreme point of the sacred junction of the rivers. The booths extend the whole distance, composed of mud walls, covered with mats, or thatched. This fair lasts about two months, and attracts merchants from all parts of India, Calcutta, Delhi, Lucknow, Jeypore, &c. Very good diamonds, pearls, coral, shawls, cloth, woollens, china, furs, &c., are to be purchased. Numerous booths display brass and copper vessels, glittering in the sun with many brazen idols: others are filled with Benares' toys for children. Bows and arrows are displayed, also native caps made of sable, the crowns of which are of the richest gold and silver embroidery.

The pearl merchants offer long strings of large pearls for sale, amongst which some few are fine, round and of a good colour. The natives value size, but are not very particular as to colour; they do not care to have them perfectly round, and do not object to an uneven surface. They will allow a purchaser to select the best at pleasure from long strings.

The deep red coral is valued by the natives much more than the pink. I bought some very fine pink coral at the fair: the beads were immense; the price of the largest, eleven rupees per tola; *i.e.* eleven rupees for one rupee weight of coral. The smallest, six or four rupees per tola; it was remarkably fine. Some years afterwards the Brija Bā'ī, a Mahratta lady, a friend of mine, called on me; she observed the long string of fine pink coral around my neck, and said, 'I am astonished a mem sahiba should wear coral; we only decorate our horses with it; that is pink coral, the colour is not good; look at my horse.' I went to the verandah; her horse was adorned with a necklace of fine deep red coral. She was quite right, and I made over mine to my grey steed.

Some of the prettiest things sold at the Melā are the tīkas, an ornament for the forehead for native women. The tika is of different sizes and patterns; in gold or silver for the wealthy, tinsel for the poorer classes; and of various shapes. The prettiest are of silver, a little hollow cup like a dew-drop cut in halves: the ornament is stuck with an adhesive mixture on the forehead, just in the centre between the eyebrows. Some tīkas are larger, resembling the *ferronière* worn by European ladies.

The Allahabad hukāks are famous for their imitation in glass of precious stones. I purchased a number of native ornaments in imitation of the jewellery worn by native ladies, which were remarkably well made, and cost only a few rupees. I also bought strings of mock pearls brought from China, that are scarcely to be distinguished from real pearls, either in colour or weight.

The toys the rich natives give their children, consisting in imitations of all sorts of animals, are remarkably pretty; they are made in silver, and enamelled: others are made of ivory very beautifully carved; and for the poorer classes they are of pewter, moulded into the most marvellous shapes.

At this time of the year lākhs and lākhs of natives come to bathe at the junction of the Ganges and Jumna; they unite at the extremity of a neck of land, or rather sand, that runs out just below the Fort. On this holy spot the Brahmans and religious mendicants assemble in thousands. Each fakīr pitches a bamboo, from the end of which his flag is displayed, to which those of the same persuasion resort. Here they make pooja, shave, give money to the fakīr, and bathe at the junction. The clothes of the bathers are put upon charpāīs to be taken care of, for so many pāisa. Every native, however poor he may be, pays tribute of one rupee to Government before he is allowed to bathe.

Two boats, by order of Government, are in attendance at this point to prevent persons from drowning themselves or their children. The mere act of bathing in the waters of the Gunga, on a particular day, removes ten sins, however enormous, committed in ten previous births. How much greater must be the efficacy at the junction of the Gunga and Yamuna, which the Saraswati, the third sacred river, is supposed to join underground! The benefits arising from bathing at the lucky moment of the conjunction of the moon with a particular star is very great, or at the time of eclipse of the sun or moon.

The holy waters are convenient for washing away a man's sins, and as efficacious as a pope's bull for this purpose. Groups of natives stand in the river whilst their Brahman reads to them, awaiting the happy moment at which to dip into the sacred and triple waves. They fast until the bathing is over. Suicide committed at the junction is meritorious in persons of a certain caste, but a *sin* for a Brahman!

The holy men prefer the loaves and fishes of this world to the immediate moksh or beatitude, without further risk of transmigration, which is awarded to those who die at the sacred junction.

January 11.—Some natives are at the door with the most beautiful snakes, two of them very large, and striped like tigers; the men carry them twisted round their bodies, and also round their necks, as a young lady wears a boa; the effect is good. The two tiger-striped ones were greatly admired as a well-matched pair; they are not venomous. A fine cobra, with his great hood spread out, made me shrink away as he came towards me, darting out his forked tongue.

There were also two snakes of a dun yellow colour, spotted with white, which appeared in a half torpid state; the men said they were as dangerous as the cobra. They had a biscobra; the poor reptile was quite lame, the people having broken all its four legs, to prevent its running away. They had a large black scorpion, but not so fine a fellow as that in my bottle of horrors.

The mela is very full; such beautiful dresses of real sable as I have seen to-day brought down by the Moguls for sale! Lined with shawl, they would make magnificent dressing-gowns. I have bought a Persian writing-case, and a book beautifully illuminated, and written in Persian and Arabic: the Moguls beguile me of my rupees.

We are going to a ball to-night at Mr F——'s, given in honour of Lady Wm. Bentinck, who is expected to arrive this evening. The natives have reported the failure of Messrs Mackintosh & Co., in Calcutta; I do not think it is known amongst the Europeans here; the natives always get the first intelligence; I will not mention it, lest it should throw a shade over the gaiety of the party. An officer, who got the lākh, and 60,000 rupees also in the lottery last year, passed down the river to-day, to place it in Government security; it is all gone; a note has been despatched to inform him of the failure, and save him a useless trip of eight hundred miles; he lost twenty-five thousand only a few weeks ago, by Messrs Alexander's failure. Lachhmi abides not in his house.

12th.—The ball went off very well, in spite of Messrs Mackintosh's failure being known; and people who had lost their all danced as merrily as if the savings of years and years had not been swept away by 'one fell swoop'!

20th.—It is so cold to-day, I am shivering; the cocoa-nut oil in the lamps is frozen slightly; this weather is fit for England. I must get all the bricklayer's work over before the hot winds, that I may be perfectly quiet during the fiery time of the year.

THE CHOLERA

It was hammered upon my forehead.
i.e. it was my destiny.

Where is the use of taking precautions, since what has been pre-
ordained must happen?

1833. August 8th—The same terrible weather continues, the thermometer
90° and 91° all day; not a drop of rain! They prophesy sickness and
famine; the air is unwholesome; the Europeans are all suffering with
fever and ague and rheumatism. The natives, in a dreadful state, are
dying in numbers daily of cholera; two days ago, seventy-six natives in
Allahabad were seized with cholera—of these, forty-eight died that day!
The illness is so severe that half an hour after the first attack the man
generally dies; if he survive one hour it is reckoned a length of time.

A brickmaker, living near our gates, buried four of his family from
cholera in one day! Is not this dreadful? The poor people, terror-
stricken, are afraid of eating their food, as they say the disease follows
a full meal. Since our arrival in India we have never before experienced
such severely hot winds, or such unhealthy rains.

'Every country hath its own fashions.' The Hindoo women, in the
most curious manner, propitiate the goddess who brings all this illness
into the bazār: they go out in the evening about 7 P.M., sometimes two
or three hundred at a time, carrying each a lota, or brass vessel, filled
with sugar, water, cloves, &c. In the first place they make pooja; then,
stripping off their chādars, and binding their sole petticoat around their
waists, as high above the knee as it can be pulled up, they perform a
most frantic sort of dance, forming themselves into a circle, whilst in the
centre of the circle about five or six women dance entirely naked,
beating their hands together over their heads, and then applying them
behind with a great smack, that keeps time with the music, and with the
song they scream out all the time, accompanied by native instruments,
played by men who stand at a distance; to the sound of which these
women dance and sing, looking like frantic creatures. Last night, returning
from a drive, passing the Fort, I saw five or six women dancing and
whipping themselves after this fashion; fortunately, my companion did
not comprehend what they were about. The Hindoo women alone

practise this curious method of driving away diseases from the bazār; the Musulmāns never. The men avoid the spot where the ceremony takes place; but here and there, one or two men may be seen looking on, whose presence does not appear to molest the nut-brown dancers in the least; they shriek and sing and smack and scream most marvellously.

The moonshee tells me the panic amongst the natives is so great, that they talk of deserting Allahabad until the cholera has passed away.

My darzee (tailor), a fine healthy young Musulmān, went home at 5 P.M., apparently quite well ; he died of cholera at 3 P.M. the next day; he had every care and attention. This evening the under-gardener has been seized; I sent him medicine; he returned it, saying, 'I am a Baghut (a Hindoo who neither eats meat nor drinks wine), I cannot take your medicine; it were better that I should die.' The cholera came across the Jumna to the city, thence it took its course up *one side* of the road to the Circuit Bungalow, is now in cantonments, and will, I trust, pass on to Papamhow, cross the Ganges, and Allahabad will once more be a healthy place.

'Magic is truth, but the magician is an infidel.' My ayha said, 'You have told us several times that rain will fall, and your words have been true; perhaps you can tell us when the cholera will quit the city?' I told her, 'Rain will fall, in all probability, next Thursday (new moon); and if there be plenty of it, the cholera may quit the city.' She is off to the bazar with the joyful tidings. [. . .]

August 17th.—The new moon has appeared, but Prāg is unblessed with rain; if it would but fall! Every night the Hindoos pooja their gods; the Musulmāns weary Heaven with prayers, at the Jamma Musjid (great mosque) on the river-side, near our house—all to no effect. The clouds hang dark and heavily; the thunder rolls at times; you think, 'Now the rain must come,' but it clears off with scarcely a sprinkling. Amongst the Europeans there is much illness, but no cholera.

22nd.—These natives are curious people; they have twice sent the cholera over the river, to get rid of it at Allahabad. They proceed after this fashion: they take a bull, and after having repeated divers prayers and ceremonies, they drive him across the Ganges into Oude, laden, as they believe, with the cholera. This year this ceremony has been twice performed. When the people drive the bull into the river, he swims across, and lands or attempts to land on the Lucnow side; the Oude people drive the poor beast back again, when he is generally carried down by the current and drowned, as they will not allow him to land on either side.

TEMPLE OF BHAWANI AND SUTTEES ALOPEE BAGH.

Temple of Bhawani and Suttees Alopee Bagh

During the night, my ayha came to me three times for cholera mixture; happily the rain was falling, and I thought it would do much more good than all the medicine; of course I gave her the latter.

Out of sixty deaths there will be forty Hindoos to twenty Musulmāns; more men are carried off than women, eight men to two women; the Musulmāns eat more nourishing food than the Hindoos, and the women are less exposed to the sun than the men.

1834, *June*.—It is scarcely possible to write, the natives are making such a noise overhead, repairing the flat roof of the house, which is made of flag-stones, supported by large beams of wood; over that brick-dust and lime, mixed with water, is laid a foot in depth, which they are now beating down with little wooden mallets, holding one in each hand.

August 9th.—This is a holiday, the nāg-panchamī, on which day the Hindūs worship a snake, to procure blessings on their children; of course, none of the carpenters or the other workmen have made their appearance. The other day, a gentleman, who is staying with us, went into his bathing-room to take a bath; the evening was very dark, and, as he lifted a ghāra (an earthen vessel), to pour the water over his head, he heard a hissing sound among the waterpots, and, calling for a light, saw a great cobra de capello. 'Look at that snake!' said he to his bearer, in a tone of surprise. 'Yes, sāhib,' replied the Hindoo, with the utmost apathy, 'he has been there a great many days, and gives us much trouble!'

September 11th.—We purchased a very fine pinnace, that an officer had brought up the river, and named her the *Seagull*. She is as large as a very good yacht; it will be pleasant to visit those ghats on the Ganges and Jumna, during the cold weather, that are under the sāhib's control. The vessel is a fine one, and the natives say, 'She goes before the wind like an arrow from a bow.'

The city of Allahabad, considered as a native one, is handsome: there are but few pukka houses. The rich merchants in the East make no display, and generally live under bamboo and straw. The roads through the city are very good, with rows of fine trees on each side; the drives around are numerous and excellent. There is also a very handsome sarā'e (caravansary), and a bā'olī, a large well, worthy a visit. The tomb and garden of Sultan Khusrau are fine; a description of them will be given hereafter. The fort was built by Akbar in 1581, at the junction of the Ganges and Jumna. Within the fort, near the principal gateway, an enormous pillar is prostrate; the unknown characters inscribed upon it are a marvel and a mystery to the learned, who as yet have been unable to translate them. The bazār at Allahabad is famous for old coins.

MATILDA SPRY

The important dates of the 1857 Mutiny in Allahabad are 12–14 May, 6 June, and 11 June. News of the events in Meerut and Delhi, following the episode of the greased cartridges, reached Allahabad on 12–14 May. Initially, the news appears to have had little effect, but as the days went by the European residents of the city became apprehensive and said as much in their letters to the press. A consequence of it was that the government ordered extra troops to be sent from Chunar, which, when they arrived on 23 May, turned out to be sixty-five invalids. On 6 June the 6th Regiment Native Infantry, whose loyalty to the British was unquestionable, mutinied, killing all the British officers, except the few who managed to survive by escaping to the Fort. The infamous Colonel James Neill reached Allahabad from Benares on 11 June and with the help of 200 faithful Sikhs, who were garrisoned in the Fort but had themselves taken part in the looting of the city earlier in the week, took command of the station. As one contemporary British account put it, it was only after Neill's arrival that 'affairs took a turn'.

Matilda Spry's letters are in the British Library (MSS Eur. B219). They are remarkable for the account they give of how one ordinary British woman coped with events in the city in the days prior to and following 6 June 1857. They are also a reminder that life in India, then as now, with or without empire and colonization, even in the midst of terrible personal losses, revolves around thieving servants. Kate Chisholm, who transcribed the letters, has provided the following note on Matilda Spry: Matilda Spry was the wife of the chaplain to Allahabad, the Revd Arthur Browne Spry. She was born in 1814, and married in Diss, Norfolk, in 1836, travelling out to India afterwards. Her daughter, Matty, was aged nine and had not long been sent home to England, as had her two elder brothers, Arthur (nineteen) and Fred (fifteen). Herbert was aged three. He survived but his brother Walter ('Podgie'), who is referred to in the letter of 13 July, died in the Fort on 4 August 1857, aged one year and eight months. Matilda Spry died on the way home to England on 17 March 1859 on board the *Alfred* and was buried at sea in the Bay of Bengal. Her husband returned to erect a monument to her in the church at Allahabad, and spent the rest of his working life in India.

∾

'Our pretty bungalow is now a heap of ruins'

Letter from Matilda Spry to her mother and sisters (in Diss, Norfolk)
Fort Allahabad
30th May 1857
[Heavily crossed, words not completed—as if written with great weakness]

My beloved mother and sisters,
    The dreadful accounts you will have heard from India will doubtless have made you all anxious for us. Thank God we are safe and I trust now the worst is over and we may not dread an attack on this place. We have been shut up in the Fort a week, a dreadful business to me weak as I am getting here, with a sudden notice, but thank God I am as well as can be expected. I am in the Church Quarters here, the children's beds standing against the corner on rails and my couch in front of them. Such scenes and such fearful heat. My windows look on the river Jumna, the walls of the Fort rising from the river. The Fort has been filled to excess with people, some sleeping in such fearful places. The barracks

Rout of the Mutineers at Allahabad by Colonel Neill

are crowded and the open spaces covered with tents filled with people. These are fearful days but we are not so full of panic as we were about the 24th or 25th. They fully expected an attack from the City people and not trusting to our sepoys, we had to depend on a small body of Europeans and a troop of Sikhs (faithful to us it is believed). We are able to get out daily, Arthur goes to the station and most gentlemen are still there, for if they left before it was absolutely necessary the houses would probably all be robbed and burnt. I get out in the carriage every day, just outside the Fort, for it is necessary to keep up the little strength I have. Oh I am so weak and my cough is very bad. My poor chicks too feel the heat sadly. I wish my darling Herbert was in England with his sweet sister now. He is just now very delicate from the heat. We have got the plate and clothes and a few things we value with us here but if our house is burnt we shall lose our all, but we don't think of that much now. Many people are going out of the Fort now, a good sign, but it will not be altogether safe to do so until we hear that Delhi has been destroyed. The country is now filled with rebels ready to rise if they may and waiting to know how affairs go at Delhi. You will read of the fearful murders at Delhi and Meerut with horror. I could tell you much but I have not strength. [. . .] Received last night dearest Mama's, Eliza's and Gatty's [her sisters in England] affect[ionate] letters. I am thankful for three out of my five treasures are safe in England at this fearful Indian crisis.

∾

Letter from Matilda Spry to her only daughter Matty
Fort Allahabad
13th July 1857
[On small rectangle of wafer-thin pale-blue paper, heavily crossed]

My own darling girl,
Oh! That I could talk to you instead of having to write to you. Not that I would wish the chat to be in this sad country, far far from that! For I have every reason to be thankful that my precious little Matty is safe with kind friends and relations in dear happy England instead of being with us where we now are shut up in the Fort. You will I know

The Judges' Court-House and Gallows at Allahabad

be very sorry to hear how wickedly the natives have behaved, how much mischief and trouble they have brought on us. Our pretty bungalow is now a heap of ruins [burnt down on 6 June] and all in it destroyed or nearly so, but we are, so far, all well, and so, dear, we have cause for praising our heavenly father for having kept us so while many around us have suffered so badly. You will I think be pleased to hear that I am feeling a little stronger and can walk about the room without my stick. I am quite proud dearest Matty of being able to do so. Herbert also is much stronger and more like what he was when you left, but dear darling Podgie is no longer little Podgie, he has grown very thin indeed and looks very ill and is so weak, but I think he will soon get right again as Herbert did. The want of nice bread is much felt by your little brothers. Do you remember how you all used to attack the loaves and jam under the glass covers in the dining room? You three soon devoured a loaf. I have got the glass covers for they were brought back to us by some of the thieving bearers but I have no bread to put under them. All our pets were carried away or destroyed. We heard that Covic [?] Bheestie carried off the guinea pigs, only the little old pair as the young one was dead and your Papa found the empty cage afterwards in his home in the Bazaar. All our servants robbed alike and we shall never see their faces again. Fullah ran away. All of the villages have been burnt, for they filled their houses with their master's property. We have got back two of our cows and so we get nice milk now and Samuel is our cook and good Mr Willcock has lent us one of his servants who does not belong to this place [illegible]. Besides these we have Buddle and Brodor, Gunjor & his son's wife. Mr Willcock sends his love to you. He is gone to Cawnpoor, he is with the Army. [. . .]

Poor Mr and Mrs H. died of cholera one after the other in the Fort, and two or three other people. It was very bad here for a week. [. . .] We have only one room for everything and just an entrance room for the servants. I have written you a long note darling and I hope it will amuse you. I shall be very happy when I hear from you again but I fear we may not get our letters. It is a fortnight since I heard of your arrival in England. I hope poor Mrs Cusine has got a situation back to India. How sorry you would be to part from her, good creature. I wish I could get her to take your brothers home. God bless you my pet girl and may we all meet again some day.

With much fond love

I am your affectionate Mama.

Your dear little brothers send you lots of kisses.

∽

Letter from Matilda Spry to her sister Mrs Eliza Bell
Fort Allahabad
16th January 1858
[Black border, finely crossed]

My own dearest sister,

It seems long since I last wrote to you and yet I always appear to be at my English letters for the days slip away so rapidly between each mail. I have before me your dear precious little note dated Nov. 17th [. . .] I have no heart to settle again in India and yet I fully see that my dear husband cannot yet with prudence retire from the service. I will never leave him if my life is spared. Our losses are very severe and the compensation given by the Govt is absurd as *compensation*; it will be an acceptable gift tho' of £280 [worth almost £12,000 in today's money]. The Relief according to our notions is only for the destitute, but doubtless it has, and will get sadly abused, there are people who will take all they can get, fair or unfair. Arthur as a member of the Committee of the Relief Fund here and Secretary too has had a most arduous task during the last six weeks in rendering assistance and relieving the Lucknow refugees. Happily they have at last all departed and you in your quiet drawing room, dearest E [Eliza, her sister in Norfolk] can hardly understand our joy at having a little peace once more. The dozens and dozens of applications for Relief, the giving and supplying out wants to those requiring things as far as we were able was beyond everything and then Arthur was applied to for every thing & by every body.

Many of the Lucknow people arrived at this now desolate station fancying they were to find all they wanted here when we, here, have lost as much as most of them, only they poor people have undergone a long siege with fearful loss of life. They were a singular party & the troubles & sorrows & horrors they had gone thro' in most cases appeared to have made them unnaturally cold-hearted—with few exceptions you saw no real sorrowing for husbands & children. They seem latterly to have had no fear. Indeed young delicate-looking widows have told me so themselves. They were all a most cheerful party & with few exceptions you would hardly find out the widows and childless. We must not

MESS-HOUSE OF THE OFFICERS OF THE 6TH BENGAL N.I., AT ALLAHABAD.

Mess-House of the Officers of the 6th Bengal N.I. at Allahabad blame them poor creatures for their apparent heartlessness, for perhaps continued exposure to such fearful scenes caused their feelings to be blunted. It seemed so strange to see these bereaved ones walk off in parties to listen to the band playing in the Fort in the evening sometimes, when in my own case up to this day I have not the heart to go near the band. The remembrance of the past with *my own merry little group* there, enjoying the music and fun brings tears to my eyes which I cannot control. I cannot ever be really happy in India again, but whilst it is our duty to our children to remain here I will try to be as cheerful as I can. Nearly eight months now have we occupied *this* one room & I am *fond* of this room & yet I long for a change. [. . .]

Jan. 19th

[. . .] We have now only a few of the 'Lucknowites' as we call them remaining, our old friends Dr and Mrs Brydon among them. He has just been here. He is really now a fine hero—he was quite a lion at home last time. What will he be now after a second siege. He says Jalalabad was trifling compared with Lucknow. [Dr Brydon was the only man of Elphinstone's army to have survived the siege of Jalalabad during the First Afghan War.] He is only just well of a bad wound. He was sitting and eating his dinner with his wife and others and suddenly said, 'I am hit,' and got up and laid down on a couch. A bullet had passed directly thro' his body and gone out on the other side of the room—a most marvellous escape. But he looked dreadfully altered when he first reached this [word missing]. Many have wonderful escapes and heart-rending scenes have been related to me by those who were either sufferers themselves or saw the events. One mother just left a widow told me herself with tears, she was seated working, her little girl of ten by her side doing the same, a shell came in and carried off her head. The poor mother lost her nourishment for her infant baby from the shock, & . . . a few days after died of starvation. This only is one of many fearful stories. After the first week or so of the siege, they thought but little of the bullets that were flying about in all directions like hail outside, continually knocking down someone and coming into their houses every instant. I have heard the ladies say they used to look up and see where the bullets struck. Many were wounded by spent bullets, *poor babies* even got wounded and many killed. Their lives all seemed to hang on a thread and yet they were mercifully supported and cheered up. Some of the stronger ladies used to take in turns to sit up during the nights to supply the poor overworked officers with tea and what refreshment they could during their watches. They had also to help the men in various ways in their many duties. They were unable to wash their clothes a proper white and so they had to dye them a sort of stone colour which did very well for trousers, coats, etc. Dear Mrs Brydon and many others dressed the wounds etc. of those wounded about them. I assure you dear, often when I have heard these ladies talk of the past hardships and the trials, I have been obliged to exclaim, 'Why, it is wonderful that you are here to tell the tale.' Scarcely a tear have I seen shed by any of the party. But I must not entirely fill my letter with accounts from Lucknow, only I fancy these little incidents may be interesting to you all.

BHOLANAUTH CHANDER

Bholanauth Chunder (1822–1910) was born in Calcutta and educated at Oriental Seminary and Hindu College, where he was a student of D.L. Richardson. Michael Madhusudan Dutta and Bhudev Mukhopadhyay were his contemporaries in college. He worked for a British mercantile firm that imported machinery for sugar mills, and undertook some of the journeys in *The Travels of a Hindoo* (1869) on the firm's behalf. In addition to the travelogue, Chunder also wrote a biography of Raja Digamber Mitra and a treatise on the economic consequences of the Raj, in which perhaps the seeds of the Swadeshi Andolan and the idea to shun foreign goods were first sown.

Chunder made the journeys described in *The Travels of a Hindoo* at different times between 1845 and 1866. In 1860, when the memory of the Mutiny was still fresh in everyone's minds, he made his tour of the North-Western Provinces. Travelling on the Grand Trunk Road, he visited Raneegunj, Pariswath, Sasseeram, Benares, Allahabad, Cawnpore, Agra, Muttra, and Brindabun.

The Travels of a Hindoo appeared in weekly instalments in the *Saturday Evening Englishman* between 1866-67 and soon attracted public attention. As J. Talboys Wheeler wrote in the Introduction to the book: 'That the author was a Hindoo seemed scarcely open to question. His thoughts and expressions respecting family and social life were evidently moulded by a Hindoo training. . . . At the same time, however, his thorough mastery of the English language, and his wonderful familiarity with English ideas and turns of thought, which could only have been obtained by an extensive course of English reading, appear to have led some to suspect that after all the real knight-errant might prove to be a European in the disguise of a Hindoo.'

∞

from *The Travels of a Hindoo to Various Parts of Bengal and Upper India* (1869)

October 26.—Fast as four wheels and a four-legged animal could carry us, we were on our way to Allahabad. The night was high when we passed by Gopigunge, missing that place of mutiny-notoriety. By eight o'clock this morning we had glibly rolled over a road seventy-two miles long, and stood upon the left bank of the Ganges. On the other side rose in view the city of Pururava, the Pratishthana of the Aryas, the Prayag of the Puranists, and the Allahabad of Akbar. The river intervened, and on its surface lay the bridge of boats floating like a leviathan. The bridge was yet incomplete for an opening in the middle—and it told much against our patience to lose two precious hours in crossing by the ferry of a primitive age.

The first thing we did on landing was to go at once to the famous *prayag* or junction of the Ganges and Jumna. It was not until standing upon that tongue of land, where the two holy streams have met, that we felt ourselves really in the city of *Allahabad*. The Ganges at Calcutta is scarcely an interesting object to the dull eye of familiarity. The Ganges at Benaras is forgotten in the more absorbing associations of the city of Shiva. But the Ganges at Allahabad is contemplated as the eternal river, which rolls on, watering the fairest valley of the earth, and forms the imperial highway on which pass and repass ten thousand fleets through every day of the year. From the grandeur of its aspect and its importance in the economy of nature, it has become an object of the most devout veneration alike in the eyes of the Brahmaites, Shivites, and Vishnuvites. There is the floating bridge of boats—in which a warmer imagination than ours might see the fabled elephant which vaunted to withstand the force of its mighty stream.

The Jumna, a novel sight, was for the first time beheld, with enthusiasm. Deeply sunk below high craggy banks, rolled slowly on a sluggish stream of crystal blue water. This was the Jumna—the *Kalindi* of our forefathers, a name associated in the Hindoo mind with the adventures of many an ancient Rajah and Rishi—the loves of Radha and Krishna. The spot where the sister Nuddees (Greek Naiades) meet, makes a magnificent prospect. The Ganges has a turbid, muddy current— the Jumna, a sparkling stream. Each at first tries to keep itself distinct, till, happy, to meet after a long parting, they run into each other's embrace, and losing themselves into one, flow in a common stream. The Ganges strikes the fancy as more matronly of the two—the Jumna, a gayer youthful sister.

There is certainly more of poetry than philosophy in all the religions professed by mankind. The 'Swerga' of the Puranists, the 'Paradise' of the Mahomedans, and the 'Last Judgment Day' of the Christians, transcend all Homeric poetry. Religion is diffident to address itself purely to the understanding, which is cold and cautious to accept its statements. It therefore seeks the aid of poetry to help its cause. This explains the reason why lovely spots and romantic heights are particularly chosen for places of worship. There is scarcely a lovelier spot than the *prayag* of Allahabad. The broad expanse of waters, the verdant banks, and the picturesque scenery, tell upon the mind and fascinate the pilgrim. Here, therefore, has superstition fixed a place for purification, through which it is obligatory on a Hindoo to pass on his arrival at Allahabad. The purification falls little short of an ordeal. You have first to submit yourself to the application of the razor from the top of the head to the toes of the feet—the eyebrows and eyelashes even not forming exceptions; and for every hair thus thrown off, you are promised 'a million of years' residence in heaven'. Few rites are more absurd in the history of superstition, and it is unaccountable why no other has been preferred to this shocking operation—when hairs have their so great importance in physiology, and their value in the esteem of beauty. Milton has adorned his Adam with 'hyacinthine locks' and Eve with 'dishevelled tresses'. The 'Rape of the Lock' sets forth the inestimable value of a lady's ringlet. Long beards gave name to a nation—the Lombards. A Sikh is never so much offended as when you touch him by the beard—the great facial characteristic of manhood, never allowed by him to be profaned by the razor. Ask a doctor, and he will say he has known women in a high delirium refuse at the sacrifice of their lives to part with their hair, given them 'to draw hearts after them tangled in amorous nets'. But squatting in little booths erected upon the edge of the waters, and mumbling their prayers like the gibberish inflicted in swearing a jury, do the Pandas of Allahabad contrive to sheep-shear their pilgrims without distinction of sex, age, or rank. The male pilgrim strips himself almost naked, and sits to pass through the hands of the barber. There were some half-dozen men whom we saw to undergo the process of hideous disfigurement. The fellows looked, sans their eyebrows, like idiots past all hope, and unrecognizable even by their own mothers. Certainly, the ceremony is 'more honoured in the breach than in the observance'.

In the Hindoo calendar, this month of October is especially sacred for ablution. If it were possible to take in a photograph of the Ganges from the Himalayas to the sea—how its banks would present an endless succession of *ghauts*, all crowded with men and women, some dipping, others sipping, and the rest worshipping, in every imaginable form of devotion. But the especial great *mela* here is held every year on the full moon in January—*Maghai Prayagai*, as the common Hindoo saying goes. The holy fair lasts then about two months, and attracts people from far and near. The whole space that is seen to extend from the extreme point of the junction to the Mahratta Bund, is then covered with tents and temporary shops. The place is then thronged by devotees, mendicants, merchants, and sight-seers of all castes and professions. But since the mutiny, in which the high-caste Brahmins of Hindoostan made a last effort to revive their ancient hierarchy, this gathering of men has been disallowed to take place under the immediate ramparts of the fort. The priesthood at Allahabad formerly numbered nearly 1,500 families. In their numerical greatness, and impatience under the restraints imposed upon their greed, many of them presumed to take advantage of the rebellion. But by bidding defiance to the authority of their sovereign, they only placed themselves from the frying-pan into the fire. Those who had too anxiously desired to get quit of the Sahibs, whose presence hampered the free exercise of their rapacity, had to save their necks by breaking up and dispersing themselves—and who are now begging their bread in obscure towns, and hiding their heads under huts in the jungles. Their difficulty has become the pilgrim's opportunity.

After Benares, everything looks poor and paltry at Allahabad, and justifies its nickname of Fakeerabad. But when first impressions give way, the place is regarded with a better feeling. More sight-seeing really deserving of the name is enjoyed here than at the great ecclesiastical metropolis of India. There, things are seen only through the camera-obscura of religion. Here, are objects to gratify a rational mind. Allahabad is a large and straggling station. The houses are few and scattered over a considerable space. The town principally extends along the Jumna; but Daragunge on the Ganges in a populous quarter. The roads are broad, and shaded at intervals with fine old trees. [. . .]

From the Hindoo to the Mahomedan—from the Mahomedan to the English, the fort has undergone a successive modernization. In its Mogul style, it typified a heavily-accoutred and unwieldy Mogul soldier. In its present state, it appears capped and buttoned up in a tight English uniform. If the castle now has a less imposing appearance, it has certainly gained in substantial strength from a more scientific plan of defence. The lofty towers of Mogul engineering 'have been pruned into bastions and ravelins on Vauban's system'. The high solid ramparts of stone have been topped with turf parapets. Then there is a 'fine broad glacis, with a deep ditch, draw-bridges, portcullis, and all the material appearances of a great fortress'. Nature and art so fortify this renowned citadel, that standing on a point enclosed by the barriers of two magnificent rivers, it bids defiance to every Native Power in India, and requires for its reduction a regular siege, according to European tactics. To a Bengalee, with his completely anti-military head and habits, the fort appears 'A mighty maze, but not without a plan.'

The importance of the fort of Allahabad was never so apparent as in the days of the Sepoy rebellion. In an early stage of that rebellion, Sir Henry Lawrence had telegraphed 'to keep Allahabad safe'. Sir James Outram 'wrote the most pressing and the most masterly state-paper respecting the paramount necessity of securing Allahabad', and eventually it proved the ark of refuge to the English. One by one, all over Hindoostan, every cantonment had been burned, every garrison massacred, every jail let open, and every treasury plundered. Of that mighty Anglo-Indian Power, which held the heir of the house of Timoor under pension, which had overturned the thrones of Hyder and Runjeet, sold the state-jewels of Nagpore by public auction, exiled the king of Lucknow to a swamp on the Hooghly, sent an army to set up a king at Cabul, and equipped a fleet to chastize his Celestial Majesty, everything had suddenly collapsed. Throughout all Upper India, Allahabad remained the only spot for a footing. There, on the promontory in which the Doab has terminated, and behind the bulwarks round which break the foam of the Ganges and Jumna, hunted to the last asylum, the last strangers had turned desperately at bay. Though the country before them was like a raging sea upheaving with the waves of rebellion, and the country behind presented the same tempestuous scene, though the City of Refuge floated like a tossing ship that expected every moment to founder in the storm, the feeble garrison of invalids, and aged drummers, and a miscellaneous party, resolutely stood their mile and a half of ground. The eyes of all India had been turned upon the little but heroic band, playing at high stakes. Fighting against tropical heat, hunger, cannon, and enormous odds, the handful of men well sustained the hot debate—till detachment after detachment, and brigade after brigade, swelled their numbers once more to subdue Hindoostan beneath the English yoke.

Facing the fort is a fine little *maidan* which separates it from, the town. The entrance, lying through a magnificent portal, is the noblest that Bishop Heber ever witnessed for a place of arms. By itself, the gateway with its high arcades and galleries is not a contemptible post of strength. The sentinel moving beneath the archway, challenges all those under a dark skin who approach the drawbridge without a passport. Inside the fort, the several barracks, the stores of artillery, the groups of soldiers at places, and other martial rights and sounds, give to it a thorough martial character. Just at the angle of the two rivers stands the great imperial hall of Akbar, 272 feet long, which has been fitted up into a magnificent armoury. They show in this hall the traces of ancient Hindoo masonry. The Jumna rolls immediately below the buildings, and on it opens a small wicket, through which there is a little staircase of stone descending to the waters. The Mogul ladies formerly residing here used this as their bathing-ghaut. [. . .]

Great numbers of Bengalees abound in Allahabad, some six thousand. Their errands are various—health, wealth, and pilgrimage. Our doctor had a friend here with whom we were to put up for the night. In searching for his house was best disclosed to us the straggling character of the city. To the question where such a one lived, the reply was *doh coss*; where the Kydgunge, *doh coss*; where the Colonelgunge, the Chowk, the Railway station, the invariable reply was *doh coss*. Coming unexpectedly in a battalion upon our host, it did not inconvenience him in the least to give us a hearty welcome. In the true spirit of a fast money-making and money-expending Kayust, Baboo N—— is accustomed to keep an open house and table for all his friends passing on, and from, a tour to the Upper Provinces. He gave us lots of good eating and drinking, and comfortable housing in an upper-room. The night was spent up to a late hour in hearing tales of the mutiny— which is, and long shall be, the topic in every man's mouth all over the land. They speak of it as a fearful epoch of unexampled atrocities on the one side—and of an unparalleled retaliation on the other. There were the Sepoys with the blood of murdered officers on their heads, and budmashes and bullies, and cut-throats and cut-purses, all acknowledging a fraternal tie, and holding a bloody carnival. But it was impossible that twenty uncongenial parties, divided by quarrels about caste, quarrels about religion, quarrels about power, and quarrels about plunder, could long act together in an undisturbed concert. Soon as batch after batch of Englishmen arrived to re-establish the Saxon rule, they were driven like chaff before the wind. Then followed a dreadful sequel—the horror of horrors. The Martial Law was an outlandish demon, the like of which had not been dreamt of in Oriental demonology. Rampant and ubiquitous, it stalked over the land devouring hundreds of victims at a meal, and surpassed in devastation the *Rakhasi* or female cannibal of Hindoo fables. It mattered little whom the red-coats killed—the innocent and the guilty, the loyal and the disloyal, the well-wisher and the traitor, were confounded in one promiscuous vengeance. To 'bag the nigger', had become a favourite phrase of the military sportsmen of that day. 'Pea-fowls, partridges, and Pandies rose together, but the latter gave the best sport. Lancers ran a tilt at a wretch who had taken to the open from his covert.' In those bloody assizes, the bench, bar, and jury were none of them in a bland humour, but were bent on paying off scores by rudely administering justice with the rifle, sword, and halter—making up for one life by twenty. 'The first spring of the British Lion was terrible, its claws were indiscriminating.'

There came in a friend, who knew about the mutiny at Allahabad, from its beginning to the end. He then lived with his family at Daragunge, carrying on business in country produce. There were other Bengalees living about him, and forming a clique. They had been placed, as it were, upon a barrel of gunpowder for many days. The firing in the cantonments at length told them of the explosion which everybody had expected to burst. It was a signal to the *budmashes* to rise at once in all quarters. The Bengalees cowered in fear, and awaited within closed doors to have their throats cut. The women raised a dolorous cry at the near prospect of death. From massacring their officers, and plundering the treasury, and letting open the jail-birds, the Sepoys spread through the town to loot the inhabitants. Our friend, as well as his other neighbours, were soon eased of all their valuables, but were spared their lives on promise of allegiance to their government. The first shock over, the Bengalees opened a communication with those in the fort for help. But what help could be afforded by those who were in need of help themselves? They then proceeded to take measures of defence against the *budmashes*, and organized a body of forces with the aid of a wealthy Hindoostanee, who resided in their quarter. The Sepoys made many efforts to take the fort, but all in vain. During one whole week after the struggle had begun in earnest, on arrival of the first instalment of troops, people did not know where to lay their heads from the unremitting hail of shot and shell showered from the fort on the streets and bazars of the city. It might be exaggerated to have 'darkened the sun',—though the Pandies were not exactly the men to 'fight in the shade'. Familarity with danger gradually lessened its terrors—the very women grew bold in their desperation. Our friend remarked, that at last he got himself so unconcerned as to walk in an open verandah of his house, while red-hot balls passed overhead through the air. Daragunge had especially been a turbulent quarter, and it had been ordered to be burnt down. The Bengalees went on this in a body, with the most melancholy and woe-begone faces, to represent their fate. But they were told that an order could not be re-called. By much importunate solicitation, they prevailed on the officers to see that order fulfilled only in the conflagration of the outskirt huts, where lived those *budmash manjees* who had broken the bridge of boats on Neill's approach. One night our friend had to drop down through a window of his house, to save a coolie from the hands of a soldier on picquet. The coolie had been moving about in the dark without answering to the challenge of the man on duty. The soldier at last pointed his gun at the stolid fellow, when our friend, jumping out, went up to the man to explain that the coolie did not understand his challenge, and was no *budmash*.

One's blood still runs cold to remember the soul-harrowing and blood-freezing scenes that were witnessed in those days. There were those who had especial reasons to have been anxious to show their rare qualification in administering drumhead justice. Scouring through the town and suburbs, they caught all on whom they could lay their hands—porter or pedlar, shopkeeper or artisan, and hurrying them on through a mock-trial, made them dangle on the nearest tree. Near six thousand beings had been thus summarily disposed off and launched into eternity. Their corpses hanging by twos and threes from branch and sign-post all over the town, speedily contributed to frighten down the country into submission and tranquility. For three months did eight dead-carts daily go their rounds from sunrise to sunset, to take down the corpses which hung at the cross-roads and market places, poisoning the air of the city, and to throw their loathsome burdens into the Ganges.

Others, whose indignation had a more practical turn, sought to make *capital* out of those troublous times. The martial law was a terrible Gorgon in their hands to turn men into stone. The wealthy and timid were threatened to be criminated, and they had to buy up their lives as they best could under the circumstances.

Not a few Bengalees had then arrived under the disguise of Fakirs and Byragees, to seek refuge at Allahabad. Many of them had got real splendid beards, to suit the characters they shammed. From all those who had then mourned that—

> Sad was the hour, and luckless was the day,
> When from Bengal Proper they bent their way—

one noble instance stood out most conspicuous. Though a native from an obscure village on the Hooghly, and unused to the warlike mood, he held his position defiantly, organized forces, made rallies, planned attacks, burnt villages, wrote despatches to thank his subordinates, and made himself deserving to be remembered in history under the soubriquet of the 'Fighting Moonsiff'.

October 27th.—Up early is the morning. Found the compound of our lodge crowded by a large gang of rustic Hindoostanee women, who were squatting in a long row, and indulging fully in their loquacity. They clean grain at the warehouse of our host, and receive a couple of annas a day per head for their labour. They were come for their previous day's pay, and were clamorous to get it, and go about their work. Our new faces made them hold their tongues for a moment, which it is female modesty to do. Though most of them appeared to have passed their middle age, they had all of them tall, healthy frames, with a coarse set of features. Those that were widows had no bell-metal armlets or bangles on their feet and arms. One creature in the company had a tolerably good cut of face, and was by no means unpleasant to look upon, with her pair of soft eyes. Their bodies were all tattooed over in fantastic figures. This operation is undergone by them at the tender age of five or six, from time to time, on different parts of their body, when, in many instances, they have to be laid up under a most painful inflammation. It is an initiatory rite, without which food and water do not become acceptable from their hands. Contrary to our notions, they think the tattooed flowers and wreaths to add a grace to their persons— or otherwise, females would have been the last to observe a custom that interfered with their beauty.

The upward train from Allahabad starts at four in the afternoon— so the whole day is left to us to spend it in exploring the town. In many parts it still has a desolate, poverty-stricken appearance, and consists of thatched huts, with a few brick-houses at intervals. The *Duria-ghaut* on the Jumna is a sacred spot. They say that Rama, with his wife and brother Luchmun, crossed here at this ghaut, on their way from Ajoodhya to go over to the land of their exile. He passed by this place to give a visit to his friend Goohuk Chandal. But it was a long time after Rama, that the Chundail kings of Chunar made their appearance in India, and held Allahabad under their sway. There is properly no ghaut with a flight of steps at the spot to do justice to the memory of Rama. The concourse of people, however, bathing there in this holy month presents a lively scene—with groups of Hindoostanee women performing their mating rites, and returning home in processions clothed in drapery of the gayest colours. The Rajah of Benares has a fine villa in the neighbourhood of this ghaut.

Not far below the Duria-ghaut they were busy at the site of the intended railway bridge over the Jumna. In two years, they have sunk about twenty shafts. The pits, more than forty feet deep, are awful. They lie side by side of each, and have extremely narrow brinks to walk from one to the other. Three or four lives have been lost in sinking the shafts, and it is difficult to get men for the work. The diver has to remain below for half the day. One man had just been taken up as we arrived. He was below forty feet of water for six hours together. But on taking off his waterproof coat, his body was found to have been untouched by a single drop of water—only the hands were dripping and shrivelled. The face also showed a little paleness on removal of the diving-helmet. But he came to himself again after a few minutes in the open air. The shafts have collected a little *chur* about them—and this is to be the foundation for a bridge to ride triumphantly across the Jumna.

The *Jummah Musjeed*, or the Mahomedan Cathedral, is a stately old building. The pork-eating Feringhee having desecrated it by his abode, it has ceased to be used as a place of worship by the sons of Islam. But not far from this mosque do the Hindoos worship a very image of the hog, under the name of *Baraha*. The boar personifies the second [sic] incarnation of Vishnu, who raised the earth on his tusks from the bottom of the ocean. 'It were better to have no notion of God at all, than such an opinion as is unworthy of him'—than blaspheming him as a fish, a pig, and a tortoise.

In Allahabad they show the sacred *asrama* or hermitage of Bhradwaj Muni, a Hindoo sage of Vedic antiquity, and the great forefather of our present *Mookerjee* Brahmins. The spot is classic, and deserves a visit. To the *coteers* of our ancient Munis, where they lived in seclusion amidst their books and pupils, may be traced the etymon and origin of the modern European *coteries*.

One spends a pleasant hour at Allahabad in visiting the *Chusero Bagh*. The garden is a large quadrangle, enclosed by a high masonry wall, in as good an order now as when first reared. The entrance lies through a noble gateway, which is in half-gothic form. Fitting the lofty arch are enormous doors, that turn upon pointed wooden pivots in lieu of hinges. It is now two centuries and a half since the planks first left the carpenter's hands. But the strength of the Indian teak has resisted wear and tear through all this time, without any mark of decay. The space within is laid out in beautiful walks and flower-beds. The patches of turnip and cauliflower console foreigners in a strange land. The fruit-trees are various, and the groves of veteran mangoes magnificent. There is also a little labyrinth of evergreens to puzzle and amuse holiday-visitors.

In the middle of the Bagh are three mausoleums—the Princes Chusero and Purvez, and a third over the Marwaree Begum of Jehangeer. The tombs are all on the model of a Mahomedan *Tazia*. The one belonging to the lady has a little peculiarity in distinction of her sex. She reposes by the side of her unhappy son, as if tending him with her maternal care even in eternity. But they do not allow her to have a quiet sleep—the upper floor of her tomb has been fitted up into a billiard-room, and the bones of the poor lady labour under a sore incubus.

The ill-fated Chusero lies between his mother and brother, and has the grandest tomb among the group. His remains are interned in the vaulted chamber, round which spreads a square terrace forming the first stratum of the building. The small size of the sarcophagus confirms the death of Chusero at an early age. The walls of the lofty octagon rising in the middle, are outwardly ornamented with many decorations. The interior is beautifully painted, in which some of the foliage and flowers still retain their dye. The dome on the top swells beautifully out into a faultless globe. In the opinion of Bishop Heber, these mausoleums 'completely give the lie to the notion common in England, which regards all Eastern architecture as in bad taste and barbarous'.

Adjoining the garden is a spacious *serai*, which gives a specimen of the Mogul public works. The rooms all round the square are still in good order to accommodate travellers. But in the open square is held the noisy fish and vegetable market of the town. To the serai is attached a deep well. From the bottom to the top, its sides are built up with strong masonry. The part left open to go down to the waters has a large flight of steps resembling a ghaut. This well has acquired a great notoriety from the Moulivie who had set up the standard of *Deen* at Allahabad, and who so prominently figured in the scenes of rebellion enacted in that city. To take in people, he used to spread a magic carpet covering the mouth of this well, and sitting thereon rosary in hand, attracted large multitudes to witness his miracle, and hear his pious harangues against Nazarene domination. The ignorant rabble wondered at the secret of his supernatural feat, and believing invincible the man who could resist gravitation, justified his treason and eagerly embraced his cause.

Up in these provinces, the *Shoe-question* has all the grave political importance of the Slave-question in America—and the force of a statutory law in the Mofussal officialdom. Our lawyer had to attend a case before the magistrate. He was forbid to enter the Court with his shoes on. On no account would the lawyer be unshod. On no account would the magistrate give up punctilio. The lawyer remonstrated, the magistrate persisted. For full fifteen minutes the war of words went on, much to the amusement of the bystanders; till at last the magistrate proposed a choice between taking off the shoes and taking off the pugree—between bare feet and a bare head, the two opposite extremes for European and Oriental etiquette. The lawyer immediately doffed his pugreé. The magistrate forthwith resumed his courtesy—and there was an end of the *battle of the shoes*.

In the dispute about the site of Palibothra, the great French geographer, Mons. D'Anville, gave the palm to Allahabad. But there is in Strabo a very particular allusion to a grand causeway leading from Palibothra into the interior of the country. Unless this causeway had been either over the Ganges or Jumna,—where is the river, channel, or any description of water whatsoever, which could have necessitated the erection of that causeway?

Tieffenthaler saw this place full of temples and idols in his time. But in all Allahabad there now rises only a single temple to break in upon the view. There is scarcely any activity of trade in this town, any bustle upon the river, any rumbling of coaches and carts in the streets, or any throng of merchants and porters on the thoroughfares. The population is scattered, and much too thin for a city of such magnitude. The houses are are poor, and the shops mean. The native community makes no stir in any of the important concerns of life—in religion, trade, education, politics, or pleasure—everything languishes at Allahabad. But all this ennui is soon to be at an end. There is a question on the tapis to make Allahabad the seat of the North-Western Presidency. Hereafter, the excellent geographical position, the strength of the natural boundaries, the fine climate, and the great resources of the neighbouring provinces, may point the place out for the seat of the Viceroy himself. Two years ago, here was uttered the dirge over the funeral of the late East India Company—here was inaugurated the era of the Sovereignty of the Queen, with royal promises of pardon, forgiveness, justice, religious toleration, and non-annexation—and here was Lord Canning installed as the first Viceroy of India.

RUDYARD KIPLING

Rudyard Kipling (1865–1939) was born in Bombay, where his father, J. Lockwood Kipling, taught at the Jeejeebhoy School of Art. He grew up speaking and dreaming in Hindustani, and probably introduced more Indian words into the English language than any other writer. When not quite six, Kipling was packed off to England, and the trauma of the uprooting never quite left him. He wrote about it most poignantly in his short story 'Baa Baa, Black Sheep' (1888), which was first published in the *Week's News*, a weekly supplement to the *Pioneer*, the paper Kipling worked for in Allahabad.

Kipling arrived in Allahabad in November 1887 and stayed until the beginning of 1889. He did not like the city or its people, comparing it unfavourably with Lahore, where he had lived and worked for the previous five years. A fuller account of Kipling's stay in Allababad can be found in 'The Young Kipling' by Edmonia Hill, which follows this extract from Kipling's autobiography.

∿

from *Something of Myself* (1937)

In '87 orders came for me to serve on the *Pioneer*, our big sister-paper at Allahabad, hundreds of miles to the southward, where I should be one of four at least and a new boy at a big school.

But the North-West Provinces, as they were then, being largely Hindu, were strange 'air and water' to me. My life had lain among Muslims, and a man leans one way or other according to his first service. The large, well-appointed Club, where Poker had just driven out Whist and men gambled seriously, was full of large-bore officials, and of a respectability all new. The Fort where troops were quartered had its points but one bastion jutted out into a most holy river. Therefore, partially burned corpses made such a habit of stranding just below the Subalterns' quarters that a special expert was entertained to pole them off and onward. In Fort Lahore we dealt in nothing worse than ghosts.

Moreover, the *Pioneer* lived under the eye of its chief proprietor, who spent several months of each year in his bungalow over the way. It is true that I owed him my chance in life, but when one has been second in command of even a third-class cruiser, one does not care to have one's Admiral permanently moored at a cable's length. His love for his paper, which his single genius and ability had largely created, led him sometimes to 'give the boys a hand'. On those hectic days (for he added and subtracted to the last minute) we were relieved when the issue caught the down-country mail.

But he was patient with me, as were the others, and through him again I got a wider field for 'out-side stuff'. There was to be a weekly edition of the *Pioneer* for Home consumption. Would I edit it, additional to ordinary work? Would I not? There would be fiction—syndicated serial-matter bought by the running foot from agencies at Home. That would fill one whole big page. The 'sight of means to do ill deeds' had the usual effect. Why buy Bret Harte, I asked, when I was prepared to supply home-grown fiction on the hoof? And I did.

My editing of the *Weekly* may have been a shade casual—it was but a re-hash of news and views after all. My head was full of, to me, infinitely more important material. Henceforth no mere twelve hundred

The Pioneer Press (2005)

'Plain Tales' jammed into rigid frames, but three- or five-thousand-word cartoons once a week. So did young Lippo Lippi, whose child I was, look on the blank walls of his monastery when he was bidden decorate them! ' 'Twas ask and have, Choose for more's ready,' with a vengeance.

I fancy my change of surroundings and outlook precipitated the rush. At the beginning of it I had an experience which, in my innocence, I mistook for the genuine motions of my Daemon. I must have been loaded more heavily than I realized with 'Gyp', for there came to me in scenes as stereoscopically clear as those in the crystal an Anglo-Indian *Autour du Mariage*. My pen took charge and I, greatly admiring, watched it write for me far into the nights. The result I christened *The Story of the Gadsbys*, and when it first appeared in England I was complimented on my 'knowledge of the world'. After my indecent immaturity came to light, I heard less of these gifts. Yet, as the Father said loyally: 'It wasn't *all* so dam' bad, Ruddy.'

At any rate it went into the *Weekly*, together with soldier tales, Indian tales, and tales of the opposite sex. There was one of this last which, because of a doubt, I handed up to the Mother, who abolished it and wrote me: *Never you do that again*. But I did and managed to pull off, not unhandily, a tale called 'A Wayside Comedy', where I worked hard for a certain 'economy of implication', and in one phrase of less than a dozen words believed I had succeeded. More than forty years later a Frenchman, browsing about some of my old work, quoted this phrase as the *clou* of the tale and the key to its method. It was a belated 'workshop compliment' that I appreciated. Thus, then, I made my own experiments in the weights, colours, perfumes, and attributes of words in relation to other words, either as read aloud so that they may hold the ear, or, scattered over the page, draw the eye. There is no line of my verse or prose which has not been mouthed till the tongue has made all smooth, and memory, after many recitals, has mechanically skipped the grosser superfluities.

These things occupied and contented me, but—outside of them— I felt that I did not quite fit the *Pioneer*'s scheme of things and that my superiors were of the same opinion. My work on the *Weekly* was not legitimate journalism. My flippancy in handling what I was trusted with was not well seen by the Government or the departmental officialism, on which the *Pioneer* rightly depended for advance and private news, gathered in at Simla or Calcutta by our most important Chief Correspondent. I fancy my owners thought me safer on the road than in my chair; for they sent me out to look at Native State mines, mills, factories and the like. Here I think they were entirely justified. My proprietor at Allahabad has his own game to play (it brought him his well-deserved knighthood in due course) and, to some extent, my vagaries might have embarrassed him. One, I know, did. The *Pioneer* editorially, but cautiously as a terrier drawing up to a porcupine, had hinted that some of Lord Roberts' military appointments at that time verged on nepotism. It was a regretful and well-balanced allocution. My rhymed comment (and why my Chief passed it I know not!) said just the same thing, but not quite so augustly. All I remember of it are the last two flagrant lines:

> And if the Pioneer *is wrath*
> Oh Lord, what must *you be!*

I don't think Lord Roberts was pleased with it, but I know he was not half so annoyed as my chief proprietor.

On my side I was ripe for change and, thanks always to *All in a Garden Fair*, had a notion now of where I was heading. My absorption in the *Pioneer Weekly* stories, which I wanted to finish, had put my plans to the back of my head, but when I came out of that furious spell of work towards the end of '88 I rearranged myself. I wanted money for the future. I counted my assets. They came to one book of verse; one ditto prose; and—thanks to the *Pioneer's* permission—a set of six small paper-backed railway bookstall volumes embodying most of my tales in the *Weekly*—copyright of which the *Pioneer* might well have claimed. The man who then controlled the Indian railway bookstalls came of an imaginative race, used to taking chances. I sold him the six paper-backed books for £200 and a small royalty. *Plain Tales from the Hills* I sold for £50, and I forget how much the same publisher gave me for *Departmental Ditties*. (This was the first and last time I ever dealt direct with publishers.)

Fortified with this wealth, and six months' pay in lieu of notice, I left India for England by way of the Far East and the United States, after six and a half years of hard work and a reasonable amount of sickness.

My God-speed came from the managing director, a gentleman of sound commercial instincts, who had never concealed his belief that I was grossly overpaid, and who, when he paid me my last wages, said: 'Take it from me, you'll never be worth more than four hundred rupees a month to anyone.' Common pride bids me tell that at that time I was drawing seven hundred a month.

EDMONIA HILL

Edmonia Hill (1858–1952) was the daughter of the Rev. R.T. Taylor, president of Beaver College in Pennsylvania, and the wife of Samuel Alexander Hill, professor of science at Muir Central College, Allahabad. Professor Hill had been appointed by Lord Salisbury's government and was, in addition to his teaching duties, in charge of the observatory. He was also the meteorological reporter to the North-Western Provinces.

The Hills made Kipling's acquaintance soon after he arrived in Allahabad from Lahore in November 1887 to work at the *Pioneer*, and they became close friends. Initially, Kipling stayed at the Allahabad Club, but the following year, in 1888, he was invited by the Hills to come and stay with them at Belvedere House, next door to the *Pioneer* office. Kipling accepted the offer. In 'A Celebrity at Home', a short piece that was never printed in his lifetime and is hard to come by even today, Kipling has left a short sketch of his hosts and of the house they occupied. It is worth quoting at length, not least because it is Kipling's only descriptive writing, outside fiction, on Allahabad:

> Mrs S.A. Hill at Belvedere House, Allahabad. In the name of the prophet cows! There must be at least twenty of them—grey, slab-sided, hump-backed beasts—grazing on the triangular patch of grass opposite the two tall masonry pillars that mark the avenue of Belvedere House.
>
> Move gingerly among them for the rank lushy growth bred by the rains may have put spirit even into these starvelings, and turn into the avenue of thick-leaved Shisham trees. It is full three hundred yards long, very quiet and dappled with light and shade. There is not such another avenue in Allahabad; the houses for the most part rudely and rawly facing the road with only a mean mud wall to fence off their acreage of bare grass plots from the public eye. Belvedere stands almost a quarter of a mile away from all sound of traffic and herein says the Lady of the House lies its great charm. Others have been known to refer the attribute to far different grounds but . . . one does not dispute the word of the Lady of the House.
>
> The Avenue opens into a garden screened by heavy timber from all external observation, and abounding as saith the ancient horticulturalist Master Parkinson 'in all manner of most pleasant flowers'—tuberoses, balsams, sunflowers, and passion flowers. The house itself is roofed with brown weatherworn thatch excellent at turning the relentless rains of three months in the year. It is one-

storeyed and its front verandah where a large portion of the life of its occupants is lived is supported on octagonal pillars of red sandstone— their bases hidden among the pot and tub plants that embroider it.

The blue jay in the date-palm which overhangs the vegetable garden is crying aloud to all the world that it is morning and the gold-mohur tree has put forth its few remaining blossoms of flame in honour of the fact. Into the front verandah steps a white-robed servant with a table and tea-tray and the master of the house, clad in white samite mystic wonderful comes out for the little breakfast that precedes the big one that is the bedrock of all the day's work. He may merely read the newspaper for half an hour or so, he may taking a portentous big stick wander down the avenue which is being remacadamised with nodular limestone and exhort the idle labourers that life is real, life is earnest and that tapping road metal as though it were glass is not its goal, or he may give audience to sundry mysterious mysteries who drive up in dissolute hack carriages and discourse in low voices.

While much has been written about the American Edmonia Hill (known as 'Ted') and her influence on Kipling—she has been called Kipling's 'muse, collaborator, and confidante all at once'—S.A. Hill has remained a shadowy figure. Of Kipling's biographers, Angus Wilson, who visited Allahabad in 1973 when he was researching *The Strange Ride of Rudyard Kipling* (1977), is alone in paying any attention to him. Hill was a keen amateur photographer and, according to Wilson, his photographs together with the Hills' accounts of the Seonee jungle gave Kipling 'much of the scenic background for *The Jungle Book*'.

Adored by his students, Hill is remembered in more than one account in *A History of the Muir Central College, 1872–1932* (1938), edited by Amaranatha Jha. Rai Bahadur L. Shyam Lal, MA, who joined Muir Central College in 1888, tells the following story:

I was once preparing lemonade in the Science Laboratory and to my surprise Mr Hill happened to come in. I was in a fix. Mr Hill asked me what I was doing. I said, 'To tell you frankly, I am preparing lemonade and want to see what will be its effect on the stomach.' He smiled and said,' This is a very interesting experiment and I would like to perform this experiment myself.' He took a bottle of the lemonade I had prepared and after tasting it said, 'It does show a good chemical manipulation. I have got a hand soda-water machine at my bungalow, if you use it in this experiment you will succeed better.' Next day he brought the machine and gave it to me. From that day we used to perform this experiment at leisure and Mr Hill used to take part in it.

S.A. Hill died suddenly of typhoid fever in 1891 and Shyam Lal was among the students who rushed to Belvedere House when they heard the news. He writes,

> 'We wanted to see his mortal frame as a Darshan. The Civil Surgeon would not allow it. But Dr Thibaut intervened and we were not only allowed to see his corpse but were allowed to carry his coffin to the carriage and also from the carriage to the grave. Mr Hill used to keep a list of his students and obtained jobs for them.'

In March 1889, Kipling set off with the Hills from Calcutta on the steamer *Madura* bound for Burma, Singapore, Japan, and San Francisco. He was never to return to India save for a short visit to his parents in Lahore in 1891.

'The Young Kipling' is based on a diary kept by Edmonia Hill and on the letters she wrote to her mother and sister in the United States. It appeared in *The Atlantic Monthly*, April 1936.

∽

'The Young Kipling'

ALLAHABAD, December 1887

Dear C.—I've met an unusually interesting man with the uncommon name of Rudyard Kipling. It happened this way. We were invited to dine with the Allens, who are neighbours. Mr Allen, the proprietor of the *Pioneer* of Allahabad and of the *Civil and Military Gazette* of Lahore, is always on the lookout for the best material for his papers. Some very interesting articles have been appearing in the *Pioneer* entitled 'Letters of Marque', which were unsigned, and we were all inquiring as to the author, who had supposedly come from the Punjab.

When we were seated at table, and conversation was in full swing, my partner called my attention to a short dark-haired man of uncertain age, with a heavy moustache and wearing very thick glasses, who sat opposite, saying: 'That is Rudyard Kipling, who has just come from Lahore to be on the staff of the *Pi*. He is writing those charming sketches of the native states, "Letters of Marque", which the *Pi* is publishing.'

Mr Wright,   Mr Boutflower,
Mr Gough,   M Zakaullah,   Mr Hill.

Muir College Staff, 1889

Of course I was interested at once, for I had been fascinated by these unusual articles so cleverly written. The author has struck a new vein, and everyone was talking about the information he displayed.

Mr Kipling looks about forty, as he is beginning to be bald, but he is in reality just twenty-two. He was animation itself, telling his stories admirably, so that those about him were kept in gales of laughter. He fairly scintillated, but when more sober topics were discussed he was posted along all lines.

After dinner, when the men joined the ladies in the drawing-room, evidently the rising young author had marked me for an American, and, seeking copy perhaps, he came to the fireplace where I was standing and began questioning me about my homeland. I am surprised at his knowledge of people and places. He is certainly worth knowing, and we shall ask him to dinner soon.

Life in an Indian Station is varied, and one great pleasure is the opportunity of meeting delightful people. I must explain that the *Pioneer* is the leading newspaper of India. It is a sheet of abounding interest to all Government servants, because it publishes a list of promotions, sailings, and everything that is important for the Anglo-Indian exile to know. There are Reuter telegrams covering the news of the world, English letters by noted correspondents, local items, which, with its dignified literary style, combine to make its daily appearance an event.

January 1888

Dear People: We give a garden party to-morrow. I never saw more perfect turf. About twenty old women have been squatting down picking out each stray weed and bottling it, while Umar the head gardener looks on. There are two fine tennis courts and six badminton courts where we can accommodate six or eight players at each. A badminton court is smaller than a tennis court, the net being narrower and higher. The game is played with racquet and feathered cork and is a very merry one with good players who keep the shuttlecock over the net with many rallies. The place will look very festive with the daintily gowned women, the sporting subalterns, the serious civilians, the bountifully spread tables, and the attentive servants in their picturesque uniforms and white turbans.

We sent a note to Rudyard Kipling inviting him to come to the garden party. He replied in a characteristic note saying that the tongue of Pennsylvania was the one language he long and ardently had desired to learn. He would be late, as he had to help put a paper to bed. He does not play tennis, but is quite good at badminton. He said he was pleased to come, and if life here was to be tempered with Allahabadminton he would begin to take comfort. He has told us much of his early life at school.

March 2

Dear J.—I had a lovely surprise this afternoon. A messenger from the Pioneer office appeared bringing me a book from the young man I told you of meeting at the Allens'. We have become quite well acquainted and we both enjoy his cleverness. The title of Kipling's collection of stories, which first came out in the *Civil and Military Gazette*, is *Plain Tales from the Hills*, and it has this amusing inscription:

Between the gum pot and the shears,
    The weapons of my grimy trade,
In divers moods and various years
    These forty foolish yams were made.

And some were writ to fill a page
    And some—but these are not so many—
To soothe a finely moral rage
    And all to turn an honest penny.

And some I gathered from my friends
    And some I looted from my foes,
And some—All's fish that Heaven sends—
    Are histories of private woes.

And some are Truth, and some are Lie,
    And some exactly half and half,
I've heard some made a woman cry—
    I *know* some made a woman laugh.

I do not view them with delight
    And, since I know that you may read 'em,
I'd like to thoroughly rewrite,
    Remould, rebuild, retouch, reword 'em.

Would they were worthier. That's too late—
Cracked pictures stand no further stippling.

Forgive the faults.

March '88

     To Mrs Hill
       From Rudyard Kipling.

Our acquaintance with Mr Kipling is progressing. His parents are quite noted people who now live at Lahore, in the Punjab. The father, John Lockwood Kipling, an architect and designer, was sent to Bombay by the English Government to take charge of the art school, and while there he designed the markets and several of the noted buildings. Young Kipling's mother is very talented. She is the oldest daughter of a Wesleyan Methodist minister, the Reverend George D. Macdonald. When the Kiplings were married they spent their honeymoon beside a little lake in England called Rudyard, and so when, on December 30, 1865, a son was born to them they called him by the name of the place where they had been so enchantingly happy.

Rudyard was educated at the United Services College, the famous school Westward Ho! in Devon, where he remained four years.

His great sorrow was that he could not enter the army, owing to his poor eyesight, and it was particularly hard for him to associate constantly with those who were preparing for the Service. Here at Allahabad I have met two young subalterns who were at Westward Ho! at the same time. They say he was so brilliant and cynical that he was most cordially hated by his fellow students. He was a leading member of the literary and debating societies, and editor of the school newspaper. He says that he earned his first money for a sonnet written for the London *World*, for which he received a guinea, and never since has he had any money which has given him such joy. He fairly thrilled when he spoke of it.

It seems that after his school days he went to London and stayed with his aunt and uncle. They felt that he was seeing too much of life about town, so it was arranged with the proprietor of the *Pioneer* and *Civil and Military Gazette* that he should come out to India to work on the latter paper. In response to the message, 'Kipling will do', he, at sixteen, started out on his journalistic career. He tells amid roars of laughter how he pretended to be years older, and so had a rare time coming to India. In Lahore he was with his own people, for the Kiplings had been transferred from Bombay to the Punjab, and J. Lockwood Kipling was in charge of the art school of Lahore and curator of the museum.

Young Kipling is certainly all things to all people. He talks equally well to High Court Judge or to a scientist, and I hear he can make first-class love to the latest belle in Simla.

He soon became known from one end of India to the other by his 'turnovers'. The first page of the *C. and M.* is filled with advertisements up to the last column, and for his column Kipling wrote a story, a poem, a clever political skit, or whatever struck his fancy, so that he made quite a reputation. These articles were called 'turnovers' because they were continued to the first column of the second page, after which came the editorial.

Dear C.—I am the proud possessor of Rudyard Kipling's *Early Verses*, a small book bound in deep maroon, with back and corners of black striped with gold, about one half inch thick, 4½ by 6, published by Shamus Din, Bookbinder, Mouch Gate, Mahala Sahdman Lahore, with a small ¾-inch blue sticker in corner of cover. The inscription is 'January 1889: from Rudyard Kipling, these the first of his ventures into print'. One of the rhymes is the tale of his experiences coming out to India when he was about sixteen. He had grown a dark beard and for mischief was posing as a man of the world, making love to all and sundry aboard ship, which experience he portrays in 'Amour de Voyage'.

Mr Kipling's characters as a rule have some foundation in real life. Mrs Hauksbee is a charming personality who is well known in India. She is in appearance exactly the opposite to his description. She is wonderfully clever and a great wire-puller. She presented him with a Bible early in his Indian career with the advice to study it carefully and follow its literary style. No one is more apt than he with appropriate Biblical quotations, as all can see.

It is so interesting to us to learn the background of some of R.K.'s poems and stories. 'My Rival' in *Departmental Ditties* has much truth in it, as the two characters are his beautiful sister Trix and a delightful woman I knew at Simla who really merited all the praise that was given her, as she was so youthful and attractive. The latter is also the heroine of the 'Venus Annodomini' in the *Plain Tales*, and that is a very truthful picture too.

In 'Three and an Extra' the incident happened at Allahabad to a lady who has become one of my dear friends. I think R.K. gives his best description of Mrs Hauksbee in this story.

April 1888

I shall never forget the glee in which R.K. came in one afternoon saying, 'What do you suppose I just came across in reading the proof of this week's English letter? Andrew Lang says, "Who is Mr Rudyard Kipling?"' He was so pleased that they really had heard of him in England, for in all modesty he intends to make his mark in the world.

He has his trials in the office, as his articles and poems must be cut to fit. The foreman used to say, 'Your po'try good sir, just coming proper length today.'

One of Rudyard's stories, 'The Recrudescence of Imray', had its origin in an incident at our home. There was a strange odour in the dining room, and by luncheon time it had become stronger and later was unbearable. As the ceilings are made of cloth to give an air chamber to cool the room, the thatch man was called, and upon investigation he discovered that a wee squirrel had died under the roof. R. studied a while and then exclaimed, 'I have it,' and the result was that terrible story of the sudden disappearance of Imray, whose body sagged on the ceiling cloth and finally tumbled down on the table. His own servant had killed him because he had called his child handsome, thus casting the evil eye on him. After I came to India one of the first things I learned was to say to a mother, in order to warn off the evil eye, 'What an ugly child you have,' no matter how winning the infant. . . .

MUSSOORIE, *June*

Rudyard is called back to the *Pioneer*, and we are discussing whether we should generously offer to take him in to our house for a little while rather than to let him go to the Club in this desolate season. He has his own trap—the 'Pig and Whistle', as he calls the turnout—and his own servant, so he would not be much trouble and might prove a pleasant companion.

I don't know how we shall like it to have our home life invaded by him, but it will be impossible for him to stay at the bungalow, for the compound is dug up, preparatory to making the new lawn and it is too unhealthy for anyone to live there during the rains in this age-old country. We can give him the Blue Room for his study and the guestroom with the big four-poster mahogany bed. Did I ever tell you that this bed was brought to India in the time of the East India Company? Things which came out in the old days are passed on from one to another. A friend said when she first called that she admired a certain chair and decided to buy it when I left India.

To continue, R. can have the dressing room, bath, and east verandah, so he can be very comfortable. He can write at night to his heart's content when a story takes possession of him and 'the child must be born'. These Indian bathrooms are very different from ours at home. The floor is of hard *chunam* (plaster), with a high partition for the tub, which is filled as needed by the *bhisti* from his goatskin, which is suspended from his shoulder. The Blue Room has every convenience and is quite private, with its own verandah and entrance from the hall. Kadir Baksh can take complete charge of his master and his part of the house. His man is quite a character. He is tall and commanding in appearance and is wholly dependable, which is well, as Rudyard, who lives in the clouds, needs some earthly care.

July

The *Pioneer* publishes a weekly paper containing, stories, poems, and sketches, a kind of supplement called the *Week's News*, for which the youthful editor was expected to write a story filling several columns. His first notification of this was in seeing, as he came from the north into Allahabad, a huge advertisement in the railway stations saying that Rudyard Kipling, author of *Plain Tales from the Hills*, will write a series of stories for the *Week's News* beginning with the next number! This did not disturb the young man, whose only difficulty was in getting time from his routine work to write out the tales with which his brain was teeming. There was no extra payment for these stories.

ALLAHABAD

Dear J.—When *The Man Who Would Be King* was germinating in R.K.'s mind he was lunching with us. Suddenly he demanded names for his characters. A. promptly said, 'Well, the queerest name I ever heard was that of a missionary I met in the Himalayas when we were both tramping—"Peachey Taliaferro Wilson".' Of course Rudyard seized that at once. I could think of no name to give, so R. said, 'Well, who was the most prominent man in your home town?' Of course you know that I replied 'Mr Dravo', and sure enough he used these very names, adding a *t* to Dravo.

Later he was sitting at a desk busily writing. A. was in a big chair and I was nearby. His custom was to push off a sheet from the pad as fast as he had filled it with his tiny fine writing, letting it fall to the floor. A. picked up the sheets, read and passed them to me, our one complaint being that we could read this thrilling story faster than the author furnished it.

Speaking of 'His Majesty the King', R.K. said he had a very tender corner in his heart for little children, but there was not often an opportunity for showing it.

I never saw anyone more devoted to children, and alas there are so few in this station; all old enough have been sent to England, but Dr and Mrs J. Murray Irwin have a darling little girl who is my godchild. When she comes to the house there is nothing that R. will not do to amuse her. He plays bear, crawling over the floor, and he will endure every sort of teasing. On her birthday he wrote to accompany my small gift a gay little verse beginning:—

Imperious wool-booted sage,
Tho' your years as men reckon are three,
You are wiser than ten times your age
And your faithfulest servants are we.

At last R.K. is coming into his own, for he is permitted to collect the stories he has written for the *Week's News* into a more permanent form to be published by Wheeler, in the Railway Edition. The covers are to be a greyish blue and the pater is designing them.

The first one, of *Soldiers Three*, came for inspection and has been severely criticized by Ruddy. Mulvaney is not smart enough in the way he stands, and the barracks are not just right. I shall keep the pencil sketch, as it will be interesting to compare.

What a life he leads, all among the babblings of the Chamber of Commerce and the unsavoury detail of the days among the dockets, departmental orders, and the queer expositions of human frailty, vanity, greed, and malice that a newspaper offers. With it all he watches for suggestive ideas for his tales. For instance:

'The Judgment of Dungara' had its origin in a statement that A. made at the dinner table concerning the Nilgiri nettle, which has most persistent stinging qualities. R. made use of every item of information he could gain, and in a few days the story of the great God Dungara appeared in the *Week's News*. It has a vivid description of the loneliness of a mission station in the interior. 'Isolation that weighs upon the waking eyelids and drives you by force headlong into the labours of the day.' The missionary, besides giving his flock the Bread of Life, had taught them to weave white cloth from the glossy fibres of a plant that grew nearby. The Civil Service official was due, and the converts, usually naked, were to appear for the first time clothed in their new garments, made, alas, from this terrible nettle. It was woven fire that ran through their limbs and gnawed into their bones. Needless to say, they broke ranks and rushed to the river, 'writhing, stamping, twisting and shedding garments, pursued by the thunder of the trumpet of the God Dungara'.

The need in India for hospitals for native women is very great. Dr. Bielby, the Kiplings' physician at Lahore, was going home to England, so she was asked to present to Queen Victoria the dire necessity for some help for the secluded zenana women. She did so, and as a result the Lady Dufferin Fund for a chain of hospitals throughout India was raised by means of everyone giving a day's pay, from the richest rajah down to the humblest ryot—from the Viceroy to Tommy Atkins. This stirred the soul of Rudyard, so he wrote for the *Pioneer* 'The Song of the Women'— prefacing the poem with the address of the women of Uttarpara to Lady Dufferin which had been published in the *Pioneer*. 'Our feelings in this matter are shared by thousands of our sisters throughout the land and of this we are assured by many signs not likely to come under the observation of the outside world.'

Kipling brought the first copy of the paper just fresh from the press to us and, tossing it over, said, 'What do you think of that?' He is rather cynical about the whole matter, for the giving of money is not voluntary, but practically compulsory.

Kipling's friends felt that it was unfair to him to keep writing stories for the two papers without any extra remuneration, so he was persuaded to discontinue them. He wound up with 'The Last of the Stories'. He pictures a visit of his old friend, the Devil of Discontent, who lives at the bottom of the inkpot, but emerges half a day after each story has been printed with a host of useless suggestions for its betterment. This Devil of Discontent is the proprietor of the largest hell in existence, the Limbo of Lost Endeavour, where the souls of all the characters go. He takes the author below, where his characters are passed in review before him—till his heart turns sick. 'The Last of the Stories' closes, 'Now the proof that this is absolutely true lies in the fact that there will be no other to follow it', and there were no more for the *Week's News*—a great loss to the Indian public. He was not permitted to sign any of his work.

We invited Rud to stay at our house while we are away, as he is at the N.W.P. Club and he could have more room and also enjoy Bhoj's cooking. He has written of his good times and of his trials.

It seems that the ayah thought this was her opportunity for a tamasha, so she celebrated by having guests in the compound. That meant noisy ekkas jingling down the avenue and the night, vocal with much tinkling of anklets to the accompaniment of the *sitar*. Rud says he had no notion that forty poor rupees could create such a devilment for so long.

Evidently he is not idling, as he says Mulvaney 'came' with a rush on the blue couch in the Blue Room, and if he walked one mile up and down as he was hacking it out, he walked three. Old 'Pig and Whistle' is getting lame, so R. is pattering about in the dust, to his infinite weariness and discontent.

September

Dear Ones: You know we live in a famous old bungalow which has been standing since the Mutiny days of 1857, when nearly every house was destroyed. R.K. so appreciated the privilege of staying in our lovely home while we were away that he wrote a clever sketch for us which tells of our daily life, our occupations, and our servants. He pictures the attractive verandah where we live most of the time, the long avenue of thick-leaved shisham trees leading to the house, and he gives many amusing incidents. He calls this 'Celebrities at Home', borrowing the title from a series of articles now coming out in an English paper.

Some day maybe I'll send you the manuscript, which is at first in his fine handwriting, but toward the last is hurriedly scribbled.

December

The *Week's News* demanded a Christmas story which would fill a whole sheet of the paper. R. K. brooded over this awhile; the result was 'Baa Baa, Black Sheep', which is a true story of his early life when he was sent with his little sister to England to be educated. It is next to impossible to bring up English children in India, not because they could not have literary advantages here, but on account of the bad influence the close contact with the native servant has on the child. He is a slave to every whim, so Sonny Baba grows too domineering to suit the fancy of an English parent. No self-reliance can be learned while under the pampering care of bearer or ayah. Also, once a *chi chi* accent—as English contaminated by a native tongue is termed—is acquired, it is rarely lost even after years of later life in England, and pure speech is an essential, according to an Englishman. 'Baa Baa, Black Sheep' recounts Kipling's experiences at the hands of Aunty Rosa, the stern Englishwoman who made her living by taking in the little waifs from Anglo-India who must be separated from their parents. The hardest choice a woman must make in India is to decide whether it is best to go home with her children or to stay with her husband.

A friend took Ruddy and Trix from Bombay on the long sea voyage, and saw them established in the 'home', where little Trix was adored and petted but Ruddy was accused of storytelling. There was great jealousy of his brightness in contrast to that of the son of Aunty Rosa. He learned to escape punishment by deceit, and there was no one to teach him the difference between right and wrong. He, poor child, at six was left in the house with a servant while Trix was taken off on a holiday with the mother and her son. Ruddy read and read from the boxful of books that his father had sent him, reading from daylight to dark, till he had devoured them all; then, forlorn indeed, having strained his eyes and being utterly alone, he entertained himself by measuring the whole house hand over hand.

It was pitiful to see Kipling living over the experience, pouring out his soul in the story, as the drab life was worse than he could possibly describe it. His eyesight was permanently impaired, and, as he had heretofore only known love and tenderness, his faith in people was sorely tried. When he was writing this he was a sorry guest, as he was in a towering rage at the recollection of those days. His summing up in the closing words shows the influence on his whole life.

'We are just as much Mother's as if we had never gone. Not altogether, for when young lives have drunk deep of the bitter waters of hate, suspicion, and despair, all the love in the world will not wholly take away that knowledge, although it may turn darkened eyes for a while to the light and teach faith where no faith was.'

Rudyard was planning to go direct to England, when suddenly the idea occurred to him that he would like to see something of the world first, and as he had helped us look up routes he begged to be allowed to accompany us. Then Mr Allen asked him to write letters on the trip for the *Pi*, which would pay his expenses. We agreed to have him join us, so he writes that he will arrive 'an awful grimy dirty unshaven bricklayer and the great——will perchance come down to the station and blandly tumble over me and then go home and tell his friends that my journey is solely undertaken in the interests of the *Pioneer* and I shall loaf down the platform with an unclean pipe in my mouth and then I'll be fairly embarked on the way to the high seas.'

CALCUTTA, *March 9, 1889*

Here we are, ready to start on our long journey to climes unknown. Rud has loaded us up with a delightful array of books, and he proudly exhibits two black leather manifold books in which he plans to write his 'Sea to Sea' letters for the *Pioneer* with an occasional 'turnover' for the *Civil and Military Gazette* of Lahore, his first love.

He has just received *Wee Willie Winkie*, with its attractive cover designed by his father. This is the inscription for my presentation copy:—

I cannot write, I cannot think,
I only eat and sleep and drink.
They say I was an author once,
I know I am a happy dunce,
Who snores along the deck and waits
To catch the rattle of the plates,
Who drowns ambition in a sea of Lager and of Tivoli.
I cannot write, I cannot sing,
I long to hear the meal bell ring;
I cannot sing, I cannot write,
I am a walking Appetite.
But you insist and I obey—
Here goes!
    On Steamer *Madura*,
    Now rolling through a tepid sea,

March 10th
    to Mrs. Hill from me,
A journalist unkempt and inky
With all regards, *Wee Willie Winkie*.

The covers were torn off from the whole six of the Wheeler edition on account of some postal law, and the letter press sent on to England to Andrew Lang, so that Ruddy may be already introduced when he arrives in London.

The Babu at the Meteorological office at Allahabad will collect the 'Sea to Sea' letters as they appear in the *Pioneer* and bind them, so we can have a record of our trip without keeping a diary, though all India will be looking on.

MARK TWAIN

Mark Twain (1835–1910), the pseudonym of Samuel Langhorne Clemens, was born in Florida, Missouri, but spent his early life in Hannibal, the Mississippi River town he gives a picture of in *The Adventures of Tom Sawyer* (1876). Though known chiefly for that book and for *The Adventures of Huckleberry Finn* (1884), Twain also wrote five works of travel, of which *Following the Equator* (1897) was the last. Written to get him out of bankruptcy, the result of a disastrous investment in a typesetting machine, it recounts Twain's experiences while he was on a round-the-world lecture tour in 1895–6, focusing primarily on India, South Africa, and Australia.

India was like no other country Twain had seen. He said it was 'one vast farm—one almost interminable stretch of fields with mud fences between', but he was also beguiled by it: 'You cannot tell just what it is that makes the spell, perhaps, but you feel it and confess it, nevertheless.' More than the landscape, Twain was fascinated by the people he met. One of them was his 'bearer', whom he nicknamed Satan. The word 'bearer', in its Anglo-Indian sense, was new to Twain, but he realized that without the 'bearer' colonial life would be impossible: 'You hire him as soon as you touch Indian soil; for no matter what your sex is, you cannot do without him. He is messenger, valet, chambermaid, table-waiter, lady's maid, courier—he is everything.' Satan, who was hired in Bombay, puts in a brief appearance in the extract below.

～

from *Following the Equator: A Journey Around the World* (1897)

A great Indian river, at low water, suggests the familiar anatomical picture of a skinned human body, the intricate mesh of interwoven muscles and tendons to stand for waterchannels, and the archipelagoes of fat and flesh inclosed by them to stand for the sandbars. Somewhere on this journey we passed such a river, and on a later journey we saw in the Sutlej the duplicate of that river. Curious rivers they are; low shores a dizzy distance apart, with nothing between but an enormous acreage of sand-flats with sluggish little veins of water dribbling around amongst them; Saharas of sand, smallpox-pitted with footprints punctured in belts as straight as the equator clear from the one shore to the other (barring the channel-interruptions)—a dry-shod ferry, you see. Long railway bridges are required for this sort of rivers, and India has them. You approach Allahabad by a very long one. It was now carrying us across the bed of the Jumna, a bed which did not seem to have been slept in for one while or more. It wasn't all river-bed—most of it was overflow ground.

Allahabad means 'City of God'. I get this from the books. From a printed curiosity—a letter written by one of those brave and confident Hindoo strugglers with the English tongue, called a 'babu'—I got a more compressed translation: 'Godville'. It is perfectly correct, but that is the most that can be said for it.

We arrived in the forenoon, and short-handed; for Satan got left behind somewhere that morning, and did not overtake us until after nightfall. It seemed very peaceful without him. The world seemed asleep and dreaming.

I did not see the native town, I think. I do not remember why; for an incident connects it with the Great Mutiny, and that is enough to make any place interesting. But I saw the English part of the city. It is a town of wide avenues and noble distances, and is comely and alluring, and full of suggestions of comfort and leisure, and of the serenity which a good conscience buttressed by a sufficient bank account gives. The bungalows (dwellings) stand well back in the seclusion and privacy of large enclosed compounds (private grounds, as we should say) and in the shade and shelter of trees. Even the photographer and the prosperous merchant ply their industries in the elegant reserve of big compounds, and the citizens drive in thereupon their business occasions. And not in cabs—no; in the Indian cities cabs are for the drifting stranger; all the white citizens have private carriages; and each carriage has a flock of white-turbaned black footmen and drivers all over it. The vicinity of a lecture-hall looks like a snowstorm—and makes the lecturer feel like an opera. India has many names, and they are correctly descriptive. It is the Land of Contradictions, the Land of Subtlety and Superstition, the Land of Wealth and Poverty, the Land of Splendour and Desolation, the Land of Plague and Famine, the Land of the Thug and the Poisoner, and of the Meek and the Patient, the Land of the Suttee, the Land of the Unreinstatable Widow, the Land where All Life is Holy, the Land of

Cremation, the Land where the Vulture is a Grave and a Monument, the Land of the Multitudinous Gods; and if signs go for anything, it is the Land of the Private Carriage.

In Bombay the forewoman of a millinery shop came to the hotel in her private carriage to take the measure for a gown—not for me, but for another. She had come out to India to make a temporary stay, but was extending it indefinitely; indeed, she was purposing to end her days there. In London, she said, her work had been hard, her hours long; for economy's sake she had had to live in shabby rooms and far away from the shop, watch the pennies, deny herself many of the common comforts of life, restrict herself in effect to its bare necessities, eschew cabs, travel third-class by underground train to and from her work, swallowing coal-smoke and cinders all the way, and sometimes troubled with the society of men and women who were less desirable than the smoke and the cinders. But in Bombay, on almost any kind of wages, she could live in comfort, and keep her carriage, and have six servants in place of the woman-of-all-work she had had in her English home. Later, in Calcutta, I found that the Standard Oil clerks had small one-horse vehicles, and did no walking; and I was told that the clerks of the other large concerns there had the like equipment. But to return to Allahabad.

I was up at dawn the next morning. In India the tourist's servant does not sleep in a room in the hotel, but rolls himself up head and ears in his blanket and stretches himself on the veranda, across the front of his master's door, and spends the night there. I don't believe anybody's servant occupies a room. Apparently, the bungalow servants sleep on the veranda; it is roomy, and goes all around the house. I speak of menservants; I saw none of the other sex. I think there are none, except child-nurses. I was up at dawn, and walked around the veranda, past the rows of sleepers. In front of one door a Hindoo servant was squatting, waiting for his master to call him. He had polished the yellow shoes and placed them by the door, and now he had nothing to do but wait. It was freezing cold, but there he was, as motionless as a sculptured image, and as patient. It troubled me. I wanted to say to him, 'Don't crouch there like that and freeze; nobody requires it of you; stir around and get warm.' But I hadn't the words. I thought of saying *jeldy jow*, but I couldn't remember what it meant, so I didn't say it. I knew another phrase, but it wouldn't come to my mind. I moved on, purposing to dismiss him from my thoughts, but his bare legs and bare feet kept him there. They kept drawing me back from the sunny side to a point whence I could see him. At the end of an hour he had not changed his attitude in the least degree. It was a curious and impressive exhibition of meekness and patience, or fortitude or indifference, I did not know which. But it worried me, and it was spoiling my morning. In fact, it spoiled two hours of it quite thoroughly. I quitted his vicinity, then, and left him to punish himself as much as he might want to. But up to that time the man had not changed his attitude a hair. He will always remain with me, I suppose; his figure never grows vague in my memory. Whenever I read of Indian resignation, Indian patience under wrongs, hardships, and misfortunes, he comes before me. He becomes a personification, and stands for India in trouble. And for untold ages India in trouble has been pursued with the very remark which I was going to utter but didn't, because its meaning had slipped me: *Jeldy jow!* ('Come, shove along!')

Why, it was the very thing.

In the early brightness we made a long drive out to the Fort. Part of the way was beautiful. It led under stately trees and through groups of native houses and by the usual village well, where the picturesque gangs are always flocking to and fro and laughing and chattering; and this time brawny men were deluging their bronze bodies with the limpid water, and making a refreshing and enticing show of it; enticing, for the sun was already transacting business, firing India up for the day. There was plenty of this early bathing going on, for it was getting toward breakfast time, and with an unpurified body the Hindoo must not eat.

Then we struck into the hot plain, and found the roads crowded with pilgrims of both sexes, for one of the great religious fairs of India was being held, just beyond the Fort, at the junction of the sacred rivers, the Ganges and the Jumna. Three sacred rivers, I should have said, for there is a subterranean one. Nobody has seen it, but that doesn't signify. The fact that it is there is enough. These pilgrims had come from all over India; some of them had been months on the way, plodding patiently along in the heat and dust, worn, poor, hungry, but supported and sustained by an unwavering faith and belief, they were supremely happy and content, now; their full and sufficient reward was at hand; they were going to be cleansed from every vestige of sin and corruption by these holy waters which make utterly pure whatsoever thing they touch, even the dead and rotten. It is wonderful, the power of a faith like that, that can make multitudes upon multitudes of the old and weak and the young and frail enter without hesitation or complaint upon such incredible journeys and endure the resultant miseries without repining. It is done in love, or it is done in fear; I do not know which it is. No matter what the impulse is, the act born of it is beyond imagination marvellous to our kind of people, the cold whites. There are choice great natures among us that could exhibit the equivalent of this prodigious self-sacrifice, but the rest of us know that we should not be equal to anything approaching it. Still, we all talk self-sacrifice, and this makes me hope that we are large enough to honour it in the Hindoo.

Two millions of natives arrive at this fair every year. How many start, and die on the road, from age and fatigue and disease and scanty nourishment, and how many die on the return, from the same causes, no one knows; but the tale is great, one may say enormous. Every twelfth year is held to be a year of peculiar grace; a greatly augmented volume of pilgrims results then. The twelfth year has held this distinction since the remotest times, it is said. It is said also that there is to be but one more twelfth year—for the Ganges. After that, that holiest of all sacred rivers will cease to be holy, and will be abandoned by the pilgrim for many centuries; how many, the wise men have not stated. At the end of that interval it will become holy again. Meantime, the data will be arranged by those people who have charge of all such matters, the great chief brahmins. It will be like shutting down a mint. At a first glance it looks most unbrahminically uncommercial, but I am not disturbed, being soothed and tranquilized by their reputation. 'Brer fox he lay low,' as Uncle Remus says; and at the judicious time he will spring something on the Indian public which will show that he was not financially asleep when he took the Ganges out of the market.

Great numbers of the natives along the roads were bringing away holy water from the rivers. They would carry it far and wide in India and sell it. Tavenier, the French traveller (seventeenth century), notes that Ganges water is often given at weddings, 'each guest receiving a cup or two, according to the liberality of the host; sometimes 2000 or 3000 rupees' worth of it is consumed at a wedding'.

The Fort is a huge old structure, and has had a large experience in religions. In its great court stands a monolith which was placed there more than 2000 years ago to preach (Buddhism) by its pious inscription; the Fort was built three centuries ago by a Mohammedan emperor—a resanctification of the place in the interest of that religion. There is a Hindoo temple, too, with subterranean ramifications stocked with shrines and idols; and now the Fort belongs to the English, it contains a Christian church. Insured in all the companies.

From the lofty ramparts one has a fine view of the sacred rivers. They join at that point—the pale blue Jumna, apparently clean and clear, and the muddy Ganges, dull yellow and not clean. On a long curved spit between the rivers, towns of tents were visible, with a multitude of fluttering pennons, and a mighty swarm of pilgrims. It was a troublesome place to get down to, and not a quiet place when you arrived; but it was interesting. There was a world of activity and turmoil and noise, partly religious, partly commercial; for the Mohammedans were there to curse and sell, and the Hindoos to buy and pray. It is a fair as well as a religious festival. Crowds were bathing, praying, and drinking the purifying waters, and many sick pilgrims had come on long journeys in palanquins to be healed of their maladies by a bath; or if that might not be, then to die on the blessed banks and so make sure of heaven. There were fakeers in plenty, with their bodies dusted over with ashes and their long hair caked together with cow-dung; for the cow is holy and so is the rest of it; so holy that the good Hindoo peasant frescoes the walls of his hut with this refuse, and also constructs ornamental figures out of it for the gracing of his dirt floor. There were seated families, fearfully and wonderfully painted, who by attitude and grouping represented the families of certain great gods. There was a holy man who sat naked by the day and by the week on a cluster of iron spikes, and did not seem to mind it; and another holy man, who stood all day holding his withered arms motionless aloft, and was said to have been doing it for years. All of these performers have a cloth on the ground beside them for the reception of contributions, and even the poorest of the people give a trifle and hope that the sacrifice will be blessed to him. At last came a procession of naked holy people marching by and chanting, and I wrenched myself away.

DAVID LELYVELD

David Lelyveld (1941–) is professor of history and associate dean, College of Humanities and Social Sciences, William Paterson University, New Jersey, USA. He is the author of the classic study *Aligarh's First Generation: Muslim Solidarity in British India* (1978).

'Swaraj Bhavan and Sir Sayyid Ahmad Khan' is a modified version of his article 'The Mystery Mansion: Swaraj Bhavan and the Myths of Patriotic Nationalism', originally published in *The Little Magazine*, Vol. IV, no. 4 (2003).

ॐ

'Swaraj Bhavan and Sir Sayyid Ahmed Khan'

On a cold January day in 2003, I visited Swaraj Bhawan, the original Anand Bhawan, Pandit Motilal Nehru's grand mansion in Allahabad. The name was changed in 1930 when he built the new Anand Bhawan next door and presented his former residence to the Indian National Congress. Both houses are now museums that display the Indian nationalist movement as well as the carefully crafted adaptation of British colonial lifestyle that characterized life in the Nehru family. Swaraj Bhawan features a sound and light tour from room to room, but you have to move quickly to keep up with it. If you fall behind you're left standing in the dark. The tour starts at the entrance to what I take to be the original bungalow of a complex of connected buildings. On the left, there is a horse-drawn carriage, minus the horses. On the right, there is the following inscription:

> Swaraj Bhawan originally belonged to Sir Syed Ahmad Khan, the 19th century Muslim leader and educationist. At the house-warming party, Sir William Moor [sic] hoped that this large palatial home in Civil Lines of Allahabad would become the cement holding together the British Empire in India. Paradoxically, the house was bought by Motilal Nehru in 1900, and went on to become a cradle to the Indian Freedom Struggle which was to destroy British rule in India.

Although epigraphy, the interpretation of inscriptions, is one of the many gaps in my training as a historian, I spent a good many hours over the following months trying to interpret this particular inscription. My project was not so much to verify its accuracy as a description of events in past time, but rather to find out what it was trying to say about the nature of India's colonial experience and the place of a significant 'Muslim leader' in relation to Indian nationalism.

From the outset, I was skeptical about the truth of the inscription. I knew from my earlier research on Sayyid Ahmad Khan that he never lived in Allahabad, and I was sure that I would have come across something if he had such an extensive property there, since he was by no means a wealthy man and pretty much had to live on his salary as a sadr amin (subordinate judge) plus a significant but not munificent political pension for so-called Mutiny service of Rs 200 a month.

To pursue my inquiry, I knocked on the door of Shri S.P. Mall, the deputy director of Anand Bhawan, to see if he could tell me more about the source for the inscription. He very kindly showed me an essay written by Bishambhar Nath Pande, a well-known historian and public figure, entitled 'The House Where India was Born: Swaraj Bhawan: an Irony of History', which in turn was derived from Pande's earlier book, *Allahabad Retrospect and Prospect* (1955). I was unpersuaded. It would take more substantial, primary documentation to make me believe that the British government had given this huge mansion in Allahabad to Sayyid Ahmad Khan. Mr Mall suggested that the place to look for such sources was the Nagar Mahapalika, the municipal office building in Allahabad.

When I went to Nagar Mahapalika, I was fortunate enough to be directed to B.B. Banerjee, additional commissioner, a PhD in history, who cordially heard my story and offered to help me get to the truth of the matter. Some months later, Dr Banerjee was able to locate a relevant document, after all, in the Municipal Records: the Register of Government Property (Nazul) in Charge of Nagar Mahapalika of Allahabad. There at Serial No. 4 in the Village of Hashimpur otherwise known as 1 Church Road, Settlement No. 1 35 A.B. was apparently the relevant property, or at least a piece of it, 2 *bighas* and 9 *biswas*. I was informed there are 20 *biswa* to a *bigha*, and 32 *biswas* to an acre, that is, considerably less that the amount of land mentioned in Pande's book. One other problem was that the entry was dated 24 October 1910 and that the occupying tenant was listed as Jawaharlal Nehru, who by then had reached an age of majority. There was no information about the earlier history of the property. Perhaps I would have more luck at the collectorate, but I decided to put that off to some future visit.

In the meantime, I came across a little commemorative essay in the Nehru Library by Indira Gandhi, who was herself born in the original Anand Bhawan. 'As far as we know,' she wrote, 'the house belonged originally to Mr Justice Mahmud who sold it to Raja Permanand of Moradabad, judge of Shahjahanpur from whom it was bought by my grandfather, Pandit Motilal Nehru, in 1900.' Here then was an independent source for the connection with Sayyid Mahmud, the son of Sayyid Ahmad Khan. It gave me reason to believe that there was at least some connection and that it might be worth pursuing the matter further.

A few months later, I had the opportunity to visit the India Office Library and Records at the British Library in London. There I managed to find a few more bits relevant to my inquiry. I discovered that Sayyid Mahmud was living at a different address, 7 Elgin Road, in 1879. But then I came upon an annual publication called *Thacker's Directory* on the open shelves in the India Office reading room. For every year after 1882 well into the twentieth century, *Thacker's Directory* provides names and addresses of people living in the Allahabad Civil Lines. I discovered from this source that Sayyid Mahmud did indeed live at 1 Church Road in 1885 and 1886; then again in 1891, and 1893 and 1894. It is listed as vacant the following year, then from 1896 to 1899 is occupied by Kunwar Permanand, pleader of the high court. It is then vacant again in 1900, but occupied continuously after 1901 by Motilal Nehru, also a pleader of the high court. This was the house that later became known as Anand Bhawan and subsequently Swaraj Bhawan. So there definitely was some connection, via the son, between the Nehru home and Sayyid Ahmad Khan, though it still was a good distance from the claims of B.N. Pande and the inscription at the entrance to Swaraj Bhawan. There was still no evidence that the land and house had been given outright to Sayyid Ahmad Khan in the late 1860s or early 1870s. In 1886, when Sayyid Ahmad Khan came from Aligarh to Allahabad to serve on the Public Service Commission, he stayed in a different house with another relative, though in the same area.

Then at last, on a later visit to India, I found documents at the

Nehru Library in New Delhi that provided solid evidence about the history of the house at 1 Church Road. It turned out that there were two very fat and complete files in the private papers of Motilal Nehru (Part II: Subject Files: S. No. 6: Anand Bhawan Papers). It is a long, complex story, but briefly here is the relevant information about the connection between the house and the family of Sir Sayyid:

In 1858, the Allahabad collector issued a *parwana* that authorized Shaikh Fayyaz Ali of Allahabad to receive an 'estate', with an annual income of Rs 1000 in compensation for losses sustained during the 'Mutiny'. The U.P. and National Archives have hundreds of such cases of land confiscated and awarded in the aftermath of the rebellion, and this is one of them. Incidentally, Sayyid Ahmad Khan turned down such an estate and received instead his monthly 'political pension'. Shaikh Fayyaz Ali, like many other Muslims, did not have to wait for the British to change their policies and attitudes to get such an award. What he got, finally in 1861, was property of over 16 *bighas* in a village called Fatehpur Bishwa at the eastern edge of Allahabad's large military establishment. The land was revenue free. In addition, he received an adjoining piece of 2 *bighas* 9 *biswas* in Mauza Hashimpur. On this property he built a bungalow, known as Bungalow Fatehpur Bishwa, No. 1 Church Road. When he died in 1873, his children were still minors, so his property was administered by the Court of Wards. In 1888, at the request of his heirs, the Court of Wards authorized the Allahabad collector to sell the property. It was under these circumstances that Sayyid Mahmud, a justice of the Allahabad High Court, purchased the house for Rs 9000 in 1888. On the basis of the information in *Thacker's Directory*, we can surmise that Sayyid Mahmud had lived there previously as a tenant. Six years later, in 1894, Sayyid Mahmud sold the property to Raja Jaikishen Das, a close family friend, for Rs 13,250. The sale deed gives details of alterations and additions that Sayyid Mahmud had made while he was owner. Kunwar Permanand, a former student of the M.A.O. College, Aligarh, was Jaikishen Das's son.

So there was a connection between Swaraj Bhawan and Sayyid Ahmad Khan, but it was a remote one. Why then has the story been concocted and so prominently displayed? What purpose does it serve?

One might start with the seeds of truth that might make the story plausible. For one thing, the house was indeed owned, if only briefly and certainly not originally nor as a gift at the hands of the British authorities, by Sayyid Mahmud, the son of Sayyid Ahmad Khan. It may have been called 'Mahmud Manzil', although I have seen no contemporary documentary reference to such a name. The house that Sayyid Ahmad Khan lived in at Aligarh, which had no special name, was originally owned by Sayyid Mahmud, purchased in 1876 when he was still the only Indian practising as a high court advocate in Allahabad. It was given as *mahr*, marriage portion, to Sayyid Mahmud's wife, Musharaf Jahan Begam, when they were married in 1888, the year Sayyid Mahmud purchased the house at 1 Church Road.

It is also certainly true that Sir Sayyid Ahmad Khan was a firm supporter of British rule, though in this respect he was hardly unique in the late nineteenth century. The founders of the Indian National Congress were equally enthusiastic in their support of the British Empire and their wish to be a part of it. On the other hand, Sayyid Ahmad Khan, particularly in the decade following the 1857 Rebellion, had made a number of enemies within the British ruling establishment for his forthright criticisms of a number of British policies and attitudes towards India and Indians. His writings after the Mutiny were controversial in British circles. His account of the rebellion in Bijnore, for example, was considered by some to be written to protect his British mentor, the collector of Bijnore, Alexander Shakespeare, at the expense of Nawab Mahmud Khan of Najibabad, who, according to some officials, was unjustly convicted as a rebel. His book on the causes of the Indian revolt received a sharp retort from Richard Temple, who considered parts of the pamphlet to be 'rancorous', and characterized by 'some kind of spite or enmity'. In 1867, the year the British supposedly offered him the property in Allahabad, was in fact a year in which he was officially reprimanded for the disrespectful tone of his publication, the *Aligarh Institute Gazette*. In 1869, Sayyid Ahmad devoted much of his time in London writing a refutation of Sir William Muir's book on the Prophet Muhammad.

But it is also true, as I've mentioned, that Sayyid Ahmad was a beneficiary of British largesse in the form of a political pension, although here again he was one of many and hardly among the most prominent. His friend, Raja Jaikishen Das, who also owned the Nehru house, received the title of Raja and an estate in Moradabad 'suitable to support the dignity of the title'. He also got a large house in Moradabad city, given to him as a matter of 'sound policy . . . to locate in the midst of a large and restless Mussulman population, such a staunch supporter and loyal servant of Govt., and to strengthen the hands of the Hindoo Community. . .'. There are hundreds of such cases of confiscations and rewards with both Muslim and Hindu victims and beneficiaries, a redistribution of land and power that would be worth detailed research.

What about the idea of the house as 'cement' for the permanence of British rule in India? This is the quote attributed to Sir William Muir whose name is garbled in the inscription. If he didn't say it, perhaps someone else did on some other occasion.

There was, in fact, an event that might be considered similar in spirit, if not in detail, to the still undiscovered house-warming at 1 Church Road. When Sayyid Mahmud returned from England in November 1872, his father hosted a dinner in his honour in Benares, where Sayyid Ahmad Khan was posted as principal sadr amin. Sayyid Mahmud had eaten his dinners at Lincoln's Inn and been called to the Bar, though he had not quite finished a Cambridge degree. The following month, he moved to Allahabad where he became the first Indian advocate to practise before the high court, a position that was then restricted to barristers, that is, legal practitioners who had been called to the Bar in Britain.

A report of the dinner was printed in the *Pioneer* (4 December 1872), then reprinted, along with an Urdu translation, in Sayyid Ahmad's journal *Tahzib al-Akhlaq*. Alexander Shakespeare, formerly collector of Bijnore in 1857 and now commissioner of Benares Division, presided. The report claims that the dinner was the first public occasion in which Indians, though apparently no Hindus, 'ate at table in common with their European friends'. There is no mention of whether or not the Indians had to endure English food, but the dinner must have followed British decorum—table clothes, knives and forks, speeches and toasts, presumably non-alcoholic ones. In responding to Shakespeare's toast, Sayyid Mahmud expressed his wish 'to unite England and India socially even more than politically. The English rule in India, in order to be good, must promise to be eternal; and it can never do so until the English people are known to us more as friends and fellow subjects, than as rulers and foreign conquerors.' Although he did not use the word, one might call this 'cementing'.

This theme of 'friendship', even 'love'—*dosti aur muhabbat*—between British ruler and Indian subject is a thread that connects three generations of Sir Sayyid's family and underlies much of their hopes and frustrations with respect to the colonial encounter. In Sayyid Ahmad's account of the rebellion in Bijnore, he states that love arose like a flame in his heart to surround his British superiors and protect them from the mutineers. In *Asbab-i Baghawat-i Hind* (Causes of the Indian Revolt), he moves from personal devotion to individuals to a more abstract theory of the relationships between 'govermnent', using the English word, and subjects. He says that the lack of friendship, love and solidarity between ruler and ruled was one of the root causes of Indian discontent, and places the blame clearly on the British for failing to take the initiative in establishing such a loving relationship. This aspiration carries forward throughout the later life of Sir Sayyid but reaches a tragic conclusion at the end of his life with the humiliation of his son Sayyid Mahmud, who was forced to resign from the Allahabad High Court in 1893 for failing to observe the procedures and schedules of the Court, allegedly because of his heavy drinking.

The famous final page of *A Passage to India* dramatizes the virtual impossibility of real friendship within any system of colonial domination: 'Why can't we be friends now? It's what I want. It's what you want.' One may consider the extent to which this idea of colonial 'friendship' presupposed a project of acculturation to British social forms in the spirit of Macaulay's infamous 'Minute on Education', as for example in banquets and bungalows, and becomes a strategy for enfranchisement within the British Empire—or, perhaps, in Gandhi's words, creating an India based on 'English rule without the English'. It was the adoption of English-style clothes, food, table manners and domestic architecture that Nazir Ahmad satirized, perhaps in specific reference to Sir Sayyid and his son, in his novel *Ibn ul-waqt*, published in 1888, the year Sayyid Mahmud bought the house on Church Road. The 'paradox' mentioned in the inscription, based on Pande's book, is the distance between this aspiration for inclusion within the empire and India's freedom struggle. It takes some historical imagination to understand how ideas like 'loyalty' to the Queen Empress could have been taken seriously, but I suggest that such emotions, ambivalent and contested as they were, form part of the genealogy of nationalism, the sense of membership in an abstract national community.

When Motilal Nehru purchased the house at 1 Church Road, he was making a set of symbolic choices that had been anticipated by Sayyid Mahmud, his elder by eleven years, who had established one model for how to adapt British colonial lifestyle to Indian family life. Although Motilal had not eaten his dinners and been called to the British Bar, in 1896 he was among the first to take advantage of revised rules that qualified Indian legal practitioners to practise as high court advocates. That was twenty-five years after Sayyid Mahmud had broken the barrier as the first Indian advocate in Allahabad.

There were, in fact, deeper and more long-standing ways in which the backgrounds of the two families prepared the ground for the cosmopolitan culture that one encounters in the museum displays of Swaraj and Anand Bhawan, or the much more modest Sir Sayyid House at Aligarh, also now a museum. The families of Sayyid Ahmad Khan and the Nehrus had a good deal in common. For one thing, both were descendants of Kashmiri families that had migrated to Delhi in the eighteenth century to take service in the fading days of the Mughal Empire, and both came to identify with the Indo-Persian culture of the Mughals. For both families, the failure of a Mughal restoration in 1857 led to their separation from Delhi and their search for a way of relating to the claims of British rulers to be legitimate successors to the Mughals. Schooled initially in Persian and Arabic, both Sayyid Mahmud and Motilal Nehru acquired a comfortable command of English along with their own particular, rather expensive versions of a colonial English lifestyle, although it was only in the next generation that this style extended to the women of their families.

Sayyid Mahmud's son, Sayyid Ross Masud, probably most widely known now as E.M. Forster's friend and partial model for the character of Dr Aziz in *A Passage to India*, was in fact a significant educational leader, first in Hyderabad state, where he played a central role in the founding of Osmania University, India's first European-style university to be conducted in an Indian language, and later as vice-chancellor of Aligarh Muslim University. He was born in 1889, the same year as Jawaharlal Nehru, and went to England at about the same time, the former eventually to Oxford, the latter to Cambridge. Both became barristers, but neither took up legal careers.

What I am leaving out, of course, is that one family was Muslim and the other Hindu. I am also leaving out the fact that Motilal Nehru attended the Indian National Congress meetings in Allahabad in 1888, while Sayyid Ahmad Khan was mounting his campaign against the Congress, though it took Jallianwala Bagh, much later, in 1919 to turn Motilal into a serious, active Indian nationalist. Ross Masud, who died in 1937, did not have to face the issues of partition and independence.

Those are complex but also more familiar matters. But for now I want to return to the words engraved at the entrance to Swaraj Bhawan. What this inscription does is to set up Sayyid Ahmad Khan against the Nehrus as the embodiment of anti-national feeling, the Muslim 'other' that helps define the boundaries of the Indian nation. What I am suggesting is that the two families were not in fact so different after all, that they came out of remarkably similar backgrounds and responded to the colonial encounter in remarkably similar ways. When Jawaharlal Nehru was invited to address the Aligarh Students Union in 1933, Ross Masud pre-empted this nationalist gesture on the part of the students by meeting Nehru at the railway station and taking on himself the role of introducing him as an old friend. It is probably true that much more united than divided them. They were, in many respects, cut out of the same cloth. I can hope that the authorities in charge of the Swaraj Bhawan will take that into consideration when they come up with a new inscription.

JAWAHARLAL NEHRU

Jawaharlal Nehru (1889–1964) was born in Allahabad, the only son of prosperous parents. His father, Motilal Nehru, was a successful lawyer, and among his ancestors was a Kotwal of Delhi and a Sanskrit and Persian scholar on whom the Mughal Emperor Farrukhsiar had conferred a *jagir*. In 1905, Nehru went to England to attend Harrow School, but before that, for his first fifteen years, governesses and private tutors taught him at home. After Harrow, he read natural sciences at Cambridge University and then the law in London. He returned to India in 1912. Looking back at the man he was then, he wrote in the *Autobiography*, 'I was a bit of a prig with little to commend me'.

Though he 'was glad to be back home and pick up old threads', life in Allahabad began to pall on him. He started practising at the high court, but not with any great interest in the profession. Some evenings he went to the club, where he met the same people he had met in the morning all over again: 'Decidedly the atmosphere was not intellectually stimulating and a sense of the utter insipidity of life grew upon me.' He was drawn to politics, but politics, to him, 'meant aggressive nationalist activity against foreign rule', for which there was no scope at the time.

'Gradually political life grew again,' he wrote in the *Autobiography*. 'Lokamanya Tilak came out of prison and Home Rule Leagues were started by him and Mrs Beasant.' Nehru joined both and in 1915, in Allahabad, he delivered his first political speech: 'The occasion was a protest meeting against a new act muzzling the press. I spoke briefly and in English.' Five years later, in June 1920, he visited the villages in the interior of Partapgarh district, about fifty miles from Allahabad. He went there after he heard two hundred peasants, who had come to Allahabad to meet prominent politicians, talk about 'the crushing exactions of the taluqadars' and the inhuman treatment they received at their hands. The experience of going to those villages, his first of rural India, affected him profoundly:

> They were in miserable rags, men and women, but their faces were full of excitement and their eyes glistened and seemed to expect strange happenings which would, as if by a miracle, put an end to their long misery.
>
> They showered their affection on us and looked on us with loving and hopeful eyes, as if we were the bearers of good tidings, the guides who were to lead them to the promised land.

But Nehru, as he knew only too well, was no messiah; he was merely a casual visitor from the distant city.

The taluqadari system was abolished in 1949, but the peasants of Partapgarh district are perhaps worse off now than they were eighty-five years ago. Today, if they happen to be disgruntled they are likely to keep the disgruntlement to themselves. It is well-known in east Uttar Pradesh that a ministerial descendant of one of the Partapgarh taluqdars has a pond in which he keeps crocodiles. From time to time, when people disappear from the villages of Partapgarh, tongues don't wag nor fingers point, for fear of the crocs.

∾

from *An Autobiography* (1936)

THEOSOPHY

When I was ten years old we changed over to a new and much bigger house which my father named 'Anand Bhawan'. This house had a big garden and a swimming pool and I was full of excitement at the fresh discoveries I was continually making. Additional buildings were put up and there was a great deal of digging and construction and I loved to watch the labourers at work.

There was a large swimming pool in the house and soon I learnt to swim and felt completely at home in and under the water. During the long and hot summer days I would go for a dip at all odd hours, many times a day. In the evening many friends of my father's came to the pool. It was a novelty, and the electric light that had been installed there and in the house was an innovation for Allahabad in those days. I enjoyed myself hugely during these bathing parties and an unfailing joy was to frighten, by pushing or pulling, those who did not know how to swim. I remember, particularly, Dr Tej Bahadur Sapru who was then a junior at the Allahabad Bar. He knew no swimming and had no intention of learning it. He would sit on the first step in fifteen inches of water, refusing absolutely to go forward even to the second step, and shouting loudly if anyone tried to move him. My father himself was no swimmer, but he could just manage to go the length of the pool with set teeth and violent and exhausting effort.

The Boer War was then going on and this interested me and all my sympathies were with the Boers. I began to read the newspapers to get news of the fighting.

A domestic event, however, just then absorbed my attention. This was the birth of a little sister. I had long nourished a secret grievance at not having any brothers or sisters when everybody else seemed to have them, and the prospect of having at last a baby brother or sister all to myself was exhilarating. Father was then in Europe. I remember waiting anxiously in the verandah for the event. One of the doctors came and told me of it and added, presumably as a joke, that I must be glad that it was not a boy who would have taken a share in my patrimony. I felt bitter and angry at the thought that any one should imagine that I could harbour such a vile notion.

Father's visits to Europe led to an internal storm in the Kashmiri Brahman community in India. He refused to perform any *prayashchit* or purification ceremony on his return. Some years previously another Kashmiri Brahman, Pandit Bishan Narayan Dar, who later became a president of the Congress, had gone to England to be called to the Bar. On his return the orthodox members of the community had refused to have anything to do with him and he was outcast, although he performed the *prayashchit* ceremony. This had resulted in the splitting up of the community into two more or less equal halves. Many Kashmiri young men went subsequently to Europe for their studies and on their return joined the reformist section, but only after a formal ceremony of purification. This ceremony itself was a bit of a farce and there was little of religion in it. It merely signified an outward conformity and a submission to the group will. Having done so, each person indulged in all manner of heterodox activities and mixed and fed with non-Brahmans and non-Hindus. [. . .]

When I was about eleven a new resident tutor, Ferdinand T. Brooks, came and took charge of me. He was partly Irish (on his father's side) and his mother had been a Frenchwoman or a Belgian. He was a keen theosophist who had been recommended to my father by Mrs Annie Besant. For nearly three years he was with me and in many ways he influenced me greatly. The only other tutor I had at the time was a dear old Pandit who was supposed to teach me Hindi and Sanskrit. After many years' effort the Pandit managed to teach me extraordinarily little, so little that I can only measure my pitiful knowledge of Sanskrit with the Latin I learnt subsequently at Harrow. The fault no doubt was mine. I am not good at languages, and grammar has had no attraction for me whatever.

F.T. Brooks developed in me a taste for reading and I read a great many English books, though rather aimlessly. I was well up in children's and boys' literature; the Lewis Carroll books were great favourites, and *The Jungle Book* and *Kim*. I was fascinated by Gustave Doré's illustrations to *Don Quixote*, and Fridtjof Nansen's *Farthest North* opened out a new realm of adventure to me. I remember reading many of the novels of Scott, Dickens and Thackeray, H.G. Wells's romances, Mark Twain, and the Sherlock Holmes stories. I was thrilled by the *Prisoner of Zenda*, and Jerome K. Jerome's *Three Men in a Boat* was for me the last word in humour. Another book stands out still in my memory; it was Du Maurier's *Trilby*, also *Peter Ibbetson*. I also developed a liking for poetry, a liking which has to some extent endured and survived the many other changes to which I have been subject.

Brooks also initiated me into the mysteries of science. We rigged up a little laboratory and there I used to spend long and interesting hours working out experiments in elementary physics and chemistry.

Apart from my studies, F.T. Brooks brought a new influence to bear upon me which affected me powerfully for a while. This was theosophy. He used to have weekly meetings of theosophists in his rooms and I attended them and gradually imbibed theosophical phraseology and ideas. There were metaphysical arguments, and discussions about reincarnation and the astral and other supernatural bodies, and auras, and the doctrine of *Karma*, and references not only to big books by Madame Blavatsky and other theosophists but to the Hindu scriptures, the Buddhist *Dhammapada*, Pythagoras, Apollonius of Tyana, and various philosophers and mystics. I did not understand much that was said but it all sounded very mysterious and fascinating and I felt that here was the key to the secrets of the universe. For the first time I began to think, consciously and deliberately, of religion and other worlds. The Hindu religion especially went up in my estimation; not the ritual or ceremonial part, but its great books, the Upanishads and the Bhagavad Gita. I did not understand them, of course, but they seemed very wondferful. I dreamt of astral bodies and imagined myself flying vast distances. This dream of flying high up in the air (without any appliance) has indeed been a frequent one throughout my life; and sometimes it has been vivid and realistic and the countryside seemed to lie underneath me in a vast panorama. I do not know how the modern interpreters of dreams, Freud and others, would interpret this dream.

Mrs Annie Besant visited Allahabad in those days and delivered several addresses on theosophical subjects. I was deeply moved by her oratory and returned from her speeches dazed and as in a dream. I decided to join the Theosophical Society, although I was only thirteen then. When I went to ask Father's permission he laughingly gave it; he did not seem to attach importance to the subject either way. I was a little hurt by his lack of feeling. Great as he was in many ways in my eyes, I felt that he was lacking in spirituality. As a matter of fact he was an old theosophist, having joined the Society in its early days when Madame Blavatsky was in India. Curiosity probably led him to it more than religion, and he soon dropped out of it, but some of his friends, who had joined with him, persevered and rose high in the spiritual hierarchy of the Society.

So I became a member of the Theosophical Society at thirteen and Mrs Besant herself performed the ceremony of initiation, which consisted of good advice and instruction in some mysterious signs, probably a relic of freemasonry. I was thrilled. I attended the Theosophical Convention at Benares and saw old Colonel Olcott with his fine beard.

It is difficult to realize what one looked like or felt like in one's boyhood, thirty years ago. But I have a fairly strong impression that during these theosophical days of mine I developed the flat and insipid look which sometimes denotes piety and which is (or was) often to be seen among theosophist men and women. I was smug, with a feeling of being one-of-the-elect, and altogether I must have been a thoroughly undesirable and unpleasant companion for any boy or girl of my age.

Soon after F.T. Brooks left me I lost touch with theosophy, and in a remarkably short time (partly because I went to school in England) theosophy left my life completely. But I have no doubt that those years with F.T. Brooks left a deep impress upon me and I feel that I owe a debt to him and to theosophy. But I am afraid that theosophists have since then gone down in my estimation. Instead of the chosen ones they seem to be very ordinary folk, liking security better than risk, a soft job more than the martyr's lot. But, for Mrs Besant, I always had the warmest admiration.

The next important event that I remember affecting me was the Russo-Japanese War. Japanese victories stirred up my enthusiasm and I waited eagerly for the papers for fresh news daily. I invested in a large number of books on Japan and tried to read some of them. I felt rather lost in Japanese history, but I liked the knightly tales of old Japan and the pleasant prose of Lafcadio Hearn.

Nationalistic ideas filled my mind. I mused of Indian freedom and Asiatic freedom from the thraldom of Europe. I dreamt of brave deeds, of how, sword in hand, I would fight for India and help in freeing her.

I was fourteen. Changes were taking place in our house. My older cousins, having become professional men, were leaving the common home and setting up their own households separately. Fresh thoughts and vague fancies were floating in my mind and I began to take a little more interest in the opposite sex. I still preferred the company of boys and thought it a little beneath my dignity to mix with groups of girls. But sometimes at Kashmiri parties, where pretty girls were not lacking, or elsewhere, a glance or a touch would thrill me.

In May 1905, when I was fifteen, we set sail for England. Father and mother, my baby sister and I, we all went together.

HARIVANSH RAI BACHCHAN

Harivansh Rai Bachchan (1907–2003) was born in Chak Mohalla, Allahabad, into a Kayastha family that had lived in Chak for several generations. His father was a clerk in the office of the *Pioneer* newspaper. After receiving his early education in neighbourhood municipal schools, he transferred to Kayastha Pathshala High School, where, in the 'ninth and tenth classes [he] filled a whole exercise book with poems'. He matriculated in 1925, and two years later joined Allahabad University as a BA student, taking Hindi and philosophy as his two optional subjects. English was compulsory. Bachchan went on to do his MA in English and, in 1941, when Amaranatha Jha was vice-chancellor, he was appointed to a lectureship. In 1952 he got a scholarship to go to Cambridge, where under the supervision of T.R. Henn he wrote a PhD dissertation on W.B. Yeats. He was one of the first Indian students to complete a literature PhD at Cambridge.

Meanwhile, inspired by Fitzgerald's translation of Omar Khayyam's *Rubaiyat*, Bachchan had written *Madhushala* (1935) and it made him famous. His first wife died and he remarried. His second wife, Teji Suri, was a socially ambitious Sikh woman with a resemblance to the film actress Nargis. They had two sons, one of whom later became a film actor himself.

When Bachchan returned from England in 1954, he came back to a hostile English department. He wrote in his autobiography:

> A new reader was to be appointed in the department that year. After I returned I learned that it had been filled on the basis of formal seniority, conveniently satisfying the nepotistic urge, the vice-chancellor and head of department both being of the same caste as the candidate! Was the promotion not hurried through because I would certainly have been a strong candidate with my Cambridge PhD?

This is not all. In the staff room, his colleagues did little to hide their jealousy. They did not refer to him as 'Dr Bachchan', which would have meant acknowledging his academic achievement, but as 'Bachchanji', thus putting him in his place, which was that of a mere Hindi poet. The head of the department, Satish Chandra Deb, who had earlier obstructed his promotion, now obstructed the publication of his thesis, though there were funds available for it.

The victim of provincialism, Bachchan decided to quit his job. Jawaharlal Nehru offered him an opening as producer in All-India Radio and he resigned. It was, nevertheless, a difficult decision:

My work, field of work, and medium of working would all change in
a single day: how could I cope with the sudden transition from
teacher to producer—a job which, when all was said and done, was
essentially clerical? The irony was that at precisely the time when I
had become more fully competent in academia, fate was throwing me
far from this area where I belonged.

Bachchan lived for another fifty years but did not set foot in the university
again. His four-volume autobiography, *In the Afternoon of Time* in the condensed
English version, evokes a lost period of Allahabad as perhaps no other writing
on the city does.

∾

from *In the Afternoon of Time* (1998)

CHAK MOHALLA

In the second decade of the century, Chak Mohalla, though full of
variety, was not a big place; it was neither fully town nor fully village,
but like a part of a village in the process of turning into a town, or rather
a part of a town thrust forcibly into the midst of village fields and barns.
Radha took me on so many tours of that mohalla, first carrying me on
her back and later leading me by the hand, that its geography became
totally familiar to my fingers and the soles of my feet. I could reach any
part of the mohalla blindfold; and it wasn't just the lanes and alleys that
I knew, I knew also their inhabitants, and felt a personal affinity with
them. The mohalla has changed completely since I left it in my youth,
with new roads, new houses, new people with new ways of life and the
new thoughts of new times; but even now when I go back there, the new
things seem to slip away like an insubstantial fantasy and the old place
comes back in crisp and complete detail, holding me firmly with its
magic.

Our house was north-facing; in front lay an undulating maidan and
the remains of the compound wall of Grandfather's time, transformed
by successive monsoons into small and large mounds of stone. Beyond,
a lane running east-west, with more open space beyond that, where an

old woman of the market-gardener Kachhi caste had set up a timber store. Old she may have been, but she was also sturdy and despotic, and her woodcutters trembled in her presence, for if anyone had the temerity to show slackness during working hours, she'd bite their heads off. Beyond the timber store there was a great neem tree, and facing it the two-room cottage of Girdhari, another market gardener, who'd taken up with a low-caste Pasi woman called Mundar. Girdhari had no children. His single task in life was the growing of vegetables, and his single passion was wrestling. To the east of his house stood two awnings of thatch supported by a common mud-brick wall; one awning sheltered his bullocks and cart, and the other a first-rate wrestling arena, maintained over several generations. My own grandfather and great-grandfather must surely have shown their mettle there. Its yellowish earthen floor was smooth and soft, for several times a year, Girdhari had it sprinkled with mustard oil. A heavy stone lying beneath the neem tree represented a severe challenge for the wrestlers, whose names would be carved on it by the stonemason if they managed to lift it. Most such inscriptions were hard to read, but I saw an 'M' and wondered if my great-grandfather Mitthu Lal had been one of the successful heroes. Allegedly, when a wrestler once lifted it, a vein in his leg burst, soaking the ground with his blood. I never saw anyone lift it in my time, though at the beginning of a wrestling match the contestants would be sure to touch it for luck; the fact that it had partly sunk into the ground suggested that it hadn't been moved for years. Girdhari was short but wiry and stocky, and no less powerful were his two bullocks, which he used sometimes to set fighting in a spectacle that the whole mohalla would gather to watch. When the two bullocks became locked head-to-head with horns entangled, pushing each other back and forward, only Girdhari himself would be intrepid enough to pull them apart.

Mundar was good-looking but hardly delicate: she did all kinds of work in the fields alongside Girdhari, and when he drew irrigation water from the well, she would grasp the heavy leather bucket unaided; she weeded the fields, pulled up the vegetables and loaded them onto the cart for Girdhari to sell at the market. And when she didn't have anything else left to do, she would take on the old Kachhi woman from the timber store in a slanging match of invective and abuse, the pretext being some timber missing from the old woman's yard, or vegetables disappearing from Mundar's field. The old woman would sit on a log from her stock of timber, and Mundar on the wrestlers' stone under the neem tree, and the two of them would go at each other hammer-and-tongs for hours on end, waving their arms and shouting until their throats gave out. They sometimes seemed to fight without any reason at all, simply to pass the time as they sat opposite each other on log and stone respectively, rehearsing the entire catalogue of profanities in their vocabulary lest they forget any through lack of practice.

Beyond Girdhari's field lay Babu Mukta Prasad's house. He was an ardent Arya Samaji who worked in the office of the 'Lat Sahib', the British governor; in the hot weather he used to go to Simla—the only person from Chak Mohalla to make the annual migration to the hills—and when he came back he would talk to the people of the mohalla as if still speaking from that lofty eminence, the rest of us listening with upturned faces from the plains below. He was not a bad fellow, and it was natural enough for him to stand on his dignity somewhat after enjoying the cool Simla air while we in the mohalla had sweltered in the scorching summer winds.

The northern boundary of Chak Mohalla was marked by Mukta Prasad's bungalow, beyond which lay Mohatshimganj, generally abbreviated to 'Mosimganj'. To the west of his bungalow there stood the small mud-brick huts of Muslim artisans: water-carriers, barbers, dressers of wounds, butchers, hookah-makers, locksmiths, umbrella-repairers, tinsmiths, kite-makers, paper-toy makers, and so on. They would breed chickens in their houses, and if you passed by that way, you would hear clucking sounds emerging from this door or that, while quacking ducks sauntered freely around the area. The menfolk would mostly be out in the daytime, making the rounds with their respective trades while the women stayed at home in purdah, and even the smallest house was sure to have some kind of curtain hanging in the doorway, no matter how frayed and dirty it might be. Only little children would be visible, and if a woman ever set foot outside, she would always be covered from head to toe in a long white burqa (the Sunni women wore white ones and the Shias black; they were all Sunnis here). As a child I was frightened by these burqa-clad forms, whose tunics with their gauze-covered eyeholes concealed mysteries unknown. When I was very little I would be prevented from going out onto the street by being told that these veiled women abducted little children, hiding them in their voluminous skirts.

The favourite sport of the men in that Muslim area was pigeon-racing, and betting on fighting partridges or bulbuls; in the evening, they would go out with a bulbul on a perch or a caged partridge, looking for a wall infested with ants, their favourite food. Many houses sprouted tall bamboo frames, visible from a long way off, for pigeons to settle on, and the evening sky would be alive with flock after flock of pigeons wheeling and circling; it was always a mystery as to how people identified their own birds and laid wagers on them. And the women's pastimes? God alone knows, perhaps little at all apart from rearing children . . . but I may be doing them an injustice; perhaps they had a hundred things to do within their houses.

Now let us leave the Imambara at the northern limit of the mohalla, and the Muslim quarter next to it, and set off southwards again. Girdhari's field lies to the left of the lane while to our right is a place we used to call Kalyan Chand's garden, surrounded by a mud dike, the height of a man. The owner was a descendant of the Seth who had employed Mansa several generations earlier. The garden had three separate sections for flowers, fruit and vegetables, of which the third was rented for a nominal sum by Girdhari so that he could scuff the ground with a hoe in the rainy season and plant the grass crop that would keep his bullocks in fodder the whole year round. The ruined flower garden intimated a sense of past glories. In the north-western corner there was a brick-built well which fed a holding tank and a system of brick irrigation channels running thoughout the garden, while in the middle of the flower garden stood a high stone platform, large enough to accommodate four or five chairs quite comfortably, and provided with little steps.

In the fruit garden there were mango, tamarind, guava, black plum, myrobalan, custard apple and corinda trees which, though unwatered and untended, gave freely of their fruit when in season, and even before they were ripe, we would break off or shake down the fruits, throw them around, eat them, take them home—all this without anyone to stop us or tell us off.

Sometimes the adults would come too, and peevishly tell us to let the fruit ripen at least, but such forebearance was beyond us children:

what could grown-ups, in their ripe maturity, hope to understand of the pleasures of unripe things? There were two occasions on which the adults—particularly the women—would come into the garden. The first was to do a puja of the well if someone in the mohalla was getting married, when the dried-up garden would come to life with merriment and singing for a little while, and we children listened to the unrestrained indecent songs from our tree top haunts. One song began, 'Smear on some silky oil, good lady, smear on some oil'—and then got very obscene! The second occasion was on some particular date in the cold season, when the women would do a puja of the myrobalan trees, tying threads of raw cotton around their trunks, and then offering them to Brahmins.

But the greatest attraction was a two-storeyed house built in the south-eastern corner, complete with courtyard of four-square design, pillared hallway, open roof terraces and the like; alongside was a stable, its tall metal door secured with a rusty padlock, and a separate room for the 'syce' or groom, its doorway now walled up with bricks. Would you believe that this whole house lay quite open in its state of disrepair, all its doors open save those of the stables and the syce's quarters? As children we loved to play games of hide-and-seek in that deserted garden, climbing trees, hiding behind pillars, in hallways and on roofs, and generally getting up to all kinds of high jinks; it never occurred to us to question why this fine place had been built, only to be abandoned as though heirless . . . but one day the enigma was in any case to be revealed.

Sometimes in the summer nights, when we slept on the open ground in front of our house, I would wake up to a jingling sound from the stables. At first I ignored it, but when it went on for several nights in succession, I mentioned it to an old lady who lived nearby. She grew serious and said, 'It's not just you that hears it; there's a history to that jingling sound.' And the story that she related was as follows.

In the family of the Jain merchant of Mahajani Tola was one Lala Kalyan Chand. He was much given to the pleasures of the senses, and had inexhaustible wealth; becoming infatuated with the youthful charms of a courtesan, he had the garden laid out for her, and built her the house where she lived in the upper storey. He would visit her every evening, returning to his haveli late in the night. She was attended by many servants who lived downstairs, and the grounds were tended by numerous gardeners. The courtesan, however, became enamoured of the young syce, a slender, handsome youth who would bring the carriage out from the stables at midnight, climb onto the high driving seat, and help the courtesan clamber down; he would return her by the same route before dawn. But clandestine love is hard to hide: the merchant became suspicious, visited the garden unannounced at two in the morning, found the courtesan missing from her room, saw the carriage standing down below, and understood the whole story. The syce's room was found to be locked from inside, and the merchant's loud call went unanswered. In the morning the door was torn down to reveal the bodies of the young lovers hanging from the ceiling. Having killed themselves, dying before their time, they returned as ghosts to haunt the place: at midnight the courtesan dances before the syce in the stables, her anklets making the jingling sound that had disturbed my sleep. The merchant never came to the garden again; the syce's quarters were bricked up, and the stables put under lock and key.

The rusted frame of the carriage stood outside the stables in my childhood, and took us on countless imaginary journeys throughout the wide world, drawn by horses as fleet as the wind. The old lady told me that the syce was still to be seen taking his beloved on nocturnal rides, and although I never saw this for myself, I certainly did hear the jingling sound—even if rather more frequently after bearing the 'history' I have just recounted. [. . .]

It was while attending Unchamandi School that I made the first and perhaps the most important decision of my life. Until this time I had always obeyed my elders in everything I did. But one day Karkal brought news of a lecture that was to be given by the ascetic Swami Satyadev at the Vidya Mandir School, and he took me along to listen. There was a large crowd of students gathered in the hall. Swamiji sat on a table to deliver his lecture, his robust body clad in ochre robes, with clean-shaven head and dark glasses. His oratory was vigorous and brilliant: there were of course no microphones in those days, but his voice carried clearly through the hall. His subject was 'Hindi: Our National Language', and the speech made a deep impression on me—truth to tell, I was quite carried away by the flow of his eloquence. Sitting there in the hall I resolved to leave Urdu and take up Hindi. As we returned home I consulted Karkal, and he supported my decision; his education had begun with Sanskrit, and he had attached little significance to Hindi, but on that day he too realized its importance. I was already in the fourth grade, and changing language at this stage threatened my exam performance, but my Hindi was not too bad; I was in the habit of casually perusing *Kanya Manoranjan* and my sisters's course books, and used to look at the literary journal *Saraswati* that we subscribed to, though I had had no formal education in Hindi. Father opposed my suggestion. When I told Panditji at school of my plan, he too expressed disagreement and pointed out the difficulties involved: there were only a few months left before the yearly exams, and, in any case, a change of language medium required the consent of the deputy inspector. But when he saw that I was in no way prepared to drop the idea, Panditji consulted my father and got me to write to the deputy sahib for the necessary permission.

The deputy inspector, one Babu Shiv Kumar Singh, was himself a great lover of Hindi, and as I discovered later, was one of the founders of the Nagari Pracharini Sabha. He called me to his house, and Panditji came with me. He looked at me long and hard, then asked me some questions to which I must have given satisfactory answers; but it was my enthusiasm alone that persuaded him to let me drop Urdu and take up Hindi. My happiness overflowed. I eagerly began my formal study, and Father took on Panditji as a home tutor to give me some additional help. As the exam approached, his tutelage and particularly his encouragement spurred me on, and I began to compete with the most able boys in the class. I passed the exam with high marks; as a result of my change of languages, I achieved second place rather than the hoped-for first, but I felt satisfied that I had set off in the right direction.

Near the Unchamandi School was the Bharati Bhawan library. Once when Panditji—still a villager at heart—passed that way, his jaw dropped and he said, 'Are there so many books in the world?' One day he told me I should read all the books stocked there—as if just by reading them anyone could achieve wisdom or intelligence. But his intention was the noble one of wanting me to make something of myself, and at that age I could not see him other than as my well-wisher and guide; so I vowed that I would indeed read all the Hindi books in the Bharati Bhawan library. They weren't so many in number, perhaps three or four almirahs full, the remainder being in Sanskrit or English. Anyway, I began to read the books from one end to the other, either following the sequence of the catalogue, or just taking them in the order in which they lay on the shelves. The Bharati Bhawan consumed my evenings for many years. While other boys of my age were playing on the maidan, I was sitting in that dimly lit hall, reading books—books which threw me from subject to unconnected subject, from novels to medicine to religious instruction to poetry to biography; books that I couldn't make head or tail of; books that perhaps were suitable only for a more mature mind; and books that I shouldn't even have touched. If only I had been able to rationalize my reading! But I now console myself with the thought that perhaps all that disorganized reading was not wholly in vain.

In July 1919 I joined the sixth class in the local Kayastha Pathshala High School. It was on the road leading from the city to Katra, beyond Surajkund and before the electricity station. My father had studied there, and I still have some books inscribed with his name, class and the name of the school; I felt a natural pride and affinity in studying at the school my father had attended. Shaligram was also moved there, so that we two brothers could stay together; a second brother was allowed a 50 per cent concession in fees. Pandit Vishram Tiwari continued to tutor us at home for a year or two more, for although he could only teach us Hindi and maths, my father also valued the generally watchful eye that he kept over us.

Moving from Unchamandi School to the Kayastha Pathshala High School was like moving from a pigeon-coop into the open air: classes were held in large, brick-built rooms; there were expansive grass lawns and maidans to play on in the front and rear, and for each subject there were separate teachers who would come to class at the hour shown on the timetable. Here too the day began with assembly, but now with *Vande Mataram*, the national song whose meaning, history and significance we were to learn only later.

I was a student of the Kayastha Pathshala High School from 1919 to 1925, that is, between the ages of twelve and eighteen. This is a period when a person acquires an individual identity and consciousness, a definition of self. Yet I think of this not so much as a 'formative' period (as it is called in English), but rather as a time of self-formation, when despite the undeniable part played by the times and by context and circumstances, the crucial determinant in the formation of personality is the increasingly alert ego. Nobody can be held responsible for the manner of their childhood, but with adolescence such a responsibility does have to be accepted. Thus, although it is true that the times in which I lived, the environment, my education and school, my family and my neighbours all had a hand in my development, the greater hand in inspiring, moulding and sometimes impeding this development was my own. To feel one's own hand is a little difficult, but to write one's own history without such an awareness of self is to be either vain or pitiable, and I would wish my pen to save me from either fate. Neither is it the case that the circumstances of my life became my slaves and followed my every wish, nor is it true that they enslaved me and did with me what they would. The events of this period changed the course of the history of the country, and to some degree that of the world also. But to observe them from this global perspective is not my aim: the rays of the sun fall on the drop of dew, as well as on the ocean, and I can only hope to reflect the dewdrop's portion, hoping that this too may hold some significance of its own.

During the First World War, I was aware only that in some far-flung part of the world the English were fighting the Germans. As a result of who-knows-what subtle propaganda or self-gratifying leap of the imagination, one felt that the Germans were the bravest people in the world and that the British would never be able to defeat them. The adults read the *Pioneer* reports very assiduously, and when we overheard them discussing the changing fortunes of the war, we concluded that the fighting was still in progress and victory or defeat still in the balance. We also used to take the illustrated *Jangi Akhbar* or 'War Newspaper', with its brief Urdu-Hindi captions underneath pictures which gave us a very distorted view of the conflict, presenting it as a beautifully smooth, clean and colourful thing.

The main effect of the war as perceived by the adults was a general increase in prices, which had its own subtle effect on many aspects of our lives. I remember one specific incident at home. Every household in Prayag used Ganga mud for plastering the walls and floors, for building domestic altars, *Shiv-lings* and so on; the cost of this mud went up from one paisa a basket-load to four paise. Mother asked irritably if they were sending Ganga mud to the front line, that it should have become so dear; but Father explained that the cost of basic foodstuffs had gone up, so the mud-carters had to increase their prices in order to make ends meet.

Lokmanya Tilak had established a branch of the Home Rule League in our city; Mother and I saw it when we rode in our neighbour Madho's *ikka* to my uncle's house. I read the English signboard and interpreted it as indicating an organization demanding rule for one's own home, doubtless set up in opposition to someone else ruling it. When Tilak's greatness took him beyond the merely human—he was called *Bhagvan Tilak* or 'Tilak the divine'—then clearly an institution established by him must be dedicated to some great purpose. I doubt if there was any member of the League in our mohalla, for at that stage 'freedom' was a topic discussed only by the Civil Lines upper classes.

Mahatma Gandhi also set foot in our town. The time when people would swarm to him like locusts was still some way off, but the few hundred who saw him and heard his address had much to say about his simplicity of manner, his mildness, his saintly ethics and his firm opposition to any kind of injustice. Within a few days the fragrance of his fame pervaded the whole town: perfume is not something that has to be applied in cupped handfuls! I remember seeing his photograph in a book, sitting in a chair in a Kathiawar turban, his wife Kasturba shown separately. When I first heard of him, I assumed him to be some great poet, because important people discussed in our house were nearly always poets; now it seems I wasn't far wrong, for his entire politics constituted a symbolic poem; and all that he did and achieved seems now to have retreated into the category of the imaginary.

When the war ended, every government institution and school was sent an order to celebrate the victory of Britain and the allies. We decorated Unchamandi School with the same enthusiasm with which I used to decorate our *baithak* to celebrate Janmasthami, Krishna's birthday. Many roads and buildings were lit up, and I went out with Karkal and some other boys to see the illuminations. Portraits of George V and Queen Mary were everywhere, along with Union Jacks and the inscription 'God Save the King'. The Home Rule League office was showing lights too, but there the electric bulbs spelt out the message 'India for Indians' on a large board—a brave display for such an occasion. The next day it was discussed everywhere, as if a new and revolutionary slogan had been coined.

Gandhiji ordered a twenty-four-hour hunger strike throughout the whole country in protest against the Rowlatt Act. I had no idea what kind of peril this bill represented—the only 'bill' we knew was the Hindi word meaning the little hole a mouse lived in, but people were saying that this Rowlatt Act was no mousehole, it was a gaping chasm that would swallow up the whole country. I just laughed at this; but that day our hearth lay cold and the family fasted. In the evening all the men in the mohalla met; Pandit Madan Mohan Malaviya had come on foot from Bharati Bhawan to the Home Rule League office, with thousands of people following behind. Numerous speeches were made in the marketplace that evening, roundly and passionately condemning the government. I remember hearing Malaviyaji's own speech, delivered in serious tones and a very restrained style. His last sentence still echoes in my memory: 'We pray God to grant government the wisdom to withdraw this bill!'

While our parents must have read of the Jallianwala Bagh massacre in the newspapers, we had heard the eye-witness account of our uncle, Chhedi Chacha. How could a ruling government, one which protected life and property, commit such an atrocity on its own people? My young mind poured forth a list of such questions; and then as if to deepen the dejection in our hearts came the news that Lokmanya Tilak had died. His ashes had been brought to Prayag to be immersed in the Ganga, and the procession set off from the marketplace, bearing the urn on a wooden frame decorated with simple white flowers and a large picture of Lokmanya, and fitted with long bamboos to accommodate the maximum number of pall-bearers. I must have felt a real boost that I too, as a boy of thirteen, was putting my shoulder to the bier alongside the other menfolk. A crowd of thousands gathered bare-headed in total silence on the banks of the Ganga where Pandit Motilal Nehru stood on a little rise to give a speech; when I came back from the commital ceremony, I felt as if I were returning from a pilgrimage.

One sun had set but another was rising: news spread throughout the city that Mahatma Gandhi was on his way, and that Mohammed and Shaukat Ali—'the Ali Brothers'—were coming with him. A crowd bigger than I'd ever seen gathered on the Home Rule League maidan to see the three take their seats on the dais, a meagre Sudama between mighty Arjuna and Bhima! Gandhiji had taken to wearing his homespun cap, kurta and dhoti, and everyone was astonished that such an emaciated frame of bones could challenge the might of the British Empire. The Ali Brothers aroused a storm with their speeches, but Gandhiji spoke of measured things in measured tones, with little modulation in his voice or ornament in his style—yet with a steely determination in every word. He advocated non-violent non-cooperation, and urged a boycott of schools, colleges, courts, government service, legislative assemblies and government titles, appealing for everyone to spin, to wear homespun cloth, and to work for Hindu–Muslim unity. He ended by saying that if the people acted on the programme he had recommended, he could deliver independence within the year.

Gandhiji left expressions of fearless self-confidence, hope and a thirst for action on the faces of his audience when he went away. More and more people were to be seen wearing homespun and 'Gandhi topis'; some students gave up their studies, some lawyers gave up their practices, and government servants their jobs. News spread of local families joining the movement: one day the Nehrus, the next the Tandons, then such-and-such a family. Whatever Gandhiji said was echoed by hundreds of mouths; then news of miracles began to spread—Gandhiji had been seen speaking simultaneously in several different places (this story perhaps originated in a printer's error), or cotton had been found growing on neem trees, and the public was happy to believe such rumours.

Our family boasted no lawyer or government servant. We children yearned desperately to boycott school but were prevented from doing so, though we were free to spin and to wear homespun cloth. Mohan Chacha set up his spinning wheel and loom workshop in the house while the rest of us did what little tasks we could to achieve the inner satisfaction of taking part in Gandhiji's movement in some way or other. We went to meetings; we listened to leaders' speeches; we called out 'Victory to Mother India' or 'Victory to Gandhiji', and at home we read Gandhiji's papers *Young India* and *Nav Jeevan*, to both of which Father subscribed. We also took the *Pioneer*, and by this time I had reached the seventh or eighth standard and could read a little English myself. In the evenings I would go to Bharati Bhawan where several

Hindi dailies and weeklies were available; I would read each news item avidly to see which leader had said what at which meeting, who had been arrested and where, what punishments had been handed down, where Section 144 (restricting public assembly) had been invoked, where lathi charges had taken place, which processions had been fired on, and so forth, churning my emotions to great effect.

One day I read a report saying that the police station at Chauri Chaura had been set on fire, killing twenty or more policemen in the flames. Gandhiji called off the campaign. A few days later I read that he had been arrested; then, that he had been sentenced to six years' imprisonment; then, that he had had an operation in jail; then, that he had been released. It was now 1924, and the movement had gone cold; Hindu–Muslim riots were breaking out, and even Gandhiji's atonement fast could not stop them.

For the people generally, 1925 was a year of political stalemate.

Education in the Kayastha Pathshala was not just a matter of academic study: attention was also paid to character-building and the development of personality. Three days a week there was a period for 'drill', and three days a week a period for music. In the drill sessions we were mostly taught to march: straight-backed, straight lines, feet in step. We were drilled by a retired havildar major whom we boys addressed as simply 'Major'—perhaps on his prompting (it was only much later that we discovered that 'major' was a much higher rank than 'havildar major').

His clothing boasted both military and civilian elements, and he carried a small cane in his hand. On formal school occasions he would wear full military uniform, albeit shruken and bunched here and there, and a few shining medals on his chest.

Professor Khushhalkar, our music teacher, was a Maharashtrian and a pupil of Pandit V.D. Paluskar. He used to come suited and booted and wearing a tie, a style of dress he maintained even throughout Gandhiji's non-cooperation movement. His Hindi was of the Bombay variety, but when he taught us devotional songs his pronunciation of every syllable was crystal-clear; he would make us do voice practice to the harmonium, then teach us bhajans such as Tulsi's *Gaiye Ganapati jagabandana*, which I can still sing from memory today. He also showed us how to sing while picking out the notes on the harmonium: he would pump the bellows with one hand while the fingers of the other would run lightly over the keys, his own voice blending with that of the instrument in such a way as to achieve a sublime harmony of the inanimate with the animate; evoking a tingling emotional response. Professor Khushhalkar sowed the seeds of music in me, but regrettably I was never able to grow the plant that should have sprung from them. Still, my slight study of music was helpful in the reciting of poetry, and a little knowledge of *tala* helped me compose songs in the folk genre. I can also tap out a rhythm on a drum, but that was learnt from my mother and sisters.

There was a Hindi society at school which arranged occasional readings of poetry, short stories and essays. Among the active pupils was Thakur Vikramaditya Singh who wrote poetry in the Chhayavad style, and dramas too: I supplied the off-stage voice of God in his play *Dhruva*, as my pronunciation was considered appropriately clear. It was him I asked to revise my first attempt at a Hindi poem, and from whom I learnt versification. The Hindi society brought out a handwritten journal called *Adarsh*, for which I transcribed the submitted articles, since my handwriting was very neat, with each character a little pearl. Though unaware of it at the time, I now see that this was a useful preparation for my own original writing.

It was in the seventh standard of the Kayastha Pathshala that I wrote my first complete Hindi poem—an encomium for some teacher— though my poetry writing really began with a little versifying at the Unchamandi School: for, when Vishram Tiwari made us write essays, he would ask us to quote a *doha* at the end, and if I couldn't remember one appropriate for the subject, I would make one up myself. In the ninth and tenth classes I filled a whole exercise book with poems, for by this time I had become familiar with Maithili Sharan Gupta's *Bharat-Bharati*, Pant's poetry in the journal *Saraswati*, and Nirala's free verse from *Matvala*. But my poems were so personal that when a friend took a surreptitious look at them, I furiously tore up the whole book and threw it away; I remember the torn pages being carried by the breeze as far as Girdhari's vegetable field.

Translated from the Hindi by Rupert Snell

NARMADESHWAR UPADHYAYA

Narmadeshwar Upadhyaya (1884–1977) was born in Mirzapur in a family of zamindar-scholars. His father, Mathura Prasad Upadhyaya, wrote the commentary to *Rasakusumakar*, a work on poetics edited by the Raja of Ayodhya. The book, printed at The Indian Press in 1894, was at the time held up as a model of typography, layout, and design for the printing of Hindi books. Till the age of eight, Narmadeshwar was educated at home, where he was taught the *Ashtadhyayi*. His colonial education began a year later in Miyagunj High School, Faizabad, where his English textbook contained Addison's essays and extracts from Smiles' *Self Help* and Griffith's translation of the Ramayana. In 1900, when Ramananda Chatterjee was principal, he came to study at Kayastha Pathshala, Allahabad, and afterwards studied at Ewing Christian College. Among his books are works of poetry and translations from the Sanskrit. *Premghan Parivar* (1970) is a history of his family.

'Snippets from Memory' first appeared in *Centenary High Court of Judicature at Allahabad 1856-1966. Commemoration Volume II* (1968).

∽

from *Snippets from Memory*

I retired from the High Court Bar in 1944. When I started to practise, the district courts at Allahabad had dirty, unventilated, dingy rooms, with chairs creaking from long use, some without seats. Walking from the Collectorate to the civil courts gave a dusty lather to one's shoes. No court room, save the session judge's, was worth the name. The income to the state from the lawsuits in the local lower courts was more than one-third of the entire revenue and yet the court buildings, flanked by the Muir Central College and the Senate Hall, and under the very nose of the High Court with its massive structural beauty, were hovelish-looking.

With a sigh of relief I left the district courts. It was like waking up from a horrid dream. I joined the High Court on 4 April 1914. It was then being held in the colonnaded stone building on Queen's Road, now in the occupation of the Education Department.

The only person who gave a semblance of welcome to me was

Pandit Uma Shankar Bajpai, later a judge of the High Court. He advised me to attend the court of the application judge and very kindly showed me the court room also.

Exactly at 10 A.M., a figure appeared from behind the high-backed chair—a portly figure with a Santa Claus beard and a fat, red chilly nose, and occupied the chair. It was Sir George Knox, doing Order 41, rule 11 cases. He took his seat, a case was called. He took the brief, looked at the findings of the appellate court; but a few minutes after the counsel started the arguments, he dozed off. As soon as the counsel stopped, the judge opened his eyes and dismissed the appeal as concluded by a finding of fact. I thought, at first, that it was the cool atmosphere and the whizzing of the fan that had lulled him to sleep. But later I realized that just as you wake up when a running train stops because the rhythm is broken, the counsel's argument had lulled him to sleep, and no sooner did it stop than he opened his eyes.

When I joined the High Court Bar, the Hon'ble Sir Henry Richards was Chief Justice. Sir George Edward Knox, Sir Pramod Charan Banerji, William Tudball, Edward Maynard Des Chamier, Syed Mohammad Rafique and Theodore Caro Piggot were the judges. Knox, Tudball, and Piggot belonged to the Indian Civil Service cadre.

Sir Henry Richards was a man of uncommon intelligence, quick in grasping facts and anticipating the counsel's argument; but he was not obstructive. Two years before his retirement, he had some head trouble but he never took a single day's leave and continued to attend the court. He heard arguments holding his head with his left hand.

Sir Pramod Charan Banerji, though senior to the Chief Justice, sat as a puisne judge. He was deeply versed in law and had an unruffled temper. He would make no comments until he had heard the arguments in full. It was a treat to argue before him. The Chief Justice always consulted him before making up his mind on some fact or a point of law. But it was a pity that Sir Pramod Charan seldom sat singly.

William Tudball was a typical ICS man, with brown moustaches, cut to disclose his upper lip, and keen penetrating eyes. He was the maker of pre-emption laws which were later given statutory shape by Dr Asthana. Tudball was well-versed in local conditions, practices, and customs. He was not very learned but was intelligent and had a highly-developed common sense. He was keen to pick holes in the arguments of the counsel and gloat over these holes. If, unfortunately, one presented a criminal revision on the grounds of the severity of the sentence, Tudball's favourite remark was, 'If you were beaten with shoes with no mark of injury on your person, what sentence would you pass?' With this remark, he would dismiss the petition.

Mohammad Rafique was dark-skinned, with a well-built body and a pair of *nawab chhatari* moustaches. He would make up his mind quickly, after asking the counsel a few questions. He would then sit mum without interfering with the arguments of the counsel. If this was not enough to stop the arguments, he would tilt his chair and gaze at the walls. This practice he adopted with his brother judge also, when he disagreed with his views; but he never gave a dissenting judgment all through his career.

Chamier and Piggot, like two inseparable brothers, always sat together. Chamier was intelligent and had a quick anticipation of arguments; while Piggot, though more learned, was patient and painstaking and would not make up his mind until he had heard the counsel in full. This, at times, fretted Chamier, but Piggot remained adamant, with the result that he was generally asked to deliver the judgment. This he did slowly and in a well-modulated voice. The judgment-writer had no difficulty in taking down the judgment, which was always a long-drawn-out one.

Chief Justice Richards was succeeded by Sir Grimwood Mears. Sir Grimwood can be said to be the one Chief Justice during the long annals of the High Court who was conscious not only of the independence of the judiciary but also of its dignity. He once communicated to the Governor of the United Provinces that the judges would not attend any function during his visits to Allahabad unless the Governor made a call at the High Court. After some exchange of letters the Governor agreed. He came, received a welcome in full court, and then a dinner followed.

Sir Grimwood was a dignified, conscientious and an alert judge. He would, every day, bow with grave courtesy to the bar before taking his seat. This practice was followed by the other judges also. I wonder if the practice still continues.

Sir Grimwood came to know of Sir George's habit of snoring on the bench. To put a stop to it, he asked Sir George to sit on the division bench with him. The sixty-five-year-old Sir George saw through the game. But habit is second nature. When the arguments started, habit reasserted itself and Sir George dozed off. Sir Grimwood looked at him now and then, while taking notes of the arguments. As soon as the arguments had concluded, Sir George, as usual, opened his eyes, and Sir Grimwood, to baffle him, asked him to deliver the judgment. Sir George had the paper-book before him. He picked it up and gave, succinctly, the allegations in the plaint, the relief sought, the substance of the written statement, the issues and the findings of the lower court on those issues, and then whispered to the Chief Justice that he agreed with the lower court. The Chief Justice was so flabbergasted that he did not care to dissent.

This went on till Friday. From Monday next, Sir George again started doing Order 44, rule 11 cases. But Sir Grimwood, it is said, exercised some pressure and Sir George took leave on grounds of health; but he continued to work as English judge for some time more and then retired. [. . .]

Justice Yorke, who was from the judicial service, was intelligent, with a sense of devotion to duty that is almost unparalleled. Sitting on a division bench, at the time of the Second World War, he got a telegram from the War Office that his son had been killed in action. He quietly put the telegram in his pocket, not mentioning it even to his colleague, and continued to work till the court rose. It was only the next day that the death of his son became known to us. He retired soon afterwards.

Justice E. Bennett was an ICS man of the Tudball type; but he burnt the midnight oil and was up to date in local laws. He used his knowledge to flout the arguments of the counsel and jeer at the counsel's ignorance. He could be depended upon to take the unexpected view and provide a ray of hope in a hopeless case.

Bennett was a shikari. Once, before the rumble of trucks and traffic had not scared away our wildlife, he went across to Phaphamau for a hunt. He sighted and shot at a leopard but failed to hit him. The leopard pounced upon him and the great shikari climbed up a babul tree. It was like Greek meeting Greek. He was rescued by the villagers. His trousers were torn; but fortunately the only scars he had were those of the babul thorns. [. . .]

There is something in the English blood that makes the English lovers of flowers. They are keen to beautify their homes even though they are conscious that their stay in the country will be short-lived. In Chief Justice Tom's bungalow, which is now in the occupation of ex-Chief Justice Desai, stands a stone-carved *kolhu* [sugar-cane press]. Tom got it from some village and had paving stones of irregular shapes put round it. In this *kolhu* he would plant annuals so skilfully that it looked like a fairy abode.

Justice Kendall was also a great lover of flowers. He had planted a maze of *inga* plants that had grown to a height of about seven feet. Once you entered the maze you could not come out unless you shouted for help, which the judge, with a smiling face, would readily give.

Justice Boys, from the English bar, was the Justice Bennett type, but not as learned. He had been a criminal lawyer and was at sixes and sevens in civil law. He, therefore, used to take heavy notes of arguments by the counsel. If a ruling was cited, he would stop the counsel, read the ruling and then discuss it with him. Because of this he could barely decide even one second appeal a day. His book on the code of criminal procedure was neatly printed and very illuminating. The rulings were not cited indiscriminately. The book fetched him rich dividends.

The Gymkhana Club, of which Justice Boys was president, was exclusively for Europeans. The club wanted to go into liquidation because of its falling income. A proposal to sell the goodwill of the club evoked an offer from the late Pandit K.D. Malaviya, Mr Krishna Ram Dave, and some others. A date was fixed for a meeting in the Mayo Hall for considering the offer. At the meeting, Justice Boys enquired if anyone was prepared to take over the club and run the All-India Tennis Tournament, which was only six weeks away. I had led the delegation, as Pandit K.D. Malaviya was ill with an asthmatic attack, and stood up to show our preparedness. But Justice Boys wanted to know if we could steer a steamship if suddenly called upon to do so. I pointed out to him that the illustration was not apt and a tournament was not a steamship. In his usual gruff voice he yielded reluctantly, but wanted, first, to see a passbook of the Allahabad Bank showing Rs 2000 in the credit column, which was the money to be spent on the venture. The amount was collected the next day, the passbook was shown to Justice Boys, and the Gymkhana Club taken over at the next meeting. The tennis tournament was run better than in previous years. We provided gallery seats, advance reservation facilities, and tea stalls, and even ended up making a small profit.

AMARANATHA JHA

Amaranatha Jha (1897–1955) was one of those legendary local figures in whose honour, opposite the city bus station or facing the vegetable market, public statues are erected. At twenty, he was professor of English at Muir Central College of Allahabad University, and was vice-chancellor for three terms, from 1938 to 1946. In 1947 he was made chairman of the Public Service Commission, Uttar Pradesh. In 1948 he took a year's leave from the Commission to serve as vice-chancellor of Benares Hindu University. He was a Fellow of the Royal Society of Literature.

Jha first met Mrs Naidu in January 1917, when he was a young lecturer and she a renowned poet, her best work already behind her. They corresponded off and on for the next three decades, and whenever Mrs Naidu came to Allahabad, usually on political work, Jha made it a point to call on her. Jha's privately printed book *Sarojini Naidu: A Personal Homage* (n.d.) consists of his diary, his articles on her poetry, extracts from her letters to him, and some rare pictures of Jha and Naidu taken on various occasions. Reproduced below is a selection from the diary. No one knows what became of Jha's papers, among which was a complete translation of the seventeenth-century Hindi poet Bihari. It is safe to assume that they are either lost or have been destroyed.

∼

from *Sarojini Naidu: A Personal Homage*

1917

January 11. Wrote to Mrs Naidu asking for a contribution to the Muir College Magazine.

January 13. Mrs Naidu spoke at a public meeting addressed by Dr Polak. Mr Polak had come to India from South Africa, and as an associate of Gandhiji, was highly respected. Mrs Naidu spoke very well.

January 15. Mrs Naidu addressed a public meeting. She has accepted my invitation to address the College on the 20th. The Principal, Dr Hill, told me that he was very pleased that she was coming, but she must not speak on politics.

January 20. In the morning called on Mrs Naidu to remind her that she was to come to the College in the afternoon. She said: 'You young men never let me forget any engagement. You wrote asking for a poem for your magazine. Will it do if I send it from Hyderabad?'

I introduced Dr Hill to her. There was an immense gathering and many had to stand outside the lecture theatre. It was with difficulty that I could provide seats for the Anand Bhavan party. After Mrs Naidu finished readings from her poetry, Dr Hill called upon me, without previous warning, to propose a vote of thanks. I was exceedingly nervous, but the Principal said I spoke well.

Later we had tea with Professor and Mrs Gidwani. Jawaharlal came with Mrs Naidu. We had a group photograph. Gidwani was later well known as Acharya of a Vidyapitha.

Then to the Law College where Mrs Gidwani and Polak spoke. At Gidwani's tea she said, 'I must get back soon to Hyderabad, where my husband is waiting with a stick to beat me, for setting such a bad example for the rest of India's women.'

October 8. In the afternoon went to the Oxford and Cambridge Hostel to hear Mrs Naidu. She said, 'Of course I remember you. I hear you are a professor now. You have changed since I saw you last. You look more grave.' Her address was splendid, as usual.

1923

February 28. Mrs Naidu came to tea with me and stayed from 4.30 to 6, saying she enjoyed my sumptuous tea. Then took her in my carriage to the public meeting in Purshottam Das Park. She asked, 'What have you been doing besides gaining fame as a professor?'

March 1. Mrs Naidu's address at the Hindu Boarding House on 'The Charms of Poetry'. I presided. Among her remarks were, 'My friend Amaranatha's memory is as young as himself,' and 'Like other professors he is guilty of desecrating poetry when he analyses it.'

1926

March 26. Called at Anand Bhavan in the morning to meet Mrs Naidu. She gave me her copy of Flecker's *Don Juan*. Went with her and Krishna to the meeting of the University Union, where she spoke on 'The Heart of Youth'. After the meeting we went out for a long drive.

April 26. Tea at Anand Bhavan with Mrs Naidu and Krishna. After I had said something, Mrs Naidu exclaimed, 'You mean cat!' Apropos

Group Photograph, 1923
(Standing) R. K. Chowdhry, K. N. Wanchoo, S. K. Handoo.
(On chairs) Vishnu Sahay, A. Jha, Mrs. Naidu, P. N. Sapru
(On ground) Mohd. Hashim, Ram Nath.

of something she said, 'Life is an absurd thing.' 'What an absurd adjective to use,' I said. She went on, 'It seems snobbish to say so, but politics makes you mix with some people you would not care to know in private life.' Pandit Motilal came and joined us for a while.

1927

July 29. Mrs Naidu came to a tea party at my house and stayed on from 5 to 8. Apropos some observation I had made she said, 'That's a bad sign, Amaranatha. You are becoming a misogynist. That is an old man's way.' She was full of praise for American girls, but 'they are crazy after novelty, a lapdog or an incarnation.' Of this party, D.B. Dhanpala wrote an interesting description in *Triveni*.

1928

September 3. Mrs Naidu went to the Hindu Boarding House at 8 in the morning to give readings from her poetry. I had earmarked several pages in *The Bird of Time* and *The Broken Wing*. She said at the meeting that she had been ordered by her friend Amaranatha Jha to recite the poems he likes.

September 4. To the New Hostel (now Ganganatha Jha Hostel) to preside over Mrs Naidu's lecture. She began by referring to her earlier visits to Allahabad when 'Professor Jha was a little younger and a little slenderer than he is.' Bhagwat Dayal told me that the same day while speaking at the Kayastha Pathshala University College she said that I had thoroughly approved of the title of her new book of poems, which she proposed to call *Feathers of the Dawn*. We heard no more of this collection and it is to be feared that the poems are lost.

1931

February 1. Called at Anand Bhavan, where had tea—Jawaharlalji, Kamalaji, Betty, Mrs Naidu. Went out with Mrs Naidu and Hansa Mehta to the gates [*sic*] for a drive, where my car was missing. Learnt that to avoid the crowd Gandhiji had taken it and gone in it some distance.

February 2. Mrs Naidu came to tea at my house. Later, took her and Mahadev Desai to the Rudras for dinner. On returning to Anand Bhavan learnt that Motilalji was sinking fast at Lucknow.

1933

October 24. Mrs Naidu came to tea at my house, 5.30 to 8. Ram Kumar Varma, Bhagwati CharanVarma, and Majid recited their poems. There was some music, too.

1934

May 9. Bombay. Called on Mrs Naidu at the Taj. Met her later in the day at tea with the Ratan Nehrus. Mrs Naidu gave me letters of introduction for Bernard Shaw, Walter de la Mare, Humbert Wolffe, Mrs Munro, Laurence Binyon. Each letter was delightfully phrased. This was a day prior to my leaving for Europe on M.V. *Victoria.*

July 6. London. Bernard Shaw made kindly inquiries after Madame Naidu, regretting that on his recent visit to India (really only Bombay) he could not meet her as she was in jail.

December 9. Dinner with Mrs Pandit to meet Mrs Naidu, who related some interesting stories. She asked me about Walter de la Mare and H.G. Wells, whom I had met in England.

1935

April 22. Met Mrs Naidu at dinner with Mrs Uma Nehru. Then went to the Palace Theatre to see *Cleopatra.*

May 1. Mrs Naidu called to see me. She said she considered 'The Illusion of Love' to be her best poem. She added, 'The Queen's Rival' was the only poem that did not 'come' to me; the last part was written several years later. Leilamani as a child used to be very jealous of my shoes. And then a Persian friend told me the story of Gulnar.' 'Edward Thomas wrote a fine article on my poetry in *The Bookman.*'

We went to dine at 19 Albert Road [Sir Tej Bahadur Sapru's house].

1937

May 1. Met Mrs Naidu at lunch with the Trilokinath Madans. She gave me the American edition of her collected poems entitled *The Sceptered Flute*, published by Dodd, Mead & Co., with an Introduction by Joseph Auslander. She inscribed it, 'Amaranatha Jha, from his affectionate old friend, Sarojini Naidu'. Her eyes twinkled when I read out from Auslander's Introduction the following sentence from one of her letters: 'Of all things that perhaps life or my temperament has given me, I prize the gift of laughter as beyond price.' 'Yes,' she said, 'don't I laugh even at myself?'

July 23. Received an affectionate letter from Mrs Naidu, addressing me as 'the Grand Moghul of the University'.

1938

May 2. Received a letter from Mrs Naidu on the decision of the Executive Council that I should act as vice-chancellor during the period of Pandit Iqbal Narain Gurtu's leave.

November 18. Mrs Naidu came to Allahabad on my invitation to address the University Convocation. She said she could not possibly write out the address. Called at Anand Bhavan to take her to the P.C. Banerji and Sunder Lal Hostels to their Social Gathering. In her speech at the latter place she said how pleased she was at my election as vice-chancellor the previous day.

November 19. Mrs Naidu addressed the Convocation and defended culture. She made several graceful references to my father, who was present. She said, 'It is not enough that we should think only of how we have great industries in the country: there must be men working in the seclusion of their laboratories who should be able to give the seed of those industries. It is necessary that in the secret recesses where din and strife do not intrude, there must be dreamers and visionaries wrestling with the secrets of nature to discover what new gifts they could give so that humanity might be better. Universities, therefore, are the storehouse, the conservatory, the treasure house of all true knowledge and inspiration; the teachers must be enchanters.'

In the evening I gave a dinner in honour of Mrs Naidu in the Vizianagaram Hall.

1939

November 21. Meeting of the University Union. Jawaharlalji, Rajendra Babu, and Mrs Naidu spoke. The last referred to me as 'the popular and ever-young vice-chancellor'.

After dinner with Mr Panna Lal, Mrs Naidu, Mr and Mrs Pandit, and I went to see the picture *The Four Feathers*.

November 23. Panna Lal saw me on his return from Anand Bhavan where Gandhiji had told Rajendra Babu that the students were being unreasonable in wanting to have the Congress flag during the Chancellor's visit, and that Jawaharlalji should intervene. Jawaharlalji sent a written note stating his opinion that the students should not ask for the flag while the Chancellor was at the University, specially as I had already allowed it on all other occasions.

November 25. About an hour before the Convocation, the Chancellor, Sir Harry Haig, sent a message declining to attend and address the Convocation. The officials who were to come also kept away, except for Drake-Brockman, the Chairman of the Public Service Commission. In the Chancellor's absence I addressed the Convocation very briefly. My address was generally liked. I made no reference whatever to the Chancellor's absence.

1940

January 25. In connection with the All-India Women's Conference there was a mushaira held at my house. It was a very pleasant function and some of the ghazals and nazms were of a high order. Among those who came were Begum Hamid Ali, Mrs Naidu, Raj Kumari Amrit Kaur, Rani Rajwade, Lady Rama Rao, Mrs Rameshwari Nehru, Mrs Asaf Ali, and Jawaharlalji. They stayed from 8.30 to 12.30.

January 29. Mrs Naidu was the chief guest at the Friday Club. Then accompanied her to Phaphamow Castle for dinner with the Parakram Jungs.

1947

September 8. The Governor's Military Secretary telephoned to say that Her Excellency [Mrs Naidu was the first governor of Uttar Pradesh after Independence] would like some Allahabad poets to come to Government House after dinner on the 11th.

September 12. Government House reception. Very large crowd. Mrs Naidu came up to me and said, 'Don't stand here, smoking your big cigar. See that you have some refreshments and others have some too.'

December 12. Annual Convocation of the Allahabad University. The Chancellor presided.

December 13. Jubilee Convocation of the University. An honorary degree was conferred on me as on many others. The vice-chancellor's citation was very complimentary. The Chancellor, in conferring the degree, said many very nice things: 'Amaranatha Jha,' she said, 'has grown from power to power, from fame to fame, but for me he still remains the young collegian I met thirty years ago. If any one truly deserves a tribute at the hands of the University, it is Dr Amaranatha Jha whose name is writ imperishably on the University.'

1948

February 9. Went from the Magh Mela camp to Government House. Mrs Naidu said she had asked Lord Mountbatten to see me and had suggested that he should find out from me what he should say to the students during his visit later in the month to the Benares Hindu University. Lord Mountbatten, while discussing this, said that Mrs Naidu had suggested that he should wag his fingers at the students and exclaim, 'You naughty, naughty children.' 'But,' he said, 'I have neither the advantage of her sex nor her prestige to be able to get away with that.'

February 10. Mrs Naidu visited my camp on the banks of the Jamuna, accompanied by Padmaja, Betty Hutheesingh, Indira Gandhi, and Mrs Dutt. We spent an hour boating, after tea.

November 10. Late at night I received this telegram: 'Tried to contact you by phone. After consultation both of us agreeable to your weekend plan. Hope matter now concluded. Confirm by letter. Sarojini Naidu.'

This was to persuade me to stay on as vice-chancellor [of Benares Hindu University], combining with that post the Chairmanship of the Public Service Commission.

November 27. At the At Home after the Convocation, Mrs Naidu said that the Sirdar [Sardar Vallabhbhai Patel] wanted to see me to inquire what my final decision was about the Benares vice-chancellorship.

November 28. Met Mrs Naidu at lunch at 19 Albert Road. Mrs Naidu came to the Muir (Amaranatha Jha) Hostel for unveiling my bronze head by Sudhir Khastgir. Her eyes were swollen and she was far from well. But she said she could see me fully well with one eye alone. She made a most gracious speech, saying that I looked like a late Roman emperor. She said, 'I have the most pleasant memories of my first meeting with him in 1917; and I am extremely happy to have the opportunity of unveiling his bronze head. This Hostel is really his creation. I have very great affection for Amaranatha Jha. I don't know why; I don't know whether he deserves it. You will serve the country well if you follow the noble example of the man after whom this Hostel has been rightly named.'

1949

January 8. Lunch on the lawns of Government House to meet the members of the Central Advisory Board of Education. After most of the guests had departed, half a dozen of us sat with Mrs Naidu under a garden umbrella, talking of all things and of nothing.

January 10. Mrs Naidu came to tea and mushaira at my house and stayed from 4.15 to 7. After listening to the poems of Nooh Narwi, she turned to me and said, 'How can this language die?' I replied. 'But how many persons use such simple words?' She was pressed by many of the younger guests to read some of her poems; she said, 'Next time. I am really not well.'

January 11. Lunch at Phaphamow Castle to meet the Governor.

January 12. The Governor's At Home to the West Indies cricket team.

January 13. Cricket match, East Zone vs. the West Indies. Mrs Naidu stayed for some time, then she left for Bamrauli to meet the Prime Minister.

February 2. Lucknow. From 1 to 3 at Government House. After lunch Mrs Naidu was busy giving instructions for tomorrow's reception to the Civil Service Association. As I was leaving she said, 'You are looking very thin. I hope you are well.' These were to be her last words to me.

March 2. At 6.30 in the morning, P.D. Tandon of the *National Herald* telephoned to say that Mrs Naidu had expired a few hours earlier. I felt stunned.

SUDHIR KUMAR RUDRA

Sudhir Kumar Rudra (1891–1951) belonged to a distinguished family of Indian Christians who were originally from Bengal. His father, Sushil Kumar Rudra, was the first Indian principal of St Stephen's College, Delhi. Sudhir Kumar was educated at Pembroke College, Cambridge. In 1922, he was appointed Reader in economics at Allahabad University and was later professor there.

Based on a notebook he kept between 1932 and 1938, Rudra's unpublished diary, 'The Rudra Book', contains perhaps the fullest account we have of Indian life in the bungalow. His portrait of Master Jumman, the sweeper-boy-turned-chauffeur, suggests a character straight out of *Miguel Street*.

⌒

from *The Rudra Book*

We had been on the look out for owning a house for several years past. Our good friend Rai Bahadur N.K. Mukerji, of the Tract and Book Society, was the one most persistently at us on this subject. We secured lease of municipal plots twice but rejected both. We could not secure suitable building plots.

Two years back we thought of buying this house, but then could not strike a bargain. The Rai Bahadur again helped us. Lala Wazir Sahai, engineer, Improvement Trust, and an old student of Father's from St Stephen's College, Delhi, went over this house and approved of it. He valued it at Rs 16,000.

This year in July, through the Rai Bahadur, we again came in contact with this proposition. Mr Rao, the university engineer, valued the house, at present prices, at Rs 15,500. He put on another 1000 for electric equipment, fans, etc.

The more people I consulted, the more divergent views I was given. It thus became very difficult for me to make up my mind. I was almost hopeless about ever possessing a house!

However, on 2 September, my mother's birthday, I made an offer of 17,000 plus costs to Mr O.M. Chiene, Bar-at-law, through whom we ultimately secured this house. We are very grateful to him for all his help. After some days, my offer was finally accepted.

We moved into this house, namely, 20 Albert Road, Allahabad, on Sunday, 6 November 1932.

Mohini undertook the entire labour of dismantling our old house on 14 Muir Road, where we had lived ever since we married and Mohini came to Allahabad in January 1925. The house was then known as 12 Muir Road. All the removal was also done by her. All the credit is hers. I was much taken up during those days by the Unity Conference presided over by Pandit Madan Mohan Malaviyaji. In fact, when I left in the morning, I did not know that I would not be going back to our old house. In the middle of the conference I got a line from Mohini, telling me that I was to come to our own house and not go back to Muir Road.

I must confess I was not thrilled. Strange! The fact is that we had lived and had a very happy time at the Muir Road house. Our landlady, Mrs Emerson, and her entire family had been very good to us. Mrs Emerson, particularly, with her great experience, was very helpful in the early days of our married life. We always ran to her whenever any of our children were sick.

Also we were close at hand to out great friends, the Calebs. The Calebs were the first people with whom I stayed, both when I came to apply for the post of Reader in eonomics at the university, and when I subsequently obtained the post. I lived with them as a paying guest for several months and spent a carefree happy time with them. The Calebs I had known from my days of boyhood. Mr E. Caleb had been a professor at my father's college in Delhi. He used to take me over to his house, opposite Lala Sultan Singh's house, in Kashmere Gate, feed me bananas and other things, and show me Mrs Caleb's photo, to whom he was then engaged. I am sorry I did not then think she looked nice and beautiful, as she undoubtedly was. Mr Caleb did not enjoy my lack of appreciation of his fiancé. Then, during the great Delhi Durbar, they came and lived with us, in my father's house. I am not sure whether their eldest son, now Dr Bernice Caleb, was not born there. Anyway, my recollection of both these good and charming people is very dear and of the happiest. It has been no small matter in our entire life to have had them in Allahabad. They have been and are our nearest and dearest friends. We look upon them as our own. Bobby's friendship with Coral[1] is something very tender and beautiful. God bless it. So it is little wonder that it was with great reluctance I shifted from Muir Road. We had had such a lovely time there.

Another point about the Muir Road house was that most of the people on that road were our Indian Christian friends. Old Mr and Mrs H. David and their people, Mr B.M. Mohan, Mr Roy, the Bobbs, and the S.W. Bobbs were not far off. We were also closer to the university and the church. Friends, especially the Calebs, were always dropping in and we used to go to them.

Also, our married life began there. We came as two and we left when we had three children born to us and the fourth one was well on her way! Pramila, our third child, was actually born in that old house. For the first two Mohini went to Lahore to good old Aunty Rosie, at 17 Park Lane, Muzang, Lahore. But this time she decided to have the baby in her own home. She would not go to the hospital either. I remember vividly the evening Pilu was born! Enid Jeremy was with us then. I was very disappointed that the third child was again a daughter! She was a sweet little mite, fair and yelled lustily. It took me several months before I really took a spontaneous interest in her. Miss Clough, of the European Civil Hospital, and her daughter Cynthia, attended on Mohini. We also had a Parsi Christian from Muirabad to help. Our old ayah, Bobby's ayah, was still with us. She was a picture of crabbed age, but she was truly reliable and knew her work well. But she was very indulgent towards Rita. For Rita was a delicate baby, and she had a strong and independent will of her own. Nothing on earth could get her to move her mind, if once she had made her decision. If she refused her feed, one could never persuade her to take it again. Unlike Bobby, who was always very gentle, sweet, and obedient. So everybody bossed over poor Bobby. If she did not wish to go to bed, the old ayah would say 'Go to *ninni*' and poor Bobby would go off to sleep. But not so Rituwa. And so the old ayah, to save herself much trouble, used to be extra indulgent to her and 'khushamad karo' her. And woe betide everybody if Mistress Rita did not have her special silk hanky or silk sock to hold when she sucked

---

[1]Coral Caleb married N.K. Chatterji, who was Rudra's nephew. With Qurratulain Hyder and Nissim Ezekiel, she was editor of *Imprint* in the 1960s.

her finger! The whole household would know about it. It took much longer for her to give up this habit than it did Bobby.

There were other people sharing the house occasionally. When they gave the rooms to some Hindu TB patients, we decided definitely to shift. But till then we usually had the entire place to ourselves, except the portion occupied by the Emersons themselves, or rooms taken by friends. For instance, the Basus were once there. They had parrots. Bobby was very fond of these parrots. She went frequently to see these birds and made friends with them. Then there was a comic figure, Mr Banjo, living in the outhouses. He was dark as coal and ragged, but he called himself an African. He palled up once with a French woman, an ex-widow of an English chaplain, they say. Banjo was once hammered on account of this lady by some Tommies. Then there was a quaint and troublesome person by the name of Ruth, who also lived in the outhouses. She was a religious maniac. All these were Mrs Emerson's protégés. Then in the cottage was an old lady, Mrs Massey, and her daughter Miss Massey. The old lady was very fond of Bobby. In fact she was very grandmotherly towards us all. But her daughter, though kind, had a funny temper. And once she slapped poor Bobby. When I learnt this, I was boiling angry. For Bobby, who is the sweetest and gentlest of children, never merited punishment.

We never had much of a garden in the old house, but one thing we had there—which we do not yet have in our own house—is a sandpit. I went to the Ganges myself, and filled and carried the sand on my own back, and with the help of Jumman and Puddan chaprasi brought the sand in the car. The children greatly enjoyed this sandpit. The younger children have often asked me for a sandpit in this house.

It was also to the old house that I first returned after having lost my dearest Fathi,[2] up in Solon, Simla Hills, on 29 June 1925. Mohini could not come down with me since our firstborn was on the way. I left her in Dalhousie, with Bushy—my sister Ila. I thus had to go through the poignant grief of the loss of dear old Fathi all alone in this house. I had many regrets, very deep. One was that I did not take certain actions which may have saved Father's life, and the other that he never came and lived in my married home. He was anxious to see me settled down.

---

[2] Rudra's father.

Cartoons of Allahabad University's Economics Department
teachers by Saeed Jaffrey

And yet he never enjoyed our home-life, except such as it was up at
Solon. Of course, Fathi had been to Allahabad since my appointment.
He stayed for some time with dear old Bishop Westcott, now buried in
the cathedral compound. In fact, the good old Bishop wished me to stay
with him. I then was able to secure a house, at 8 Bank Road, and Fathi
came and lived with me there. I have happy recollections of those days.
How he wanted me to sit at the head of the table and I did not! How
pleased he was. Also how keen and active a part he used to take in
looking after the garden. He actually used to water the garden with his
own hands! He was very fond of gardening, or at least in having a good
garden. He was also a great one for a decent house. He was very
particular about this. A high plinth, airy rooms, quiet surroundings,
clean and neat, would, he said, add greatly to efficiency of work and
enjoyment of life.

I became seriously ill after my father's death. Dr B.K. Mukerji,
known universally as the 'Beloved Physician', treated me. He has done
so ever since, all of us, free of cost. We can never repay his debt of
kindness to us. He maintains that he is merely showing gratitude for all
the care he received from my maternal grandfather, Babu Ishwar Chandra

Singha, of Batala fame, during his medical college days. So thus goodness done by ones forebears help the later generations. I developed pleurisy. I had to turn out a servant—he was a Hindu—because he refused to give me the chamber pot. Jumman was there. He was then a sweeper boy. He has now blossomed into a full-fledged 'Driver Sahib' and has become a Muslim to boot.

It was to the old house that we brought our first car, a Fiat, from Delhi. This car is still going strong. It was brought with money I received in Fathi's will, so I regard it as Fathi's gift to us. And a great gift it has been too. We are greatly attached to this car of ours. Sujit Boy[3] was very fond of it. His eyes used to beam whenever Mohini brought him near it. He used to spread out his hands with great vigour to grasp the steering wheel. It was in this car I took him on his last drive to the Railway Hospital.

When we first got the car, practically every Sunday I was at it, cleaning it, etc. Then Brij Lal, the one person to whom we have always gone, said that the car always went wrong after I had been at it. I don't believe it. Anyway, it's been ages since I have done anything to the car. Then I had a man, a syce, who would come and clean it in the morning. Jumman now looks after it in a kind of way. He was good at it once, but has gone slack now.

The syce, Mithal, used to clean the saddle Jick[4] had given me. When I stayed in the YMCA on Queen's Road, Keron Benjamin and Enid's mother were living there. Keron was secretary. I was their paying guest. I used to go out riding with a fellow called Bowers. He is now assistant registrar at the Allahabad High Court. I used to ride a racehorse. One day—it happened to be Mohini's birthday—the animal bolted with me. It was on the parade ground. I just could not keep it in. He took a big jump across the nullah opposite the High Court and rushed down Elgin Road. Fortunately, here was no traffic, otherwise it would have meant certain death. At the Queen's Road and Elgin Road crossing, near the

---

[3]Rudra's son, born after four daughters. He died of bacillary dysentry in 1936, aged one year and three days.

[4]Rudra's brother, Major General Ajit Anil Rudra (1896–1993). He enlisted as a private in the 18th Battalion Royal Fusiliers and saw action in France and Flanders during World War I. In 1946 he was awarded the OBE for meritorious services.

corner of the Head Post Office, I would have dashed into a telegraph post, but with supreme effort I pulled on one side, ducked to avoid the sustaining wires, and came off. It was a miraculous escape. I attribute it to Mohini's birthday. But I was badly hurt in the head.

It was at Keron's that we had our first dinner in Allahabad. We walked across from our place, via the cemetery. The upper and lower storeys of the YMCA were lit. There was a hockey field in front. Mohini mistook the lower lights as the reflection of the top ones and the hockey field to be a tank. I must say it looked very much like that, such was the effect at night. We often tease Mohini about this even now.

While staying with Keron I fixed up the Muir Road house, and also, got the services of Master Jumman. He was a mere lad then. I did not wish to employ him, because he looked so poorly. But I thought he would become strong, and then we could train him up as we wanted. Also, when we would be old, he would still be strong and active. But this does not seem to be the case. Dr Mukherji suspected him of TB, and I believe he was right. So we gave him rest and took him off his sweeper's job. He did not wish to give this up, since he would miss his tea. I could not get him a job elsewhere. No one would keep him because he was a sweeper. So we kept him on and now he is our driver. He did not wish to remain a Hindu because it was a costly business to be one. All kinds of feasts and festivals had to be observed. Also, he believed in nothing. He says he has tried all kinds of religions, and they are all frauds. The one religion is the worship of money. He says Money is God! He says he was once, along with his family, baptized a Christian. But it meant that he had to understand a bit of the religion, and it also meant expense. Cleaner clothes, etc. His children blossomed out in shorts. And the servants began to call his wife Memsahib! I believe he eventually became a Muslim to escape untouchability. And also because our cook and our bearer were Muslims and he thought he could get more food out of them, which he does. They are naturally very happy he has become a Muslim. I have felt hurt, much.

We have a cook, Abdul, who is a funny kind of bloke. I took him on when Mohini was away in Lahore, expecting Bobby. He seemed to be a smart bearer and produced good chits. Mohini once got very angry with him and dismissed him. I am sorry I interfered and had him reinstated. Now he has hung around. He is jolly dirty, an absolute pig.

I shudder to think he is our cook! I wish we could replace him. This summer, 1938, he nearly died of enteric. Mohini looked after him personally. But for very careful nursing and feeding, the fellow would have died. Ronny Bannerji, Bishop Bannerji's son, looked after him as he does us also free of cost. Ronny is alert and keen and doing exceedingly well for a young doctor.

We had an A-1 servant in George. Absolutely first-rate. I am very sorry he left us. But he was getting a little on my nerves. He and our sweeper, Bindoo, whom we had secured in Almora, when we went up to Binsar for the first time, never pulled together, due to our ayah, Buddhiya, who was a sparkling kind of woman. George was clean, punctual, intelligent and resourceful. He could cook English and American dishes well. He replaced Ghazi when he fell ill. I should have kept him on as a cook, but he could not make Indian food properly. He was a smart and neat person to have in the house. I swore at him one day, and he went away. He worked for us for over seven years. Splendid servant. He once wished to come back. But I do not believe in keeping a man once dismissed or rather who leaves on his own accord.

I was eager to keep a Christian servant. We got one after much difficulty, Yakub. He turned out to be sickly. His wife was a grand lady. I must say he was very good to Sujit. And he liked him very much.

After Sujit's death, I took seriously ill. Yakub too fell hopelessly sick, and then turned up Kallu. He used to be our punkah-coolie boy in the Muir Road house. He began work very well. Though he is really a lazy devil. Of course, in crucial moments he is of great help. He is very fond of Mohini. But the fellow has got strictly limited intelligence.

Bobby's old ayah could not work for us after we moved into our own house. It was too far for her to come and go. So we pensioned her off. We give one month's pay for every year of service, provided the sum is not above Rs 50. We did this in Ghazi's case too. The old ayah got us Buddhiya ayah. The children and everybody else liked her. She was bright and a good worker. Nira was born when she was with us. We had to discharge her because she was suffering from a particular disease. We were sorry she had to leave.

She gave us the present ayah as a substitute. She came in a little before Sujit was born. She is old, untrained and slow. I do not know why we have kept her on. But she was good to Sujit. And he was very fond of her.

Bindoo had to go because his wife did not keep well. His home also was far away in Bijnor. He too liked Sujit. He was shocked to hear that we had lost him.

Since then we have had Ghani. Smart and clean lad. Needs watching.

Our *mali*, Gaya Din, is a humdrum kind of fellow and is always taking leave and staying away. He has killed my interest in the garden to a great extent. But he is a handy kind of fellow. He has been with us ever since we took the house.

This house was planned and owned by a Frenchman named Edward Moreau. A tennis cup in the All-India contest goes by his name. He was a very rich man. The house was built by a European firm, Firzonni & Co. It was built, it seems, during the War. The two side passages ensure a fine circulation of air. The house is picturesque, is strong and neatly built. The two outstanding defects were that the servant quarters were right in front of the house, a tremendous mistake, a second that there was no verandah. The absence of a porch is also a handicap.

On 1 December 1933 we applied to the municipality for extensions to the house. We wished to add a verandah and some rooms. Rao, the university engineer, has very kindly helped. Material and labour are cheap. Ram Lal Soni, an old Stephanian and Father's old pupil, did the work.

The plans for extension were sanctioned by Mr Bishop, the Collector, and Mr Brij Mohan Vyas, the executive officer. The matter was expedited through the kindness of Rai Bahadur N.K. Mukerji.

We started the new extension on 15 February 1934. Jick and Edith, with Lila and Asha were here. Jick helped greatly with his suggestions. I followed mostly what he suggested. The new extensions were not completed till after Jick and family left. They had all taken a keen interest in it. I got the staircase built at the express wish of Jick and Bobby. But for these two I would not have gone in for this expense.

I find that it is hardly worth my while to transcribe from the old notebook. Too much of a sweat and almost a waste of time. So please refer to the old book.

RAJESHWAR DAYAL

Rajeshwar Dayal (1909–99) was born in Nainital, where his father was a lawyer. In 1925, he came to Allahabad to do his Intermediate at Kayastha Pathshala, and the following year joined the Kayastha Pathshala University College for his BA. After doing his MA in history at Allahabad University, he sat for the Indian Civil Service examination in 1931 and was successful at the first attempt. In a long and distinguished diplomatic career, he served as high commissioner to Pakistan and foreign secretay to the Government of India. During 1960–1, at a crucial moment in the post-colonial history of Africa, he was special representative and head of UN operations in the Congo.

∿

from *A Life of Our Times* (1998)

With Bhagwat's return from England in 1924, a new dimension entered our lives. We greatly admired him for his fine mind, personality, literary tastes and culture and owed him much for the broadening of our horizons. He inspired in us a taste for English literature; he introduced us to classical Western music, and brought some Western influences into our predominantly Indian way of life.

At home we heard and spoke only in Urdu or Hindustani to our elders but in English to each other. While our Hindustani pronunciation and syntax was being constantly corrected, English manners and language were not discouraged provided we did not foresake our own. We thus lived in two worlds, not belonging wholly to either. But it certainly widened our horizons and created a greater awareness of and sensitivity to cultural influences from different sources.

We did quite well at school and our teachers, who expected much of us, were not often disappointed. In my case, it all began when I was in the third standard, aged eight or nine. I had stood second in class and proudly announced the fact at home. But instead of the expected 'Shabash' ('well done'), Mother quietly said that someone must have come first and why was it not me? This greatly hurt my self-esteem and I sulked, but something must have registered, as thereafter there were few occasions for a similar reproach. We managed to win merit scholarships both in the Junior and Senior Cambridge examinations which helped comfortably to meet our fees up to the university level. As I had secured a high position in the school-leaving examination with distinctions in mathematics, English and Urdu with a handsome scholarship, it was thought that I should take up a science course, which the brighter students were expected to do. It was also decided that I could telescope a two-year course in one year; I was soon to prove how mistaken these assumptions were. The Intermediate College at Allahabad—the Kayastha Pathshala—which I joined, was a devastating experience from the start. An untidy jumble of buildings, the place had a shoddy and unkempt appearance. There was an air of languor and neglect about everything. The classrooms were laden with dust and a large punkah swished overhead trying unsuccessfully to stir the torpid air. The students were of a piece with the surroundings, hailing mostly from villages and regarded me with not a little curiosity. For my part I found their habits of sitting cross-legged on the benches, scratching themselves, and behaving in a generally uncouth fashion rather obnoxious. The teachers seemed to share in the general apathy and were an uninspiring and dispirited lot. They rattled off their lectures without much regard for their audience and left. The English teacher, a venerable Bengali gentleman in pince-nez spectacles, had a totally unintelligible pronunciation. The authorship of the only essay I wrote, which was on Charles Dickens, was questioned by him as having been plagiarized. The portly and turbaned physics and chemistry teacher was more interested in the shop that he ran in Katra bazaar than in his students. Soon, I too began to be infected by the general lassitude and, to make matters worse, I was completely at sea with the science and mathematics I was reading.

Dr Tara Chand, the principal, tried valiantly to dispel the listless air of the institution by prescribing uniformity in dress which would smarten up the students and staff. Everyone was required to wear khaki shorts and white shirt. The result was bizarre. The principal himself set the example and other teachers and students had to conform, despite their protests. The science teacher's outfit was crowned by his familiar bulky turban, but his legs, used to squatting, hardly seemed able to sustain his weight. The students looked a motley crowd, their newly-exposed and little-exercised legs hardly providing an aesthetic sight. To further activate students and staff, there was compulsory parade in the afternoons, and we were formed into platoons. Our drill-master was none other than the science teacher. He and the other teachers had been given some instruction in elementary drill. All we could do was to stand to attention and form fours, or to about-turn and march (generally out of step). The different platoons would snake around the limited grounds, intersecting each other. After half an hour of this ordeal in the sun, we were too hot and bothered to pay much attention at class.

In the Intermediate examination I barely scraped through with a second class. That made me decide to take up arts at the university, which I looked forward even more eagerly to joining. The impressive buildings, the quality of the professors and their teaching fully justified the high reputation of Allahabad University as one of the very best in the country. Many of the teachers were eminent scholars and authors of considerable distinction and some of their original research had won wide acclaim.

The new K.P. University College, which I now joined, faced the grand University Senate Hall; it pioneered the holding of tutorials on Oxbridge lines. Forsaking the rough-and-tumble of the Bar, my brother Bhagwat had joined it as the warden, his heart being more in education than in law. Dr Tara Chand had moved over to be the head of the college. The new college attracted good students and athletes and soon acquired a fine reputation. As some form of sport at the university and college was obligatory, and not being an athlete, I plumped for the University Traning Corps.

A British Staff Sergeant, who had a particularly salty vocabulary and was a martinet for discipline was in charge of our training. The recruits assembled at the armoury at the dot of 6.30 A.M. and were issued used uniforms and equipment, evidently leftovers of World War I. The uniforms were hopelessly oversized, but somehow, with belts and braces, we managed to defy gravity. Woollen stockings, puttees, heavy hob-nailed and well-worn ammunition boots, webbing belts and straps which were our harness, completed our outfit. Before parade, there would be much polishing of brass buttons and buckles and much effort to coax some shine out of the old boots whose tough leather often needed softening with oil. After being put through our preliminary paces with much bantering and hectoring in his strong Yorkshire accent, Staff Sergeant Giles would ultimately pronounce us as no longer being a total rabble. In due course we were issued dummy rifles and later qualified in the use of bayonets against stuffed gunny bags. Our drill and marching reached a point when, with bayonets flashing and to the accompaniment of our own bagpipe band and with much energetic drumming, we were thought fit for public exposure and taken for long route marches.

The two-week winter camp in bitter cold and rain was, however, a rough and rugged experience. There was much parading, night and day marches, sundry exercises and games which occupied all our days. Sentry duty at night was a particularly unpleasant chore. We slept crowded, eight to a small tent, on the damp ground on thin tarpaulins and blankets. The food was execrable, always gritty, the lavatory arrangements were nauseous, while only the hardiest would dare a shower in the open in icy cold water. Despite four years in the training corps, I could never rise above the rank of lance corporal and it was no consolation that Napoleon made all his great conquests rising from that lowly rank.

There was a strange sequel to my none-too-glorious soldierly career. There had been a great agitation in the Indian Central Assembly and press about the almost total exclusion of Indians from the officer ranks of the Indian Army. A Royal Commission was accordingly appointed to enquire into the matter under General Sir Andrew Skeen. On one particularly torpid and humid afternoon, while a lecture on some dull branch of economics was in progress and I sat drowsily at the back of the classroom, there was a sudden flurry of activity which jolted me to wakefulness. General Skeen and members of his Commission walked in and after some conversation with Professor Rudra and between themselves, started peering at the students. Suddenly, I heard my name called out; when I stood up, I was asked to see the General in the professor's ante-room. I followed doubtfully, wondering what it was all about. The General, after eyeing me, asked what career I intended to follow; I replied hesitantly that I supposed I would take one of the competitive examinations. What if I did not succeed, asked the General. I said I had not thought about that. I was then asked whether I would like to join the Army. Quite taken aback, I stammered that I had not thought of that either. The General said reassuringly that if I would like to be considered, I should let him know at next morning's parade, which he would be inspecting. I made no further contact with him, nor he with me. I was certainly not cut out to be a soldier and I shudder to think what could have become of me—or of our Army—had I said 'yes' to the General.

The Indian Army was officered entirely by British officers, from subalterns upwards, a sort of 'apartheid' being practised in it. It was put out that no British officer would condescend to serve under a superior Indian officer; accordingly an 'Indianized' unit, the 4/19 Hyderabad Regiment, was assigned for the appointment of Indian officers which they joined as Second-Lieutenants, the senior officers still being British. Those who managed to survive the gruelling training course at Sandhurst, which was beset with discriminatory hurdles, had a rough run when they joined their segregated regiment in India, then posted at Allahabad. There were many casualties among our friends, some having been sent down from Sandhurst, others cashiered and sacked later. Two of the great soldiers of the Indian Army—Field Marshal Cariappa and General Thimayya—were junior officers in Allahabad at the time and we used to hear from them of their harsh treatment. All this offered little encouragement for a military career even for those who had an aptitude for it.

When the BA results came out, I acquired an entirely meretricious reputation for scholarship. Having wasted much of my time during the year, I was assailed by pangs of conscience a couple of months before the examination. I then got down to leafing through the yet unread prescribed volumes, working from dawn to midnight, keeping at hand some classic textbooks for the essential facts. I thus managed, before each paper, to refresh my memory and to regurgitate all that I had ingested the previous day. This technique, born of sheer panic, stood me in good stead at the examinations. I got a high position in the BA, winning the history and economics prizes, medals and a merit scholarship. In the MA in history I also managed to pull off a surprise by standing first in the university. I do not consider that these feats made me a good student as I took no part in debates or dramatics and was indifferent at sports and games.

The Civil Disobedience Movement was raging and there was a great ferment among the students, many of whom were torn between joining the agitation and abandoning their studies, or trying to qualify for a living.

Many great political leaders came to address the students. We were thrilled by the eloquence of Sarojini Naidu, greatly excited by the stirring words of Netaji Subhash Chandra Bose, whom I drove in my brother's car from one meeting to another. Jawaharlal Nehru was the spoilt darling of the students, who accepted anything from him. On one occasion, trying to leave the Senate Hall he was mobbed by the adoring students; in a display of his famous temper and petulance, he lashed out to left and right with his baton. His sister, Krishna, was adopted as a sort of mascot and half the students seemed to have fallen in love with her. Also some of the revolutionaries who believed in the cult of violence were much admired.

The student community watched with fascination and sympathy the frequent protest meetings and processions led largely by the Nehru family, but not many joined the movement. The call to abandon schools and colleges, law courts and offices, etc., and to offer civil disobedience, largely fell on deaf ears at the university. The students were more preoccupied with the need to qualify for earning a livelihood than with anything else. Nor were they disposed to burn foreign goods or clothes as they could not possibly afford a second wardrobe. Since not many avenues of employment were open to educated young men at the time, the scramble for government jobs continued unabated. Also, the prospect of being submerged in an anonymous mass of processionists and braving police beating, and spells in prison, was less than alluring. Therefore, while the students were greatly moved by the swelling mass agitation, they were unwilling to become insignificant drops in an ocean of faceless humanity. There were, of course exceptions, sometimes even among non-Indians. A young Ceylonese freshly returned from Oxford, who was staying with us, was so taken up by what he witnessed that he decided to join the movement forthwith. Clad precariously in an unfamiliar khadi dhoti, he made a bundle of his Oxford suits and blazers to which he added his English tennis racquet for good measure, and flung the lot into the smouldering bonfire of foreign things. After this purificatory sacrifice, he joined the processionists led by Krishna Nehru and shared in their daily travails. After some months of this and considerable personal experience of the attentions of the Indian police, his enthusiasm waned and he took off for his own country. It was said that his devotion to the cause was exceeded only by that to the enchanting Krishna.

What really thrilled the students was the cold courage and self-sacrifice of the revolutionaries, the votaries of violence. At the very gates of the university a great drama took place when an epic battle was fought to the death between an intrepid revolutionary, Chandrashekhar Azad, and the British Superintendent of Police, which ended only when Azad, his ammunition exhausted, was shot down. Stories of political assassination attempts, mostly in Bengal, some successful, received much attention and applause. The Communists attracted a certain following but not many continued with the movement on leaving the university.

Yet another political tendency which found favour chiefly among the educated and professional and propertied classes, was represented by such patriotic figures as Sir Tej Bahadur Sapru, M.R. Jayakar, Hriday Nath Kunzru, Rt. Hon. Srinivasa Sastry, Sir Surendra Nath Banerji, Sir Pherozshah Mehta, to name a few. They believed in a policy of constructive cooperation, the establishment of a parliamentary system of government responsible to the people, and independence within the Commonwealth. They advocated the entry of Indians in increasing numbers into the senior administrative services and the armed forces. Their methods were constitutional with due respect for the law, and they believed in achieving their objects by a process of peaceful negotiation. They were skilled negotiators and constitutional and legal experts of eminence. By these means, Indians could be enabled to penetrate the citadel of power from within rather than attempt to assail the impregnable fortress from without. They joined issue with the Congress on boycotting educational institutions and resigning from government jobs and professions as this would only deprive the country of talent and experience which it sorely needed. They also cautioned against the breaking of laws, civil disobedience and jail-filling, as this would breed habits of lawlessness and indiscipline which would indubitably endure even after independence and make the country ungovernable. All other political movements were, however, eventually swamped out by the Congress flood.

After doing my MA I applied to take the forthcoming examination for the Indian Civil Service (ICS) in January 1931 and was asked to appear before a Medical Board at Lucknow in August. Its Chairman was a Colonel Townsend, the Civil Surgeon there. As the candidates were numerous, they were divided into batches, I falling in a group headed by a Major Salamatullah, a man of enormous proportions who was the Jail Superintendent. To my dismay, I was declared to be anaemic and therefore medically unfit. This caused much disappointment among family and friends and plans began to be discussed about my taking the London examination which, incidentally, offered many more vacancies and was regarded as easier than the Delhi examination which had only three or four places. To avoid a similar mishap, I went for a medical examination to the Civil Surgeon of Allahabad, who, unknown to us and by a stroke of fortune, turned out to be none other than Colonel Townsend, recently transferred there. He found me one hundred per cent fit. When told that only a couple of months previously his Board had rejected me, he was shocked and indignant, and fair-minded man that he was, he immediately sent a strong letter to the head of his department in Lucknow demanding a rectification of the mistake. The wheels of government thus being set in motion, I heard after some time that I would be permitted to appear again before a board set up for the benefit of the half-a-dozen failed candidates from London who were returning to take the Delhi examination. When I again appeared before Major Salamatullah, who had obviously received a reprimand, he was all smiles and remarked how well I now looked. I was passed, and in early December, informed that I could appear at the January examination.

In the doubt and confusion of the previous few months, I had abandoned whatever preparations I had begun and felt most diffident about taking a gruelling test with such little preparation as the limited time would permit. But Mother, with her unerring instinct, gave me heart to make the attempt, which would at least provide useful experience. The examination, held in the stately Metcalfe House, was abuzz with candidates from all parts of India engaged in animated discussion. Many of them, smartly turned out, seemed very knowledgeable and confident. After the paper, they again engaged in an animated post-mortem. I had offered many papers in Indian, British and European history, besides political organization and political theory, all of which required much study. The examination stretched over three weeks, and the frequent gaps of half a day to a whole day between papers provided some opportunity for preparation. When the ordeal at last ended, it left me exhausted and without hope as I returned home to Allahabad.

SURYAKANT TRIPATHI 'NIRALA'

Suryakant Tripathi 'Nirala' (1899–1961) belonged to a family of Kanyakubja Brahmins who had migrated from the Kanauj region of Uttar Pradesh to the small princely state of Mahishadal in Bengal, where his father was a court official. Thanks to the geographical accident of his birth, Nirala grew up speaking two languages, Baiswari, which was the language of his home, and Bengali, in whose literature, especially Tagore, he was deeply read. Standard Hindi he taught himself later, by studying back issues of magazines like Chintamoni Ghosh's *Saraswati*, published from Allahabad.

Family tragedy dogged Nirala from an early age. He lost his mother when he was two, and though there followed some carefree years during which he got married, had children, and flunked his matriculation examination, for which he got thrown out of the house, tragedy struck again. He lost his father in 1917, and his wife, brother, and sister-in-law in the influenza epidemic of 1918. Not yet twenty, he had two of his own and four of his brother's children to parent. Leaving his children with his wife's parents in Dalmau, he moved to Calcutta, where he became editor of a magazine brought out by the Ramakrishna Mission. In 1923 he became editor of a new journal, *Matvala*, in which his first poems were published.

In 1935 Nirala's nineteen-year-old daughter died. His elegy for her, 'Saroj-smriti', introduced a new note of direct speech into Hindi poetry. Written in the same year, 'Breaking Stones' has the same directness. It is the first Hindi poem to call Allahabad by its Mughal name; a lesser poet would have chosen the older and more elevated 'Prayag'. Nirala lived in Allahabad, in the Daraganj area, from 1941 until his death.

In a literary career spanning four decades, Nirala published novels, short stories, and books of essays, in addition to a dozen volumes of poetry. He is regarded as the greatest Hindi poet after Tulsi Das.

✵

Breaking Stones

By a road in Allahabad
I saw a woman
        breaking stones.

No tree to give her shade,
A dark skin,
Firm tightly-cupped breasts,
Eyes fixed to the ground,
Thoughts of the night before
Going through her mind,
She brought down the heavy hammer
Again and again, as though it were
A weapon in her hand.
Across the road—
A row of trees, high walls,
The mansions of the rich.

The sun climbed the sky.
The height of summer.
Blinding heat, with the *loo* blowing hard,
Scorching everything in its path.
The earth under the feet
Like burning cotton wool,
The air full of dust and sparks.
It was getting to noon,
And she was still breaking stones.

As I watched,
She looked at me once,
Then at the houses opposite,
Then at her ragged clothes.
Seeing no one was around,
She met my eyes again
With eyes that spoke of pain
But not defeat.

Suddenly, there came the notes of a sitar,
Such as I had not heard before.
The next moment her young body
Quivered and as sweat
Trickled down her face, she lifted
The hammer, resuming work,
As though to say
                    'I'm breaking stones.'
     (1935)

Translated from the Hindi by
Arvind Krishna Mehrotra

NAYANTARA SAHGAL

Nayantara Sahgal (1927–) was born and raised in Allahabad. She spent part of her childhood in Cawnpore Road bungalows and part at Anand Bhavan, the ancestral home of the Nehrus. Her mother, Vijaya Lakshmi Pandit, was Jawaharlal Nehru's sister, and her father, R.S. Pandit, was a Sanskrit scholar and lawyer, who for a while practised at the Allahabad High Court. In the Introduction to the 1961 reprint of *Prison and Chocolate Cake*, Sahgal says that the 'provincial grace of the small town' she grew up in has 'served as [her] model for civilized living'.

Widely regarded as the finest novelist of her generation, she is also the most political. Her novels include *A Time to be Happy* (1958), *Storm in Chandigarh* (1969), *Rich Like Us* (1985), the third being about Indira Gandhi's Emergency, *Mistaken Identity* (1988), and *Lesser Breeds* (2003).

∼

from *Prison and Chocolate Cake* (1954)

Allahabad, our home, has changed now, become, shabby and uncared for, but in our childhood it was a serene city of gracious homes and well-kept gardens. For those who preferred the atmosphere of a metropolis, it was a dull place. Its charm lay in its tranquillity. Its life was geared to the high courts, the university, and the intellectual and cultural activity that men like my grandfather, Motilal Nehru, Sir Tej Bahadur Sapru, and Pandit Madan Mohan Malaviya, all eminent lawyers, inspired around them—for in those days the legal profession offered the highest rewards to men of culture. Allahabad had always been an honoured city to Indians. Later, it became famous as one of the centres of the national movement.

Mummie had grown up in this very town, in Anand Bhawan (Abode of Happiness), the beautiful home of her parents, brought up in the care of an English governess, and educated at home by private tutors. At this very house she was married; afterwards she and my father continued to live in Allahabad, though in their own home.

After my grandfather, whom we called Nanuji, gave up his fabulous law practice to join the national movement, he gave his grand old home, as he had already given his time, his fortune, and himself, to the nation, and Anand Bhawan came to be known as Swaraj Bhawan (Abode of Freedom). It was used partly for Congress Party offices and partly as a medical dispensary, which dispensed services free of charge; but three quarters of the enormous house lay empty and unused. The indoor swimming pool, which had been the first private pool in Allahabad and the scene of many festive gatherings, was also left to gather dust and cobwebs.

Across the road from Swaraj Bhawan, Nanuji built a smaller house, the new Anand Bhawan. Although I was born in Swaraj Bhawan, in the very room where my mother had been born, and Lekha and I had been left there with our grandparents when Mummie and Papu went on holiday to Europe, we were, of course, too young to have any recollections of the old house. It was the new Anand Bhawan that we knew and loved, and that became our home when in 1935 we went to live there with our uncle.

Both houses were, and still are, places of pilgrimage for the nation. Not a day went by without crowds of people streaming in at all hours of the day to see the home of the Nehrus, the house that Motilal had built and Jawaharlal had lived in, to slide loving hands across the smooth floors and pillars of the veranda and—when Mamu was at home—to pierce the air with cries of '*Jawaharlal Nehru ki jai*!' till he had to come out and with folded palms acknowledge their greeting.

The chowkidar (watchman) employed to steer the crowds and to keep them from swarming joyously into the house had grown old in the service of the family, but he had not been able to devise any argument to convince people that they must confine their sightseeing to the outside of the building. It was no use. His pleas were never heard. And often, when we were eating or sleeping, curious visitors would appear in the rooms, eager to see what was going on. These occasions would be more frequent during the season of the Magh Mela in March each year, when pilgrims would come to Allahabad in their hundreds of thousands to bathe at the confluence of the two sacred rivers. After completing their holy pilgrimage, they would throng to Anand Bhawan, a vast marching column of humble folk.

One afternoon, I was lying on a divan in the drawing room. It was a hot day, and the whirring fan had lulled me to sleep. Suddenly, a peculiar noise entered my consciousness, and by the time I was fully awake its rhythmic beat had turned to thundering cries of '*Panditji ki jai!*' I got up and peeped out through the window. I saw men, women, and children clambering eagerly onto the verandas. I shivered in spite of the heat for it was awe-inspiring to see a mammoth crowd moved to adoration.

They did not stop roaring till Mamu came downstairs and spoke to them, his usually grave face lit up by his radiant smile, his low voice asking quiet, interested questions, making humorous remarks, laughing with them; till, listening behind the window, I had a queer sensation. All at once I became one of those anonymous faces outside, gazing with complete belief and affection at the man who stood before them. The little girl behind the window was on the wrong side of it. She should have been out in the garden with those others, with whom she felt a strange and sudden kinship. It was a miraculous accident that she lived in the house with Jawaharlal, accident that he played with her, and that she called him her uncle. For actually she was one small ripple in the sea of humanity that looked trustingly to him for inspiration and guidance.

We were brought up by a series of governesses—I think there were eight in all—who kept us on a strict regime of boiled vegetables, custard puddings, regular walks, and early bedtimes. On Sundays we visisted our grandmother and great-aunt at Anand Bhavan. For these visits we dressed up in saris, which we tore off when they became too cumbersome for our games; ate rich Kashmiri food, which Mummie deplored; refused to take our afternoon naps; raced around in the hot sun shouting like hooligans; and came home hoarse, stuffed, and exhausted. Going to Anand Bhavan was always an eagerly anticipated event because of the unlimited freedom we were allowed there.

Our grandmother, whom we called Nanima was tiny and doll-like, with a Dresden china perfection about her. She had the fair complexion and hazel eyes common to Kashmiri women, and her hair had been a rich chestnut brown before it turned grey. She had small, beautiful-shaped hands and feet, and a sharp, imperious manner that was a result of long years of frail health.

Life had been kind to Nanima. It had given her a husband whom she adored, three lovely children, great wealth, and a famous name. But it had also demanded a great deal of her. Born and bred in luxury, a typical example of the flower of Kashmiri womanhood, helpless, beautiful, and pampered, she had willingly given up all her comforts and shed generations of orthodoxy to follow her husband when he joined Gandhiji's ranks. Uncomplainingly she had discarded her lovely clothes for coarse white khadi, had seen her husband, son, daughter-in-law, and daughters go to jail, and had herself proudly courted arrest and imprisonment at a time when her age and ill health could well have excused her from taking an active part in politics.

Nanima disliked all children except those of her own family, and made no bones about it. Towards us her manner was one of humorous tolerance rather than the demonstrative attitude of most grandmothers.

When we arrived at Anand Bhawan, we were always greeted at the front steps by the old gardener, Datadin, who, with a smile creasing his grizzled face, would present us each with a nosegay of flowers. Bibima, our great-aunt, would come hurrying out to meet us and take us to our grandmother. Already tired of my enveloping sari, I would start dragging it off, trailing it behind me as I ran, emerging in my finger-tip-length cotton frock.

'Be careful your frock doesn't trail in the mud,' Nanima once cautioned me dryly. 'It's even longer than usual today.'

I sneezed and sniffed. Our governess always pinned a handkerchief on the front of our dresses with a large safety pin, but it was too much trouble to unpin it when we wanted to blow our noses. I sniffed again against the back of my hand.

'In heaven's name, what is the handkerchief for?' asked Nanima, waving her exquisite little white hands in despair. Turning to Bibima, she added: 'No wonder these children are always sniffling. Look at their absurd high frocks.'

Our beloved Bibima, widowed at an early age, had devoted her life to the care of her fragile younger sister. Her apartments were a separate unit a short distance from the main house, and she lived a serene, peaceful life of worship and service. Bibima cooked her own food, as she did not eat meat and would not touch the semi-European food cooked in the main kitchen. In her Indian kitchen with its spotless, swept floor and its neat small earthen stoves, we had our Sunday lunches, sitting cross-legged on little bamboo mats while she gave us piping hot *puris* and delicious vegetable concoctions fresh from gleaming copper and brass vessels.

After lunch we would lie under a tree in the garden if the weather was cool, under a fan indoors if it was hot, while Bibima sat beside us, chopping areca nuts with her large, heavy *sarota* and peeling cardamoms and arranging them in piles on a tray. All afternoon she told us stories from her endless store, holding us enthralled in an atmosphere of princes and princesses, of animals who lived and spoke like human beings. This way we learned not only fairy tales but the colourful stories of our epics, the Ramayana and the Mahabharata, and other classics. We loved folk tales too, and among our favourites was one I have often thought of since.

'Once there was an old woman,' began Bibima. We stretched out on our full tummies, our chins propped on our hands.

'I want an animal story,' I objected.

'Just wait,' said Bibima; 'soon an animal will come into it. Well, this poor old woman had no child, though she had prayed for one all her life, and because she had lived such a good life, at last the gods took pity on her and decided to reward her piety. One day she was sitting beside the little stove in her hut, cooking her lunch, when a drop of hot fat jumped from the pan and splashed onto the back of her hand. It made a big blister, and before she could even cry out in pain, the blister burst, and out popped a frog!'

I shuddered. 'I don't want a story about a frog,' I said. 'I want real animals like lions and tigers.'

'Well, I want to hear this one,' said Lekha firmly. She was deeply interested in frogs, and poked and prodded the ones she found in the garden.

'After this I'll tell one about real animals,' Bibima compromised. 'Just wait, this one is very interesting.'

'Frogs aren't interesting,' I persisted. 'Do princes and princesses come into it?'

'Of course,' said Bibima. 'Now listen. Well, this frog jumped out, and the old woman was overjoyed because the extraordinary manner of his appearance could only mean that the gods meant him to be her son. So she brought him up and lavished love on him, and he learned to read and write. And though everybody laughed at her for treating a mere frog like a son, she did not mind.

'One day, when the frog was grown up, a royal messenger came to the old woman's town bearing the proclamation that the king's daughter's *swayamvara* (the ceremony of choosing a husband) was going to be held. All the young men who wished to compete for her hand were invited to assemble at the palace on the appointed day. Of course the invitation was intended only for the wealthy nobles and princes, but the frog also began to prepare for his trip to the palace.

'Now the old woman was very upset. She knew that other people did not look upon the frog with the same loving eyes that she did. Others would only laugh at him if he went to the *swayamvara*, and she wanted to save him this unhappiness.

'My son,' she pleaded, 'you have been a good son, and you are enough for me. I do not crave a daughter-in-law. Why must you go to the *swayamvara*?'

'I must go, Mother dear,' said the frog happily, and a dreamy, faraway look came into his eyes, 'for they say that the king's daughter is as beautiful as the crescent moon. I must not lose this opportunity to win her.

'In vain did the old woman try to stop him. Off he went, dressed in the finest robes he could afford.' Bibima paused to pop some areca nut into her mouth.

'Well, then what happened?' we clamoured impatently.

'The frog arrived at the palace and was given a seat among the princes and nobles of the realm. They were dressed in rich garments and jewels, and they were all accompanied by retainers carrying costly presents for the king's daughter. When they saw the frog, they burst out laughing. But he held his head high and paid no attention. At last the princess came out.'

'How old was she?' I breathed.

'Oh, about fifteen or sixteen.'

'And what did she look like?'

'Well her skin was the colour of golden-brown wheat, and her eyes were large like a deer's and almond-shaped. When she walked, she swayed gently as if she were walking to music, and her anklets tinkled as she moved. Her hair was threaded with pearls, and her clothes shimmered with precious stones. In her hand she carried the *jaimal* (garland of flowers) with which she was to indicate the suitor of her choice.

'She passed before each suitor and, to the amazemeat of everyone assembled, she stopped in front of the frog and placed the garland around his neck. Everybody laughed, thinking it was a joke, and the king told her to repeat the ceremony. The second time she again chose the frog. The king was angry and puzzled, and told her to try a third time. But the last time she again placed the garland about the frog's neck. There could be no mistake. The princess had chosen the frog for her husband. The king was enraged and the nobles humiliated, but they were helpless to prevent her. The age-old custom of the *swayamvara* gave the princess the right to choose whom she liked. And then a miracle happened.'

'Oh, I hope there will be a happy ending,' I interrupted anxiously.

'Oh, yes,' Bibima said, 'a very happy ending indeed. Well, the miracle was this: suddenly the frog, the ugly, squat creature, turned into a young prince. So beautiful and strong was he in his glittering robes, and with his shining sword at his waist, that he put the rest of the company to shame.'

We gasped in unison.

'He smiled at the princess, who had lowered her eyes before him, and said: "A spell had been cast on me that I would remain a frog until a lovely princess looked upon me with love. Your beauty and love and kind heart have released me from it forever." And so they were married with fitting pomp and pageantry, and lived happily ever after. And the old woman lived with them in comfort all her days.'

'Oh, how wonderful!' I sighed: 'Tell us another.'

We did not let a minute elapse between the telling of one story and another. And Bibima would gladly have continued had it not been time for us to drink our milk and leave for home with our governess, Miss Collins, who had come to fetch us.

On the way home I would complain: 'I'm getting a headache.'

'To bed the minute you get home,' Miss Collins would say briskly. 'It's all this heavy food, and no naps during the day.'

'No,' I would object in irritation. 'It's not so bad *now*. It's just *starting*, and by tomorrow it will be really bad.'

I regularly developed a headache on Sunday nights. The thought of school on the following day was a hateful one.

'Well, we'll see when tomorrow comes,' Miss Collins would say unsympathetically.

Bibima taught us more than stories. She made the Hindu approach to life a reality for us; not through words, for she was not a learned woman, but through her own extreme simplicity, her deep religiousness, and her tranquil calm faith in the goodness of God. I trailed around after her devotedly, and sometimes she took me to the temple with her. But better than this, I liked her *puja-ghar*, her room of worship at home. It always smelled of fresh flowers and mild incense. Often I was given the happy task of picking flowers for her worship and staying in the room while she prayed. Guided by her, I began to believe in the nearness of God.

When Bibima died, just twenty-four hours after my grandmother's death (for the shock of her beloved sister's death had been too great for her), I suffered my first irreparable loss. Day after day I sat in the deserted little *puja-ghar*, convinced that if I waited long enough she would return, for she had always come to me when I had needed her. Perhaps it was a good thing that my earliest loss should have been of someone I loved so dearly, because I quickly learned that she was not lost to me. To this day her memory revives the charmed hours of childhood and the belief that goodness prevails and that the world goes on because of it.

KATE CHISHOLM

Kate Chisholm (1952–) grew up in north London and read history at Edinburgh University before training as a copy-editor at Cambridge University Press. She has published a life of the eighteenth-century diarist and novelist, Fanny Burney (1998) and a book about anorexia, *Hungry Hell* (2002). In 1998, she visited India for the first time with her father who was born in Allahabad. Her grandfather travelled to India in the 1910s to work on the *Pioneer*, and while there he married her grandmother, who was born and brought up in Allahabad. 'Best Bakery in Town', which was written specially for this book, follows the disparate threads of a British family's connection with India across several generations.

∾

Best Bakery in Town

When my godmother died, my parents and I had to clear out her home, a dark mansion-block flat in Turnham Green, underneath the embankment along which the Piccadilly and District Line trains wend their way to Heathrow and beyond. We found hat boxes, suitcases, trunks still covered with their scuffed P&O labels—Aden, Port Said, Marseilles, Bombay, Liverpool—and boxloads of papers and photographs. One set of photographs in particular made me wish that I had talked more with my godmother about the life she had lived before she came to England in 1946.

They were wrapped like a child's keepsake in a brittle sheet of paper torn from an exercise book and tucked inside an envelope marked '14 Canning Road, Allahabad'. Tiny black-and-white views taken from every angle, as if on a last farewell glance.

Number 14, they revealed, was a long, low, whitewashed building set within a vast expanse of elegantly mown lawn. It's a picture-book version of a colonial bungalow with its ornamental balustrade, impressive porch and deep, colonnaded verandah, shading the rooms inside from the intense glare of the sun. A turbaned servant peers out from the darkness, watching perhaps the departure of the last guests.

There were once hundreds and thousands of similar buildings planted throughout British India during the years of the Raj, the uniform of occupation. But Number 14 Canning Road boldly declares its distinction with signs in large capital letters announcing that this is BARNETTS & CO, THE HOUSE OF CONFECTIONERY.

I had heard of Barnetts and knew that it was in Allahabad, where my godmother, Rosemary Barnett, had grown up and where my father was born in 1923. But I had never seen a photograph of it. It was so much larger than I had imagined; palatial, almost. So different from the modest flat in which my godmother and great-aunts lived in England and which I used to visit as a girl.

I kept looking through the photos. Their poignancy was tangible. But why, I wondered, were these faded sepia images of another life, a different world, so potent to me?

I had always been fascinated by the flat in Turnham Green; by the rosewood cabinet filled with Eastern curiosities—a porcelain Buddha, cowrie shells, a brass lion—and the watercolour painting of steps leading down to a muddy river. But I was even more intrigued by the silver tea set, the crumpet-warmer and the beaded mat that covered the sugar bowl. My godmother and great-aunts took so much sugar in their tea, and always in lumps, which I had never seen. Their home was exotic to me not so much because of its mementoes of their Indian life, but because of this confusion between their outward appearance of Englishness and their passion for India.

In some ways they were much more aware of being English than we were. They loved to watch TV—*Z Cars*, *Dr Kildare*, *Coronation Street*—and to read Georgette Heyer and Agatha Christie as well as Jane Austen, Shakespeare and Robert Herrick. They admired the royal family and were punctilious about the correctness of their English style dustcoats in summer, cardigans in winter, and always a hat, lipstick and earrings. And yet they all smoked non-stop, hooked on nicotine, quite unlike my mother's family or the women I knew from the church where my father was an Anglican priest. They were unusual, too, in their addiction to cricket. Rosemary and her mother, Rose, and Rose's sister Ruby avidly followed the Test Match scores, especially when the Indians were playing.

Conversations in their flat revolved around their memories of the snake charmer who haunted the front gate of Barnetts, the luscious juiciness of freshly picked mango, languorous afternoons waiting for the monsoon to arrive—even though they had left Allahabad many years ago. Their obsession with India puzzled me. A chance remark would lead to a flood of reminiscences, all of which insisted that everything there was perfect. But how could this be? Surely, the heat must have been unbearable? No, I was told, it was exhilarating, cleansing, and quite different from the dull, oppressive heat of an English August. The long wait for the monsoon was part of the rhythm, the texture of their life, which now had lost its meaning. Anyway, they could always escape to the hill stations, to Mussoorie, Nainital or Simla. They would tell stories of how ill they had been, and how afraid of being sick, but they were proud of the way their self-dosing led to recovery, using a mixture of conventional (quinine powders) and unconventional (champagne) cures.

As far as I can recall (and perhaps I, too, became bewitched by their tales of the exotic, by the idea of difference), they never criticized anything about India, nor did their life there have any negative associations. Even if something had gone wrong, they always remembered it as a joke, something to laugh about. 'Oh,' with a slight chuckle, 'do you remember when the white ants got inside the trunks and ate through Rose's trousseau?'

Shiva Naipaul once described the peculiar, obsessive, almost wilfully blind regard which the English often had, and still have, for the countries which they travelled to in search of land, wealth, meaning or escape. He was writing about the colonists he met in Africa, but it applies just as much, if not more so, to the British who once lived in India. 'Beauty—the word rarely fails to crop up in conversation with the long-settled expatriate,' wrote Naipaul. 'But it is not an ordinary "beauty" that is being referred to; nor a straightforward aesthetic response that is being described. It is a special form of perception, of yearning, that is almost an illness.'

My godmother, by the time I knew her, had a stimulating and well-paid job in advertising, and yet she still talked with huge nostalgia about the excitement of writing for the *Pioneer*. A clever, bright, sparky woman, she was confident of her abilities and enjoyed a relaxed, jokey camaraderie with the men in her West End office. Tall and large-boned, her legs were shapely enough to have been spotted by one of her firm's clients, Pretty Polly (famous for stockings), who wanted to use them as advertising copy. She refused. She never married, devoted always to the memory of the boyfriend who was killed in the war, shot down by the Japanese, and left behind in a cemetery in Burma when the British, including my godmother and great-aunts, retreated from their Indian possessions.

She was very well read and had become fascinated by the story of London, compiling volumes of facts and anecdotes about its social history. As a child I was taken by her to the ballet, the West End theatre, and to the British Museum to see the Assyrian exhibits. But when we came home, she talked not so much of what we had seen but of her life at Barnetts, and at school in Mussoorie in the foothills of the Himalayas.

Rosemary came from a family who had lived in India for generations. Her great-grandfather, Thomas Winter Gregory, arrived in Bengal in 1849, after enlisting in the East India Company's Artillery. Like most families who lived through the Mutiny of 1857, the Gregorys had their own story of 'miraculous' survival amid the horror. An aunt was so terrified of being raped by the rebels that she threw herself off the flat roof of her bungalow in an attempt to kill herself. But as she fell the hoop of her crinoline caught on an iron hook protruding from the wall and she found herself dangling precariously above the ground unable to move. There she waited, saved from the Mutineers by a quirk of Victorian fashion, until some British soldiers arrived on the scene and rescued her. (Nothing was ever said about the brutality of some of the British officers, most notably Colonel James Neill, who in retaliation scoured the villages surrounding Allahabad, torturing, raping and hanging.)

Rosemary's mother, Rose, and her sister Elvira Phoebe, my grandmother, socialized with middle-class Indians, and became friends with the daughters of the Nehru family, who also lived in Allahabad. Their sister Ruby once taught the daughters of the Wali of Swat as part of her mission to bring education to those Indian women who were living in purdah. The family all spoke Hindustani fluently; when they had need of a lawyer, they went to an Indian barrister.

It was not that they were conscious of their Englishness in contrast to the Indians; quite the reverse. They believed themselves to belong to India just as much as the Indians. This, of course, is now regarded as typical of the arrogance of the English. But in the case of families such as mine, they *did* belong to India; they had grown up there. It was home to them in a way that England could never be. That's what felt so odd to me as a girl when I listened to them talking about India. They appeared to be so unlike the world they were describing. How could these elderly women in their woollen cardigans once have spoken Hindustani as fluently as English?

At first I was enthralled by their stories of a life so different. But later, as a teenager in the 1960s, I began to feel uncomfortable with the way they talked about India. Their memories of Allahabad were all about the social whirl of the English community: tennis parties, church socials, Gilbert and Sullivan, the choir. They said nothing about the India of the *ragas* or temples; nothing about the sadhus and holy men; nothing about the swirling colours of the street markets. My father would tell me about his *ayah* who sang lullabies to him in Hindustani, and the drumming in the village that kept him awake as a boy. He remembered being deafened by the monsoon rains beating on the tin roof of their bungalow in Mussoorie, where he grew up, and how he had only ever played with other Indian boys, chattering in Hindustani. But he also admitted that he had always thought of himself as 'the Sahib', taking the lead and telling his friends what to do.

I suppose I was gratified by the idea of my family's Indian connection, by the exoticism it endowed, and yet a little discomfited by it. By the time I went to school, and later university, most of the British colonies had regained their independence. We were taught that the old maps with their vast swathes of pink to show 'British possession' were relics of a past and inglorious era. That my family had once belonged in India, where they had servants and thought of themselves as the superior, ruling class, was something I did not wish to recognize as being part of me too.

Some of my contemporaries at university headed off on the road to Kashmir, but I only got as far as Istanbul and into Anatolia, my first encounter with Asia. It was enough of a shock to make me realize that what I had heard about the East was only half the story. Nothing they had told me prepared me for the noise, the bustle, the chaos of the bazaars. The hubbub and exposure of lives being lived in the open, on the street. The air so heavily scented with a mixture of spices and dung. The sense of being lost in a foreign culture. But after the first few days of feeling dazed and confused, I began to feel oddly at ease, as if part of me was more at home within that cultural atmosphere than back in London.

This sensation of an unreal, alien, and yet very tangible 'tranquillity' is captured by Paul Scott in his quartet of novels about the English community in India during the years leading up to Independence. He writes about one of his characters, 'For all his doubts about its present source he had long since learned to appreciate the sensuousness of the East, and how it could set mind and body at ease. He enjoyed a sensation almost of tranquillity.' When I read this I began to wonder whether this was what my family missed most about their life in India. Perhaps this is what they could never recapture? This curious 'sensation of tranquillity', of belonging to a world that was yet so utterly different from their cultural and social aspirations.

My family, however, were never part of the 'Raj', at least as it was depicted in the television series *The Jewel in the Crown* (based on Paul Scott's *The Raj Quartet*), which made such an impact in Britain in the 1980s. They were of English origin and as such were part of the colonizing hordes, but they did not belong to the ruling elite. They were never members of the Club.

I was surprised by my godmother's lack of interest in the series. Surely this was a story about her? But when I asked her why she did not want to see it, she explained to me, as if I should have known better, that it was not about our family. We were not of that class. The Gregorys ran a business in which they worked as servants of the servants of Empire.

Barnetts Hotel began life as a pharmacy called Buncombe's in a bungalow on Edmonstone Road that had once been owned by the East India Company. My godmother remembered how as a girl she used to trace with her fingertips round the words etched on one of the windowpanes— 'John Company', the name by which the company was known by those who worked for it. Thomas Winter Gregory bought Number 24 Edmonstone Road in 1878 and continued to run the pharmacy, selling pills and potions to the increasing numbers of British civilians living in Allahabad, by then the governing city of British India.

In 1884, he retired, handing over the business to his son Charles and wife, Elvira Henrietta. Elvira gave birth to six surviving daughters—

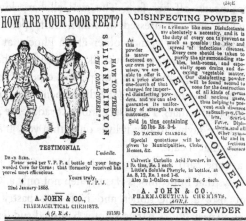

Rose (my godmother's mother, who was born in 1886), Kitty, Elvira Phoebe (my grandmother), Olive, Ruby and Coral—and one son, Vernon. A framed photograph of the family used to hang on the wall of my godmother's sitting room, just behind her chair. Whenever I visited, I found myself constantly drawn to it, as if it could explain my connection with that Indian past. Their statuesque stillness. Those deepset, all-knowing eyes.

They appear to be a typical Victorian family. Charles Winter is a stern, imposing figure in white collar and drooping whiskers; Elvira seems more approachable, though tightly buttoned into her lacy bodice, her hair swept neatly off her face. The girls all have long, trailing, whimsical ringlets and are dressed in white, fluffy petticoats—even Vernon, aged about six. My grandmother Elvira Phoebe at thirteen or fourteen, despite the ringlets, looks just like my sister at that age. The resemblance is disarming, unnerving, compelling, especially since I only remember my grandmother vaguely (she died when I was nine but was ill for many years before that). The past cannot be evaded, the photograph seemed always to be saying to me; it lives on within you. It's up to you to find out what that means.

I found a trade card among my godmother's papers from about 1910 which shows that Buncombe's was by then not only a 'Chemists & Druggists' but also 'a confectioner and high-class pastry cook . . . Wedding cakes a speciality'. Charles Winter had died suddenly, leaving his widow to carry on running the business with her daughters, who were by then in their late teens. The pharmacy had never been a success, but my grandmother was a talented cook, with a gift for decorative icing and the patience to produce trayloads of tiny confectionery. Soon her cakes and sweets were in great demand. When Rose married George Barnett, in December 1917, pride of place among the wedding photographs was a huge three-tiered wedding cake, extravagantly iced and decorated with roses, the creation of my grandmother and the inspiration for what was to become 'Barnetts of Allahabad: The House for Fresh Confectionery'.

George and Rose met one hot summer's evening at the YMCA. George, who had arrived in India as a non-commissioned officer with the Royal Fusiliers, was on duty, running the social club for British troops stationed in India; Rose, a fine singer with a pure soprano voice, had been engaged for the musical entertainment. George must have been a genial, sociable man for he became a well-known and much-liked figure in Allahabad's English community. The *Pioneer* reported that he was 'welcomed as a friend wherever he went'.

On 23 June 1914 he organized the YMCA's celebration dinner for 'The King Emperor's Birthday'. The temperature in the dining room, even after dark, would have been over 40°C; those attending were in full dress uniform. The only air-conditioning was from the huge canvas *punkah* hung from the ceiling, swaying gently to create a cooling breeze. As the reporter in the *United Provinces Times* concluded: 'The idea of a members' dinner is something to be proud of in weather when it is even a trouble to think.'

Shortly afterwards George rejoined his regiment in Calcutta to serve in the 1914–18 war and was posted first to Palestine and then Egypt. His departure was noted in the *Pioneer*: 'He was now going,' says the paper, 'to take up an even higher and nobler work for the Empire.'

All the surviving photographs of George show him to be a neat, dapper man, not much taller than his wife. He's always smiling, relaxed, at ease; in one picture he's lounging on an easy chair, roaring with laughter. His daughter, my godmother Rosemary, adored him, and always talked about how he teased her, laughed with her, taught her to take life as it comes. Rose, his wife, has the strong features shared by all the Gregory girls—shapely lips and deep-set eyes with a prominent forehead and well-defined eyebrows. Her hair is bushy, extravagant, uncontained, and her eyes look dreamy, but this is belied by the firmness of her expression. As the eldest of the sisters she was used to being in charge, and of having her way. Before he meets Rose, the photographs of George show him sporting a thin and rather unattractive moustache; it soon disappears.

In 1918, with the war over, George returned to Allahabad and he and Rose took over the responsibility of managing Buncombe's. By this time Elvira Phoebe had married my grandfather, Thomas William Henry Chisholm, a journalist who worked on the *Pioneer* as a subeditor. They soon moved away, first to England so that my grandfather, who came from a family of priests and missionaries, could train for the Anglican ministry, and then to Mussoorie, where my grandfather served as pastor to the English community, taking services in Christ Church.

George and Rose were an unusual couple for their time, running Buncombe's strictly as a partnership, jointly signing all the correspondence. Rose was obsessively neat; making lists of everything. George, too, had incredibly precise handwriting, very small, rounded and fluent. Like Rose, he kept scrupulous accounts of everything he spent, down to the smallest purchases. Despite this, Buncombe's was constantly in debt. A note in the family papers suggests that it became difficult to import medicines from Europe and America in the 1920s. But this explanation seems unlikely. I suspect that George and Rose, despite their impressive neatness and appearance of organized efficiency, were not good at business. They were too anxious to acquire a 'high-class' reputation, and had not inherited the money to make this possible.

George was forced to take a job in Calcutta selling cars for Allenberry's, agents for General Motors in India, taking his wife and their young daughter, Rosemary, with him. By 1928 they were back in Allahabad, having saved enough money to take over the lease of a bungalow in Canning Road owned by Lala Bihari Lal, who at first charged them rent of 125 rupees per calendar month.

Number 14 Canning Road was part of the new Civil Lines, built as colonial Allahabad expanded after becoming the governing centre of British India in 1858. The road had been named after the first Viceroy, Lord Canning, who on 15 November 1858 read out the proclamation in Allahabad that British India would no longer be under the governance of the East India Company but under the direct rule of the Crown, the jewel of Queen Victoria's Empire. Mark Twain, who visited Allahabad in the 1890s, described the British cantonment as 'comely and alluring, and full of suggestions of comfort and leisure, and of the serenity which a good conscience buttressed by a sufficient bank account gives'.

The British population in Allahabad continued to grow, especially after the East India (EI) Railway was built between Calcutta and Delhi, and so did the grandiosity of the buildings. The family albums are filled with photographs of the High Court (serving the whole of northern India), Government House, the Law College, Mayo Hall—huge buildings designed in a hybrid Mughal/Gothic style. A marble statue of Queen Victoria, canopied with Gothic tracery, was erected in Alfred Park, which was 'the chief ornament of the Civil Station' according to an article published in 1910 in *The Modern Review*. Victoria's statue was matched later by one of her grandson's George V, with a plaque beneath dedicated to the 'King Emperor 1910–1936'.

Alfred Park, named after Queen Victoria's son who toured India in 1869, was laid out as a vast municipal park with flower beds and promenades. The Gregorys remembered it as the venue for the annual Flower and Dog Show and the All-India Lawn Tennis Championship. A fading photograph shows its acres of grass covered with hosts of what look suspiciously like daffodils.

Allahabad's huge Gothic cathedral, which was consecrated in 1887, stands in the middle of a huge roundabout at the end of what was then called Canning Road. With its flying buttresses, perpendicular arches and stained-glass windows, it would not look out of place in East Anglia. Dedicated to All Saints, its design was modelled on the east end of Canterbury Cathedral, although once inside there are telltale signs of an Indian influence. The stone screens between the sanctuary and apse were copied from examples at Fatehpur Sikri, and marble from Jaipur was used to pave the choir. As they listened to the weekly sermon, the congregation could watch the patterns of light cast by the Indian sun shining through stained-glass windows brought from England.

The Barnetts, however, did not worship in the Cathedral, perhaps because its congregation came mostly from the Club. They preferred the smaller scale of Holy Trinity, which was built in 1826, along neoclassical lines. Inside is a memorial plaque dedicated to those 'who were killed in the station and district of Allahabad between the 6th and 10th days of June 1857 by Sepoys of the 6th Regiment Native Infantry and other mutineers and rebels'. The plaque was erected 'by the surviving residents of Allahabad'. It's a salutary reminder of the back-story to Allahabad's imposing Victorian architecture. The fear that such violence could erupt again provided the impetus for a flurry of building; an attempt to provide concrete foundations for the imperial dream.

Many English visitors to India passed through the city on their Grand Tour of Empire. In 1912, E.M. Forster stayed at Laurie's Great Northern Hotel, 'a bad place'. Perhaps this was the same hotel which Edward Lear had enjoyed in 1872, 'admirably managed' by a Mr and Mrs Laurie, a German couple, who gave Lear 'a super good breakfast'. Lear spent the day on the verandah reading *Roderick Random* and sketching the water-carriers who passed by, before catching the night train to Bombay. On another visit, he stayed at Kelner's Hotel, where the young children of the house asked him to draw for them the owl and the pussy-cat celebrated in his nonsense rhyme. 'On inquiry,' he wrote in his journal, 'I found that she and all the school she went to had been taught that remarkable poem!'

Forster did not have a good time in Allahabad. His first few weeks in India had been spent in the native states, staying with Indian acquaintances he had made in England. It was, he says, 'a piece of luck that comes to very few Englishmen'. In Allahabad, he was thrown amongst the British, and he did not like it. At dinner with the Collector and his wife, 'neither nice', he was shocked by their attitude to 'the natives', as if they despised them.

He hired a bicycle and with the head of the Public Works Department, Ahmed Mirza, visited the principal buildings, 'all of which were new and one of which—very beautiful—he was superintending'. The next morning Ahmed brought him a basketful of guavas wrapped in a towel, for which, he tells his mother in a letter, Allahabad was famous. I have a photograph of a 'tope' or grove of guava trees that must have been taken at about this time, as well as the label from a bottle—'Guava Cheese. Made in Allahabad'.

Two years earlier, Allahabad was the venue of the All-India Exposition (modelled on the Great Exhibition of London in 1851). The exhibits were a bizarre mixture, exposing the contradictions implicit within the imperial project. Displays of native crafts and produce gathered from all over India were juxtaposed with jungle scenes filled with the shikar (hunting) trophies of the colonial administrators, including 'no less than four fully set-up tigers according to an article in the *Hindustan Review*, which was given the title 'A Bird's-Eye View of Allahabad's New White City: The United Provinces Exhibition'. (The 'White City' in London was a stadium and pleasure ground created for the Franco-British exhibition of 1908. At its centre was a lake with illuminated fountains surrounded by Indian-style pavilions.)

Most thrilling of all the entertainments was the air show, the first such event on the subcontinent, with demonstrations by the famous French aviator, Monsieur Pecquet, of his magnificent flying machine. My godmother was the proud possessor of a stamped envelope, addressed to 'Charles W. Gregory, Esq, Buncombe & Co, 24 Edmonstone Road, Allahabad', marking the world's first-ever air mail flight, from the exhibition site in Allahabad to Naini.

Despite all this expansion, Allahabad in the 1920s and 1930s was still a small city, green, verdant and full of trees and open spaces. Its British residents, proud of its university, colleges and libraries, thought of it as 'the Oxford of India'.

The bungalow on Canning Road had not been designed as a hotel. George and Rose adapted the building, creating eight bedrooms with private bathrooms. Very soon they were writing to their landlord, Lala Kamta Prasad Tandon of Rani Mandi, Allahabad (who had taken over from his uncle Lala Bihari Lal), for permission to build an extension within the compound so that they could accommodate more guests. The Grand Trunk Road across north-west India from Calcutta to Peshawar ran through Allahabad, as did the EI Railway, and there was no shortage of travellers, needing a place to stay en route. This increased when in 1933 Bamrauli aerodrome, eight miles outside the town, was opened to commercial aircraft. George Barnett, ever willing to make the most of an opportunity, was appointed agent for Imperial Airways, and also for KLM (the Dutch airline) and Air France, who began operating routes from London, Amsterdam and Paris to Australia, Batavia and Rangoon.

The first Imperial Airways passenger flight left London airport (then based at Croydon) for Calcutta at 12.30 P.M. on 1 July 1933, travelling via Paris, Brindisi, Athens, Alexandria, Cairo, Gaza, Baghdad, Basra, 'Koweit', 'Bahrein', Sharjah (in Oman), Gwadar (in Muscat), Karachi, Jodhpur, Delhi and Cawnpore before touching down at Bamrauli at 12.30 P.M. the following Saturday and reaching Calcutta that evening. The fare from London to Calcutta was £122 (worth about £5,000 in today's money), with an £8 reduction for those travelling only as far as Allahabad. For the first time it was possible to post a letter in Calcutta bound for London and to receive a reply in just sixteen days! Three years later the Empire flying-boat service was inaugurated, the lumbering 'Coolong' aircraft flying over Bamrauli aerodrome to land on the Jumna River 'alongside a large pumping station whose twin towers provide an easily distinguishable landmark from the air'. The Imperial Airways passenger guide to the flight describes Allahabad as '*The Abode of Allah*'.

Luncheon for ongoing passengers and the crew was provided at Bamrauli by George and Rose, who on all their correspondence with the airlines sign themselves as 'the proprietor and proprietress' of Barnetts & Co, continuing their unusual husband-and-wife partnership of equals. George built a 'Barnetts' trailer and converted his 1928 Chevrolet to handle it, driving out to the aerodrome daily with provisions from the Canning Road kitchens. An airport restaurant was built, with a bar. Some aircraft stopped only to refuel, giving the passengers just enough time for a quick G&T and snack; others remained overnight, the passengers travelling into town to stay in the hotel. Many years later, Lord Mountbatten spent a quarter of an hour at Bamrauli changing planes on his way to Nepal 'to get another medal'. George was away in England (he and Rose travelled by boat) but his manager, Mr Barkworth, reported that he had served the future Viceroy with a glass of lemonade; it was 'a doubtful pleasure'. (Mountbatten was not popular with the British in India, who believed that he favoured the cause of the nationalist Congress Party rather than their own interests.)

Those travellers who stopped off in Allahabad would have been served tea and fancy cakes in the hotel lounge followed by a five-course dinner in the evening. Rose was immensely proud of the high standards maintained at Barnetts, and the superior quality of her menus. Forster, in his novel *A Passage to India* (published in 1924), mocks the English for their appalling culinary pretensions and their desperate attempts to hold on to what they considered to be English 'civilization'. At dinner in the fictional town of Chandrapore, he writes, the menu would inevitably be: 'Julienne soup full of bullety bottled peas, pseudo-cottage bread, fish full of branching bones, pretending to be plaice, more bottled peas with the cutlets, trifle, sardines on toast: the menu of Anglo-India . . . the food of exiles, cooked by servants who did not understand it.'

Rose would have been horrified to read this. Only one menu from the Barnetts regime has survived; a dual menu, one version for vegetarians, the other for meat-eaters (they were obviously expecting to entertain both Indian and English guests), from a dinner held by the Allahabad Gymkhana Club celebrating the completion of the All-India Lawn Tennis Championships on 24 January 1937:

Fruit cocktail	Fruit cocktail
Tomato cream soup	Tomato cream soup
Curried beans on toast	Fillets of Rohu à la Marie Louise
Lentil rolls	Mutton sauté
Vegetable cutlets	Roast guinea fowl
Peas pillau—Vegetable curry	Pillau—Madras curry
Duchess cream	Duchess cream
Cauliflower au gratin	Cauliflower au gratin
Dessert	Dessert
Coffee	Coffee

Notepaper from the heyday of Barnetts shows that the business had the imperial seal of approval: 'Barnetts. The House for Fresh Confectionery, Allahabad. By appointment to His Excellency Sir Malcolm Hailey, GCSI, GCIE, ICS, Governor of the United Provinces of Agra and Oudh'. But the Barnetts logo paints a different picture. A doll-like figure with her chef's toque worn at a jaunty angle grins out at us cheekily, poking fun at Sir Malcolm's pompous title. And the advertised goods for sale—small cakes and pastries, dessert confectionery, 'our renowned butter toffees, nut hardbakes and butterscotch'—are suggestive less of pomp and circumstance than of the tuck-box of a child pining for some home comforts.

I was intrigued by all these contradictions. On the surface the story of my family's life in India appeared to tally with the history of the Raj as it has been told since post-colonialism. A cultural imposition. An almost paranoid adherence to the essentials of Englishness. An ignorance of native ways. And yet, certain things did not quite fit. Perhaps, I began to wonder, there is another way of telling the story about the British in India. This version of the Raj would not be one of despising and misunderstanding but would reveal connections and exchanges—just as can be shown about those first decades of the imperial project in the mid-eighteenth century when English scholars translated Hindu texts and commissioned works of art to explain the incarnations of Vishnu. Perhaps beneath the broad sweep of exploitation and subjugation there are less visible but no less valid truths?

Not long after discovering my godmother's photographs, I came across a novel, *The Romantics*, by an Indian writer, Pankaj Mishra, set not only in Allahabad but also in Mussoorie, the two places in India associated with my family. It felt as if chance, fate, destiny, karma, call it what you will, was prodding me, reminding me of what I must do.

Pankaj told me that Barnetts still existed—just. He sent me photographs of it, taken from every angle, and looking more or less as it had done in 1946. It was too much of a coincidence. I knew that I had to see Number 14 Canning Road for myself, to look beyond the verandah, before it was demolished by one of the new future-loving entrepreneurs.

'Cultures are so different,' said the young Indian army officer whom I met on the North-East Express from New Delhi to Allahabad. He could not comprehend why I was still unmarried (at 51, I was obviously well past marriageable age). 'People in India just get married,' he told me bluntly. 'It's expected of them.'

He was on leave, travelling back from the border with China to be with his wife who was just about to have their first child. This is how it is in India, was his message; and your attitude to family and tradition is disrespectful. Our conversation stopped abruptly, but not before he had told off the carriage attendant for bringing me a crumpled sheet and grimy pillow.

His reproof hit a nerve. What was I thinking of? My family had left India almost sixty years ago, and in any case had lived in a world that they had superimposed on India. What foolishness to think that I could renew their connection with the subcontinent.

I arrived at Allahabad junction in the midst of a tropical storm— torrential rain, shriek of lightning, and thunder that drum-rolled continuously for most of the night. Although Barnetts still existed, I had been advised not to stay there. The hotel, which had been renamed the Hotel Harsh (pronounced 'Hursh' and meaning 'joy', 'rapture', 'delight' in Hindi) by its present owner Harsh Tandon, had become part of his chain of shops, and its rooms were more often used as a saree emporium than as bedrooms for paying guests. But I had written to Mr Tandon explaining that my family had once owned Barnetts and that I hoped to meet him while I was in Allahabad. Was he related, I wondered, to the K.P. Tandon, banker, landlord, contractor and proprietor of the Jubilee

Hosiery Factory at Rani Mandi in Allahabad, who had rented Number 14 Canning Road, to George and Rose?

In my rucksack were copies not just of the photographs of the bungalow taken by my godmother in 1946 but also of the correspondence between George and Rose and K.P. Tandon in the 1930s. I wanted to show them to Harsh Tandon, who was perhaps his son, nephew, grandson or great-nephew. Such a meeting, I hoped, would forge a direct link back to Barnetts and the Allahabad my family once knew and loved.

Next morning I woke early to brilliant sunshine, anxious to get out of my hotel room. As soon as it was a reasonable time to make a phone call, I tried Mr Tandon's number. No answer. I tried again. Still no answer. At last after three attempts someone eventually picked up the phone.

'Hello. Good morning. I . . . I . . . I'm Kate Chisholm,' I announced tentatively. 'I wrote to Mr Tandon. Is it possible to speak to him?'

'Mr Tandon is not available.'

'When will he be back?'

'At 1.30 try again.'

I could see from the map that Mahatma Gandhi Marg (the post-Independence name for Canning Road) was only 15 minutes' walk from my hotel. Would Barnetts still look just as it did in 1946?

I set off purposefully down the road, but as soon as I left behind the cool, air-conditioned vestibule of the hotel I knew that I should have asked the receptionist to find me a bicycle rickshaw. It was still only ten o'clock but the sun was already high in the sky. I was dazed after only five minutes.

The road was busy. There was no pavement. It was dusty, pitted with rubble, a pig darted past. I began to walk but kept having to stop as scooters loaded with children, cycles, bullock-carts, rickshaws and cars brushed past me. Other women were out and about, on their own, walking along the roadside, but I was taller and whiter. My trousers and top could not conceal that I was different.

At the first roundabout I tried to cross the road, watching how the other pedestrians just weaved their way through the moving cars without changing pace. I waited for what felt like ages until I could see an obvious space and then darted across, provoking hoots from every passing car and narrowly missing being hit by a scooter that I had not heard coming up from behind.

I felt incongruous, misplaced. My godmother, my grandmother and the great-aunts had been born into it; this was their country, their home. But they would never have attempted to walk along the road—and would not have gone out without a hat. I retreated back to my hotel room, feeling foolish.

At 1.30 P.M. I tried Mr Tandon's number, and missed him again.

'He's at his jewellery shop.'

I had allowed myself four days in Allahabad before returning to Delhi to meet up with friends. Perhaps my letter had not arrived. Perhaps Mr Tandon was just not interested in the story of Barnetts. How, I wondered, could I change his mind?

Before leaving London I had also made contact with Action Aid, the charity which my godmother had always supported, in the hope of visiting one of their projects in the Allahabad district. They put me in touch with Uttara Ratna, whose father established the Viklang Kendra Rural Research Project to help disabled children and their families. A commanding but warm-hearted woman in her early forties, Uttara was thrilled by the views of old Allahabad that I had brought with me, and took me for dinner with her parents so that they could see them too.

Dr Banerjee and his wife lived in a large bungalow, simply but well furnished—stone floors, rugs of carnelian red, firm, upright sofas and statues of Ganesh. After looking through the photographs, he told me that some thirty or more years ago he had bought just such a bungalow and had pulled it down so that he could build a new house on the site. 'Maybe I regret that now,' he reflected.

Dinner had been prepared by Uttara's sister-in-law. After a selection of deliciously simple vegetarian sauces with rice, she shyly presented dessert—a trial run for the Annual Cake Competition, which took place the next day. Orange Cheesecake, decorated with those tiny segments of tinned mandarin orange that were a special treat when I was growing up in the 1950s. The cuisine of Empire. She could have found the recipe in the *Mrs Beeton's Family Cookery* book that was lying at the bottom of one of my godmother's trunks—with a section on 'Indian Cookery' that begins: 'House-keeping in India is totally different from housekeeping in England. The mistress cannot undertake the personal supervision of her kitchen, which is not in the house or bungalow, but outside, and often some distance away. . . . Indian servants are good, many of them; but they cannot be trusted, and will cheat if they have a chance.' It makes very odd reading now, and I wish I could have asked my godmother what she thought of it.

Next morning Uttara took me on a tour of Allahabad, haphazardly driving a van belonging to the project. She wanted me to see for real the buildings of which I had brought photographs, and to help me find some connection to the life my family had lived in the city.

'We need to find our roots,' she told me.

She had been born years after my family and most of the English community had left Allahabad, but the city in which she grew up had been shaped by them. The landmarks she knew were the Cathedral, the polo grounds, the High Court and the minarets of Muir College. We discovered a shared belief in the importance of the past and how we are moulded by it. But not just that. We shared something of that past. Our roots were intertwined. My great-aunts might well have known her great-aunts.

Every so often I caught a glimpse of what Allahabad might once have been like—a grassy alleyway leading to a patch of open ground; a cluster of trees; the huge, deep sky falling into darkness as we rowed out to see the Sangam, the meeting of the waters of the Jumna and the Ganges Rivers.

By some lucky coincidence Uttara had a Christian friend Lydia who worshipped at Holy Trinity, where my family had once been members of the congregation. Uttara had taken on my quest as if it were her own, and she arranged not only for the church to be unlocked but also for the *chowkidar* to bring with him keys to all the cupboards so that we could search the vestry for the registers of births, marriages, deaths.

Holy Trinity is a huge Georgian-style building furnished just like an English metropolitan church with its rows of wooden pews, brass eagle lectern and wooden hymn board. Once inside, the congregation must have felt as if they were in comfortingly familiar surroundings. And yet there was something very different about the light as it blazed through the open door and the sound of the birds chattering in the trees outside.

The *chowkidar* took us into the vestry and brought us cups of hot, sweet, spicy tea. He opened up a dilapidated wooden cupboard and took out a couple of ancient leather-bound volumes, nibbled round the edges, inscribed on the front, 'Register of Marriages'.

I leafed through the pages from the first entry dated in 1855, hoping to find a familiar name. At last, on 5 June 1917, I read that my grandmother Elvira Phoebe Gregory had married Thomas William Henry Chisholm. I recognized my grandfather's handwriting immediately from the letters he wrote to me as a child, signed 'Yours affectionately, Grandfather'. Six months later, I discovered the entry for Rose Mary Gregory, a 'spinster of no occupation' of Allahabad, who, on 26 December 1917, married George Henry Barnett, 'bachelor, soldier of Bangalore'.

It was very quiet in the vestry. In a flash, I realized that I was sitting exactly where George and Rose (and also my grandparents) would have sat when they signed the register. The sun would have shone upon them in just the same way. I could almost hear the restless murmur of the congregation as they waited for the couple to walk back down the aisle. Suddenly I could see them, George, stiff and upright in his military uniform, Rose in layers of floaty white lace.

That afternoon I ventured out on my own again, determined this time to walk as far as Barnetts. I had grown more accustomed to the rush of traffic, and to the knack of walking across the road without pausing, confident that everything will miss you, just.

Uttara had already driven me past the front gates. At first glance the bungalow looked unchanged, if less well-kept. The same colonnaded verandah, porch and crenellated balustrade. Take away the 'Hotel Harsh' signs and reinstate 'Barnetts & Co' and you could almost be in 1946.

But as I stood at the end of the drive looking in, I noticed that new buildings were going up on either side, concrete blocks six or more storeys high, overshadowing the bungalow and encroaching on its grounds. The once-elegant lawn was covered with trellises and fading flowers left over from a wedding party. No one was about, except an elderly man in charge of a towel sale that was being held on tables set out on the verandah. The bungalow looked smaller than the photographs had suggested, and less imposing. There was no bustle of guests arriving, no sense that the Hotel Harsh was the busy social hub that Barnetts once had been.

I stood there for some while, looking in on my godmother's old world. It should have been a thrilling moment but, disappointingly, nothing happened. Barnetts did still look the same, but too much else had changed, and I was too unaccustomed to Indian life to appreciate the experience.

I suppose I should have walked through the gate and up the drive to the porch. But I didn't. It was not just an unwillingness to arrive unannounced (Mr Tandon had not replied to my phone calls, and whenever I phoned he was always on his way to one or other of his business interests). But much more the fear that there would be nothing much to see beyond the verandah, nothing to remind me of my godmother, no sign that my family had once belonged there, and so no real point in my being there.

Instead, I wandered round the outside, tracing the undulating shape of the old boundary wall, which could still be seen through the layers of cheap brickwork added on over the years. As I turned into the alleyway at the back with my camera slung round my neck, a group of young boys who had been playing cricket surrounded me, demanding with beaming smiles that I take their photograph. My godmother would have loved it.

When I arrived back at my hotel, some visitors had arrived to see me, relatives of a friend in London, an elderly lady with her grey hair tied back in a bun, with her daughter and grandchildren. Mrs Singh, the grandmother, asked me why I had come to Allahabad, where she had lived all her life. I explained that my father had been born in Allahabad, as well as my godmother, and I began to tell her the story of Barnetts.

'Barnetts?' she repeated, slightly hard-of-hearing. 'It was the best bakery in town . . .'

'So you remember that the hotel used to sell cakes and chocolates?'

'Oh yes,' she said. 'We bought their cakes for birthdays and special treats.'

The thought crossed my mind that as a girl Mrs Singh would have eaten cakes baked in the Barnetts kitchen, perhaps by the Indian cook whom Rosemary told me about, rolling out puff pastry for the cream horns. Another fleeting connection.

I wanted to hold on to the moment, let the conversation continue. But Mrs Singh's daughter, who was too young to remember Barnetts in its heyday, was anxious to leave.

After they had gone I reread the email that Pankaj had sent me describing his friend Arvind Krishna Mehrotra's encounter with the novelist Angus Wilson in the 1970s. Angus Wilson was researching a biography of Rudyard Kipling, and stayed at Barnetts. He told Arvind Krishna Mehrotra that the puddings he had tasted there reminded him of his childhood in South Africa, the 'cuisine of Empire'. So Barnetts was for years the best bakery in town, and Rose and George's reputation lingered long after their departure for England.

In October 1948, George Barnett wrote to the new owner of Barnetts from west London, where he and Rose were trying to build a new life:

> I should like to come back for a time to see the dear old place—
> though I would be very sad to have to turn away again—they were
> very very happy years and I shall never forget or regret one moment
> of them. I don't think I shall ever be so happy again as I was there,
> with all its worries and problems and anxieties—life was more
> worthwhile there.

The Second World War and Indian independence combined to ensure that Barnetts, hotel and restaurant to the British community in Allahabad, was no longer a viable business. George and Rose, just turned sixty, were forced by circumstance and common sense to set sail for Southampton. For them, to stay on in India was not possible; Barnetts had been losing money for several years and there was no way they could stem the flow.

As early as July 1940 George had written to his landlord K.P. Tandon, confessing that he was 'desperately worried' about the future. 'Everything has gone to pieces,' he said. Sixty per cent of Barnetts' business had vanished overnight when the European airlines suddenly stopped all flights to the East. With no warning, two days after Hitler's troops invaded the Netherlands in May 1940, the KLM flight to Jakarta just never turned up. A few weeks later, Paris fell to the Nazis, preventing all passenger flights out of France.

Many of the British in Allahabad, sensing that a major European war was brewing, had already left for home before September 1939. There were few people left to order wedding cakes; no one to buy cream fancies and Victoria sponges, or organize the tea dances or garden parties catered for by Barnetts. George was forced to discharge half the hotel staff.

With great resourcefulness, he responded to the UK's rationing crisis by setting up a food-parcels service. Boxes of Barnetts' goodies were sent home to the UK by sea. The 'Winston', costing seven rupees, offered two cartons of toffees and hardbakes. The 'Empire', slightly more expensive, consisted of an 'uniced' fruit cake, weighing two pounds.

There were many more selections: the 'Princess', the 'Duchess' and the 'India', which cost twenty-one rupees and included a three-pound, 'iced' fruit cake, one pound of crystallized fruits, one pound of toffees and hardbakes, and fifty cigarettes. But George knew in his heart that their time was up. 'Things are changing,' he wrote to a friend in England, some months after the end of the war and the reopening of the air routes to the East in November 1945. 'You just can't get along with good business—there are too many interferences.'

At the end of March 1946, the Govermnent of India 'in view of the acute food shortage' had disallowed the dispatch of food parcels to England, with the exception of tea and cigarettes. No more Winstons, and certainly no more Empires. Meanwhile, the rent on Barnetts, in accordance with the United Provinces Rent Control Act, had been increased by 25 per cent, a response to 'the general high level of prices'.

George and Rose's original plan was to retire to England, leaving the business in the hands of an Indian manager, who would in time be invited to join them in partnership. But on 29 March 1947 George wrote that 'the government's decision to quit on a definite date has jerked our plans'. Without warning, the viceroy, Lord Mountbatten, had brought forward the date when power would be transferred from the British Crown to the new Constituent Assembly in Delhi to midnight on the 15th of August. Uncertain of what the handover of power would mean for the British still living in India, George sold off Barnetts in a rush—to Mr Nanak Singh Datta and Mrs Nirmala Verma.

The deed of sale, dated 1 May 1947, valued the contents (beds, cake moulds and adjustable toffee cutters) at 44,000 rupees and the 'goodwill of the business' at 26,000 rupees. More than half the hotel's value depended on its reputation: 'Barnetts—Best bakery in town'.

Once the sale had been agreed, the Barnetts were homeless. George had written to P&O asking for a passage home at the earliest opportunity, but in the run-up to Independence the shipping lines were inundated with such requests and by the last week in April George still had not received confirmation that he had secured a cabin. Ever optimistic, he arranged on 24 April for most of their luggage to be sent ahead by goods train to Bombay—a lifetime of personal effects in just eight boxes. A week later, on the day that Barnetts changed hands, George received a telegram from P&O offering him a cabin on the *Georgic*, which sailed from Bombay on 19 May. He and Rose left the next day, taking with them Rose's eighty-four-year-old mother, Elvira Henrietta (Charles Winter Gregory's widow), who, until then, had never left India.

George wrote to a friend in London, while at sea, halfway between Bombay and Southampton: 'We sold out—the offer seemed good, so after some haggling we came to terms. . . . It's sad, of course, to cut off all those years of work and fun, but—withdrawal now seems inevitable.'

For the first few months George continued to write from London to the new owners of Barnetts, offering them advice and encouragement, as if unable to let go. 'I'm glad business keeps something above normal during the hot weather,' he told Mr Datta. 'With the Club and the Alliance finished [they had both been closed down once independence was declared], you have no appreciable competition.'

Mr Datta was evidently trying to find new ways of making money out of the hotel: 'The dances are an experiment—good luck—my only fear when I heard of them was that they might inconvenience the regular hotel residents. But these matters are your pigeon—when I was boss, I did as I wanted to, and took risks.' He added, 'I hope the Indian staff are being good—they are a good bunch of fellows, but they are very human—I must admit that they have slogged for me for more years than I can remember.'

A year later, and still struggling to settle themselves in bomb-scarred London, George told Mr Datta: 'I am not sure that I like this life . . . frankly, I should like to get back to India and do something there. . . . Our kindest regards to the Vermas, Tandons, Agarwalas, and so on—I wish I was back among them, alternately loving them and fighting them.'

Mr Datta replied: 'It will give us a great pleasure if you come back for a time to see your dear old place being run exactly according to the sentiments which you expressed at the time of the sale. Your good name is being kept up in running this business untarnished.'

George and Rose never did return to Allahabad. Nor did George find other employment. His letters reveal his increasingly desperate search for something, anything, to do. He tried to resume the food-parcels business, compiling a list of firms—Barnetts & Co., Allahabad; Newmans Fruit Market, Srinagar; Indian Mildure Fruit Farms, Renala Khurd, Montgomery, Punjab; Taj Mahal House, Bombay—and printing order forms. The 'Empire' parcel, he noted, would have to be renamed. The surviving stationery suggests that it became the 'Dominion'.

He advertised in the *Statesman*, offering his services as an agent for firms wishing to export to the UK ('Business man, 30 years Indian experience, seeks contacts as UK representative . . .'), and received replies from a carpet-maker in Mirzapur, from a warehouse for dried fruits in Kurseong, north Bengal (who in return wanted motorcycles and bicycles for their representatives in Afghanistan), and from Universal Industries Corporation of Calcutta, manufacturers of 'incandescent lanterns'. But nothing came of anything.

Then he looked for a property to buy in Hertfordshire, just outside London—'on the main road where restaurant and tea-garden business could be done with the summer motor traffic, with a front shop room suitable for a confectionery, stationery, library, books, newspapers, tobacconists' business'. By December 1950 he was writing to the organizers of the Festival of Britain, asking whether they had 'need of any further staff—office management, or anything other than sheer physical labour'. 'I am tired,' he said 'of suburban idleness.'

A year later he was dead, of cancer. Rose was devastated, and came to rely increasingly on her daughter Rosemary. By the time I knew her she had retreated to her bed, an invalid with no discernible illness except a lingering malaise, a homesickness for Allahabad.

On my last evening in Allahabad, a big party was held in the hotel where I was staying (a 50th birthday party for the manager's son). Uttara told me she had been invited, that Harsh Tandon would be there. They were at school together. She promised to introduce me.

Lights had been threaded through the trees surrounding the garden, marigold wreaths suspended from the branches, and petals spread in patterns on the marble floors. It looked like the party scene in *Monsoon Wedding*. Most of the guests arrived early, the women in a dazzling array of saris—ruby-red, scarlet, electric blue. Uttara, whom I had only seen in her working clothes—a plain cotton saree, woolly cardigan and trainers—appeared in the best Kashmiri silk, burnished gold with a delicately embroidered border.

She spotted Harsh in the distance, with his wife, a tall, steely-eyed woman in a shiny, brilliant-green saree and dripping with gold bangles, gold earrings and gold neck chains. Harsh, much shorter than his wife, was in a light-grey, Italian-wool suit, his hair cut short and well-oiled, a heavy gold signet ring on his little finger. I was not sure how to greet him. Should I shake his hand or make *namaste*. He gave me a limp handshake and attempted a smile.

'How nice to meet you. Did you get my letter? I've rung several times,' I blurted out, wishing as I spoke that I had found a more polite way of saying how disappointed I was that he had not replied to my messages.

'I rang the hotel,' he replied with excessive politeness. 'But you were not there.'

His wife said nothing, her eyes darting round the room.

I couldn't think of anything else to say, and they moved away.

For me, the Barnetts bungalow resonated with family history: my godmother triumphantly standing beside her first bicycle, aged ten, having just learned to ride it; George, lounging on the verandah smoking a pipe; Rose, in the office with her spectacles on, writing up the accounts. Their memories also taught me something about the way in which history impacts upon individuals. For Mr Tandon, I suspected, Barnetts is merely a business opportunity and the bungalow itself is only important for what it represents—the prospect of a different future.

The entertainment arrived—a pop group in tight white-satin suits—and began belting out Western-style music of no fixed identity. The young, rather plump female singers were clutching scraps of paper from which they sang the words. Conversation became impossible and we retreated back to my room so that Uttara's young son could watch the cricket (the World Cup was in progress). India was playing England.

By half-past ten most of the guests had mysteriously vanished. It seemed strange. The party was over before it had really begun, and the hosts were left standing around wondering where everyone had gone.

Before I left Allahabad, Uttara took me to meet some of the villagers who have been helped by her father's project. We set off by jeep, a two-

and-a-half-hour journey, she warned, to Koraon, jostling and bumping along pot-holed, muddy roads. On either side the fields stretched for miles, flat and lush-green with the new growth of spring.

Our first stop was at a specially summoned village meeting, held on a patch of grass outside the school. One of the men, full-bearded and with a scarf tied round his head like a tribesman from the hills, spread a large mat on the ground and we all sat down, men and women, cross-legged in a close-knit circle, Uttara insisting that I should join in. At first I was uneasy, reluctant to intrude—the English outsider—but that feeling soon gave way to a curious sense, almost of belonging, as if I knew them, had been with them before.

The discussion was fraught—VKRRP has been so successful in encouraging the villagers to set up their own community council and in enabling the disabled children, that Uttara was planning to withdraw its funding. Her visit was intended to reassure the villagers that they could manage the change. An old man with a grey beard, wearing a white shirt and lungi, warned her, 'Shake the tree, not the branches.'

We visited a school, where the children drew pictures for me—a Diwali lamp, a mango, the Indian national flag—and a workshop where crutches, wheelchairs and prosthetic limbs were being made out of local bamboo and leather. Most of the conversation was in Hindi, which I do not understand, but a young man, the technician, designing simple aids for each individual child, talked to me in English about writing poetry and reading Premchand.

On the way home the jeep broke down, a puncture in the rear tyre. The driver had no spare. We were miles from anywhere, and a deep, velvety darkness had fallen. A lorry driver stopped to offer us a lift, five of us crammed into his cab, crushed against the windscreen, almost no room to breathe, bowling along at 50 mph. We were now so late in returning that we had to join the queue of traffic trying to cross the Yamuna Bridge back into Allahabad, built by British engineers. I recognized it from the photograph in my godmother's album.

The lorry driver dropped us outside the city and we squashed into a rickshaw bus. I sat opposite an elderly couple, baskets of shopping on their laps. We smiled at each other, and then, in perfect English, the husband asked me where I was from.

I said, 'London, England.' But I'm still not sure what that means.

SAEED JAFFREY

Saeed Jaffrey (1929–) was born in Maler Kotla, Punjab, the son of a medical doctor. After attending public schools in Mussoorie, he joined Allahabad University. He was there from 1946 to 1950. Later, he took a degree in drama from the Catholic University of America. Though Jaffrey has acted in theatre and television for several decades, in India he is known chiefly for his work in films like *Shatranj Ke Khilari* (1977), *Gandhi* (1982), and *A Passage to India* (1984).

∽

from *An Actor's Journey* (1998)

Allahabad—pronounced *Ilaha-baad*—was at that time considered the Oxbridge of India; it is also considered a holy place by the Hindus, because it has a *trimoorti*, a triumvirate, where the two big Indian rivers, the Jamuna and the Ganga, are joined by the mythological river, Saraswati, from the centre the earth. In the mid-Forties Allahabad University was considered to be the best in India. It had some of the best professors teaching there; in sports, especially in cricket, its teams excelled; and most of the men selected for India's administrative and foreign services came from there. And because I had excelled in my intermediate exams from Manor House and obtained a first class, I was lucky enough to gain admission. Not only that, I was also admitted to the best hostel there which was called Muir Hostel. But I had to share my room with another Muslim boy. The two of us could not have been more dissimilar; we were really poles apart. He came from Lucknow, and had never been to any other city, let alone to an English public school like Wynberg-Allen in the Himalayan hills. He sported a priest-like *maulvi* beard, covered his head with a white *dupalli* topi, wore a *sherwani* and prayed five times a day! He hardly spoke any English and was deeply prejudiced against the Hindu boys. Thank God this term of torture lasted only a year. In 1947, a Christian friend of mine belonging to an affluent family, called Nicholas Macedo, from Manor House, asked me to share a flat with him in the Civil Lines, just a cycling distance away from the university. And, for a little over a year, we two

Manorites shared this flat, with a garden, which was a part of a house that belonged to a famous Christian tailor. We were informed by reliable sources that all of Prime Minister Nehru's clothes were stitched in this tailor's house.

In Mussoorie I had barely touched a cigarette, but at Muir we had a rather large-nosed and pompous megalomaniac from the famous Doon School in Dehradun. Doon is where rich Indians, to this day, send their sons to study; the late Rajiv Gandhi and his brother, Sanjay, went there. So, this braggingly rich Doon product used to flaunt his fifty-cigarette tin of 555s. He was always entertaining fellow students in his room—he was rich enough to have a single one, as opposed to us double chaps. He would open his tin of cigarettes and pass them round. 'Cigarette, cigarette, cigarette, cigarette,' he would say haughtily and, when he got to me, he would laugh sarcastically and say, 'But you're just a kid, a mere *buccha*, you're too young to smoke!' It was true that I looked very young; indeed, all my life, thank God and touch wood, I have looked years younger than my real age. But this Doon smoker's insulting insinuations were too much to take. So at one of these soireés in his room, I couldn't help bursting out, 'No, I'm *not* too young and I *do* smoke!' And, even though my head was spinning, I finished an entire cigarette and cheekily asked for another! But once the dizziness had gone I became a regular smoker. The cigarette had captured almost all my senses; the sense of taste, smell and touch. On the meagre allowance Papa used to send me—I think it was something like one hundred and fifty rupees a month—I could hardly afford the British 555 tins, but I did start smoking the much cheaper Gold Flakes.

And it was now that I got my first silver medal for acting. Playing an old man and a young girl in a play in Hindustani, I won the Muir Hostel annual drama competition, and Dr Katju, who later became the governor of West Bengal, awarded me a beautiful silver medal.

The most prestigious meeting place for us university students in Allahabad was the Friday Club. It was considered a great honour if you were invited to join so I was delighted when our vice-chancellor, who was also the president of the Friday Club, Dr Amaranatha Jha, invited me to join. One gained a lot of information, especially about English literature, in this Club, and one had the opportunity to mix with one's professors socially every Friday. There I met the great Urdu poet, Firaq

Sahab, though I must admit I was a little frightened of him because it was rumoured that he had an eye for pretty boys. I met the delightful Parsee professor of English, Dr Dustoor; and I met a girl called Coral Caleb, who was later to join my theatre company in Delhi and, of course, I met the impressive, cigar-smoking, vice-chancellor, Dr Jha. Years later, I was destined to work with Dr Dustoor in All-India Radio in Delhi and it was also my sad duty to announce the death of Professor Jha when I was an English newsreader at AIR.

Allahabad in those days had a huge Anglo-Indian community and most of the men worked in the railways. So there was a railway colony with lovely bungalows and a club with a large dance hall, and monthly balls. I made many friends there, like the charming and affectionate Mr and Mrs Callaghan, whose younger daughter Dierdré I met, after all these years, in Toronto a few years ago. Then there was the friendly Giddens family with their two daughters, Dulcie and Mavis. Waheed moved to England and married Mavis. The Bassetts were there and I had a secret crush on their pretty daughter, Rosie, but she preferred the company of a close friend of mine, Sonny Pillai. But perhaps I was closest to Muriel and her sister Violet and their cousin, Mickey Thomas. It was with Mickey, while playing hide-and-seek in the darkness of her house one evening, that I discovered the delicious sensuousness of a French kiss. It never went beyond that, alas, though she was my official girlfriend for a while. But that dark erotic corner of her house, the sudden heavy breathing and the passionate feel of her lips on mine are memorable. Rather reminiscent of my pigeons kissing in Aligarh. But, except for the odd kiss and embrace, we both remained virgins till quite a few years later.

Another Anglo-Indian girl blew into my life around that time. Her name was Mary Lee; she had married a GI during the war, gone with him to America, and was visiting her uncle in Allahabad. We became passionate at a picnic and after that would go to cafés and cinemas on my bicycle. The Callaghans, bless them, even provided us with a rendezvous in the bedroom of their house. But, for some inexplicable and stupid reason, despite the most imaginative and erotic attempts on her part, I hung on to my virginity! Maybe it was because she was the wife of another man and had a little daughter by him. Anyway, in sheer disgust I suppose, Mary retaliated by going out with the acknowledged playboy of the railway colony and made sure that their passionate kisses and embraces were witnessed by me. We parted friends though; saw together that lovely film, *Pride and Prejudice*, with the effervescent Greer Garson and the dashing and handsome Laurence Olivier, and passionately kissed each other goodbye when she went back to the States. I will always be grateful to Mary for introducing me to American music. Through her I received a pile of V-discs which used to be given to the GIs during the war. So I discovered and fell in love with 'St Louis blues', 'I hate to see the evenin' sun go down', the boogie-woogies and 'Honky-tonk train blues', played on the piano by Meade Lux Lewis, and all those jazz improvisations from New Orleans. Years later I was to visit this great southern city while touring with an American Shakespeare company, and spend many a late night in the jazz joints of New Orleans.

A girl I used to ask sometimes to accompany me to the cinema was Yvonne Abel. Her father was a brilliant saxophonist and, while playing with the Railway Club band, would often make his instrument laugh. Perhaps it was more like a giggle—'heh, heh, heh'. He was very amiable and, with a name like Abel, must have had Jewish ancestors. But Yvonne's mother was a rather racist Anglo-Indian lady. One evening I was waiting for Yvonne in the drawing room, while she was getting ready in her bedroom. We were to see an Errol Flynn film that evening. And then I heard the mother reprimanding the daughter in a low hoarse voice: 'But why do you still go out with him? He's not one of *us*; he's just a *wog*, mun. Yeah, a wog, that's what he is.' And, bless her, Yvonne defended me in a manner that I shall never forget: 'Oh, Mummy, what are you talking, mun! I swear, put him behind a curtain, and hear him *speak*. You'd *swear* he was an *Englishman!*' This platonic friendship continued for a while till another occasion when Mumsie played a trick on Yvonne, probably in the hope of wrecking our friendship. Yvonne and I had planned to go and visit some friends who lived a small train journey away from Allahabad. We went to the station and were told that the train had left an hour earlier. Mrs Abel had given us the wrong time and when, frustrated, we came back to the Abel bungalow, you should have heard the furious Yvonne speaking to her mother. I had not, till then, heard such a choice collection of four-letter words—in English and in Hindustani. Only once before had I heard such picturesque abuse delivered by a girl. That was in Mussoorie, when our beautiful, honey-haired, hazel-eyed and honey-skinned sweeper's daughter, Mano, discovered that someone had beaten up her little brother—'Mother-f, sister-f, bastard!' The street below The Acorn resounded with Mano's four-letter words! But they were in Hindustani and I bet she never knew the true meaning of the words she was yelling; she was only sixteen and I'm sure, like Yvonne, still a virgin. [. . .]

My subjects for the BA degree were English, history and, believe it or not, economics. The first two were my choices, the third was Papa's—a slight compromise for someone who was so weak in maths! Papa still hoped that his good, obedient son would eventually appear for the IAS or the IFS exams for the administrative and foreign service posts in the government. He didn't know that his good, obedient son had other ideas. I hated economics; so boring, so dull. I cannot even remember who taught that subject. But I do remember my English and history professors very distinctly. Besides Dr Dustoor, we were taught English literature by a gentle-voiced, bespectacled gentleman with sharp features whose name was Mr Mehrotra. I can still hear him and his upper-class English accent: 'We seek him heah, we seek him theah, is he in heaven or is he in hell, that demmed elusive Pim-per-nel.' Professor 'Kelly' Mehrotra had a rather chubby Irish wife who looked after him like an indulgent mother, and always wore white saris. Some of his favourite students, like me, were even invited to his house for afternoon tea. He loved the English language and I learnt a lot about Wordsworth, Keats and Shelley from him, even Byron and Tennyson. Alas, not enough of Shakespeare was taught, nor did we dwell as much as I would have liked on the works of George Bernard Shaw.

Three professors taught us history; one was quite ordinary; one was flowery and flamboyant, but my favourite was the bald, *paan*-chewing, and totally delightful Dr Tripathi. He taught us medieval Indian history, all about my ancestors, the Mughal emperors. He would bring the characters from history totally alive. Talking about Emperor Babur's son, Humayun, he would describe the time when his younger brother had mutinied in this manner, in his dulcet Purabiya (eastern UP) tones: 'So Humayun sent a message to his brother Askari and said, "I say, look, you are my younger brother. You are being a bit cheeky rebelling against me. But younger brothers are known to make mistakes after a sudden rush of blood. So, being your Bare Bhai Sahab I shall forgive you. Come home and be a good boy." But Askari was adamant. So Humayun said, "To hell with you," sent his troops to Gujarat, defeated Askari, brought him back to Delhi and threw him into prison.'

Looking back, it seems very odd that till Allahabad I knew nothing about the Hindu religion or its mythology. But, by talking to my Hindu friends, reading books, and going to some temples I more than made up for this lack. Which religion has God as a lover in one of his incarnations? The Hindu religion has Lord Krishna, who had a wife and a special mistress called Radha, and made love to and enchanted several milkmaids in his Brindaban forest! Little did I know that years later, I was destined to play Lord Krishna in the Canadian film, *Masala*. In Allahabad I learnt about another *trimoorti*, a three-headed god that can create, preserve and destroy the universe. I learnt about Lord Shiva who meditated for centuries in the Himalayas and his wife, the Earth goddess, Parvati, and about Kama, the god of love. I learnt about the most Christ-like Hindu god, Ram and his devoted wife, Sita; and I learnt about his brother Lakshman and the king of Lanka, Ravan, who could appear in numerous disguises.

Two weeks before my BA exams, Violet, Muriel, Mickey and her mother, and I went one night to the Railway Club Ball. It was a hot April night in 1948 and the ceiling fans were on. A blond boy was also with us and I found out that he had had a secret crush on my Mickey. He, Mickey and I sat at one end of the table, and facing us was Muriel— who had announced her decision to become a nun—next to her, Mickey's cigarette-smoking mother, and at her side, teenager Violet. Mr Abel and his band were playing, and couples were waltzing away when suddenly I heard Muriel saying, 'Look, Auntie, I think I'm on fire.' As she got up, I saw that her dress was indeed on fire and flames were reaching up to her breasts. The music stopped; someone had the sense to stop the ceiling fan above us. I took the jacket of my new suit off, went over and covered Muriel with it to put out the flames. We rushed her to the hospital, but she already had third-degree burns. She was a very slim girl. I can still remember gently slapping a hysterical Mickey that moonlit night in the garden of the hospital, I can still hear Muriel saying, 'St. Peter, St. John, wait for me, I'm coming, I'm coming'; and then she died. I cried and cried and cried. And so did Violet and Mickey. Everyone except Mickey's heartless mother whose cigarette

must have been the cause of the accident. After we buried her, Violet
told me that Muriel had been deeply in love with me all the time we had
known each other. It was only because she felt that she had no future
with me that she had decided to join a nunnery. Her death was such a
traumatic experience for me that I couldn't sleep and I couldn't
concentrate on my studies. Poor Nick, my flatmate, tried everything to
cure me, large doses of rum, long lectures on how I would be wasting
a whole year and my father's money if I did not appear for my BA
exams. Nothing worked. Then one night, a week away from the exams,
through the mosquito net of my bed in the garden of our flat, came
Muriel! I was wide awake, but I can still feel the touch of her hand
stroking my hair; I can still hear her comforting voice saying, 'Don't
worry, Jeff, my darling, don't worry about me. I'm in heaven with the
saints. Do me a favour. Please do your BA exams. For my sake, darling,
I swear I'll bring you luck.' While she was alive she had never spoken to
me like this, never called me darling. And, then she disappeared. Like a
comforted child, I slept soundly that night; and, with the help of my
classmate, a girl called Bobby Rudra, I mugged up my history, English
and economics books for the next six days. And, God bless Muriel, I got
a first-class degree and came third in the university!

Some new friends came into my life around that time. Reggie
Carapiett, his two brothers, Eddie and John and his sister Thelma; and
the Tobit brothers, Bunny and Hugh. Nick gave up the flat after his
bachelor's degree and moved on to the United States, but his mother
and sister lived in the poshest hotel in Allahabad. All of us spent
wonderful evenings in that hotel. I didn't want to go back to Muir or to
any other hostel, so Dulcie Giddens came to my rescue. Her boyfriend,
whom she later married when they emigrated to England, was a tall,
handsome lad called Richard Burgess. He and his brother Sidney lived
in a small bungalow with their widowed mother and her friend and
confidante, Grace. Mrs Burgess was an undertaker. I became the Burgess'
house guest. I had a large room, with a conservatory to study and sleep
in, and I had my meals with them. I also found a companion in their
servant, Moti, and perfected my Purabiya accent listening to him:
'*Hamaar mehraaroo kahath hain, paisa dabe, paisa dabe. Kayhuur say
paisa dabe? Hamaar toh hooliya hee tait hoee gawaa!*' Translated it would
go thus: 'My wife keeps saying, "Give me money, give me money."

Where can I find the money to give her? Mine is such a tight situation.'
So, wherever and whenever I could, I used to help him out so he could
give some pocket money to his *mehraaroo*, his wife.

Dick and Sidney Burgess became great friends of mine and we had
some marvellous times together. They thoroughly enjoyed my mimicry,
and I became almost like an adopted son of the family. I used to sit and
study, even entertain sometimes, in the conservatory, and sleep in the
adjoining room. It was in the conservatory that I was paid one of my
best compliments by a young and beautiful girl, though we never even
spoke to each other, and didn't even know each other's names! Some
poor people lived a short distance away. One day I spotted a most
beautiful young girl. She had been married off to a man old enough to
be her father. She would clean the room, wash the clothes, hang them
up in the sun, and cook the meals. The only source of water was a hand-
drawn pump outside. There was no privacy for the poor girl; she would
sit near the pump, pour water over herself and have a bath fully clothed
in her sari. She would then go into the room and change into a new sari.
I would sit in the conservatory and watch her, totally fascinated. I truly
appreciated her youth and her beauty and this admiration must have
communicated itself to her. Now comes the compliment! She started
timing her baths to coincide with my arrival from the university. Not
only that, knowing that my non-voyeuristic and non-lustful eyes were
watching her, she devised a way to reveal every inch of her body to me.
She would create a see-through shield with four charpoys around the
pump, take off her sari completely and bathe totally in the nude, singing
merrily away! We never officially met, never knew each other's names,
but we did have this secret tryst of mutual admiration on several
occasions.

The Tobit brothers, Bunny and Hugh, became a very important
part of my life. Bunny used to play the guitar and he became the darling
of the Anglo-Indian community in Allahabad. God only knows how
many ladies he seduced with his charming smile, curly hair and adorable
manner, but it didn't matter. There was no jealousy and women of all
ages were willing to share this musical, sexy toyboy. Hugh was totally
mad. He must have been a Cancerian—a Moonchild, as they are called
in America—because on full moon nights he used to go completely
mad, laughing and giggling and actually talking to the moon in the sky.

He had several talents, though. He was a very good jazz drummer and would often play with the local band. He was also a good short-story writer. He was deeply impressed by the American writer, Damon Runyon, and I remember listening to his Runyonesque prose on many occasions. The locale of the stories was not India, but some other area of the world, where people spoke in Brooklyn and Harlem accents! Waheed and I often played billiards with Hugh in the local YMCA club. Hugh Tobit always used to say to me in his Harlem tones, 'Come on, man, I'm bored with this shanty town. Come on, let's hit the big city.' [. . .]

As for my MA degree, I almost missed getting it altogether. The charm of Dr Tripathi's manner of teaching had so seduced me that when father insisted that I read history for my MA rather than English, which was my choice, I voted for medieval Indian history. Tripathi Sahab, I knew, would teach me, for he was considered a great authority in that field. Also, I would learn a bit more about my Mughal ancestors.

In April 1950, a little over a month away from my MA exams, I received a letter from Papa in which he accused me of extravagance. I was deeply hurt because I had always been extremely careful not to ever exceed the meagre monthly pocket allowance that he sent me. So when Hugh came over to my place one night urging me to 'hit the big city', I found myself saying to him, 'Yeah, man, let's go and *really* hit the big city.' We took a few summer shirts and slacks in a joint suitcase, plus our shaving necessities and with three hundred rupees in our pockets—about thirty pounds which was a lot of money then—we boarded the train to Calcutta. The city was quite dangerous in those days; there were riots and Hindus and Muslims were fighting with each other—yet another legacy of Partition. I was fairer than Hugh and, though I was twenty, I looked like a fair, Anglo-Indian boy of fifteen. Hugh was taller, darker and more muscular. In some ways, I used to look up to him for a lot of things. He could push his way forward, talk to anybody and gave the impression of being a sophisticated grown-up who knew his way around the world; I on the other hand was shy and sensitive, and still a virgin.

Crowded Calcutta was a real challenge. It made me adventurous. For the first four days we tried our best to get a job and learn to stand on our feet. I went to several shops and asked them if they wanted a window-painter and cleaner. I felt I could use my painting and drawing powers to earn a few rupees. No one wanted me. We scoured the night clubs and asked if Hugh could play the drums for them. One or two clubs let him play a few numbers, but they didn't pay him anything. They did treat us to a few beers, though. So, on the fifth night, tired and frustrated, we came back to our cheap and seedy Sind Punjab Hotel, absolutely convinced that we had seen enough of the big city and that I should go back for my MA exams. When we entered our room we discovered that we had been robbed. Someone had stolen into the room while we were out and taken all the rupees we possessed! We complained to the slimy manager but he was totally unsympathetic and wanted to know how and when we would pay his bills for five days' stay. I lied and dropped the name of Dr Katju who was now governor of West Bengal. I said I would borrow the amount required from him. This is how I was able to avoid us being thrown out.

We went back to the room, and big Hugh suddenly lost his stature and his swagger and, looking ever so small to me, burst out crying like a baby. My mind was working overtime to find ways of getting out of this tight situation. Hugh was saying, 'Come on, Jeff, mun'—gone was the Harlem imitation and back had come the Anglo-Indian accent—'Come on, mun; we've been disgraced. Let us jump off the Howrah Bridge and drown in the Hooghly River.' I had no such intention; I wanted to live. I said, 'Don't be silly, Hugh. We're too young to die. We have a life to live. Wait a minute,' and I started looking in the pockets of our dirty slacks. *Voila!* In one of the white trousers I found twelve annas, almost a rupee! I took out the blade from my razor and said to Hugh, 'Come to Chowringhee Bazaar with me, mate, and I'll show you how we tackle the big city.' And off we went. I bought a drawing book, a rubber and a soft drawing pencil, and I still had two annas left. We went, armed with my drawing artillery, to a place called the Nizam Teahouse and ordered two cups of tea. In those days you could get two cups for just two annas. I took out the drawing book and drew a portrait in pencil of the man sitting at the next table. I showed him the portrait; he was deeply impressed and wanted it. He asked me how much I wanted for it. With not a penny or *paisa* in my pocket, I smiled modestly and said, 'Whatever you like, kind sir,' And, bless his heart, he took out fifteen rupees—three five-rupee notes—and put them in my hand. 'Keep up the good work, son, you're extremely talented,' he said.

Electricity ran through my entire body and my fingers were itching. For the very first time in my life, I had earned some money through my own efforts. I had learnt to stand on my own two feet, and earn. For the next ten days, at that teahouse and in bars, I drew hundreds of portraits, sold them and made about fifty to sixty rupees a day, half of which I used to give to Hugh. I found out later that he would foolishly spend a lot of it on drink. I, on the other hand, had even cut down on my cigarettes, and, like a true Capricorn mountain goat, could survive on very little, often just a sandwich or two and a few cups of tea. [. . .]

Not having heard from Hugh and me all that time we had been in Calcutta, everybody in Allahabad was convinced that we had been killed in the riots. I shall never forget the look on the faces of Waheed, Mavis, Dulcie and Richard, Sidney, Mrs Burgess and her friend Grace—even the servant, Moti. It was the look at first of disbelief and then enormous pleasure and gratitude to God, as though I had been resurrected, had risen from the dead, and they were witnessing a miracle.

When I got to the university, a bureaucratic clerk informed me that, because I had missed almost a month of 'class attendance' (his expression), I would not be allowed to take my MA exams! So, I ran to Professor Mehrotra and Dr Dustoor and told them the entire story of growing up in the big city. Overnight, I became a hero; and everyone in the university was singing Saeed's praises. I studied solidly for a week, did my exams and just missed getting a first-class MA degree.

ESTHER MARY LYONS

Esther Mary Lyons (1940–) was born in Calcutta. Her mother, who was of part Muslim descent, was from Latonah, Bihar; her father, a Jesuit missionary, was from Detroit, Michigan. Her parents first met in 1929, when her father, who was working for the Patna diocese, visited the Catholic Girls' School in Bettiah, where her mother was a student. They were married ten years later. From 1942 to 1945, her father worked for the US Federal Economic Administration, helping it to locate beryllium, a critical component in the manufacture of nuclear bombs, in India. He returned to the United States in 1946, abandoning his family. Esther Mary Lyons now lives in Sydney, Australia. 'Railway Colony' is excerpted from her two works of autobiography, *Unwanted!* (1996) and *Bitter Sweet Truth* (2001), in which, by telling an extraordinary personal story, she also tells the story of one of India's lost communities.

◌

Railway Colony

In 1950, when I was ten years old, we moved from Chunar to Railway Colony in Allahabad. Uncle Eddie, who was a friend of my father, had got a job as a cane supervisor in a sugar factory some sixty miles from Gorakhpur. The factory was still British-owned and only Anglo-Indian and European families of the employees were allowed to live there. Though Uncle Eddie was Anglo-Indian, his wife, Aunt Natasha, was not. She was an Indian Christian, and therefore ineligible to live in the factory. An exception was made for children, but since their daughters were still very small and needed their mother, Uncle Eddie asked Mr de'Cunah if he could help them out with accommodation. Mr de'Cunah had been a contemporary of his at Gresham's School, Kalimpong, and was a conductor guard in the railways in Allahabad.

Mr de'Cunah did not have any children of his own. He was separated from his wife and never talked about her to anyone. He was a lonely man and happy to have his friend's family staying with him. My mother, too, at the time, needed a place for my sister and me. She was taking a course in nursing in Allahabad and had to stay in a hostel with other nurses, where children were not allowed. My mother arranged with Aunt Natasha for us to move in with her and her two daughters. She paid her a fixed sum every month to cover our expenses. Mr de'Cunah (whom we children called Uncle Dick) seemed not to object to this.

Uncle Dick lived in a two-storey building that had four flats. He occupied one of them. There were six such buildings on either side of a narrow street. The Railway Colony consisted of many such buildings, all of them painted the same off-white colour. The flat was small and could barely accommodate all of us. It consisted of two biggish rooms, a storeroom, and a bathroom. One of the rooms was used as a bedroom. Two double beds, placed side by side so that they formed one large bed, occupied the centre of the room. Along a wall were two wooden wardrobes and a dressing table. Aunt Natasha and Uncle Dick slept on either side of the joined beds. Aunt's two daughters slept in the middle. My sister and I slept in a *khatiya*, for which place was found in the same room. Uncle Dick was mostly out on night duty and sometimes he was away for two or three days at a stretch. Whenever Uncle Eddie came home from the sugar factory, he slept next to Aunt Natasha. He was home for about six months of the year, when the factory was closed after the crushing season.

The storeroom was to the right of the bedroom, and to the left was the bathroom, with a metal bathtub. On one side was a pedestal-type toilet. The water supply often did not reach the first floor because of low pressure, and Uncle Dick had a number of metal buckets for storing water. Daily, a woman would come to sweep and mop the house. She also swept and mopped the stairway and the bathroom. She used phenol as a disinfectant. The sweeper and her family lived in one room in the servants' quarter, and every time the toilet was used we would yell out to her from the verandah to come and clean it. I don't remember where she disposed off the soil from the toilet. The sweeper and her family did all this in return for free accommodation.

The other room was used as a dining-cum-drawing room. There were verandahs in the front and back. Uncle Dick had a hat stand in the front verandah, on one side of which was a door that led to another flat. The door was always locked. When Uncle Dick was not on duty, he sat in the front verandah drinking rum. He had it with ice. He had three or four glasses of rum every evening before dinner. He would then have his dinner and go to sleep. The apartment had electricity and every room had ceiling fans.

The kitchen and pantry were downstairs. They formed a separate block, adjacent to the four flats. Often, the pantry was used as a servants' quarter. The servant received a small salary, in addition to free accommodation, so long as he worked for the sahib.

Uncle Dick's cook was called Cheronji. He was a big, dark-skinned man who did his cooking on a raised *chulha*. He used coal and wood to cook European and Anglo-Indian-style food. Anglo-Indian-style food is a mixture of two cuisines, Indian and European. In the morning, he brought us bed tea. It was followed by breakfast, which consisted of toast, fried eggs or an omelette, porridge, and tea. The food was covered with a lacy cloth and carried up in a tray. At 12 noon, he brought boiled rice with yellow *dal* and a mild curry. Dinner consisted of soup, meat cutlets, mashed potatoes, boiled vegetables, and pudding. Once a day, Uncle Dick gave him money to do the shopping, but he never asked for accounts nor told him what to cook.

Not long after we came to stay with Uncle Dick, Aunt Natasha made Cheronji build a second *chulha* in the back verandah. She said the food always got cold while it was being brought up from the kitchen downstairs. Besides, she was certain that they were being shortchanged. Uncle Dick soon made her in charge of running the house. He gave her money for housekeeping and she bought the groceries herself every month. She gave Cheronji money to buy meat and vegetables and kept a close watch on the accounts. There was always a dispute over a few paisas or annas. She did not trust him, nor did she trust the vegetable and fruit vendors who came to the door. She was certain they were cheating her as they did all their calculations in the head, with nothing written down. In those days, wheat, rice, and some of the lentils could be had only against ration cards. The rich, however, preferred to buy their groceries on the black market, where they got the same things but of superior quality.

The Anglo-Indians would say, 'There is nothing left for us in India. Who would want to work under Indian babus or Indian officers?' They were not happy with Independence and the change of government. The ability to speak English, having a European name, belonging to the Christian religion, and education up to middle school was sufficient to land them good jobs in the railways or in British-owned companies.

The Anglo-Indian guards in Railway Colony had a 'Western' lifestyle, and since we were now living in Uncle Dick's house, we too adopted it. We sat at a dining table and ate with a knife and fork. We had to be on our best behaviour during meals. Uncle Dick sat at the head of the table and Aunt Natasha sat at the other end. We said Grace before every meal. Every Sunday, we walked about five kilometres to the church in the Cantonment. We attended church twice on Sundays, once for the service and again in the afternoon for benediction. Every night at eight before going to bed, we all knelt in front of the little altar where the statues of Jesus and Mary were kept, and said our rosary. We wore our best clothes to church. In those days, the dresses the women and girls wore were taken from English fashion books. The Muslim tailors who made the dresses preferred to come home and work from the verandah. They were paid according to the number of dresses stitched per day.

After the service, while Uncle Dick and Aunt Natasha chatted with other families from the colony, we stood still and waited for them in silence. The servants and shopkeepers called us 'Baby' or 'Missy Sahib'; they called Aunt Natasha 'Memsahib' and Uncle Dick 'Sahib'. I liked being called 'Missy Sahib'. The local Indians treated Anglo-Indians very much as they did the British.

One Sunday after church, Aunt Natasha met a young lady, Mrs Medley, whom she thought she recognized. She later told Uncle Dick that the lady was Violet Collis, an ex-student of hers and Mum's from Bettiah. She and her sister, Mrs Mackrot, were the daughters of Mr Collis, who used to work in an indigo factory in a small village in Bihar. Mr Collis was British and had fallen in love with a local woman. After the factory closed down he bought some land and settled down in the same area, adopting the ways of Indian village life. They had many children together, all of whom turned out to be fair-complexioned and beautiful. Since some of the children had been born before the marriage, they were sent off to Christian orphanages and homes to be raised. That's how Violet and her sister, Helen, or Mrs Mackrot, came to the mission school in Bettiah. Later, an old aunt of theirs who was married to a railway stationmaster arranged their marriage to two Anglo-Indian railway guards, who were now posted at Allahabad. Violet and Helen became good friends of Aunt Natasha and Mum and we visited them often, until the time came for them to migrate to England. One of their brothers, Edwin, who was about twenty-three years old, was a regular visitor to our place. He would tease me, saying he wanted to marry me. I found him most disgusting for saying this, but Aunt Natasha thought it was funny. I started to avoid him. Being only eleven years old, I had no idea what marriage was.

A fortnight before Christmas, Uncle Dick would enroll us for the Christmas tree at the Coral Club. The club was only for railway employees and their familes. Mum and Aunt Natasha gave in our gifts on the 22nd to be placed under the tree. On the evening of the 23rd we all went for the function. We wore our new dresses to it, which were all frills and bows, as was the fashion then. The hall was decorated with paper streamers, and Christmas carols played on the gramophone. After some time, one of the Railway officials, dressed up as Father Christmas, arrived in a tonga and presented us with our gifts. He also gave us a guava each and a packet of peanuts. Throughout the Christmas season we had small groups going round Railway Colony singing carols.

Patience was a beautiful young woman of thirty-five. She lived with her brother and sister-in-law in Railway Colony. She was known as the merry widow. Her husband had died suddenly and she had a five-year-old son. Patience, who loved to dress in the latest fashion, was a regular at the church and at Coral Club. She had a job as a receptionist in a tobacco firm owned by a Muslim and had many Indian admirers, with whom she went out for meals frequently. Anglo-Indians like Uncle Dick disliked her for going out with Indians.

I heard Uncle Dick say to Aunt Natasha once, 'She is giving us Anglo-Indians a bad name by mixing with these wogs and wearing their wog clothes. She goes out with them because they have the money, but she does not realize that none of these men will marry her. They only like to fool around with our girls because they think us to be cheap.' But I thought Patience was gorgeous. She had beautiful white skin and a slim figure. I did not understand why it was wrong for her to go out with Indian men. There were, in those days, not many European or Anglo-Indian men left in Allahabad, since most of them had migrated in search of a better life. By and by Patience too migrated, along with her brother and his family.

The Du'Casses lived opposite us. Their apartment was on the ground floor. Their eldest daughter, Emily, was the same age as my younger sister and we went to the same school. Emily had two younger sisters and four younger brothers. Mrs Du'Casse was always busy with the children and the housework. They had their fireplace on the floor in the back verandah. Mrs Du'Casse sat on the floor blowing into the coal fire, her white face black with soot, a baby feeding at her breast. She did not have any servants except for the sweeper woman. Her flat was very untidy, with her children's dirty clothes littered everywhere.

Mr Du'Casse loved only two things: alcohol and gambling. On payday, he would go straight to the Coral Club after work and spend most of his salary on 'Housey', rummy, and drinks. He would come home late that night, completely pissed and with very little money. He and his wife would then have a big fight and scream at each other. It would end with Mrs Du'Casse crying out in pain, because Mr Du'Casse had hit her and she was bleeding from the nose and mouth. Emily and her brothers and sisters would quietly sit through the fight, watching from their beds. They knew from experience that their parents would make up the next day and behave as though nothing had happened. For the rest of the month Mrs Du'Casse would buy grocery on credit from a little shop round the corner. The children attended Catholic schools where they were exempted from paying school fees.

Uncle Dick had started to kiss my sister Violet and me in a peculiar way whenever he found us alone. He would put his grubby rum-smelling mouth on our lips and push his slimy tongue right inside our mouths. Then he would pat us on our cheeks and say, 'If you need anything, just tell me.'

Violet and I hated his kissing, and could only avoid it by keeping out of his way. Violet did tell Aunt Natasha about it once, but all she said was to avoid him and not let him find us alone.

'Perhaps he just means to show affection,' she said.

Uncle Dick did not like gambling in any form, but he liked his drink. He was also a strict disciplinarian. Once we had two young girls come and stay with us over a weekend. Their father was a friend of Uncle Dick's and lived in a remote town. The girls said they had come to attend the Christmas dance, but Uncle Dick was far from happy about this.

He said, 'Other people's daughters are too much of a responsibility. I do not want to be blamed for anything they do, or if anything happens to them. Besides, I don't like the way they dress. It's asking for trouble. When I was young, girls used to be chaperoned and never went out to public places alone, specially if they were dressed the way they dress now.'

He had told the girls that they were to be back by twelve midnight, and when they did not he was mad with anger. At three in the morning we heard them banging outside the door to the staircase. Uncle Dick had locked the door exactly at midnight and told Aunt Natasha she was not to open it after that. The banging and calling out went on for a while, but no one dared go down to open the door. The girls must have spent the rest of the night sitting out in the cold and left for the station in the morning. We never saw them or heard from them again.

On 15 August 1955 Uncle Dick turned fifty-five. It was time for him to retire. We celebrated his birthday and retirement by going to a Chinese restaurant called Nanking in Civil Lines. The retirement also meant that Uncle Dick had to vacate his flat in Railway Colony. In the five years that we had lived there, we had seen many changes. The colony now had more Indians living in it. The Anglo-Indians we knew had either retired or were about to retire; some took early retirement and emigrated to Australia or England. The Coral Club continued as before, with the same facilities, but they now also celebrated Hindu and Muslim festivals, in addition to Christmas.

Since both Uncle Dick and Uncle Eddie were Anglo-Indians, they were allowed to move into the Anglo-Indian Trust Property on Thornhill Road, where they rented part of a bungalow called Anthony Cottage. Uncle Dick moved there first, along with all of us, and Uncle Eddie, who was still in Gorakhpur, joined us later. The Trust Property was an open unfenced tract of land, with a club in the middle, the Bundhwah Club. A large old building with a colonnaded verandah along the front, the club was known all over town for the dances that were held there at Christmas, New Year, Easter, and on Independence Day. Scattered around it were cottages, some of red brick with gable roofs. Most cottages had a servant's quarter attached to them.

Next door to us lived Mrs Annie Clarke, a teacher at St. Mary's Convent, who had taken it into her head that I should look like an Anglo-Indian. One fine day she came with a hairdresser, a Mrs Beveridge who lived in one of the cottages, and, after taking Aunt Natasha's permission, got my beautiful long brown hair that reached to my knees cut to shoulder length. She also saw to the shaving of my arms and legs.

'An Anglo-Indian girl', she said to me, 'should look like an Anglo-Indian and not like a *chowkri* girl with pigtails.'

We had been in Anthony Cottage for about a year when Uncle Dick decided to migrate. He had lived in India all his life but thought England was the right place for him. He said India was going to the dogs and that he could not take it any more. Uncle Eddie, on the other hand, though his sugar factory was now Indian-owned, had no desire to leave the country. He thought we were all well settled in Allahabad and going to England would mean uprooting ourselves unnecessarily. According to him, those of us who had migrated to England would have a lot more adjustment to do than we over here, who only had to adjust to a change in govermnent. Aunt Natasha agreed with him and so did Mum, who had joined the Kamala Nehru Memorial Hospital and loved her nursing profession. It seemed like the best decision at the time.

After he had been in England for three months, we got a troubled letter from Uncle Dick. He wanted to return to India. 'It is very cold here,' he wrote. 'I was better off in India. I miss the food and the luxury of having faithful servants to look after me.' Before going to England, he had sold off everything he possessed, and I don't know if he had the money to return. In any case, a year later we heard that he had died.

VED MEHTA

Ved Mehta (1934–) was born in Lahore, Pakistan, one of seven children of a public health officer of the Indian govermnent. He has been blind since the age of four. In 1949, Mehta left for the United States to attend the Arkansas School for the Blind. He continued his education at Pomona College, at Balliol College, Oxford, and at Harvard. In 1959 he joined *The New Yorker* and was staff writer with the magazine for over thirty years. His first book to appear in its pages was *Walking the Indian Streets* (1960), a rumbustious account of a summer spent in India. During 1965–66 Mehta made a prolonged visit to his native country, travelling from Kashmir to Kerala and from Bombay to NEFA. He also came to Allahabad, where he spent many days tramping about the Kumbh Mela, meeting the holy men and women congregated there. His report on what it was like to be at the biggest freak-show-cum-hustle on earth is still the most vivid and detailed we have.

In addition to several books on India, Mehta has written *Fly and the Fly-bottle* (1963), a report on contemporary philosophers and historians in Britain, and *The New Theologian* (1966), a report on Protestant thinkers in the United States and Europe. The Continents of Exile series is a work of autobiography consisting of eleven volumes, the final book of which is *The Red Letters* (2004).

༄

from *Portrait of India* (1970)

THE LOINS OF THE EARTH ARE
BETWIXT THE GANGA AND THE YAMUNA

Today I am in Allahabad, which, like the other Indian cities, is a jumble of British, Muslim, and Hindu influences. The British Allahabad, which now exists only for the benefit of a few educated Indians, takes in the military and civil cantonments, the race course, the clubs, and the university. The Muslim Ilahabas is well represented by Akbar's great fort, which lies three miles to the east of the city, but the wedge of land has by now been so eroded that the water flows very close to the embankment, leaving a correspondingly larger sandbank at Jhusi, across the Ganga. The ancient Hindu Prayaga can be observed in the parched, dusty, but joyful faces of tens of thousands of pilgrims coming to the city on the Grand Trunk Road—some in buses, tongas, ekkas, and bullock carts, some on bicycles, horses, and even elephants, but most on foot, patiently trudging, with loads on their head, as if they had been walking for years.

The country is in mourning for the death of Prime Minister Shastri, at Tashkent, but the *mela* goes on, and at one point on the day before Amavasya I find myself resting in a tent—pitched near the *sangam*—which I have reserved in advance, and composing a letter to Roy and Miss Devi, who print in *Kumbh* a letter to a friend relating some of their experiences at the Purna Kumbh *mela* of 1954:

> I have heard from you such a lot about the *sadhus* you have met [their letter says] that I may as well return the compliment by telling you about a few *we* have had the good fortune to contact here—at the Kumbh *mela*.
>
> What we have seen at this great congregation of *sadhus* and pilgrims has moved us to our depths. We were given, as it were, a glimpse into the heart of Reality, the Great Reality that *is* India— where dreams come true and the dynasty of the holy still abides! We may well be proud. But to begin . . .

And my letter, never sent, begins, 'Once, in your book, you resorted to a letter, as though that perfunctory but intimate form were the best you had at your disposal for conveying an impression of the *mela*. I have just spent some time at Jhusi, which is one vast stretch of saffron tents interrupted by straw huts, by sheds roofed with sheets of corrugated iron, by bamboo towers, and by bamboo poles flying the flags or signs of every imaginable sect of *sadhus*. And though I am not clear yet about what those dreams are that come true here, at times I did feel as though I were sleepwalking through some celestial bazaar. Or was it a medieval battlefield with hordes of Saracens in disarray? No, perhaps it was an ancient camp of Hannibal. Every man or beast was covered with dust. In front of the tents, which seemed to extend nearly to the horizon, camp fires burned. By the camp fires, beneath the open sky, were huddles of squatting *sadhus* and milling or motionless crowds of pilgrims. Now and again, I passed an elephant, festooned with flower garlands and embroidered rugs. All along the way, beggars held out their bowls, into which pilgrims dropped coins or grain. There were naked *sadhus* and *sadhus* opulently robed. There were *sadhus* wearing dhotis and marigolds, with horizontal stripes of ash on their foreheads. There were *sadhus* with ash-smeared naked bodies, offering *ghi*, *jaggery*, and *sesamum* to a sacrificial fire that crackled in a brazier, and chanting 'Hare Ram. Hare Krishna. Hare Om.' Elsewhere, *sadhus* were shaking bells or clapping tongs or cymbals, or were singing or haranguing crowds over loudspeakers, or were leaping up and down, or were hanging by their feet from trees. Here was *sadhu* reclining on a bed of thorns; there was a *sadhu* waist-deep in mud; nearby, a *sadhu* stood on one foot, and opposite him another balanced himself on one arm; farther along were *sadhus* fixed in still other yogic contortions. Beyond, a man wearing a skimpy loincloth was in the middle of a ritualistic dance to the music of a harmonium. Then, there was a group of seated men, each with a finger pressed to his lips. Opposite them sat other men, each with his forefingers in his ears. The names of the sects of sadhus were as endless as the ways they conceived of God: for the Vedantists, it was as the One; for the Vaishnavas, as all things; for the Shankarites, as the self; for the Tantriks, as the doctrines in their sacred books; for the Shaktas, as Kali; for the Shaivas and Avadhutas, as Mother Ganga—all, of course, overlapping even as they asserted their contradictions.

Since at the *mela* anyone can go anywhere and talk to anyone, I visit a number of the *sadhus'* camps at Jhusi. On a *gaddi* (Hindi for 'cushion') of straw in one tent, pitched a little apart from the others, a man sits silent and withdrawn, like a *guru*. Near him sits a fast-talking man who is answering questions addressed to the silent man by an Indian filmmaker.

'Looking at your face, I get the impression you have achieved great peace,' the film-maker is saying, in Urdu. 'In your eyes there is this wonderful glow of happiness. How do you achieve this peace?' He adds, 'This question may seem very foolish to you, but I would like to know if you encounter any difficulty in keeping your vow of celibacy.'

'How do I know you're not a spy?' the fast-talking man asks.

'Spy for what?' the filmmaker cries.

The man on the *gaddi* seems about to say something, but the fast-talking man speaks up again. 'You could be a spy for another *akhara*, or a spy for the government,' he says.

The film-maker courteously identifies himself as Habib Tanvir and explains that he is shooting a documentary on the Kumbh *mela*, which he hopes to sell to the BBC.

The fast-talking man listens warily, and then says, 'The question you ask about peace would take months to answer, because the answer is very difficult, and I would have to go through many highways and byways. As for the other matter, if you have had that experience, it's much more difficult. It's not at all difficult for us, because we have never had that experience.'

One large colony of tents is marked by a sign that reads, 'Spiritual Regeneration Movement Foundation of India'. This is the headquarters of Maharishi Mahesh Yogi. I know of him, or know the few available facts about him (all uncorroborated): that he was born around 1910; that his father was a revenue inspector; that he attended Allahabad University; that he worked in a factory for a time; that for some years he studied in the Himalayas with the Jagadguru Shankaracharya of Badri ka Ashram; and that, unlike most Indian sages, who use one religious title, he prefers to use two—Maharishi, which is Sanskrit for 'great seer', and Yogi, which is from the Sanskrit '*yoga*', meaning 'effort'. Inside the first tent, which is packed with such items as tomato sauce, cornflakes, soap, tooth-paste, and chewing gum—all imports, to judge from the labels—a man in a brown lounge suit and with a vermilion mark on his forehead comes up to me. He tells me his name and continues, in English, 'I am America-returned. I am MA and PhD in public administration from the States. Guruji has fifty-four *chelas* from distant foreign lands here at Kumbh. I myself am going to he initiated on this Amavasya, when Guruji will recite some *mantras* to me by the side of Mother Ganga, and I will recite them back. I met the Guruji only a month ago. After I set my eyes on Guruji, I left my five children to follow him.'

He takes me to an open area among the tents, where many Westerners, some in Indian dress, are standing around a serving table finishing a meal of macaroni and custard. I accept a small dish of custard from a girl in Western dress. She has very long eyelashes and the slightly bored expression of a fashion model.

'Where are you from?' I ask her.

'From Canada,' the girl replies. 'Guruji is a fact, and, like a fact, he manifested himself to me in Canada.'

When I ask her to tell me something about the Spiritual Regeneration Movement, she says tersely, 'You must address any questions you have to Guruji himself.'

An Englishwoman joins us. 'Guruji has been around the world six times, and now we have a half-dozen Spiritual Regeneration Movement centres in Britain,' she says. 'They teach Guruji's simple technique of meditation.'

The members of the group start moving into a tent. They arrange themselves as best they can on the floor in front of Maharishi Mahesh Yogi, a merry-looking little man with smooth skin, blunt features, and long, well-oiled hair. He is dressed in a flowing cream-coloured silk robe. Three tape recorders stand near him on the floor, as sacred books might surround another guru.

Maharishi Mahesh Yogi urges the audience to ask questions, and I ask a general question about the nature of his movement.

He asks me to identify myself, and when I do, he says, in English, in a soft, rich, bemused voice, 'All I teach is a simple method of meditation. We are all conscious on a mundane level, but beneath that consciousness, in each one of us, there is an ocean vaster than any in the world. It's there that most new thoughts originate. The bridge between the mundane level of consciousness and the ocean is meditation—not reading, because if you read you can have only second-hand thoughts. Meditation expands the consciousness and leads to the greatest production of goods and services. The ultimate test of my method of meditation is therefore its utility—the measure of the usefulness of people to society. Through my method of meditation, the poor can become as rich as the rich, and the rich can become richer. I taught my simple method of meditation to a German cement manufacturer. He taught the method to all his employees and thereby quadrupled the production of cement. As I said when addressing a meeting in the Albert Hall, in London, my technique does not involve withdrawal from normal material life. It enhances the material values of life by the inner spiritual light. My method is, in my London example, "like the inner juice of the orange, which can be enjoyed without destroying the outer beauty of the fruit. This is done simply by pricking the orange with a pin again and again, and extracting the juice little by little, so that the inner juice is drawn out on the surface, and both are enjoyed simultaneously."'

During the rest of the session, which goes on for a few hours, with the tape recorders running, Maharishi Mahesh Yogi expounds on his simple method of meditation. He has a way of dismissing everything.

Not only does he rule out at the start all questions concerning morality, theology, and philosophy—implying at one point that men are free to do anything in their personal lives, to themselves or to others, as long as, by the technique of meditation, they experience the bliss that is within themselves—but he seems to remove himself from the whole process of intellectual discourse by giggling at every question put to him and then at his own answer to the question, so one feels that no matter how long one talked to him one would come away with, at worst, chagrin at having been ridiculed and, at best, vague excitement at having been tantalized. He does not satisfactorily answer any question. (If by a few minutes of meditation a day the poor can become rich, why do they continue to he poor? Maharishi Mahesh Yogi's answer is that they are too indolent to master his simple method of meditation.) [. . .]

By one of the tents, a number of *nagas*, all quite rotund, sit around a smoky fire. Most of them have mischievous expressions, though their eyes appear glazed. 'Join in! Join in!' they call out to me, in Hindi, as I approach. Every one of them is ebulliently puffing a hookah or a cheroot, and the atmosphere is a little dizzying. 'Come and sit a while,' one of them says. He wears a bracelet made of hippopotamus hide, as a talisman against illness, and by nodding frequently he jangles three silver chains around his neck, from one of which hangs a flaming-red stone. He is called Bhola Nath, he tells me.

'How did you travel to the Kumbh?' I ask these men, sitting down among them. Their nakedness, I know, must have prevented them from using public transport.

Some of them nudge each other with familial camaraderie. Bhola Nath breaks into a grin, and asks, 'How did you come to the Kumbh?'

'By train,' I say. The reply arouses general mirth.

'We came on the power of *ganja*, *bhang*, and *charas*,' Bhola Nath says, referring to three narcotics made from the hemp plant and commonly eaten or smoked. 'Would you like a dream smoke?'

I decline, with thanks.

'Then we came on the backs of elephants and horses,' Bhola Nath continues.

'Where do you make your home?' I ask.

'On the backs of elephants and horses,' Bhola Nath says. He adds, becoming a little more serious, 'The villagers along the way always give all the *sadhus* lodging and food. They know we are coming when they hear our conchs and gongs.'

'You spend all your time travelling?' I ask.

'We sleep on the backs of elephants and horses,' Bhola Nath says. 'We must travel all the time, because we go to every Kumbh—Hardwar Kumbh, Nasik Kumbh, Ujjain Kumbh, and Prayag Kumbh.'

'But the *mela* comes only once in three years,' I say. 'The distances between these places could be covered in a few weeks.'

'But *we* take three years to get from one Kumbh to another,' Bhola Nath says emphatically. 'We travel very slowly. You know how elephants travel? We travel like them.' All the *nagas* around around the fire laugh.

'Why do you go naked? What is the theory behind it?' I ask the assembly.

'As a baby, you have no shame,' Bhola Nath says affably. 'You snuggle happily in your mother's lap. That is the age when you are most loving and affectionate. You love your mother and father without self-consciousness, and you instinctively know the oneness of life. You grow up, you start giving yourself airs, and you reject your mother, who brought you into the world. You start wearing pantaloons and shoes, and you think there is something sinful about sitting in your mother's lap. You are no longer innocent. You have shame, because you've become guilty. You can't love your mother any longer. Now, take you. You've become a babu. No doubt you wear fancy suits, you have a lot of education, but you are full of shame and guilt. We are not full of shame and guilt, because we go naked.' He buttresses his argument with a bit of verse:

You move from fifth standard to sixth standard,
You go from more awareness to less awareness.
You move from sixth standard to seventh standard,
You go from less ignorance to more ignorance.

I am now in a tent filled with serene-looking women. They are sitting at the feet of another woman, who looks to be in her seventies. She is bundled up in a coarsely-woven black blanket, which is faded, dirty, and patched. Her face is fine and bright, with the sweet expression that elderly ladies in India seem to acquire like gray hair. Everyone addresses her as 'Mataji' (Hindi for 'Mother'). When I am presented to her, she invites me to sit down.

'Ask Mataji something,' the women in the tent say, almost in unison.

'I have been living abroad, and the question I want to ask you may sound a little strange,' I say hesitantly. 'But all the while I've been walking through Jhusi, the question that has been going through my head—'

'Ask your question,' the chorus cuts in.

'Well, I've been wondering how one gets *chelas*—how one becomes a guru,' I say. 'I would like to know how your sect got started.'

'Our sect is called Kali Kumbli Vali, child,' Mataji says. She speaks rustic Punjabi. 'And Kali Kumbli Vali, as you know means "the lady of the black blankets". I am the Kali Kumbli Vali. I was born into a very good family in Rawalpindi. Some of my relatives were doctors and lawyers, and one of my close relatives was a judge. I was married into a very good family, too, and my husband also had relatives who were doctors and lawyers, but my husband died when I was ten years old. And, child, as you should know, in our country marriage can be entered into only once, so, a widow of ten without education but with much life before me, I had nothing to do. I started sitting with some ladies who were my neighbours and who knew about godly matters. So I came to know about godly matters, too, and some other widows and such ladies started coming and sitting with me. And so I fell into the godly way. Now Kali Kumbli Vali is known in the four corners as a refuge for widows, and when mothers lose their husbands and want to follow the godly path, they ask their way to my abode, in Hardwar. Many know about me, and they direct the good widows to me.'

'She has *shakti*,' the chorus says. ('Shakti' is Sanskrit for 'capability', but sometimes also means 'female essence'.)

A demure young disciple adds, 'She has *shakti*, so people follow her. We don't have *shakti*, and no one follows us. But everyone follows and obeys Mataji.'

Another disciple, who is toothless and seems to be the oldest member of the congregation, says, 'You see, most people are born upside down, and they haven't any *shakti*. A few people are born with their feet first, and they have *shakti*, and they show the way. Most people are so unfortunate that they can't even find someone who was born feet first to follow. Mataji is one with *shakti*, for she was born feet first.'

ARVIND KRISHNA MEHROTRA

Arvind Krishna Mehrotra (1947–) was born in Lahore and grew up in Allahabad and Bhilai. He is the editor of this volume.
'Partial Recall' first appeared in *Civil Lines 1* (1994).

ᗐ

Partial Recall

The brand-new cricket bat, with Len Hutton's signature inscribed near the top of the blade, where it joins the handle, stood in a shallow pan half filled with linseed oil. The bat was supposed to soak up the oil through a tiny hole in the bottom, and I went and checked it from time to time. When at the end of three days I saw that nothing was happening, I took the bat out of the pan and vigorously rubbed the oil into it with a cotton rag. Finally, I took a cork ball and bounced it off the blade, each thud leaving a dark sunken mark on the smooth surface. Looking at the disfigured face of the bat afterwards, I almost regretted what I'd done.

Whenever I made it to a cricket eleven, it was more on the strength of the equipment I brought along than for any cricketing abilities I possessed.

I don't recall my boyhood, uneventful though it was, as being particularly lonely. Without telling our parents, we'd go swimming in the lake. It was full of tall, offensive weeds that came up almost to the water's surface. We'd strip to our underpants and, from a concrete platform that abutted the lake, jump into the water. The weeds seemed to follow us around, and I was afraid they might, any moment, grab hold of my leg and drag me to the bottom. I'd thrash about violently if one of them so much as brushed against my skin. We'd sit on the embankment to dry ourselves, then go home.

The boys I played cricket with, or hockey, or soccer, or with whom I went swimming, have today become unsubstantial as ghosts. Ask me their names. or what they looked like, or their fathers' professions, and my mind, more or less, is a blank. The person who still seems real from that time is someone I didn't know at all. She was a businessman's daughter I was in love with in school. We never talked, but on some pretext or other I would frequently go past her classroom, trying hard not to look in its direction; in the recess I would follow her around; and before going to sleep at night, in the privacy of the mosquito net, the bedside lamp switched off, the pedestal fan purring, my eyes half-closed, I would murmur her name to myself over and over again. But there were also nights, specially in the summer, when the full moon would creep up the window and refuse to go away, throwing its unwanted light both on the world I was about to shut out and the hidden one I wished to enter, trapping me between them. I lay as though suspended in the air. If I attempted to bring the darkness back by covering my eyes with a pillow, the moonbeams pinned my arms down so I couldn't move.

The evenings, too, went in trying to catch a glimpse of her face, for which purpose I would go past her house on my Raleigh bicycle at regular fifteen-minute intervals. She had large black eyes, high cheekbones, sloping shoulders, wide hips, and a slow, deliberate walk. Her complexion was the colour of wheat, and often, even at home, she wore the white blouse and sky-blue skirt of the school uniform.

A bicycle may be a noiseless way of getting around, but whenever I approached the street where she lived, the tires (as if I'd upset a basket of snakes) began to hiss, the leather saddle creaked, the chain rattled against the chain guard, and it felt as though I was travelling in a fire engine instead. If there was a light in her window, I'd turn back and cross it a second time, all the while looking out for her cousin, who was the same age as me and suspected what was going on. But he also knew that my evening routine was harmless and didn't interfere with it.

Despite the hundreds of hours spent in this pursuit, had she and I met by accident somewhere, say on a desert island, I wouldn't have known what to say to her. I was unused to her presence, whereas her absence summoned all my latent powers. I believed she could be conjured up, like the pigeon the magician makes appear simply by passing a cloth over his hand, and I was the one to do it. Sitting in class or fielding at deep third man, I'd snap my fingers and look about me to see if her languid figure had materialized, but except that words disappeared from the blackboard before I took them down or I gave away an extra run, little else happened. I realize now that I was driven not only by my infatuation with her, but also by some image I had of myself, an image that formed only when she became the looking glass.

We were living in Bhilai, a city designed by a pencil stub and a six-inch plastic ruler. It was all parallel lines. The tribal village that gave it its name was nowhere to be seen, and in its place, in the middle of the mineral-rich Deccan Plateau, a region that once formed part of the hypothetical continent of Gondwanaland, stood rows of mostly one-storey houses with flat concrete roofs. There were so many houses to a street, so many streets to a sector, and ten sectors made the township, at one end of which, next to the lake where we swam, a steel plant was being built with Soviet aid.

The pencil and ruler that planned the city also drew its houses. They were toy houses really, rectangular in shape and coloured yellow, pink, or brick red. Ours was a semi-detached in Sector 10. It consisted of a living room, two ten-by-ten-feet bedrooms, a kitchen with a cement counter, a porch just big enough to accommodate one rattan chair and some flowerpots, and an enclosed backyard on whose whitewashed walls no papaya tree cast its thin shadow. There still lingered in the rooms the wholesome smell of sawdust and fresh paint when we moved in, and some of the paint was splattered on the floor, forming strings of islands. Blobs of grey plaster clung to the window bars. You looked out and saw that for miles around there was nothing outlined against the sky. The sky itself was flat, straight, and like a weight, kept pressing everything down into the earth—houses, fences, utility poles, everything. This is not all. The place had the stillness of a morgue. There was little traffic on the roads, and none whatsoever in the air. No butterfly flitted past, though you could have sat in the porch all afternoon. At such times, the only movement was that of your eyes, when they blinked; the only sound came when someone cleared a spot of phlegm from his throat, and Bandhu Ram cleared his constantly.

Like a stain preserved in cloth, Bandhu Ram is preserved in the folds of my memory. Half-crouched and without making a sound, he approaches the coal enclosure. Behind it a chicken, which a minute ago was fluttering all over the yard, has hidden itself. Bandhu Ram was a slender, dark-complexioned man who didn't speak even when spoken to. His family since his grandfather's time had worked in the kitchens of regimental messes, and from it he had inherited the art of baking vegetables, steaming puddings, and making clear soups that sometimes tasted like hot water. He used to be our cook in Allahabad and came to

Bhilai with us when my father, who was a dentist, took up a job in a newly opened hospital there. Once a month, he would bring a postcard and dictate a message to his family: 'Bandhu Ram conveys his greetings to everyone. . . .' The contents never varied, and soon I knew them by heart.

From the doorway I had watched the chicken's flight and capture. Bandhu Ram went outside, holding the chicken upside down in one hand and a rusty knife in the other. He had his back towards me. I wanted to go and stand near him, but didn't have the courage. Then I saw him wipe the knife on the grass. Around him lay stiff white feathers. I was watching his face when he came in, but it was impassive, as my own must have been when afterwards at dinner I sucked on the wishbone.

Unlike us, the Soviet engineers lived in air-conditioned apartments from which, when the door opened, came the smell of frying. Without realizing it, we were a nuisance to them. Every schoolboy in Bhilai was an ardent hobbyist and had picked up enough Russian to ask for postage stamps, coins, and brooches (depicting naval ships, Lenin, the hammer and sickle), and say thank you. An afternoon of knocking on doors seldom produced more than a few postage stamps, though on lucky days one or another of those oversized Soviet women would give us a one-kopeck coin, and sometimes a crumpled rouble note. Limited though our contact with them was, even as children we could see that between them and us language was not the only barrier. My badminton partner in the club was a Russian. A thickset man with short hair and the grace of a battletank, he seemed to want to crush the shuttlecock whenever he made contact. We became friends, though only on court. Off it he refused to recognize me. By and by we found out more about these strange people. We learnt they ate red meat in enormous quantities; they had bad teeth (this detail was contributed by my father); they did a lot of shopping, epecially for footwear; and they put up their binoculars and cameras for sale before they left.

Though aboard the stamp album's magic carpet I made frequent visits to the Union of Soviet Socialist Republics, and less frequent ones to Borneo, Cameroon, Formosa, Gold Coast, Madagascar, Rhodesia, Siam, Tanganyika, and Zanzibar, it was not philately or even the sight of blast furnaces and coke ovens that was the highest point of my otherwise plain boyhood. That dot on the contour map still belonged to the girl I had partly daydreamt into existence. Was I sorry to see my boyhood end? Not really, for whatever the *rites de passage* might say, I never did believe it had ended.

In July 1963, just out of high school and after five years of living in a steel town, I found myself on the train back to Allahabad. No two cities could be more different. One had not yet made it to the map of India, the other had been a continuous settlement for thousands of years, visited by mythological heroes and ancient travellers, and mentioned in sacred texts; one adjoined a man-made lake, the other lay at the confluence of three rivers, the Ganges, the Jumuna, and the invisible Saraswati; one was small but cosmopolitan, the other large but provincial, a one-horse town of half a million souls; one was in the process of coming up, the other, described even by local journalists as a dead place, content to remain in perpetual decline. I fell in with its ways almost at once.

In Allahabad I had spent my childhood, attended my first school, Boys' High School, and made my first friends, some of whom I was eager to see again, so my return was a homecoming. The city's tree-lined roads and high-ceilinged colonial bungalows were as familiar to me as the night sky is to a stargazer. In a poem written while pacing up and down a studio at Yaddo in the summer of 1972, I discovered, quite by chance, that local history and private memory are intersecting lines:

> At seven-thirty we are sent home
> From the Cosmopolitan Club,
> My father says, 'No bid,'
> My mother forgets her hand
> In a deck of cards.
> I sit on the railing till midnight,
> Above a worn sign
> That advertises a dentist.
>
> I go to sleep after I hear him
> Snore like the school bell.
> I'm standing alone in a back alley
> And a face I can never recollect is removing

The hubcaps of our dull brown Ford.
The first words I mumble are the names of roads,
   Thornhill, Hastings, Lytton . . .

The roads are now called after Hindu nationalists or provincial leaders, but their new names are far less resonant, good only for aiding postmen. I cannot imagine any child reciting them.

Atop a bookcase in my room is a photograph showing three rows of solemn-faced Allahabad University students, Class of '28. The men are all wearing jackets, their trousers are tight and narrow, and some are wearing caps; the women are in white saris, their heads covered. I've never paid much attention to the photograph, and were it not for its wooden frame, a floral design carved along the edges, and one slender bespectacled figure standing in the back row, fourth from left, I would have thrown it away. He is Kewal Krishna, my father's elder brother. After taking his degree, he went to Oxford and wrote a dissertation on *The Castle of Otranto* and the Gothic novel; he also fell in love with an English girl, Phyllis Ravenscroft, and decided to marry her. In the late Forties Uncle Kelly showed the first signs of multiple sclerosis, a disease that severely disabled him for the remaining twenty years of his life. During this period Aunt Phyllis ('More devoted to her husband than Indian woman') functioned as an extension of his limbs. Together with a battalion of loyal, light-fingered, hierarchy-conscious servants, she bathed, dressed, and fed Uncle Kelly, drove him to the university and pushed his wheelchair, chased away the mosquitoes that settled on his arm, and turned the pages of the book he was reading. But it was Aunt Phyllis alone who got up two or three times each night, and seeing that he was lying in one stiff position, gently turned him on the other side.

Uncle Kelly and Aunt Phyllis lived on 20 Hastings Road. To my parents they had written saying that for the three years I would be going to college and university they expected me to stay with them and not in a student hostel, so on reaching Allahabad it was to Hastings Road that I asked the rickshaw to take me. The bungalow I entered I'd often visited as a child. Built in typical colonial style, it was set in the midst of extensive grounds in which grew neem, custard apple, jackfruit, guava, and jujube-berry trees. In one corner was a dusty badminton court. The lawn was a patch of brown. All day a blind gardener, sprinkling-can in hand, moved among the flower beds. A wide verandah ran along the entire front of the house. The bedrooms were large and stuffy and lay on either side of the living room. Each dressing room had a chest of drawers, into which everything from torn tablecloths and runners to used copybooks went. In my earliest memory of the place, there was a thunderbox near the bathroom window, and though a toilet bowl had replaced it, nothing else had changed. The heavy brass tap was still there in the wall, and under it stood a metal bucket and dipper. From time to time there issued from the tap a thin trickle of water. Termites had eaten away the doorframes, and during the rains it was not unusual to find a snake leaving the bathroom. Less disconcerting was the presence around the house of vagrant cows. They wandered in through the front gate and destroyed what little garden there was. Sometimes a cow was caught and tied to a tree, and an excited Aunt Phyllis would wait for the claimant to turn up. If by evening none did, the animal was given a few kindly whacks and released.

My favourite room in the house was the study. Neither of my parents was fond of reading, and except for those condensed by the Reader's Digest, I had not known many books in Bhilai. Afterwards, when my father became interested in Hindu religion and philosophy, commentaries on the Gita and the paperback lives of sundry saints, mystics, yogis, and gurus were added to the memoirs of field marshals and the accounts of World War II naval battles. We also possessed some books on shikar, a three-volume set of Somerset Maugham's stories, a biography of Napolean Bonaparte printed in double columns, and Gray's *Anatomy*. As a boy, the only book I consulted was *Anatomy*. It always opened on the page containing an illustration of the female pudendum, and I looked at it whenever my parents were out of the house.

The study was where, during winters, Uncle Kelly took his morning tea, and where he received visitors. Tall book-cases lined the walls, and someone gifted with a sensitive nose could also catch the dry smell of foxed paper and calf bindings in which diligent maggots had bored tunnels. Behind the safety of undusted uniform editions lay clusters of identical taw-sized gecko eggs. In one corner was kept an easy chair, and sitting in it I felt like a general on horseback. From that coign of vantage, in the light of a forty-watt electric bulb, I surveyed the enemy:

books. My ill-planned raids into that articulate territory never came to very much, and I soon felt defeated.

The truth is that even before I could acquaint myself with the titles of the books that surrounded me, I became impatient to write one. Looking out the dressing-room window at the row of yellow oleanders outside, their leaves wet with rain, or while turning the virgin pages of an economics or a geography textbook, I would dream of publishers' imprints, of a spine and title page with my name on them. It was as though the tongue had acquired new taste, and so it had. One day I found it saying,

> Four hundred miles away,
> Beyond many moons you stay.

The lines, which completely took me by surprise, were addressed to the businessman's daughter in Bhilai.

There is another photograph. It is pasted on a student ID card and bears the signature of the proctor of Government Intermediate College, Allahabad, in one corner. I thought I'd lost the card, indeed I'd forgotten all about it, when the other day it waylaid me again. Taken in 1963, the year I returned to Allahabad, the photograph shows a smooth-chinned sixteen-year-old who is half man and half boy. His thick black hair is neatly parted, and he is wearing a white terylene shirt and a narrow tie. But hold the photograph at a distance, and you'll see the boy's confidence comes from inexperience, that behind the pleasant door-to-door salesman's face is the face of a narcissist. Nothing seems further from his mind than writing poetry, and yet it is just the kind of thing he might do very soon.

The first poem was something given, something received. It wrote itself. I then wrote several more. It was as though I had lifted the sticky lid of a tin box and the brown-winged insects breeding inside had rushed out, their numbers such that I thought I wouldn't see the last of them. The poems brought about a change in my appearance. I was writing, but I was also being written. The change happened slowly and over a period of time, at the end of which it was visible to everyone except me that whereas others wore clothes, drab everyday shirts and trousers, I went about in costumes. Ochre cotton had replaced white terylene.

The Royal typewriter I used was my maternal grandfather's gift to my parents. Bought second-hand in Simla from an Englishman who was selling his effects prior to leaving the country, it was a portable model that had the weight of a saddle quern and came in a high black case. When I thought I had accumulated enough poems to fill a small volume, I typed them up and took the pages to the nearest bindery. Two days later the mournful-looking cloth-bound object I held in my hand was narrower than a paperback and barely possessed a spine; it had neither jacket nor publisher's imprint, and yet bore some resemblance to a book of poems. I brought it home and hid it between the college textbooks on economics and geography.

In the house adjacent to ours, similar to it architecturally but with a tile roof and bigger windows, lived my closest friend, Amit Rai. He and I would stand on either side of the low wall that separated our compounds and talk for hours. Alongside the wall grew large, thickly foliaged trees, their trunks hidden by the underbrush. Getting to the wall was not easy, and I had to back my way through a tangle of branches. Once there, amidst the trees and closely planted shrubs, it was like being inside a tropical forest. This forest often rang with laughter. We laughed for no reason at all, and there was nothing we didn't laugh at. We once laughed at a man merely because he was bald and drove a grey car. He was a phoney, which is what we felt about most people we knew, whether it be somebody's senile grandfather, who daubed his clothes with Dettol before he put them on; an honest classmate, whose ambition in life was to join the civil service; or a puffy-faced university lecturer, of whom it was said that once a month, leaving his wife and three small children at home, he dined by himself in Kwality's restaurant and smoked a Gold Flake cigarette afterwards. We looked at them, as we did at ourselves, with unsparing eyes.

Our attitude of rebellion was shaped by our reading, just as much as it was reflected in the books we read. The word *phoney* had entered our vocabulary through *The Catcher in the Rye*, and when we were not trying to speak like Holden Caulfield, we recited passages from *Penguin Modern Poets 5*, where, for the first time, we had come across poems that were funny, clever, sad, irreverent, and though written in a style that looked as natural and easy as breathing, left us in a state of euphoria—Gregory Corso's 'Marriage', Lawrence Ferlinghetti's 'Underwear', and Allen Ginsberg's 'America'.

Perhaps not so surprisingly, the ineffable longings of Rabindranath Tagore and Kahlil Gibran—and not the profanities of the Beat Generation—prompted my first published work. This was a group of five poems, titled 'The Soundless Flute' in the March 1965 issue of the *Allahabad University Magazine*.

> Let not the cloud remain and dirty the sky, let it not shade the sun,
>   let it not he tossed about by the wind or be pecked by the birds. Let
>   it merge into the bigger cloud that will carry it with its own strength,
>   or else let it rain and die.

I wrote about twelve such poems in all, and learnt a few things about poetry I didn't know before. I came to know that you could say the most trivial things in it, but they would still come out sounding like profound truths, or at least to my ears they did.

One humid September afternoon, some six months after the poems appeared, as Amit and I were bicycling down from the university, the thought came to us to start a magazine. In an issue of the *Village Voice*, sent by his maternal uncle, Vijay Chauhan, from New York, we had read about *Fuck You/a magazine of the Arts*. We now decided to steal the name for ourselves, modifying it slightly. Amit's father, a publisher, had converted a part of the front verandah of his house into an office. In it, among the wooden tables and chairs, stood a Gestetner mimeographing machine, covered in dust and seldom used. We had it cleaned and learnt how to operate it. After applying ink from a large tube to the roller, we rotated the drum a few times to let the ink spread evenly. We then fastened the stencil, fed the paper and watched nervously as the printed sheets rolled out.

The first number of *damn you/ a magazine of the arts* contained ten pages and had a pale green cover. It carried poems by its three editors, the third editor being Amit's brother, Alok. The back cover mentioned the price, which was 'Anything commensurate with your dignity—and ours,' and gave the address, 18 Hastings Road, Allahabad. There was also an editorial, called 'Statement', in which, while putting a brave face on it, we nevertheless confessed to the misdemeanour of writing and selling verse:

what about? long-term policy? general objectives? that's not even
funny. besides, we wouldn't know. the basic point is that all of us
write—more or less—and would like being read. hence *dy*.

this statement is here because we thought we might explain
things a little before flinging poetry at you. who knows, perhaps it is
needed. the explanation or the flinging? *dy* shall be issued as frequently
(or seldom) as we feel. what is more, we'll even try and get some
money off you for it. the financial benefits are not meant for ourselves.
poor boys' fund. vietnam. (before you pigeonhole us, we didn't
specify which side.)

Not just the editorial, but almost everything else in the magazine was
printed in lower case. This was partly a matter of breaking conventions
and partly of being with the times, for poems that used capital letters
looked so old-fashioned.

My handwriting kept changing. There were several styles to choose
from, and I tried all of them out. I'd adopt a schoolgirl's round hand
one week, then give it up for flat, angular strokes that I thought suited
me better, or else, in imitation of Aunt Phyllis, add a little flourish to the
letters, a flowing curve that made them look like birds in flight. For the
poems, likewise, there were models (Tagore, Gibran, and a score of
others), and I served my apprenticeship copying them, and sometimes
failing to, as happened with X.J. Kennedy's 'Nude Descending a Staircase',
which I first read in Donald Hall's *Contemporary American Poetry*
anthology. I would on occasion catch myself humming it, but the
rhythmic modulations that made it so hummable also made it difficult
to imitate. I had one go at the poem and did not try a second time.

The models I followed had little in common. They belonged to
different traditions, and if to the same tradition, to different schools.
This eclecticism came with the discovery itself, for having stumbled
upon the kingdom of verse I was impatient to explore its several regions,
even the most remote, and inhabit each as my native place. Though
which treacherous region was I exploring in these nine lines is anybody's
guess:

> my breath
> flees downward
> down butterfly hill

> the red rocks
> and the blue rocks
> it meets and kisses
>
> my breath
> bleeds to pieces
> on the white rocks below.

Reading through *damn you/1* again, it appears my role in it was to strike anguished poses, and Amit's to write the poems. Their manner is not derivative, and their themes, unlike mine, have less to do with the artificial wilderness beloved of artistic souls and more with the time and place we lived in. He wrote about young people having fun at a party, a sixth-century Buddhist site near Allahabad, a dead paratrooper:

> is it not beautiful
> to come billowing down in silk
> what your little son would tell
> the neighbour's boy if he saw you do it
> and he can't
> where is your comrade who got pleasure
> from making paper dolls
> and he who yet felt happy
> when any said he needed a shave
>   parachute   trouble
>   machine gun   trouble
>   dead.
>   dead . . . can you imagine
>   eyelids that won't blink
>   when the raindrops
>   drop on them . . .

We couldn't have printed more than a hundred copies of the first issue. I took one to Uncle Kelly, who, when he saw what the magazine was called, raised his eyebrows, a wrinkle of disapproval forming on his forehead. Then he looked up, and his face broke into the thinnest of smiles. One or two English department lecturers we knew bought copies, and said 'Damn you' as they paid for it, but most of our friends just stared at us in disbelief and walked away. Writing poetry belonged to that phase of their lives they had sidestepped altogether, and they had no wish to be reminded of it. Though our age, they already were grown-up men, preparing to enter their fathers' professions or professions their fathers had chosen for them. Their future looking secure, they sometimes worried about the world's.

Our obsession was poetry, and the world, we found, has only one side, the funny side. For the rest, Amit and I were like other students, conscientious and keen to do well. Admitted to the University of Allahabad in July 1964, we were required to take three subjects and pursue them for two years. Both of us offered English (a play each by Shakespeare, Shaw, and Galsworthy, and Romantic and Victorian poetry) and ancient history, and while Amit took philosophy, I had economics as the third subject. We didn't much care for history, ancient or any other, but took it all the same because the subject was 'scoring', which is to say the examiners were believed to be liberal and award high marks to every script they read. (In contrast, those in medieval history and political science were well known for being stingy.) Scoring in ancient history was easier said than done, for the next thing we learnt was the marks awarded depended on the length of the answers rather than what was written in them.

The first ten weeks of classes did little to kindle our interest in the ancient world. We realized that what the lecturers were telling us we could find out on our own, in half the time. Moreover, who could have wanted to hear about the Hittites, say, when there was a roomful of lovely provincial girls with freshly talcumed faces to look at? They would troop into the classroom, sit in the area reserved for them, listen to the lecture, and troop out, without our getting a clue to where they came from and where they went. Finally, I made eye contact with one of the girls, a plain-looking, heavenly creature with thick black eyebrows and a low forehead. Having repeated the contact over many days, and having noticed that her eyes lingered over me just as mine did over her, I plucked up courage and asked her for a book. It was the beginning of a romance. I started going over to her place, and as the months passed the visits became more frequent. She lived with her old parents in a large two-storey house that had countless small rooms, and as soon as she and I were inside one of them, we behaved as if her parents were not just old but also deaf, blind, and crippled. Amit would be kept informed of these developments. At home, after returning from the university, he and I would kick a ball around or play a game of badminton, and when it grew dark, stand near the boundary wall and talk into the evening, till one of Aunt Phyllis's servants came and said dinner was on the table or we heard the ayah call out to Amit. Reluctantly, we would leave the strip of forest that lay on either side of the wall and go into our lighted bungalows.

Though the BA Part I exams were not until the following summer, we had begun studying for them in all seriousness. Perhaps studying is the wrong word to describe what we did, for most of our time went in making 'notes'. This was true about history particularly. The history syllabus covered ancient India and the ancient world, and while books on ancient India were available in every shop and kiosk, and under every tree on University Road, those on the ancient world were hard to come by. Our familiarity with them did not go beyond knowing their authors' names, which, presumably, were British or American, and their resounding titles, such as *The Conquest of Civilization*. The handful of teachers and students who possessed copies scarcely wanted to lend them out, and if they did, it was only for a few days. So making notes in fact meant copying at high speed whole chapters in longhand, the drudgery made worse by the condition of the books, whose every page was heavily underlined in red pencil or royal blue ink, usually in both, and whose margins had 'Imp' scribbled in them. Since one person, however fast he copied, could not copy everything, Amit and I had decided to divide the work. He took responsibility for half the syllabus and I for the remaining half.

I spent the autumn vacation in October with my parents, taking the 3 Up Howrah–Bombay Mail out of Allahabad and reaching Bhilai twenty-eight hours later, after two changes. The Royal typewriter now went everywhere with me, and I was carrying it when I got down from the train. Though not intending to write any poems, I still wanted to have the machine around, just in case. In Bhilai I received two letters from Amit. 'Vinoo *dear* (I don't mean it),' the first letter began (Vinoo is my nickname), 'By God! What bloody notes! What notes? Egypt. Great. Burns, Breasted, Swain, Finger. And this bloody Egypt is worth at least two other civilizations, so please add one more civ to your list. Well, I'm not working too hard . . . I play three solid hours of squash every day.' Immediately after this he wrote, 'In ancient India I have completed religious movements of the sixth century BC. Will proceed further. What about you? Going solider than ever?'

In all his letters to me, Amit would have something to say about Peeks, as Piyush Kanta Verma was called. The three of us had known each other from the time we were in Boys' High School, where Peeks and I, aged nine and eight respectively, had fought for the hand of an elflike seven-year-old Anglo-Indian girl, June Cearns. I never saw him speak to his father, a high court judge, without first rising to attention, and Amit and I were convinced that he also sirred him. He later went into the civil service, to nobody's surprise. Peeks wasn't interested in literature and didn't write poetry. Nevertheless, he saw nothing wrong with those who did. Like us, he had spent the vacation transcribing books. 'Peeks is going very solid,' Amit wrote, and signed the letter 'Mulk Raj Anand (author of *Crows and Pigeons*)'.

After four days, on 13 October, he wrote me again. 'You don't really expect me to believe,' he said, referring to my economics course, 'that you have done only Indian population, do you? I have completed Egypt today. I move over to pre-history. Brother Peeks is going super-super-solid . . . By the way, I am glad you have given up heavy prose. Your poem is horrible—what about the other one?' Of the poem I have no recollection. Was it about adolescence in the unrestrained voice of adolescence? Or a piece of shamming, a pseudo-poem, a laboured imitation of an admired work? Or something composed in a frenzy, supernaturally inspired, as though dictated from above? But whatever it was, his letter when it came that day thirty years ago must have made me quite miserable.

Suddenly the neem trees looked very bare. Their scythe-shaped leaves fell in ones and twos, then in great masses, the wind scattering them all over the compound. The sweeper-woman, with her twig-broom, would go about collecting the leaves into small heaps, which she would burn. Then new shoots appeared overnight on the branches. The heat gradually intensified. We opened the skylights, but they only let in more hot air. The ceiling fans, even at top speed, rotated slowly. Whiskey, Aunt Phyllis's ancient Pomeranian bitch, repaired into a bathroom for most of the day. By the second week of April the beds were out and we were sleeping on the lawn, under mosquito nets. Dew had fallen, and inside the nets the white sheets were cool. Lines of camels passed, headed for the river, where they were loaded with watermelons. A pleasant breeze would blow, though not for long. The nights were getting shorter, and with sunrise, when the same camels made the return journey, the heat started building up again. By nine the roads would be deserted, and whoever ventured out saw mirages in the distance. We took salt tablets with breakfast to prevent sunstroke. It was the middle of summer and examination time.

The changing season saw us change too. If we still met near the boundary wall, it was to assess how well we were prepared for the exams, the thought of which made us rush back to our desks. We slept less, and at odd hours, and when awake had our eyes glued to books, continuing to read even at the dining table during meals. Quite apart from the hundreds of pages that had to be crammed, we had dates in history and quotations in English (Graham Hough and Maurice Bowra on the Romantics, A.C. Ward on Shaw) to commit to memory. And on top of this I had economics to cope with, a subject I felt remote from and should not have offered. We studied selectively of course, like everyone else. There were parts of the syllabus we left out and others we mugged up, depending on the 'guess papers' in each subject. To make a guess paper we scrutinized the previous ten years' questions, available in inexpensive booklets with flimsy pink or yellow covers, on University Road, and after taking into account the hints dropped by teachers and the gossip among students, and after listening to our own inner voices, we drew up a list of questions that were likely to be asked.

Peeks went a step further and enlisted divine help. He arrived on the morning of the first exam wearing a tilak on his forehead, and it looked as though he had come straight from a temple. Conveniently, the temple was located inside his house. It was like any other room, but furnished with the pictures of gods and goddesses instead of almirahs and beds, and the tilak was applied by his mother. It took only a minute, Peeks said, and could do no harm.

I was in Bhilai when the results were declared. There was a brief telegram from Uncle Kelly followed by a letter from Amit, giving details. The letter is undated, but was written in the first week of July 1965. 'And what a huge fake it is,' he wrote, 'that ancient history is more scoring than medieval history. We both did our papers very well, and yet you just get 100 [out of a maximum of 150 marks] and I 96. Peeks [who had medieval history] mucks up one question solid and generally has poorer preparation, and slogs 112!' The letter contains one more surprise, the marks of the girl with the thick black eyebrows and a low forehead. She got 122. Since that day I have mistrusted examination results and had a little more faith in the influencing power of framed oleographs.

In English and philosophy also, Amit's marks were less than what he expected. In the letter he sounded lonely and despondent, which was unusual for him, and asked me to return to Allahabad sooner than I would have normally. 'Vinoo, even though the university opens late, can't you come back early? I miss you a lot. Even Peeks is not here.' Greatly disappointed though we were with the results, we were too young, too alive, too disdaining of authority to let them affect us for long. At the same time, if unknown to ourselves, we were trusting and innocent, still very much the boys who stand first in class and on Annual Day walk away with all the school prizes. When the university reopened we resumed copying chapters out of textbooks. As resolutely as on ancient Egypt earlier, we now started making notes on Greece and Rome. We were in BA Part II.

The dual lives we led, of ambitious terrestrial students and rebellious subterranean poets, continued to run side by side and on the whole peacefully, one part of us concentrating on the campaigns of Alexander the Great, the Punic Wars, the rise of the Guptas, the significance of the opening scene in *Macbeth*, and the other reading the *Village Voice* and declaiming 'Underwear' ('Women's underwear holds things up/Men's underwear holds things down') and 'America' ('America when will you send your eggs to India') from *Penguin Modern Poets 5*. According to the date below my signature in the title page, I had bought the book in August 1965. That September we had brought out the first issue of *damn you*.

Even we realized that the magazine, if it was to continue, would need contributions from poets other than its editors. Our difficulty was that sitting in Hastings Road, Allahabad, we didn't know where to look for them. The English poets we were familiar with were the sort who have their monuments in Westminster Abbey, and it did not occur to us that we could ask Indian poets to contribute. This left the United

States, a country just fifty yards down the road, and at whose entrance stood not the famous statue but a bright red letter box nailed to a neem tree. Into it Amit dropped an aerogramme addressed to Vijay Chauhan in New York.

Vijay, or Chhote Bhaiya (Younger Brother) as everybody called him, was at the time studying international relations at Columbia University on a Fulbright. He was a short, compact man with large bulging eyes, a carefully trimmed beard, and a receding hairline. He wore blue jeans and T-shirts, smoked Charminar cigarettes, and liked his rum, which he poured out of a silver hip flask. He was a bachelor. At Sagar University, where he taught political science and directed contemporary American plays for an amateur group, he was seen by some as an oddball, whereas to others, his students mostly, he was a hero figure. He was certainly one to us. Amit's letter to him, written on 30 October, reads, in part:

> We are now getting down to the second issue of *dy* and are trying to increase its scope. You once said that there were some magazines in the Village whose contributors would have no objection to contributing to us also. But that is not the point of this letter. You also said you had the addresses of these magazines. But even that, if you ask me, is not the point of this letter. If you can, will you please send us the addresses of these people.

Early in November, just days after he posted the letter, Amit fell ill. He came out of philosophy class complaining of pain in his arms and went home. The pain persisted and a blood test was done, after which the doctor treating him suggested he be taken to Bombay where better diagnostic facilities were available. In a stream of letters he wrote from there, Amit sent us an almost day-by-day account of his illness. 'My disease is to be finally diagnosed on Tuesday,' he wrote to Peeks and myself on 17 November in one of his first letters. 'They took the live marrow from my bones to test and boy! did it pain. Ammi/Mama [his parents] are worried, but curiously, it did not matter to me much whether I had cancer or no. I am somewhat having the Kay Kendall feeling, the difference being that I know everything.' Seven months later, on 21 June 1966, in Bombay's Tata Memorial Hospital, three weeks after his eighteenth birthday, Amit died of leukaemia. His last letter, to Peeks, was written on 9 June:

Dear Piyush,

I have not written for so long because I was in no physical condition to write. I have recently been subject to very severe pains and have lived my last few days under morphia. I don't write this to get sympathy but to make a thoroughly silly sentimental confession. You remember in November (note the rhyme) I said cancer does not make any difference to me. Believe me I was sincere, but now I beg to withdraw the statement. Vinoo was here today and said *quote* grotesque rumours were going through Allahabad *unquote*. It was his unominous way of saying that people in Allahabad were already convinced that I was dead. Well I am not dead as yet and still I am not so frightfully keen to survive. No emotions involved, what I want is a decision one way or the other. 'One way' would be preferable, but 'the other' too is fine by me.

PEEKS! My muse is awake. First the first verse—

> remember
> in november

and then the singularly rhyming one—

> Amit Rai
> is going to die . . .
> I'll cry . . .
> I'll try . . .

O Brother! I'm still a poet after all.

There had in those seven months been a brief period of about eight weeks, from the end of February to the end of April, when Amit returned to Allahabad. Looking at him, one could hardly say anything was wrong. We laughed and talked as before, and he joked about all the phoney sympathetic letters he had received in Bombay. He stayed away from the university for the same reason, to avoid meeting people who would ask about his health. Some of them, since I was a friend of his, would come and ask me, and I would shrug them off, believing Amit had been cured. One way of shutting up these solicitous people, we thought, would be to bring out the second issue of *damn you*.

It appeared that March, without the Greenwich Village poets, but in a new A4 format. On the cover it said 'poems & sketches', and inside were contributions by the editors and their relatives and friends. There was a story, 'Lucky Horace', by Amit's cousin Sara, aged ten; an oil company slogan, 'I'll put a tiger in your tank', became the first line of a pastiche by Vijay Chauhan; and there were haiku-like verses and imitations of T.S. Eliot by the less philistine of our university friends. Amit had a poem on a family picnic ('my brother alone half-heartedly sings/yippi yippi yai'), and I contributed a reflection in poetic prose on the human condition. I had no sorrows to speak of, yet always wrote as though I had been stabbed through the heart. It played havoc with my grammar. Among the sketches, one showed a nude woman lying inside a bubble, and the acknowledgement below it said, 'Courtesy: Bugger'. It was meant to shock. The price of *damn you/2* was one rupee.

There were to be four more issues of the magazine before it ceased publication in 1968. The sixth issue listed in the back some of the little magazines and small presses that exchanged with us: BB Books, *Trace*, *University of Tampa Poetry Review*, *Wormwood Review*, *Elizabeth*, dustbooks, *Manhattan Review*, *open skull*, *El Corno Emplumado*, *Hyphid*, *Iconlatre*, Openings Press, Hors Commerce Press, *Camel's Coming*, *Beloit Poetry Journal*, *Loveletter*, *South Florida Poetry Journal*, *Outcast*, *Klactoveedsedsteen*, Broadside Press, Smyrna Press, *Poetry Australia*, *Poetry X/Change*, *Tornado*.

For years afterwards, university libraries abroad would write asking for back issues of *damn you* for their special collections, but our calf-time was behind us and their letters remained unanswered.

The Ozark Airlines plane that took my wife and myself from Chicago to Cedar Rapids, Iowa, was no bigger than a Greyhound bus and less comfortable. The flight was short, but that is not the only reason why for the first time in forty-eight hours I breathed a little more easily. *At least planes like this one don't crash*, I remember telling myself, and indeed the aircraft seemed to cover the distance without leaving the ground.

Coming inside the airport lounge, we were met by Elliott Anderson from the University of Iowa's International Writing Program. Not many passengers had got down at Cedar Rapids, so it wasn't difficult for him to identify us, two tired, nervous foreigners. We put our bags in his station wagon and sped off towards Iowa City. Night having fallen, we saw little of the landscape. What did I know that even if it had been daylight, there would still be little to see. Elliott brought us to an apartment building called the Mayflower, and said he'd be back after an hour to take us out for dinner. We went to a Chinese restaurant just outside Iowa City, in Coralville, and were joined there by the emigré Czech novelist Arnost Lustig and his wife Vera. The food was unfamiliar, but more than this, Coralville seemed to be an unreal sort of place. Too many red and green neon signs, too few people, almost no noise, and no permanent residents or buildings.

Next morning, my first morning in America, as I emerged from a bank at the corner of North Dubuque and Washington, I heard someone call out 'Vee-noo'. I froze on the sidewalk, and the same instant plunged down a shaft of time, passing certain gateposts, bungalows, armchairs, verandahs, treetops, as I fell. Then I saw Arnost. He was standing some twenty yards away, outside a drugstore, chuckling to himself. I remembered his asking me at dinner the previous evening if my friends in Allahabad addressed me by another name. By calling that name out now, he had only wished to make me feel at home. As I walked toward Arnost, Washington Street merged into Hastings Road, and there was a neem tree near where he stood. I wondered then if some of us can ever leave the places we've grown up in.

The Roys

We've rented a flat in Ghosh Buildings, Albert Road
And the Roys live across the street. Mr Roy,
General Merchant, dresses in white
Drill trousers, long-sleeved cotton shirts,
And looks like a friendly barn-owl.
His sons are in school with me. Ganesh,
The eldest, has a gleaming forehead,
A shelled-egg complexion, a small
Equilateral mouth; he belongs to a mystical
Group of philatelists. Together with Shaporjee,
The tallow-white Parsi next door, and Roger Dutt,
The school's aromatic geography teacher, he goes up
In a hot-air balloon and, on the leeward
Side of a Stanley Gibbons catalogue, comes down
Near a turret in Helvetia or Magyar,
Stamp-sized snowflake-like countries
Whose names dissolve like jujubes on my tongue.
We play french cricket, seven-tiles, I-spy, and Injuns.
Our tomahawks are butter knives, our crow
Feathers are real, and riding out from behind
Plaza Talkies we ambush the cowboys of Civil Lines.
Ganesh doesn't join our games. The future,
He seems to say, is not a doodle on the back
Of an envelope but a scarp to be climbed
Alone. He attends a WUS meeting in Stockholm
And opens a restaurant in the heart of town.
I go there in early youth for Jamaican coffee,
In early middle age to use its toilet.
Without getting up from the cash desk he shakes my hand,
'How's the English Department?' he asks, 'How's
Rajamani? Is Mishra a professor now? Is it true?
What are things coming to.' While I listen to him
My piss travels down the left trouser leg
Into my sock, and then my restless son drags me

Towards a shoe store and buys his first pair of
Naughty Boys. Seen from the road,
Mr Roy's shop is a P & O liner anchored in midstream.
Inside, it's an abandoned coal pit. A film
Of darkness wraps the merchandise; a section of the far
Wall conceals the mouth of a cave, leading
To an underground spring; the air, dry and silvery
At the entrance, is moist and sea-green, furry
To the touch; the display cases, embedded
In the floor, are stuffed with a galleon's treasure;
Finned toffees peer at customers through glass jars.
Every afternoon Mr Roy goes home for his
Siesta and Ramesh, his second son, still wearing
A crumbled school uniform, takes over the town's
Flagship. At 3 P.M. the roads melt, becoming
Impassable, and canvas-backed chicks
Protect shop-fronts against heatstroke.
For the next two hours the sun, stationed above
A traffic island, lays siege to the town, and the only
Movement is of leaves falling
So slowly that midway through their descent their colours
Change. The two waxen shop-assistants
Melt in their sticks, Ramesh sits beside
The cash box with an open sesame
Look in his eye, and I have the well
All to myself. Looking up its bejewelled
Shaft, I make out, in the small
Light coming in through the well-mouth,
Bottles of ketchup, flying cigarillos,
Death-feigning penknives, tooth powders, inexpensive
Dragon china dinner sets, sapphire-blue packets
Of detergent, wooden trays holding skeins
Of thread, jade-coloured boxes of hosiery, rolled-gold
Trinkets, mouth-watering dark tan shoe polish, creams,
And hula hoops. Driven by two ceiling fans,
The freighter moves. Land drops from sight.
Though binoculars are trained on the earth's dip,

The eye is monopolized by after-images of land:
I hold a negative against the light,
And now I'm received into the negative I'm holding.
At 5 P.M. the spell is broken. The sun
Calls it a day and goes down and Mr Roy comes
To clear away the jungle that has grown around his shop and I
Run out with a stolen packet of razor blades.
Where stealing's easy, hiding stolen goods is tough.
A pink stamp issued on Elizabeth's Coronation
Cannot be traced to a cigarette tin buried among
Clothes, but what do I do with an album that has
The owner's name rubber-stamped
All over it? I give lessons to five-year-old Suresh
In the pleasures of stealing.
For each first-day cover he brings, I press
My View-Master against his mongoloid eye
And let him look through it once. Then one day, while we're
Having lunch, I see a policeman framed in the door.
The food in my mouth hardens into a lump
Of plaster of Paris. Afterwards, I lose my voice
And so does everyone around me. Believe me when I say
That nothing's more sad than a tropical evening,
When auctioneers buy dead advocates' libraries
And there's all the time in the world and nowhere to go.
Anil, their cousin, takes out his autograph-book.
'Just in case,' he says, 'you become famous.'
He has said this to every boy in school.
'Do you think,' he asks me, 'I can get Peeks's
Grandfather's autograph?' Peeks's grandfather is a retired
Chief Justice and gets his pension in sterling.
Anil squints at a marble
In the hollow of his palm
But can't make out if it's an oblong. His sister, hairy
As a sloth bear, sits in the verandah, absorbed
In our game. Her mind, too, is half her age.
Through broken tiles in the roof
Sunbeams let themselves down and she screams

Before they strike her. She vanishes
Inside a blackbeetle and crawls on my skin;
I smell the bouquet of my spittled thumb
And it works like hartshorn. Charlie Hyde, nicknamed
Bony Arse, is the only other person
To so affect me. We go our different ways and sometimes
We cross Albert Road together or meet outside
A chemist's. Anil has a tabletop head and bulging
Irisless eyes. He nods; I nod. It's like watching
From a distance two men one doesn't know
Recognize each other. Anil sets himself up
As a dealer in office equipment
And then as a distributor for Number Ten cigarettes.
He fails at both jobs and is given shock therapy.

PANKAJ MISHRA

Pankaj Mishra (1969–) grew up in the small towns of north India and was educated at Allahabad University and Jawaharlal Nehru University, Delhi. In a personal communication he says, 'I was at Sir Sunder Lal Hostel [Allahabad University] from 1985 to 1988. Exactly three years, but they felt longer.' He has written about Allahabad both in *The Romantics* (2000) and *An End to Suffering: The Buddha in the World* (2004).

∾

from *An End to Suffering* (2004)

In 1985, when I first visited Lumbini, the birthplace of the Buddha, I was a sixteen-year-old student in Allahabad. I hadn't imagined the birthplace of the Buddha to be a real, accessible place until Vinod, a fellow student at Allahabad University, told me about it; and although Vinod got the whole trip going with an invitation to his ancestral house, which was not far from the Indian border with Nepal, he wasn't much interested in visiting Lumbini, which he had already seen and had found very drab.

He, like me, wanted to go to Nepal because it was the only foreign country we hoped to visit. There were other students in Allahabad who went on tours to southern Nepal—tours that were more like sorties since after two days and nights of ramshackle country buses and cockroach-infested 'guest houses', you never really got much beyond the border. The mountains remained on the distant horizon; and most people returned trying to suppress the disappointment of having found Nepal as flat and dusty as the part of north India they themselves lived in.

Nevertheless, the visit to Nepal retained its glamour. The richer students bought themselves Chinese-made Walkmans; and almost all of us who managed to go returned from the trinket-selling shacks at the border with at least one garishly printed baseball cap which we wore gratefully for a year or two, trying to overcome, but more likely setting off, the shabbiness of our terylene pants and shirts.

Vinod might not have been much interested in the baseball cap. It wouldn't have gone well with the embroidered Benares-silk kurtas and tight churidars he usually wore; it would have added an unnecessary frivolity to his serene good looks, to the slightly hooded eyes under the broad forehead that seemed to meet the world with gentle scepticism. Compared to the general run of students at the university—people from impoverished rural or semi-urban families in the Indo-Gangetic Plain— he seemed well off. He was, I had heard, the only son of a rich landlord. He lived in a three-room house outside the campus while most of us lived—two or sometimes three to a room—in one of the dingy university hostels.

Most of us hired bicycles at 75 paise an hour to move around the city while Vinod had a rickshaw waiting outside his house at all times of day and night, along with a driver, a low-caste boy in his early teens, who seemed to pedal with extra vigour when he brought prostitutes to Vinod's house, twisting and turning through the potholed alleys with such abandon that it was hard to distinguish the ringing of his bells from the jangling of the heavy silver bangles and anklets worn by the very young women he carried.

Vinod, who was much older than I, had a fully realized personal style—or so it seemed to someone as timid and inexperienced as myself, who had freshly emerged from a constricted life at home. I remember that I would visit him in the afternoons so as to catch a glimpse of the women. Often, the boy resting on the rickshaw would stop me from going upstairs, and I would hang around the dusty deserted alley, the solemn tones of All-India Radio newsreaders leaking out of the shuttered windows, until the woman had emerged from the narrow staircase, freshly and clumsily lipsticked, blinking in the harsh sun.

All the forbidden deliciousness of sex lay in Vinod's dark bedroom when I went upstairs. It was present in the mixed smell of sandalwood incense and cheap lipstick, on his dimpled bed, the discarded strings of jasmine flowers, which were already wilting as Vinod, still in his sleeveless vest, his handsome face perfectly composed, leaned over a small table and cut a guava into thin little slices.

'*Aaiye-ji, aaiye-ji*, come in, come in,' he would say, the '*ji*' always an unaffected part of his courtesy. '*Paan layngay na, aap*? You will have some paan, no?' I rarely had any paan and did not much like chewing either the betel leaf or the tobacco. The first couple of times I had met him had been at a paan stall near the university, and he never lost the notion that I was an addict. He would walk up to the window, open it, and then instead of shouting for attention—for the boy below never seemed to take his eyes off the window—calmly place his order. Closing the window—the room made enigmatic again after the moment of drab light—he would turn to me and ask, 'What are you reading today?'

He himself was a fanatical reader. Like many students wishing to demonstrate a modern outlook and intellectual maturity, he possessed the Hindi translations of Sartre and Camus. But much of the shelf space in the rooms was taken up by the lectures of 'Osho' Rajneesh, the international guru of the 1970s and 1980s, who exalted both sex and meditation, and whom Vinod thought of, he once told me, as a great philosopher. There were books by J. Krishnamurti and several pamphlets by Swami Vivekananda, the nineteenth-century monk and thinker, who in 1893 had introduced Hinduism to the West at the World Parliament of Religions in Chicago.

He also had different books on the various systems of Indian philosophy. But they had more to do with his course work as a postgraduate student, which he neglected, staying away from classes and living, from what I could see, a life of willed leisure: he read in the mornings; the women in the afternoons were followed by long sessions of body-building at an *akhara*; the women sometimes returned at night, with the boy driving more cautiously, and the rickshaw hood up.

The question about my reading was how he attempted to respond to my fascinated interest in him. Otherwise, he asked me few questions about myself. He seemed self-contained, fully consumed by the present moment, and with none of the anxiety with which the rest of us—poor students with uncertain prospects—darkened the future.

I tried to escape my own insecurity through obsessive reading. But very little of what I wished to read—literary fiction and criticism, poetry, history, western philosophy—was easily available in Allahabad. The old, wood-panelled bookstores near the campus mostly stocked *kunjis*, pamphlet-sized 'study guides' aimed at students wanting to dispense altogether with their textbooks. Nothing expressed the city's decay as vividly as the Allahabad University library, whose contents, supervised by idle and obstructive babus, were a mystery to students and, as I learnt later, teachers alike.

I often travelled to the British Council library in Lucknow. I couldn't afford to buy a train ticket; and so, on the early morning Ganga–Gomti Express, I kept four or five steps behind the ticket conductor as he shuffled sleepily through the coaches. I spent an exhilarating day at the library, reading the *TLS*, *The Spectator*, the *New Statesman*, and whatever else I could find. Returning late in the evening to Allahabad, I was seized by melancholy again as the train clattered across the bridge over the Ganges to the deserted railway station at Prayag.

On long, empty afternoons in Allahabad, I cycled down the broad avenues of Civil Lines—past the extravagantly marbled Hanuman temple, which Vinod visited every Tuesday, and where I often stopped on summer days to drink sugar-cane juice and to feel the cool stone against my feet—to the A.H. Wheeler's bookstore in Civil Lines. There, among dusty and often poorly lit but remarkably well-stocked shelves, I browsed for an hour or so under the benign if watchful gaze of an elderly man in a dhoti. Occasionally, after I had skipped a few meals at my hostel mess, I had enough money to buy one of the Penguin Modern Classics with grey spines I had handled longingly for months.

It was how I came to read Thomas Mann (*The Magic Mountain*, *Buddenbrooks*, *Death in Venice* and *Selected Letters*)—and then, as though tracing Mann's own intellectual trajectory, Schopenhauer and Nietzsche.

I wasn't aware then of Nietzsche's reputation as an adolescent favourite in Europe and America—indeed, few students around me at the university in Allahabad would have known who Nietzsche was. I found his short aphorisms about art, death and boredom easier to grasp than the elaborately conceived attacks on Socrates, Christianity and Kant, or his frequent if cautious praise of the Buddha.

I was held by the inner drama he frequently confessed to—the loneliness, the urge for self-knowledge and self-overcoming—the drama that culminated in his mental collapse twelve years before his death. One statement particularly stood out. He had written it one bright winter in Genoa, after a period of pain and sickness: 'No, life had not disappointed me. Rather, I find it truer, more desirable and mysterious every year—ever since the day the great liberator overcame me: the thought that life could be an experiment for the knowledge-seeker.' Vinod asked me often about him. He had become curious after reading about him in a book by the self-styled God, 'Osho' Rajneesh. He was much taken by an aphorism I once read out to him. 'Life,' Nietzsche had written, 'is essentially appropriation, injury, overpowering of what is alien and weaker; suppression, hardness, imposition of one's own forms, incorporation, at least, at its mildest, exploitation.' Vinod immediately copied the lines down in a small notebook he carried in the pocket of his kurta. But when he asked me to explain more about Nietzsche's philosophy, I floundered. I was too ashamed to tell him that I didn't understand most of what I read in Nietzsche, or that I had the greatest trouble with the word he appeared to use most often: nihilism.

Nietzsche often implied that a belief in historical progress and modern science—articles of faith for me, and for educated Indians like myself—was a form of nihilism. This was as puzzling as the character Bazarov in Turgenev's novel *Fathers and Sons*, who was defined as a nihilist not despite but because of his belief in progress and science.

More than what he wrote about, it was the image Nietzsche presented—the solitary thinker, struggling with what Thomas Mann in *Death in Venice* had described as the 'tasks imposed upon him by his own ego and the European soul'—that was initially attractive. He was part of my high idea of Europe and the West in general—the idea which Vinod also had, and from which he drew his conclusions about the role of people like the Buddha and Gandhi in India.

Years later, while I was living in London, this romantic image of Nietzsche began to dissolve. I knew more about Europe's nineteenth century: how it had shaped much of the world, and thus my own circumstances. The physical and emotional landscape Nietzsche had moved through became more vivid. I began to see what he had meant when he compared his position in modern times to the Buddha's in classical India: how both of them had lived at a time of tumultuous change, and confronted, in different ways, the phenomenon of nihilism.

The significance of what Vinod said to me—on the roof of his parents' house on the evening we returned to India from Lumbini—also came back to me. It was his own experience of nihilism, which I was too young to understand then, but which stayed in my memory for a long time afterwards.

On the way back from Lumbini, our bus had broken down, and we had to wait for a couple of hours before being rescued by a passing truck. It was not until late the next morning that we reached the town where the smuggled goods from China were sold. There, I bought a red baseball cap while Vinod looked on slightly mockingly. We then travelled to the border, from where another bus took us deeper into India, on increasingly narrow and broken country roads. It stopped just where late monsoon rains had washed away a bridge over what was usually a narrow river. An improvised ferry took us across the brown silt-laden waters of the river. A tonga stood on the other side.

It had rained early that afternoon. The thatch-roofed huts of the villages looked battered; the ponds under the clump of mango trees were full and muddy, and deceptively shallow pools had gathered on the ruts and potholes of the road, in which the tonga's large wheels plunged with a terrible crunching sound. The driver cracked his whip then, and the horse swayed angrily to one side, and swished his tail, spraying us with water.

The few pedestrians walked very slowly, prodding the ground with large tattered black umbrellas, carefully raising their dhotis with one hand. Naked children floated paper boats in the larger potholes on the road; mud draped their brown legs as cleanly as breeches. They looked appraisingly at us as we approached—in what was in those parts a rich man's vehicle—and their furtive eyes seemed fearful as we drew close.

The power had failed and lamps were being lit at Vinod's house when the tonga finally drew up outside it. I dimly saw the outline of a rectangular double-storeyed white-painted building with a flat roof, standing in the middle of a large treeless compound.

Vinod shouted a few names into the darkness, and servants—silent white-clothed apparitions—abruptly emerged to take our bags. In the first room we entered, a man sat on a low wicker chair, his long thin shadow splayed across the wall by the lantern kept next to him. He got up as soon as he saw Vinod.

Vinod's father was tall, with an unexpected shock of white hair and lined face that suggested a great and tormented old age, although he couldn't have been more than fifty. The gesture he made towards his son was one of respect and deference. Vinod made as if to touch his feet, but then walked past without saying anything. I had taken off my new cap as soon as I saw Vinod's father. I now followed Vinod somewhat embarrassedly, past his father and into the inner courtyard.

Tiny candles fluttered bravely on the parapet of a well, outlining a large tulsi plant and making the abraded plaster on the whitewashed walls of the house look like a gigantic scab. Each room opening out into the courtyard seemed to contain its own small glow and flickering shadows. In the room I was shown to—bare except for a string cot with a rolled up mattress—a candle rested along with incense sticks on a rack under the framed and garlanded picture of a young woman. The garland was of plastic; the light under the photo exposed the dusty cracks in the flowers. The beauty of the dead woman, her large liquid eyes and full lips, seemed to dominate the room.

The woman was Vinod's sister. He had a smaller framed photo of her hanging in his room in Allahabad. I had noticed that Vinod kept it face down on a table while he was with a prostitute. I had once asked him about her, and Vinod had seemed not to have had heard my question. It was too obviously something he did not want to talk about.

Vinod and I bathed in the open courtyard, next to the well from which a servant drew pails of cold refreshing water. Vinod's father came out and watched us as we dried ourselves, with an expression of tender solicitude on his face. Here, too, Vinod barely acknowledged his presence.

We later ate in the long narrow kitchen, sitting on low stools on the stone floor. In the far corner, an old man turned rotis over a wood fire, his brown skin glistening with perspiration. Vinod's mother sat before us, in a posture suggesting both resignation and ease, one hand supporting her head and the other slowly twirling a coir fan. She asked us questions about our journey, about life in Allahabad. Vinod barely said a word. I found myself replying to her, slightly disconcerted by her resemblance to her dead daughter.

Later, we went up to the roof. The clouds had vanished, and the night sky glittered indifferently over us. Strange noises kept erupting in the undergrowth, dogs howled in the far distance, and then it was quiet and the only sound was of the water dripping off the roof to the wet ground.

I felt a shiver of loneliness, and in that feeling was blended the strangeness of the evening in the large gloomy house in the middle of nowhere, the doting parents and their silent son. And, perhaps, it was the setting and mood it engendered that made me ask Vinod what I wouldn't have dared to ask at any other time about the woman whose photo hung in my room.

He was silent. And then when he began to speak, he didn't stop, and spoke much more frankly than he ever had. He didn't wait for my response, but I don't think I could have said much anyway.

He said, 'I know you have asked me this before. What can I tell you about that photo? It is of Nirmala, my sister who was married to a businessman in Bombay. She was harassed by her in-laws and husband for not bringing sufficient dowry, although my parents had given them a car, several hundred thousand rupees in cash, and then one day, a year after her marriage, they poured kerosene over her and burnt her alive. There was a police case, but the in-laws claimed that she had committed suicide. They bribed the coroner. Her husband remarried.

'But I don't want to shock or upset you. That's why I didn't tell you before. And also because I came to feel that there is nothing shocking about her murder. It happens every day. It is part of our world. And there is nothing we can do about it.

'I have many friends in Allahabad who ask me the same question about the photo. I have never brought them here. I know they will ask me the same question and I know that they won't understand why we couldn't do anything either to save her life or to punish the husband. Some of them think it is a question of family honour, which you can settle with a gun. But this is primitive feudal thinking, which brought us to this pass in the first place.

'Perhaps you will understand what I mean. You will understand what I mean when I say that all of us are born with certain advantages and disadvantages, and then it's up to you to make something of them. I didn't lack much where I was born. You see this land, this house that my forefathers built. For you who have seen other places, big cities like Delhi, it may seem nothing, but for people here, these things mean wealth and achievement. You saw how people looked at us when we were travelling on the tonga. They knew who I was, who my father was. This is the kind of reputation my family has had.

'When I was growing up, I took our power for granted. I went to school in a nearby village. The master used to take his class under a big pipal tree; we used to sit before him on the ground with our chalk and slates. He used to beat the other students with a *beshram* stick at the slightest provocation, but he was always sycophantic towards me, always trying to please me. The tehsildar brought boxes of sweets to the house on Diwali and Holi. The local MP and MLA came asking for money during elections and touched my father's feet. The peasants in the field trembled at my father's approach. My uncle kidnapped the daughters and sisters of his farm workers and raped them. He murdered two low-caste peasants who had dared to attack his friend, an upper-caste landlord. The police registered a case, the people in the murdered men's village went to Lucknow to complain to the chief minister of Uttar Pradesh, but no one could do anything.

'Times may change fast in the cities, but life in these parts stays more or less the same. Even today the position of my father is unchanged. The local MP and MLA still pay him tribute; ask him for donations and votes. I could have stayed here and inherited all this power. I know people in this region who have built upon their fathers' position, who are now in politics, in crime, who are running big smuggler mafias. But for little accidents of fate, I too could have stayed here, lived that kind of life, picked up the pretty girls in the fields and raped them.

'I think it was my cousins from the big town who first gave me a sense of where I was. They used to come during school summer holidays from Gorakhpur. They used to love doing all the things that bored me: swimming in the nearby canal on warm evenings, throwing stones at the mango and tamarind trees in the morning when it wasn't very hot.

'But they also had things I envied. They wore readymade clothes and bought shoes from the Bata shop instead of having them stitched by the local *mochi*. All we had by way of entertainment was a radio, but they went to the cinema once a month and spoke intimately of heroes and heroines I knew only by name. I wanted to be like them. I think it was during those holidays when I began to think of the world outside and grow dissatisfied with the place I had grown up in.

'What did I see when I looked around? I saw all this land and the workers on it, the servants, and my family's authority that had been maintained for decades for no other reason than that no one had challenged it. I left this compound and what did I see? I saw those half-naked boys and those wretched huts we saw on our way in. I went inside those huts and they were crammed with children that no one knows what to do with. There is not much to eat, so they die fast, but more are born each week.

'There is no one to tell their parents what to do. There is a family planning centre not far from here but it is closed for much of the month. The man in charge of the centre collects his salary and pays a commission to his boss, and no one says anything. So the poor go on reproducing and suffer malnutrition and disease, and then if they manage to grow up, they suffer cruelty and injustice.

'This is not what they taught me at school. This is what I learnt to see later. I saw that I went to school but my sister had stayed at home, and learnt to cook in that little kitchen we ate in. A pandit had taught her to read the Hindi alphabet and that was all she could do. She had girlfriends in a nearby village who knew no more than she did. She grew up a simple girl, with no knowledge of anything outside her home, and then one day her marriage was arranged into a family in Bombay who said that they were looking for exactly that: a simple girl from a village. My parents were flattered by their attention. They were high-caste people like us, rich, living in a big city, and respected within the community. My parents had no idea of the people they were marrying their daughter to. They had no idea because they had let themselves remain simple, they had trusted in obsolete things like God and society and morality. They barely knew what was going on in their own world.

'I would have been like them if I hadn't realized that this life of farming wasn't for me. I didn't want to grow up like my uncle. I saw how people my age could go and rape some low-caste woman in the fields and think nothing of it. I don't know where the feeling came over me but suddenly I didn't want to be like them. I wanted to go to a city and study there.

'As I say I don't know where I got these ambitions. My father certainly didn't understand them. He wanted me to do what he and his brother did. He wanted me to take over the running of the estate. He was getting too old. He wanted to retire and devote his life to religion. He couldn't understand why I even wanted to finish my schooling. One day he saw the schoolmaster and asked him why he had put strange ideas in my head. The schoolmaster got so scared that he told my father that he would have been ready to confine me to the same class for a few years on his instructions and that would have killed my desires for further education. But when I insisted my father finally sent me to the nearest high school, which is in a *kasba* called Mehmoodganj. It wasn't much of a school. The teachers rarely turned up, and then often dismissed the class because so few students had come. On examination days they helped the students cheat.

'How can you learn anything in these conditions? I didn't and I began to try to persuade my father to send me to Allahabad. I had heard so much about it from one of my cousins, about the grand buildings the British had created. I remember how impressed I was by the university when I went to get admission there. I saw that they were indeed palaces, with domes and towers.

'But perhaps they were fit for only kings to live in; they weren't for students. And not such students as you found in Allahabad: boys from poor families whose fathers were breaking the bank to give them higher education so that they can get a degree and be eligible for a job somewhere with the government. I went with such high expectations but it was the same story at the university: teachers not showing up for classes, the exams being delayed for months, sometimes years.

'Criminals roamed the campus with guns and homemade bombs. Some of these were boys who came from my own district. I tried to do what I could. I read on my own and took private classes from the same teachers who did not show up for classes at the university. I was very privileged. You have seen my house. How big it is. But these privileges didn't help. What can you do if you haven't got a decent basic education? I found myself working very hard, but I felt unmotivated. I asked myself: What was I working so hard for? The British had created universities like Allahabad so that they could get educated Indians to help them exploit this country. And now people went there so that they could get a job with the govermnent, become part of the elite class, and plunder the country just as the British used to. I didn't want to work for the government. I wasn't interested in making money. I hoped I could do something else.

'I had also started reading other books. These weren't things I had ever found in Gorakhpur where the bookshops had cloth editions of the

Mahabharata and the Ramayana. Nothing I had read had told me about my own world. In Allahabad, I discovered Osho Rajneesh, I read Swami Vivekananda. These philosophers taught me to think, to see things in a new way. I felt on my way to some kind of personal liberation.

'I began to see how much of what I had grown up with and come to accept as common sense was ignorant prejudice. For instance, our society had arranged things that you could not satisfy your sexual urge outside marriage. The sexual repression in our society kills so many sensitive and intelligent people; that is also why you have so much rape and violence against women. I think from Osho I gained at least the knowledge that sex is a natural thing and nothing to be ashamed of.

'Swami Vivekananda taught me to see that our society has grown corrupt and feeble, how it had lost its manhood. Of course this wasn't just something I got out of books. You can see it in the world around you. The peasants breed mindlessly, live in poverty and disease, and then die as ignorant and trampled-upon as ever. The shopkeeper adulterates the food and oil he sells. The policeman wants a bribe before he can register your report, and will implicate you falsely for the sake of money. The student is not interested in education; he only wants a degree. The teacher will supply it to him at a price. And he will become a govermnent official. What will he do then? Go to the civil hospital. Go to the district collector's office. The men working there collect their salaries, like the family-planning man, and they extort money from the poor people who come to them for help. They have lost all idea of what they are supposed to do.

'It is people like Gautama Buddha and Gandhi who have misled us. They have taught us to be passive and resigned. They have told us of the virtuous life; they have told us to deny ourselves in order to be content. But they haven't told us how to live in the real world—the world that grows bigger and bigger and more complex all the time. This is why Vivekananda is important. He could see why the old habits of fatalism and resignation—the habits of village people—wouldn't work anymore. He saw that they had made us the slaves of the Muslims and then the British, why these people coming from outside could rule over India for so long. He was totally unsentimental, and he was brutally frank. He told us that we were sunk in *Tamas*, darkness. There was no point in trumpeting our spiritual success, our philosophical wisdom. All that is past. It was meant for primitive people. This was now the age of big nations. India was one such nation but it was way behind Europe and America. The West had technology, it had mastered nature, it had exploded nuclear bombs, it had sent people to the moon. When someone asked Gandhi what he thought of Western civilization, he made a joke. He said that Western civilization would be a good idea. But Vivekananda knew that the West had much to teach us. The first lesson was that we have to be materialists first. We have to learn to love wealth and comfort; we have to grow strong, know how to take pleasure in things, and recognize that there is no virtue in poverty and weakness. We have to know real manhood first. Spirituality comes later, or not at all. Perhaps we don't need it.

'I wish I had known this before. I could have avoided much confusion and pain. I could have seen the hollowness of the life and the value I had known. Perhaps, it is not too late to make something of myself. I fear sometimes that I will have to make my peace with what I had. But if I can't go forward, I can't go back either. I can't unlearn anything I have learnt. And now with these different ideas I have, the new vision of things, I find it very hard to come back home and find the same old complacency. The fields are still ours, the peasants still work on them, the servants haven't left, the house still stands. But people don't even know where they are in the larger scheme of things. They have no future. They need to change but don't know how. The world has moved on. People have gone to the moon, they are conquering space and time, they are living in the nuclear age. We are stuck in our old ways. You saw my father and mother. You must have wondered about my silence before my parents. But I find it too hard to say anything to them, and then I feel ashamed of the impatience and contempt they provoke inside me. They have spent the last five years mourning my sister, and will mourn her until the day they die. But she is not going to come back to life, and for me the worst thing is that they don't, they can't, even see what killed her. They have no idea of the world outside their little fiefdom here. In Allahabad, I took a course in Western philosophy and the first thing I learned was about Plato's cave. I thought then that my parents were like the people in Plato's cave who watch shadows and images on the walls and imagine that there is a clear sky and sun outside the cave and the shadows they see are reflections of the realm of eternally true laws and ideas. They think that there are rules out there, some kind of divine morality, governing life and society. But they are mistaken. And perhaps this is what I discovered for myself. There is no clear sky and sun out there, no great ideals or values to appeal to. You have to live in the dark cave and there are no rules there except those that strong men make for themselves and enforce upon others.'

It was in this mood Vinod spoke again about Gandhi and the Buddha: as luxuries India could not afford. It was why, he said, he had not been interested in visiting Lumbini. He said that he had been once to Kushinagara, the town where the Buddha is said to have died. He had seen a huge brick mound over the supposed site of his death. There were people worshipping there—people from South-east Asia and Western countries, but not, as far as he could see, from India. He thought it fitting that the affluent countries should rediscover the men whose ideas of self-denial and passivity were no longer relevant in India and make them their own.

I listened, but didn't feel I had much to add. What I knew of Gandhi and the Buddha resonated as little with me as with Vinod. It was hard to see, while living in Allahabad, much virtue in poverty and weakness. Perhaps, Vivekananda's ideas could better illuminate our peculiar circumstances and show a way out of them. But I didn't know enough about him to speak confidently.

We left the next morning for Allahabad. I had expected Vinod to stay a little longer. But he was in a hurry to leave. He was already dressed and packed and had ordered the tonga when he woke me up. I came out of my room to see him watching his mother praying before the tulsi plant in the sun-drenched courtyard. He said nothing to her, only touched her feet as she pulled the edge of her sari back from her head, and then before she could even ask where he was going, he turned his back upon her and walked out of the courtyard.

I followed him after a swift embarrassed *namaste* in his mother's direction. I passed his father sitting where I had first seen him the previous evening, in the room that was still dark and gloomy, although the light outside was dazzling. He came out, walking slowly with his stick, and then as the tonga lurched off, he stood there for what seemed like a long time, a small diminishing figure against the white house.

The autumn sun was warm. The bare-bodied men in the stripped-down rice fields looked exposed; and the pipal trees with their ample spread and shade stood even more self-assuredly in the vast flatness. It was the same landscape we had passed through before. But the twilight and the rain of the previous evening had given it a gentle aspect. In the bold exposing sunshine it was touched by what Vinod had told me. Poverty and disease and neglect seemed to mark the low huts with the bare front yards where low-caste peasant women in colourful saris sat slapping together cow-dung patties, and children who had been playing with paper boats the previous day looked underfed and malnourished with their rust-coloured hair and protruding, hard bellies.

Vinod sat next to me on the tonga and then the bus. But he didn't speak much during the rest of the journey back to Allahabad. We met again several times. I went to his flat and found myself staring at the photo of his sister. We talked about Vivekananda; he gave me pamphlets and booklets to read on the subject of India's regeneration. But we never talked about that evening.

At the end of three years, I left Allahabad, and moved to Delhi. I heard intermittently about Vinod. He had become a lawyer; he had married; he had become a social worker; he had become very devout. It didn't surprise me much when I heard that he had become a politician and joined the Hindu nationalists who were then rising to power on a wave of anti-Muslim violence all across north India and would soon form the federal government in New Delhi.

It was many more years later that I began to see differently the thoughts he had expressed that evening, and I realized that the certainties he longed for could have been supplied to him only by a radical political ideology.

I realized, too, that no one had ever spoken more directly to me of my own situation than he had that evening on the roof of his house. There were the obvious similarities in our circumstances: I had no difficulty in recognizing the picture of the colonial-age university, the sense of futility and doom the students lived with. But I had also heard for the first time a description of my own young life—of growing up bewildered and ignorant and frightened.

KAMA MACLEAN

Kama Maclean (1968–) was born in Sydney, Australia. She has a degree in Hindi and politics from La Trobe University, and completed a PhD on the history of the Allahabad Kumbh Mela in 2003. She currently teaches South Asian and World History at the University of New South Wales. 'On the Modern Kumbh Mela' is a modified excerpt from her article, 'Making the Colonial State Work for You: the Modern Beginnings of the Ancient Kumbh Mela in Allahabad', originally published in the *Journal of Asian Studies*, Vol. 62, no. 3 (August 2003). Her book *Power and Pilgrimage: The Allahabad Kumbh Mela* is forthcoming.

∾

On the Modern Kumbh Mela

At the height of the Kumbh Mela, in late January 2001, *India Today* breathlessly reported that

> In Prayag, Allahabad for modern India, it's the biggest show on earth, conceived by Hinduism's antique memory, conscripted by mythology, history and tradition, and enacted by keepers of wisdom and seekers of moksha. It's the costume drama of nirvana and the passion-play of the East and the naked dance of asceticism and the hara-hara delirium of the hippie and the raw picturesque of pure faith rolled into one oversized panorama of India in its divine diversity—even in the digital age.

Of course, this conception of the Kumbh is not exclusive to *India Today*. It is broadly believed that the Allahabad Kumbh Mela is an ancient religious festival, or that it is 'ageless', that its roots lie obscured in 'time immemorial'. Editorials and articles in the press at mela time lyrically emphasize the continuity of the pilgrimage throughout India's past, find inspiration in its durability and apparently changeless character, and marvel at the anachronism of an ancient festival, thriving in the modern world. There is no better example of this than the oft-quoted section of Jawaharlal Nehru's will and testament, in which the avowedly secular modernist explains his desire to have a portion of his ashes scattered at the triveni sangam, the confluence of the Ganga and Yamuna rivers, the site of the Kumbh in Allahabad:

> I have had an attachment for the Ganga and Yamuna ever since my childhood, and as I get older this connection strengthens. [. . .] The Ganga is a symbol of India's age-long culture and civilization, changeless, always flowing, but always the Ganga. [. . .] Of course, I have abandoned the old-fashioned traditions, and I want to break the chains which constrain India and oppress innumerable people and which prevent the development of their minds and bodies. But even though I want all of these things, I cannot completely separate myself from these old traditions. It is a great source of pride to me that this magnificent succession of heritage is ours, and will always be uniquely ours, and I know very well that I, like all of us, am a part of this chain, which will never, ever be broken, because this chain has gone on since the beginning of India's eternal history. I could never break this chain, because I see such unbounded worth in it, and it gives me inspiration, courage and spirit.

This passage eulogizing the triveni has been reproduced in many Kumbh Mela-related publications; Nehru's affection for the site is powerful, especially because it is so palpably at odds with his political being. In Nehru's articulation, modernity struggles with tradition, and in the opposition between what Dipesh Chakrabarty has called 'the rational and the affective', it is surprising to find the secular Nehru we presume to know so well succumbing to the emotion inspired by 'this chain that has gone on since the beginning of India's eternal history'.

Such is the attraction and impact of the timelessness that is popularly attributed to the Kumbh Mela. Yet while the agelessness of the Kumbh is an important component in the way pilgrims perceive it, its actual historiography, generally speaking, is not. As one writer puts it, 'the historical origin of the Kumbh Mela is an open and indeed almost uninvestigated question'.[1] It is not entirely remarkable that the history of the mela has not been investigated—with reference to Eliade, J.E. Llewellyn points out that 'people seek in the sacred something

---

[1] Sax, William. 'Kumbh Mela'. *Encyclopaedia of Religion*. Ed. Mircea Eliade. New York: Macmillan, 1987, p. 402.

transcending history, beyond profane duration'.[2] Yet clearly the history of the mela *is* important, for the ways in which the mela is remembered and interpreted rely upon an abstract notion of time and history as inferred in the phrase, so often used to describe the mela's continuity 'from time immemorial' (*pracheen kaal se*). The agelessness of the mela, in combination with its enchanted Puranic origins and related stories— such as the presence of the unseen Saraswati river, which converges with the Ganga and Yamuna to form the three braids of the famed triveni— combine to inform pilgrims of the festival's sanctity.

While scholars have been suggesting that the Kumbh Mela in Allahabad is no older than the seventeenth century or eighteenth century, there has been no further attempt to pinpoint a precise date and manner in which the festival began.[3] This article therefore attempts to isolate the genesis, or at least the beginning of the popularization, of the Kumbh Mela in Allahabad. It is argued here that the Kumbh Mela was applied to Allahabad's existing Magh Mela in the 1860s by Prayagwals—river *panda*s of Prayag—working upon and within the limits imposed by the colonial state and its discourses. This process was inadvertently aided by the British, and the resulting mela was affirmed by sadhus and pilgrims. The 'ageless' Kumbh Mela in Allahabad was therefore made by a combination of actors, responding to the aggrandizement and growth of the modern state, particularly its infrastructure, administration and preference for well-controlled, predictable, orderly and 'traditional' manifestations of religion. In this sense, the making of the Allahabad Kumbh is not merely another example of an 'invented tradition'; indeed, had it been suspected that it was 'invented' in any sense, it would not have been accommodated by the British to the extent it was. The Kumbh in Allahabad offers a complex illustration of how Indian actors, working with and reacting to British Orientalist assumptions, cast a major cultural and religious event. In carefully constructing a 'religious festival', they created for

---

[2]Llewellyn, J.E., 'Kumbh Mela: Festival of Discord', 1999, Unpublished MS., p. 7, courtesy of the author; also, Eliade, Mircea, *The Myth of Eternal Return, Or, Cosmos and History*, Princeton: Princeton University Press, 1954.

[3]Krasa, M., 'Kumbh Mela: the Greatest Pilgrimage in the World', *New Orient*, Vol. 6, 1965, p. 180.

themselves a sphere in which they could enjoy some autonomy in the atmosphere of an increasingly repressive colonial state, whose post-Mutiny promises of freedom were in many ways hollow. By couching the modern Kumbh Mela in terms of an ancient tradition with a well-known past, Prayagwals ensured that it was not vulnerable to the intervention of the state, which had demonstrated its preference for tradition over innovation. The ongoing strength and dynamism of the Kumbh Mela in Allahabad is an example of how Orientalist ideas 'were adapted and applied in ways unforeseen by those who initiated them',[4] as colonial conceptions of Hindu religion, holy men and pilgrims emanating from modes of British administration were appropriated by Indian actors to create a positive entity that, in turn, relied significantly upon British infrastructure and government to succeed.

MELA STORIES AND HISTORIES

An article in a scholarly book on Allahabad embarks upon its history of the festival with the words 'Kumbh Mela started from the date of sea-churning ceremony',[5] and another posits that 'the historical origin of the Kumbh Mela is lost in legends'.[6] To dismiss this simply as 'belief' will not do, for belief accounts for a considerable portion of what holds together the Kumbh. The *sagar manthan* story, which appears in a number of Sanskrit texts including the Mahabharata, the Ramayana and several Puranas, is said to provide the textual basis of the mela's origins. It tells of the battle between the gods and the demons for the nectar of life (amrita), which was produced from the churning of the milk ocean and placed into a pot (a kumbh). The coveted kumbh was spirited over India by Dhanvantari, the physician of the gods, who, en route to Paradise stopped in Prayag, Hardwar, Ujjain and Nasik to rest, giving the mela its four venues.

---

[4]King, Richard, *Orientalism and Religion: Postcolonial Theory, India and 'The Mystic East'*, London and New York: Routledge, 1999, p. 86.

[5]Singh, Pramod and L.N. Gupta, 'The Kumbh', in Pramod Singh (ed.), *Urban Environmental Conservation*, New Delhi: Ashish Publishing House, 1990, p. 134.

[6]Sinha, Surajit, and Baidyanath Saraswati, *Ascetics of Kashi: An Anthropological Exploration*, Varanasi: N.K. Bose Memorial Foundation, 1978, p. 161.

However, in studies attempting to uncover the history and origins of the Kumbh Mela, it has been strongly argued that these stories have been relatively recently applied to the festival.[7] Bhattacharya concluded that 'the Puranic legend has been forcefully grafted on the Kumbh fair in order to show Puranic authority for it. Though the incident of *amrita manthan* [churning the nectar], has been stated in several Puranic works, "the fall of amrita in four places" has not been stated in any of them'.[8] Mention made of 'kumbh' (pot, pitcher) in various Vedas, Puranas and *mahakavyas* has also been taken to refer to the mela, but this is taking considerable licence in translations.[9] It is interesting to note that the *Matsya Purana*'s fulsome descriptions of the holiness of Prayag in the *Prayag Mahatmya*, which is generally accepted as an authentic text, mention its superlative sanctity in the month of Magh but neglect to mention any Kumbh.[10]

The word *Kumbh* refers not only to the pot of nectar spilt on its way to the heavens, but to the astrological sign Aquarius, which also equates as the water-carrier in Western astrology. In relation to the apparent astrological authority for the festival, Bhattacharya noted that 'it is of great importance to note that there is no clear mention of the Kumbhayoga in astronomical works, dealing with the yogas [defining when a Kumbh Mela takes place]. It appears to be a later conception'.[11] Furthermore, there is considerable disagreement amongst joshis, Hindu astrologers, regarding the incidence of the astrological constellation which ushers in a mela. This disagreement has resulted in two Kumbhs being held twelve months, not twelve years, apart, such as in 1941 and

---

[7]Bonazzoli, Giorgio, 'Prayag and its Kumbh Mela', *Purana*, Vol. XIX, No. 1, January 1977, p. 117; Bhattacharya, R.B., 'The Kumbhaparvan', *Hindutva*, Vol. 7 (9–10), December 1976/January 1977, pp. 1–9; and Dubey, D.P., 'Kumbh Mela: Origin and Historicity of India's Greatest Pilgrimage Fair', *National Geographical Journal of India*, Vol. 33, no. 4, December 1987; Sax, 'Kumbh Mela', p. 402.

[8]Bonazzoli, 'Prayag and its Kumbh Mela', p. 5.

[9]Dubey, 'Kumbh Mela'.

[10]Taluqdar of Oudh (trans.), *The Matsya Puranam*, Vol. 1, Allahabad: Indian Press, 1916.

[11]Bhattacharya, 'The Kumbhaparvan', p. 7

1942; and in 1965 and 1966 in Allahabad. There is also the frequent incongruity that the Kumbh Yoga constellation for the Allahabad mela does not coincide with the month of Magh, in which case it is the Magh calendar which is upheld.[12] Nor are the Kumbh festivals in each of the four cities necessarily held every three years, as is often stated. The last Hardwar Kumbh was in 1998, and the Allahabad Kumbh was in 2001, but the Nasik mela was held in 2003 and the Ujjain mela in the following year, 2004. The only Kumbh Mela of the four cities to be celebrated featuring Aquarius (kumbh) astrologically is the Hardwar mela, which has led to scholars convincingly arguing that the mela first began there.[13]

The other three festivals, it would appear, have had the Kumbh tradition and story applied to pre-existing local bathing festivals by enterprising *pandas* competing with India's other *tirthas* (holy places) for sacred status. The British took a condescending view of religious flexibility of this kind. 'The practice of giving to favourite spots the names of celebrated foreign sacred places is common in Oojein and elsewhere,' explained a lieutenant in the nineteenth century, with some deprecation. 'By this simple process, the Hindu thinks to concentrate a quantity of holiness into a small space, and needy, feeble, or business-bound piety indulges in the plausible consolation of worshipping at home and at ease, the objects of a difficult and expensive pilgrimage.'[14] Like Allahabad, Nasik and Ujjain are noted in nineteenth-century literature to be pilgrimage sites of long standing, but their melas are not specifically designated as Kumbhs. In fact, both the Ujjain and Nasik melas are still locally known as Singhasth Mela, in reference to the prominence of Leo in their respective constellations; the 1975 *Nasik District Gazetteer* does not speak at all of a Kumbh Mela in its jurisdiction,

---

[12]N.Rathnasree, the director of the Nehru Planetarium, Delhi, writes that according to the Kumbh Yoga, the mela in 1989 should have begun in mid-March, not in the beginning of January. Rathnasree, N., 'Kumbh Mela: The Astronomical Connection', *India Perspectives*. March 2001.

[13]Bonazzoli, 'Prayag and its Kumbh Mela', p. 118; Bhattacharya, 'The Kumbhaparvan', p. 9.

[14]Connolly, (Lieut.) Edward, 'Observations upon the past and present condition of Oojein or Ujjayani', *Asiatic Journal of Bengal*, Vol. 6, Part 2, 1837, p. 815.

indicating that the Kumbh tradition there has not been broadly accepted. Despite academic aspersions that the ocean-churning story and the Kumbh Yoga have been relatively recently adapted or adopted for the purpose of mela-making, in Allahabad, the annual Magh Mela has become known as Kumbh every twelve years, and Ardh (half) Kumbh every intervening six.

The ancientness of the Kumbh Mela in Allahabad is usually sealed with reference to the account of the Chinese pilgrim Hsiuan Tsang in the seventh century. However, his record that the festival he witnessed in Allahabad occurred every five years has raised doubts that it was a Kumbh that he described. Translations of the pilgrim's memoirs describe the festival as one of alms-giving, rather than of bathing in a holy river, which characterizes a Kumbh Mela today. In addition, Hsiuan Tsang does not use the word kumbh in his account; the festival was convened by the Emperor Harsha, not by sadhus or brahmins; and the festival he describes is Buddhist in nature, with an image of Buddha central to the rituals, and Buddhist monks being favoured over 'heretic' Hindus.[15] Interestingly, when arguing in legal battles for their historically established right to conduct rituals and accept donations from pilgrims, Prayagwals have used the account of Huan Tsang, not to establish the historicity of the Kumbh Mela per se, but the very existence of a 'religious fair' in 643 CE.[16]

Many historians and translators have presumed that evidence of any mela in Allahabad must necessarily indicate a Kumbh. The conflation of the Magh and Kumbh Melas has become quite common, and has been reiterated so many times that it has become widely accepted that the Kumbh Mela is as old as the Magh Mela, as evidenced by Jawaharlal Nehru's musing in the *Discovery of India*:

> In my own city of Allahabad, or Hardwar, I would go to the great bathing festivals, the *Kumbh Mela*, and see hundreds of thousands of people come, as their forebears had come for thousands of years from all over India, to bathe in the Ganges. I would remember descriptions

[15]This insight is from James Lochtefeld, 11 October 2001.

[16]Caplan, Anita Lee Harrison, 'Pilgrims and Priests as Links between a Sacred Centre and the Hindu Culture Region: Prayag's Magh Mela', PhD thesis, University of Michigan, 1983, p. 179.

of these festivals written thirteen hundred years ago by Chinese pilgrims and others, and even then these festivals were ancient and lost in an unknown antiquity. What was the tremendous faith, I wondered, that had drawn our people for untold generations to this famous river of India?

Other historical accounts which have been used to infer the antiquity of Allahabad's Kumbh Mela have also proved to refer in the original source to the Magh Mela. An example of this is the frequently made claim that the Bengali mystic Chaitanya visited the Kumbh Mela in 1514. However, when one takes the trouble to consult the original Bengali, it is to be found that Chaitanya visited the Magh Mela.[17] Similarly, Fanny Parkes's account of the Magh Mela in the 1830s has a reference appended to it by her twentieth-century editor, who helpfully informs the reader that every twelve years, the mela is a Kumbh and is consequently much larger, but there is nothing in Parkes's account which so much as hints this.[18] Thus, Kumbh melas have been written into the past where they may not have existed at all.

There are several references to an annual mela, as opposed to a duodecennial mela, observed in Allahabad, in texts such as Tulsidas's sixteenth-century *Ramcharitmanas* which states: 'In Magh, after the harvest, when the sun enters Capricorn, everybody goes to the lord of all pilgrimage places, Prayagraj. Gods, demigods, divinities and men gather and bathe in the Triveni with great reverence (Balkand, 43).' The *Khulasat-ut-Tawarikh*, a description of India under Aurangzeb composed between 1695 and 1699, also mentions a yearly mela in Allahabad; significantly, the same text acknowledges the Hardwar Kumbh Mela in an earlier passage. The *Yadgar-i-Bahaduri*, dated c. 1833 (1249 Hijri), also discusses Prayag's sanctity at length, and clearly states that the mela takes place every winter in Magh, 'when the sun enters the constellation of Capricorn'. It appears that there is evidence enough to suggest that the Magh Mela, or at least, the tradition of a religious festival at the triveni, is exceedingly old, but that the Kumbh Mela at Allahabad is much more recent.

---

[17]This was also pointed out to me by James Lochtefeld.

[18]Parkes, Fanny, *Wanderings of a Pilgrim in Search of the Picturesque*, London: Oxford University Press, 1975, Vol. 1, p. 488.

A related problem in historiography, and also evident in Nehru's musings, is the sweeping conflation of the Hardwar Kumbh Mela with melas in Allahabad. It was expedient for British administrators in Allahabad to draw on century-old examples of disorder in Hardwar without differentiation, when ruminating on the possible dangers of melas at Allahabad and advocating for tighter controls there. This failed to concede the fundamental differences in the respective histories of the two melas, some elements of which were still evident, particularly in the early nineteenth century. In Hardwar, Kumbh Melas were characterized as large religious meets, where the trade of valuable commodities, such as livestock, was a significant component of the activity. The Kumbh at Hardwar was controlled, until the cession of the region to the British, by akharas of militant sadhus who contested for this privilege in battles of truly alarming scale. By contrast, Allahabad's sacred ground was located at the base of the Fort of Allahabad. The literally towering presence of this base of military power over the sangam made a considerable impact on the nature of the mela in Allahabad. Built by Akbar between the years 1574 and 1583, the fort remained a key strategic economic and military stronghold for Mughal rulers and its subsequent tenants; in 1765 the East India Company were successful in negotiating the establishment of a garrison there and it was ceded to them, along with Allahabad, in 1801.

Akharas naturally found Hardwar a more appropriate place to joust and contest hegemony, where they would be unchallenged by any third party. There is much evidence to suggest that sadhus in large numbers visited and worshipped at Allahabad prior to the region being ceded to the East India Company, and some akharas were (and indeed remain today) based in Allahabad. I shall return to the role of sadhus in establishing a Kumbh in Allahabad after explaining the post-Mutiny politics of Prayag's *panda* community.

PRAYAGWALS AND PILGRIMAGE

Prayagwals, also known as Pragwals, are the brahman priests that service pilgrims visiting Allahabad; their primary function is to guide the pilgrims through the rituals associated with a visit to Prayag. Prayagwals establish their exclusive right to serve pilgrims at the triveni with reference to a firman by Akbar, dated 1593.

Festivals such as the Kumbh Mela are generally not organic, spontaneous observances somehow embedded in the religious psyche of the people, as pondered by Nehru, but the result of long and hard orchestration by the *pandas* of the locality, whose business it is to serve the incoming pilgrims. It is a profitable enterprise, and it has always been in the interests of these brahmins to create and maintain traditions and practices centring around their tirtha. Accordingly, as described above, scriptures have been drafted or interpolated into and circulated extolling the sanctity of Prayag, describing everything from the religious ceremonies to be observed, to precise descriptions of the payment to be given over to the officiating *panda*.

Recent scholarship indicates that during the period of colonial rule, great importance was placed upon the written word in Hindu practice, leading to a growth in interpolation into religious texts. The British expected that Indian religions ought to be explicable in Christian terms; that the importance of the Bible in Christianity ought to have its equivalent in Hinduism, and if it did not, this was seen as a deficiency in the 'native' religion. All Hindu practice, reasoned Orientalist scholars, must find sanction in a holy book; if it was not written, it was wrong, and should probably be stopped. The most relevant example of this is the regular complaints of British administrators against the practice of sadhus parading naked at the mela. Because they could find no scriptural sanction for what they saw as an indecent, unnecessary display, many a Brit thought that the processions should be banned immediately (the impossible implementation of such a scheme clearly won the day each time this issue was raised).[19] The point is that under the colonial regime, practices recorded in texts were much more secure from colonial deconstruction; in this light, the attempt to find scriptural authorization for the Kumbh Mela was most likely intended to shore up the practice.

In Allahabad, as elsewhere, the regular observance of melas was predicated on effective advertising done by priests and their agents,

---

[19]Prior, Katherine, 'British Administration of Hinduism in North India, 1780–1900', PhD thesis, St Catherine's College, Cambridge University, 1990, p. 187.

known to the British as 'pilgrim hunters', who regularly penetrated villages across the breadth of the country, alerting prospective pilgrims to a particularly auspicious forthcoming mela. The British recognized that the Prayagwals were the driving force behind melas, with one Christian missionary optimistically noting in 1840 that 'in a few years this great folly [i.e. pilgrimage to Allahabad] will get out of fashion, especially if the crowds of brahmins lose their interest in keeping it up'. On the contrary, in the face of mid-century fears regarding the spread of Christianity and the corresponding decline of Hinduism, Prayagwals fought back remarkably well, and they did this utilizing an excellent working knowledge of the mechanisms of government.

Conflict between the river *pandas* of Prayag and the British began with the latter's attempts to regulate and profit from melas, when Allahabad was ceded to the British in 1801, and along with it the right to collect taxes from pilgrims at the sangam. Following the established custom, the British outsourced the collection of the tax to 'a native', preferring not to intervene in the complexities of the tax collection, both practically, for the tax system inherited was not straightforward, and symbolically, in order to escape accusations in England that the Company was upholding 'heathen' practices. However in 1806 these reservations were set aside and the Company took over the collection of the Pilgrim Tax, set the tax rate at one rupee per person (vehicles and other conveyances extra), and proscribed the collection of 'all other duties, fees, or gratuities at the ghaut within the fort' other than those of the government. 'Every man, even the veriest beggar, is obliged to give one rupee for the liberty to bathe at the holy spot;' wrote Fanny Parkes, a resident of the Fort in the 1830s, 'and if you consider that one rupee is sufficient to keep that man in comfort for one month, the tax is severe.'

The Prayagwals viewed the Pilgrim Tax in the same manner in which they viewed the British government—as contrary to their interests. On the British side, it was thought by many—especially local administrators, who found organizing the mela onerous—that the expense of the Pilgrim Tax deterred pilgrims from making the journey to Allahabad. At the same time, the British recognized that they were reliant on the Prayagwals to ensure a good crowd from which the revenue could be exacted, which somewhat compensated for the burden that the mela represented; thus there was an uneasy reliance of the Company on the Prayagwals. The former detested the latter's ruthless attempts to extort the maximum sum from pilgrims. Prayagwal avarice became legendary, but this was equalled by the government's determination 'in squeezing those who come for salvation', as a British writer noted in the 1830s.

But it would be facile to reduce the resistance of pilgrimage priests to mere economics, as it would be to interpret these spiritual specialists as mere cash registers, dispensing holy goods and services according to demand. To accept such a position would be to accept uncritically the discourses of those colonialists and missionaries who were keen to emphasize the material over the religious in Hindu practice. Prayagwal objections to the British presence were not merely economic; a good deal of their resistance was in response to the challenge to their hegemony at the sangam. This resistance can also be interpreted in devotional terms.[20] Ritual is known to be 'less efficacious when on land where another is sovereign',[21] and the objection to interference by those insensitive to specific needs and practices was to become a familiar refrain in Prayagwal memos to government.

Therefore, the insertion of the British authority into a Hindu landscape—the sangam—was clearly a disturbance for the *pandas*, who had enjoyed some freedom from intrusion during Nawabi rule, and to those wishing to perform devotions there, as the British attempted to constrain the pilgrimage trade, by levying taxes and applying legislation. The Prayagwals' resistance to colonial authority was noted (and the awareness of their vital role in attracting a desirable revenue for the government revealed) in 1815, when in response to a new chowkidari system of policing instituted by the British,

> the class denominated Pragwals, who perform the religious ceremonies
> at the junction of the great rivers, to the number of 4 or 5,000,

---

[20]I am mindful here of Pinch's articulate polemic against 'the subordination of *bhakti* to a world of power, of domination and resistance' in historical analysis. Pinch, William R., '*Bhakti* and the British Empire', *Past and Present*, no. 179, May 2003, p. 168.

[21]Bayly, C.A., 'Pre-History of Communalism?', reprinted in *Origins of Nationality in South Asia: Patriotism and Ethical Government in the Making of India*, Delhi: Oxford University Press, 1998, p. 219.

shewed a determination to resist, threatened to cease to officiate, and withdrew altogether, which would have caused a loss to the Government of the Pilgrim Revenue. Many other conspiracies to arrest the progress of the arrangements took place, but by patience and firmness were ultimately dissipated or suppressed.[22]

The tension between the government and the Prayagwals reached a peak in June 1857, when during the general confusion in Allahabad following the mutiny of the 6th Native Infantry, Prayagwals joined the rebellion.

Before the outbreak, Prayagwals were said to have been involved in perpetuating unrest in Allahabad by 'playing upon the passions of people and making propaganda that the aim of the British Government was to convert people to Christianity'.[23] This is significant, because if Prayagwals had been mobilizing people in Allahabad, we can assume that in all probability, they were conveying this to their clients the pilgrims, so that this unrest would have spread effectively across India; recent studies show that pilgrimage networks serve as effective conduits of information.[24] *'The Brahmins amongst the Hindoos, the Moulvies and others amongst the Mussulmen, have, it is well known, proclaimed that it is decreed that British power is to close this year,'* wrote the besieged Magistrate and Collector of Allahabad, underlining his words for emphasis. 'The poorer classes are thoroughly imbibed with this belief and as a consequence they work against us.' As these words were being written, Colonel Neill was embarking upon his notoriously brutal 'pacification' of Allahabad.

Acting upon the animosity they held for the missionaries who competed, often rather aggressively, at the mela for the attention of pilgrims, during the rebellion Prayagwals targeted and destroyed the mission press and churches in Allahabad. From the relative security of the cholera-ridden fort, Owen, a missionary with the American Board of

---

[22]Hamilton, Walter, *A Geographical and Historical Description of Hindostan and the Adjacent Countries*, London: J. Murray, 1820, p. 299; and Hamilton, Walter, *East India Gazetteer*, London: Parbury, Allen and Co., 1828, Vol. I, p. 34.

[23]Srivastava, M.P., *The Indian Mutiny 1857*, New Delhi: Chugh Publications, 1979, p. 68.

[24]Bayly, C.A., *Empire and Information: Intelligence Gathering and Social Communication in India 1780-1870*, London: Cambridge University Press, 1996.

Missions, noted in his journal that upon entering Allahabad city, Neill's first action was to attack Daragunj, where 'a nest of pryagwalas [sic] has been very troublesome in stopping the communication over the Ganges' by taking control of the bridge of boats. Days later, Owen reported that another Prayagwal settlement on the Yamuna was fired at and many buildings destroyed, their inhabitants dispersed. Once British control had been re-established over the city, Prayagwals were persecuted for their acts; some were convicted and hanged, and others were forced to flee Allahabad 'to save their necks'. According to Bholanauth Chunder, Prayagwals had been resentful of the 'restraints imposed upon their greed', and 'had too anxiously desired to get quit of the Sahibs, whose presence hampered the free exercise of their rapacity'. Many of their number, estimated by Chunder to be nearly 1,500 families, were thereafter forced to live as beggars in obscure towns and in jungles to evade capture. 'Their difficulty,' remarked Chunder, 'has become the pilgrim's opportunity.'[25]

The surviving Prayagwals were persecuted by a government devoid of proof enough to convict them but nonetheless convinced of their complicity in the events of 1857. Large amounts of Prayagwal land in Kydgunj, in proximity to the *pandas'* place of work, the sangam, were confiscated and incorporated into the landholding of the Fort cantonment; it is likely that some of the confiscated land constitutes today's mela grounds. After the Rebellion, contending with rumours that the government intended to convert all Indians into Christians, the Prayagwals, reduced in number, were left to rebuild their businesses. And they fought back admirably. It appears that there was no formal mela held in 1858 due to the general turmoil, but by 1859 press reports reveal that there was a small Magh Mela, although governmental records confidently, but unconvincingly, deny it. In March 1860, after a large and successful Magh Mela, a report in *Allen's Indian Mail* noted, with not a little revulsion, that the Prayagwals' flags bore anti-British signifiers:

> The spot opposite the confluence is covered with rude flagstaves; and
> it is strange that upon the flags themselves there are many allusions

---

[25]Chunder, Bholanauth, *Travels of A Hindoo to Various Parts of Bengal and Upper India*, London: N. Trubner & Co., 1869, Vol. 1, p. 305.

to occurrences which one would little expect to see commemorated close to the fort, and just under the muzzles of its guns. One flag represents a set of black soldiers, whom it is easy to identify as pandies, portrayed in the act of triumph over fallen enemies, and the faces of the slain are *white*. On another flag are seen a group of artillery men, engaged with a fort, which it is plain to see was intended to represent an English one. In every place are to be seen symbols of the bloody and cruel nature of heathenism, and it is not difficult to divine, from the scowls and mutterings of men as Europeans pass by, what they would do if they dared.

Flagstaves are used at the mela so that pilgrims can locate in the crowd the Prayagwal that keeps their family records, and each Prayagwal has a distinctive symbol. It would appear from this account that the images of the rebellion had been incorporated into the Prayagwals' insignia; even today there is a *panda* flag depicting a row of sepoys. The currency of the flags is an interesting one—Prayagwals were exploiting their part in the Rebellion apparently in the belief that anti-British flags would excite more business. More interesting is the bravado with which these flags were openly displayed in such close proximity to things British, particularly Allahabad Fort, which during the rebellion had proven itself as the base of British military power in the North-Western Provinces; had the British not held the fort, the operations to regain supremacy in north India would have been seriously compromised.

The following decade was to be a time of partly proactive, partly defensive actions for the surviving Prayagwal community. In 1860, the Pragwal Sabha was formed and registered with the government, with the stated aims of protecting and preserving the 'rights of its members to conduct rituals and accept donations' at the sangam.[26] Clearly, this was the action of a community under threat, attempting by organizational means to fight back government attempts to curtail their traditional occupation, after the revolt had failed.

---

[26]Caplan, 'Pilgrims and Priests', p. 179.

TRACING THE BEGINNINGS OF THE KUMBH IN ALLAHABAD

It would appear that it was at this time that Kumbh Melas were instituted at Allahabad, and if not instituted, then popularized. No governmental record that I have consulted before the 1860s mentions the word 'Kumbh', in any of its variant spellings, in relation to melas in Allahabad, nor even that every twelve years the mela in Allahabad had any special significance. Given the depth of knowledge that the British sought about the Allahabad mela, necessitated by the perceived need to effectively tax and control the festival, so dangerously close to the Fort, this is noteworthy. Legislation had been passed in regard to the Allahabad mela, notably *Regulation XVIII of 1810* describing methods of taxation at Allahabad, and *Act XII of 1840* proscribing it. Yet in the volumes of surrounding debates, never is it noted that every twelve years a mela occurs of such special significance that crowds are enlarged, and along with them, revenues and the scale of arrangements. Similarly, various gazetteers describe a mela at Allahabad but not a Kumbh; nor do missionaries, who attended the mela from the early 1830s mention the duodecennial event; nor interested and inquisitive Europeans, such as Fanny Parkes, who lived in, or passed through Allahabad at the time of Magh Melas. Petitions from Hindu princes for permission to enter British territory and attend the festival repeatedly use the word Magh, not Kumbh, to describe the mela. Bhartendu Harishchandra wrote an essay on the importance of Magh Snan in 1873 without so much of a mention of Allahabad or the superior Kumbh Mela indicating (apart from the writer's Benares roots), that the Allahabad festival had yet to reach monumental proportions.

Given the amount of material covered, the absence of the nomenclature 'Kumbh' applied in relation to Allahabad, together with the failure of any of these sources to note a twelve-yearly mela cycle in Allahabad before the 1860s, is meaningful. By contrast, many writers in the early nineteenth century mention a twelve-yearly festival in Hardwar, variously describing a 'Cumbha-Mela'; 'Koom'; 'koombh ca Mela'; and 'koomb ke mailah', to name a few.

So when did every twelfth Magh Mela in Allahabad become recognized as a Kumbh? The first mention of a Kumbh Mela in Allahabad that I have been able to find is in the closing discussion of an

1868 report into pilgrimage and sanitation controls, now in the British Library, in which the magistrate of Allahabad wrote:

> In going through the correspondence that has taken place during my absence from the district, relative to the large native fairs held periodically in different parts of India, I have observed an omission in the correspondence which I now make haste to rectify. It is this— that in January, 1870, or 25 months hence, there will be the Coomb fair at this station, and the concourse of people will certainly be very great. [. . .] I witnessed the Ad Coombh four years ago when the concourse was immense. [. . .] The whole space below the bund to the confluence of the rivers, and for a great distance above the bund, was a mass of human beings; and owing to the proximity of the fair land to the fort, city and station, and the very narrow limits where all feel bound to congregate to bathe, the risk of an outbreak of disease is very great [. . .] these fairs are European nuisances.

It is interesting here to note that Ricketts is informing others in the provincial government about the Kumbh at Allahabad, then the provincial capital. Had the festival been well-established, an inquiry into pilgrimage and sanitation in the North-Western Provinces could not have proceeded very far without its mention.

If there was a Kumbh Mela earlier than 1870, it would have fallen, depending on how you make your astrological calculations, in 1858. In the aftermath of the turmoil of the rebellion, it is difficult to discern what precisely happened that year. In March 1860, *Allen's Indian Mail* reported that that the Magh Mela of that year was 'the largest to take place for the last five years. There was none the year after the Mutiny, and a very poor one last year—the concourse of people near the fort being probably considered dangerous.' In none of this discussion is there mention of a scheduled Kumbh Mela, nor in any Indian writings are there lamentations of a Kumbh foiled by the Mutiny. Quick calculations indicate that an earlier Kumbh Mela in Allahabad would have fallen in 1846, but it is difficult to discern whether it was a Kumbh on the basis of crowd size, in the absence of any other evidence. The crowds in the 1840s were noted to be 'ever increasing in number since the Government withdrew the pilgrim tax' to the point that, in 1843, for example, the volume of pilgrim traffic was so great that the *Agra Akbar* noted that the 'Magistrate permitted them to pass for five hours over the bridges without paying' the usual toll.

In 1864, there was mention of an 'exceptional' crowd, which would have been the Ardh Kumbh Mela referred to by Ricketts, although this term was not so entrenched that it was used in the government report. Therefore it is not unreasonable to assume that the first Kumbh to be celebrated in Allahabad was in 1870, and that the Prayagwals had put in enough work to attract large crowds of pilgrims to it and the Ardh Mela before it. In the 1870 report of the Magh Mela, the commissioner of Allahabad wrote that 'this year, being a "Koombh", attracted an unprecedented crowd, [and] has passed without serious incident'. Interestingly in the same year the *Pioneer*, the voice of the British (at this stage still based in Allahabad), still referred to the Kumbh as the 'Magh Mela', when dryly commenting that the 'very large surplus' that the mela had produced ought to be spent in Allahabad on 'well-directed activity towards averting, or at any rate mitigating, the ravages of disease' that the mela attracted. There was still some British administrative confusion on the subject of melas in 1874, when Ricketts, by then Allahabad's commissioner, complained in the Magh Mela Report of that year: 'We are in possession of very little information as to the causes which bring about a greater or less attendance at the fair in one year than in another, beyond the fact that every 7th year is more sacred, and there is a more numerous attendance of pilgrims and visitors, and consequently of merchants.'

THE ROLE OF SADHUS IN KUMBH CREATION

What defines a Kumbh from a Magh Mela today is that the former is characterized by the institutionalized processions of sadhus, which are allowed, by a convention established by the British, on three bathing days over the period of the mela (Makar Sankranti, Mauni Amavasya, and Basant Panchami); these sadhu processions are an attraction for ordinary pilgrims, and in more recent years, the media. It is highly likely that the 1870 Kumbh Mela was the first to be celebrated in Allahabad, for all of the reasons given above, and because its report details the establishment of the order for processions of sadhus. The officiating magistrate in 1870, Robertson, was openly relieved to have had a Hindu in Inspector Narain Singh, negotiate with the sadhus the order of procession. The order decided upon was close to the one observed in Hardwar, established as a result of the pitched battles between akharas, and so probably translated, as was the mela itself, from there. By establishing a Kumbh Mela in Allahabad, Prayagwals were able to maintain and expand their festival in the face of a hostile government that might have been tempted to place a lid on the festival they deemed to be 'a European nuisance'. By elevating the status of the Magh Mela from annual market-cum-bathing festival to renowned Kumbh, Prayagwals forced the British into a position where banning or minimizing it was well-nigh impossible.

In this process, the sadhu akharas played an important role. In previous centuries, the Hardwar Kumbh Mela was the arena in which sadhu akharas fiercely battled for economic and spiritual supremacy, with the victorious sect winning the right to control the mela and collect lucrative taxes. It is significant that the battles between akharas in the eighteenth century are said to have characterized Kumbh Melas, yet none of these battles are reported to have taken place at Allahabad. Montstuart Elphinstone wrote that at the Kumbh in Hardwar in 1760, 'An affray, or rather a battle, took place between the Nagas of Shiva and those of Vishnu, in which it was stated on the spot that 18,000 persons were left dead on the field.' The body-count was so high that Elphinstone dismissed it as an 'exaggeration', but contemporary reports attest to the scale and intensity of the conflict.

Had any such 'affray' taken place at the sangam, we can be fairly sure that it would have been recorded and reproduced in British records, as any conflict of such a scale as that described by Elphinstone, in the close vicinity of the Fort of Allahabad would certainly have attracted attention and alarm. In the Company's early forays into the region in the late eighteenth century, papers from the Secret Department at Fort William reveal that there was some consternation that, 'under the pretence of pilgrimage', 'the provinces [of Korah and Allahabad] have been annually visited by the sunnassies and in former times they have appeared in it in bodies of 50,000 men, but their ravages have never been marked by any very bad effect on the collections or the peace of the country'. Yet aside from British reports of 'cold' conflict between akharas on mela days in the late nineteenth and early twentieth centuries, in which shoes are thrown and insults traded, there are no inter-akhara battles recorded to have taken place in Allahabad.

While sadhus no doubt attended melas at Allahabad in large numbers before the mid-nineteenth century, it is evident that the trade component of that fair was rather petty, comprising trinkets, homewares and 'articles of the most trifling value, but of every possible description',[27] in comparison to the elephants, camels, bullocks and horses that were on sale in Hardwar. This explains in part why Allahabad did not attract as large a gathering of trader-sadhus, and as a result it escaped the sadhu battles that Hardwar was synonymous with in the eighteenth century. Furthermore, the scale of the Hardwar festival before the 1800s, and the corresponding reward if an akhara was to win the right to tax the pilgrims, inflated the stakes of sadhu warfare. By contrast, in Allahabad, the rulers ensconced in the Fort had established the right to tax pilgrims, or to waive that tax, as some Mughals did. That this had not been questioned by militant sadhus in Allahabad indicates that the mela was so comparatively small and the Mughals so well entrenched—the Fort of Allahabad looming above the sangam declaring their sovereignty—that stakes there were not worth fighting for, even by the most skilled sadhu warriors; this may even have diminished the ritual value of the landscape in their eyes. Here lies another indication that the Kumbh Mela was not established in Allahabad before the conquest of the East India Company.

The position of the sadhu in Indian society changed with the encroachment of the East India Company. Originally a trading enterprise, the East India Company altered trading terms and conditions in such a way that the position of sadhus as wealthy traders began to decline. With their fall in economic status followed an inevitable dip in their social standing. Having eroded the sadhus' social and economic role in Indian society, the only arena in which they could enjoy their former status was in the Kumbh Mela, which, as a religious event, enjoyed a degree of immunity from governmental intrusion, within the limits described above. At the Kumbh Mela, sadhus were allowed to parade

---

[27]Compare the accounts of Davidson and Mundy, who visited both Allahabad and Hardwar fairs. Davidson, C.J.C., *Diary of Travels*, Vol. 1, pp. 316–27; Mundy, (Captain) Godfrey Charles, *Pen and Pencil Sketches, Being the Journal of a Tour in India*, London: John Murray, 1832, Vol. II, p. 147.

Contemporary Print of Tirtha Raj Prayag

naked and bear their arms, which by the twentieth century had become largely ceremonial. Periodic and prudish attempts by the government to wind back these privileges at the Kumbh were persistently met with defiant resistance by sadhus insistent of their autonomy in this space alone. The Kumbh Mela was an arena of status communication for sadhus, as it was for other elites, such as notables who publicly distributed charity at mela time. Consequently, the creation of any new Kumbh Melas would have been met with approval by the sadhus, and their presence at the melas boosted their importance in no small measure for pilgrims. The British, keen to redefine the sadhus' role from militant trader-ascetic to one of holy monk, tolerated and accommodated venues such as the Kumbh to give an arena to the latter.

The Kumbh Mela has been successfully adapted to Allahabad, and has become the greatest mela in modern India. While there are many religious and sacred elements at work that emphasize Prayag's sanctity, we cannot ignore the temporal forces that have promoted the Kumbh Mela in Allahabad. By transcribing the Kumbh Mela festival onto the Magh Mela in the mid-nineteenth century, Prayagwals were adapting their tirtha to suit the changing political and economic climate which otherwise may well have left them behind. Prayagwals reinvested the Magh Mela and related it to the Kumbh tradition, which had a history well recognized by the British, and as the major event that is the Kumbh Mela, it came to affirm Prayagwal, pilgrim and sadhu aspirations. Because these aspirations were articulated in the religious genre of the mela, an element of sovereignty was conceded to them by the British in recognition of the importance of religious freedom, or rather, in fear of the consequences if certain aspects of Indian autonomy within such a sanctified space were denied. Paradoxically, even the needs of the sarkar were fulfilled by the new Kumbh. Organizing the mela to the satisfaction of pilgrims ingratiated them to the foreign power, and the creation of an arena in which the theatre of sadhu hegemony could be periodically rehearsed under controlled conditions partially served to contain the sadhus' potential as subversive elements of society.

GYANRANJAN

Gyanranjan (1936–) was born in Akola, Maharashtra. He grew up in Allahabad, where he also went to university. He took his MA in Hindi in 1957. Since 1960, he has lived in Madhya Pradesh, mainly in Jabalpur, from where he edits the Hindi literary magazine *Pahal*. Many of his early stories, collected in *Fence ke idhar aur udhar* (1968), are set in Lukergunj, Allahabad. In his fiction, Lukergunj is a place of dimly lit houses, peeling walls, and dark noiseless streets, where people lead humdrum lives. The only events in them are a father bathing himself in the courtyard under a tap or a son making a routine visit home. A selection of his stories, *Pratinidhi kahaniya*, appeared in 1984 .

'Vagabond Nights' first appeared in the Hindi literary periodical *Tadbhav* in 2002.

༄

Vagabond Nights

A recent visit to Allahabad has left me with conflicting thoughts about the city, a place to which I have been returning for more than forty years. One image is of a city that is constantly changing and renewing itself; the other is of a city that has already been destroyed. Some aspects of Allahabad appear to have remained the same; but if time is measured by the movement of clocks and changing calendars, the city has been left behind.

Those things which move forward until they die a natural death do not call for attention. It is those things which remain where they are that give the impression of having died. But then everything in Allahabad seems to foretell its ending, even that which appears to have life. A famine-like situation prevails. People vanish, as if by magic. They are here one minute and gone the next. It's as though nothing leaves a mark, never made a mark. Are all cities like this, or is it just Allahabad?

My memory keeps returning to the days gone by in Allahabad, in the same way that any work of fiction by Nirmal Verma is a version of his novel *The Days Gone By*. I cannot understand this obsession of mine. At my age, men usually have other things to occupy the mind. Yet it is old haunts, old friends, old books and their authors that obsess me.

To some extent, the history of modern Hindi literature begins in Allahabad. Ajit Kumar, Dharmavir Bharati, Vijay Deo Narayan Sahi, Jagdish Gupta, Vipin Kumar Agarwal, Malayaj, Sumitranandan Pant, Laxmikant Verma, Shriram Verma and Shivkutilal Verma were some of the poets who lived in Allahabad. Among the prose writers who belonged to the city were Amarkant, Kamleshwar, Markandeya, Shekhar Joshi, Bhairav Prasad Gupta, Upendranath Ashk, Amrit Rai, Balwant Singh, Doodhnath Singh, Shailesh Matiyani, Ravindra Kaliya, Mamta Kalia and Ramnarayan Shukla. When Ramswaroop Chaturvedi said that the history of New Poetry in Hindi is synonymous with that of the literary group called Parimal, he came in for severe criticism from Kamleshwar. It is strange that there should have been such a division of opinion between the poets and the prose-writers. Both camps had their own journals and forums, and each exercised its own power over the Hindi literary establishment.

For centuries, men and women have wandered, covering vast distances, and they still do. In my desire to arrive at the meaning of the mysterious city of Allahabad, I too pored over municipal maps, often getting lost in my explorations. In the process, I looked with fresh eyes at even its most obvious aspects, at those with which I had always assumed I was familiar. It is important to look at the same scenes again and again. Countless times I walked the length and breadth of the city, never bored; I could never have enough of it. Often, during my lonely perambulations, the only sound to reach my ears was that of my own footsteps.

More than anything else in my youth, I was in love with Allahabad. I recall the innumerable shops and roadside restaurants, where I was treated not like another customer but as though I owned the place, and the homes in which I was received as a member of the family and not as a guest. I could always be relied upon because I was always around. Maybe I gave the impression that I had money in my pocket but, if the truth be told, the pocket always had a hole in it.

Allahabad, the city and its writers, must take some of the blame for the unrelenting hold that the modern has over me. The town has none of the qualities of Benares. Looking back, I now think that allowing myself to be so influenced by its prevailing atmosphere was perhaps a mistake. Modernity constituted my entire mental world. I read not only the leading writers of the Chhayavaad and Progressive schools, but also went through the entire gamut of Western writers. My days and nights were spent churning over in my mind a heady cocktail of Baudelaire's poems, Modigliani's biography, the suicides in Osamu Dazai's *The Setting Sun* and the bleakness of Dostoevsky. The mixture, like a drug, went to my head, and I stopped thinking about what I had read in the past or would read in the future.

But with visitors, who came to Allahabad and wanted to know about the city's past, we behaved as though we were the guides to some historic place. We pointed out the chair in the corner of the Coffee House where Sahiji or Laxmikant Verma came and sat. We took them to the Jain Betel Shop, Dharmavir Bharati's favourite haunt, where he would always try to get change for a currency note of large denomination. We would move on to the *mithai* shop patronized by Niralaji because his credit there was always good. There was also Jagdish Gupta's house with its panorama of the Ganges. Then it was on to Nyaya Marg, on the old Hastings Road, to Amrit Rai's house, and from there to Mahadevi Verma's.

We would arrive at the turning that led to Harivansh Rai Bachchan's house, and then go past Rajapur Cemetery to Markandeya's and Onkar Sharad's house on Minto Road. Naresh Mehta used to live in this lane, Bhairav Prasad Gupta in that one, and facing the historic wall of Khusrau Bagh was Upendranath Ashk's residence. Unorthodox weddings and romances took place there, and it was the scene of some wild literary fights. It was also where the magazine *Sanket* was published.

Firaq Sahab did not vacate his house on Bank Road, even after he retired from the university, but no one complained. The Annie Besant Memorial Hall where Parimal held many important functions was on Lowther Road. The old bungalow with its tiled roof was the editorial office of Balkrishna Rao's magazine *Madhyam*, and behind it was the Leader Press, from where the magazine *Sangam* was published. Illachandra Joshi was its editor. Vachaspati Pathak's haunt was there too; a meeting place for writers seeking literary gossip, or who just wanted to have some innocent fun. The offices of the publishers Bharati Bhandar, which published major figures like Jaishankar Prasad, Maithilisharan Gupta and Nirala, were situated in the same compound.

As a rule, people in Allahabad stayed in the same house throughout their lives; there were few changes of address. Mamta Kaliya and Ravindra Kaliya did move from Rani Mandi to the banks of the Ganges, but only after many decades of staying in one place. They used to live in a predominantly Muslim locality, at the end of the lane in which *Shabkhoon* is printed. During the sectarian riots, curfew was imposed on the area. However, the Kaliyas continued to live there in safety, and ate there some of the tastiest biryani they'd ever had. After giving the matter a lot of thought, Doodhnath Singh has finally moved from Shambhoo Barracks on Cassels Road to the other side of the Ganges. Most of the characters in his stories, however, continue to belong to this side of the river. Giriraj Kishore stayed next to the Coffee House throughout his years in Allahabad. His house was a solace to me in my penurious days; he was the only friend I had who was doing well.

Not more than a hundred yards from our house in Lukergunj was 'Padamkot', where Shridhar Pathak lived. The grand building is fast turning into a ruin, its magnificent architecture unable to keep misfortune at bay. It is not clear to me why Sumitranandan Pant left the scenic mountain surroundings of Kausani to settle in hot, dusty Allahabad, but he must surely have been inspired to make the move because Allahabad was the centre of literary activity at the time, in the same way that Delhi now is. Pantji's house, where he stayed to the end of his days, was near the Masonic Lodge on Stanley Road. The Lodge, which had something mysterious about it, used to cast ghostly shadows on the house. Only two or three people lived in the house, all of them unmarried, which made the place seem unusually quiet. Pantji, it was said, was so delicate that even the prattle and laughter of children could injure his ears. It was a little puzzling to me why he made up for the absence of a woman in the house by wearing his hair long; his curls were of shoulder length. I only caught a glimpse of him a few times. Certainly I was no Dante and he no Beatrice, but there was something attractive about Pantji.

Sometimes I passed his house while returning from the university. It was a quiet area with many trees and few people, and not without a certain grandeur. We had bicycles in those days, but that was a time when possessing a bicycle was not a reflection of one's status in society. I would stand in front of Pantji's house for a long time, rather in the way that people once waited in front of the film actress Suraiya's flat on Marine Drive, or today wait outside Amitabh Bachchan's bungalow in

Juhu. I hoped that he would suddenly open the door and make an appearance. But Pantji was always busy inside, writing one poem after another. He was the kind of person who could do nothing except write poems. It is hard now to understand the curiosity I had about him, the sense of excitement. I seem to have wasted my youth in waiting for a glimpse of him.

One day I heard from Prabhat, who was a friend of mine, that Pantji would be visiting the offices of Lokbharati, his publisher, to release his new book. The news spread like wildfire among the students at the university. Some of us, riding two to a bicycle, raced to the Darbari Building on Mahatma Gandhi Road, where the offices were located. Pantji, who knew astrology, had chosen the time of the release, 11.40, only after doing mathematical calculations to ensure that it was an auspicious time, just as Hindi film producers do when they launch their films. His faith in astrology had worked miracles for him. It had brought him success. He was certainly more successful than Nirala. Sadly, by the time we reached Lokbharati, Pantji had left.

My way of life had by then taken on an element of the absurd, and this had rubbed off on my creative work. A kind of clownishness had surfaced in my dealings with people. It made me look like a barbarian in the sophisticated society of Allahabad. It was as if I'd come from another planet.

I enrolled at the university in 1953, my heart full of trepidation. I thought people would look upon me as a bumpkin, a villager. Someone pointed out to me the house of the great mathematician Pyarelal, and the house where Satya Prakash of the chemistry department lived, and the medieval historian Ishwari Prasad. Dhirendra Verma lived in front of the Senate Hall, at the head of the road that led to Allengunj. Ramkumar Verma's house was called 'Saket'. His image, with his silk tie fluttering in the wind, does not leave my eyes. Today, the tiled roofs of these houses are broken, the hedges are untrimmed, dogs urinate on the gateposts, and mongooses run about in the gardens. It is impossible to stem the decline; things cannot be changed back. These bastions of grand living have fallen. The children of the old Allahabad families, even those who are doing well in Delhi, Ahmedabad, Calcutta and Bombay, appear not to have the money to whitewash their ancestral homes, or to have the leases renewed.

Allahabad has built new walls around itself to keep this indignity hidden. An odd kind of westernization has crept into the city. It is as if neither the indigenous *jalebi* is allowed to survive, nor Domino's Pizza to come in. In the meantime, the decline continues. Plaster falls off the walls, which themselves are crumbling away. Paan shops now operate from within the bungalows, or else tailors and dhobis are living in them, paying minimal rent. Allahabad is beginning more and more to look like any other town in eastern Uttar Pradesh. The village has edged its way into India's largest and most impressive Civil Lines, and everywhere one sees lawyers in black coats sidling out from behind the corners of houses.

I left Allahabad on 14 August 1960. On the innumerable occasions that I have been back since then, I've come away with the feeling that I've barely touched its core. People still seem to speak the same language. I cannot comprehend how the dialect has survived. I have certainly heard it in Daraganj and in Loknath, but also, early in the morning, in Alfred Park. Of course, one lifetime is not enough to know all there is to know about a city. Something always remains to be learnt.

There have been many occasions when I have tried to kill the Allahabad within me. Once you start living in another city, the people there want you to belong to them. When I am in Jabalpur, I don't talk of Allahabad. Dharmvir Bharati, too, did not return to Allahabad once he moved to Bombay. Hariprasad Chaurasia came back a few times, to visit his friend Vishwambhar, who ran a *malai* shop, but then he, too, bade farewell to Allahabad. It is impossible to have two lovers, or to love two cities. Exceptions apart, it's not possible to write in two languages, either. Ultimately, Allahabad also took leave of those who had left Allahabad.

A town cannot really be divided into two equal halves but, if Allahabad were divided, Mahatma Gandhi Marg, or Canning Road as it was called, would be on one side and the Grand Trunk Road on the other. The beautiful, affluent, glitzy Allahabad is quite distinct from the poor and crowded older town of the Grand Trunk Road. The two halves are as different from each other as the water of the Ganges is from the water of the Yamuna. One is a muddy brown, the other is green.

The difference between the two halves of Allahabad, the old and the new, is too stark for it not to be noticed. On one side are the railway station, the telegraph office, the clubs, the hotels (especially the Royal and Barnetts), the university, the High Court and the imposing buildings of the accountant-general's office, the police headquarters and the Board of Education. Here, too, are radio and television stations, the colonial-style bungalows, the cantonments and parks. There is nothing like this on the other side; only roadside shops selling spices, grain, utensils and vegetables. The town has its kitchen on one side, its dining room and drawing room on the other.

In contrast to the respectable, moneyed bourgeoisie on one side are the clerks and small artisans who live in the crowded streets of the other. This is a world of poverty, narrow lanes and sarais. Here, there is little to tell a Hindu locality from a Muslim one. Starting with Sarai Akil, Sulem Sarai and Garhi Sarai, the sarais extend into the heart of town. Whether it's the crowds of the Kumbh Mela or those of a Moharram procession, they pass through the same lanes. At the mouth of each lane is a tea shop. I came across similar tea shops in Tashkent and Tajikistan, even at the airport. They serve whole-wheat biscuits, and the kettle is always on the boil.

Birds hop about on stone platforms in front of the shops or inside cages, pecking at the grain which is put out for them. Till late in the evening, paper kites, kite reels and kite string are sold outside shops that have closed for the day. The clinking of iron griddles can be heard, and the air smells of kebabs being roasted on skewers. Horses drink water from stone troughs, and ekkas do the rounds between Manauri and Sangam. Cotton is carded and the dyers are at work, standing over huge vats of boiling dye. The clothes already dyed are hung out to dry. Perfume is sold in small bags made of catgut. Fruit-sellers, sitting on watermelons, using them as stools, fan themselves in the heat. These people never leave the Grand Trunk Road to go to Civil Lines. They know only one world, the world they live in, and are never bored with it.

The area perpetually has the look of a fairground, and the people, because of their great numbers, move as if in slow motion. Just as all great European novels, even those by Camus, seem to end on a note offering the consolations of Christianity, in the same way, hidden in the crowd near the City Kotwali, there used always to be found an evangelist, spreading through a loudhailer the message of Christianity and offering hope to the passing Dalits. The church there always looked abandoned. This went on for about twenty-five years, then the man disappeared, taking the loudhailer with him. Evangelists are a patient lot.

There are churches everywhere in Allahabad. They're painted white, brick red, yellow—and then there is All Saints Cathedral, which is built of stone. They are some of the largest and most beautiful churches in the country, now only a shadow of what they once were. Their bells can be heard ringing at Christmas time, but are otherwise silent. No one attends to their upkeep, and the day cannot be far off when some crazed mob will tear them down. Churches may be destroyed or allowed to fall into ruin, and yet the power of the Church has increased. Everywhere places of worship are deserted, but religion's hold over the political process is on the rise.

I had thought Allahabad would survive, come what may. I was wrong. The fact that the Saraswati river disappeared from here so many centuries ago should have told me that the Allahabad I knew would not remain either. There is a story told about the ancient banyan tree inside the Fort. It is believed to have survived the Great Deluge. But the tree has turned out to be a fake. In any case, it cannot come to the rescue of the drowning. Allahabad used to be a quiet, easy-going sort of place. A person could get by on very little. A four-anna coin could see one through an evening in the Coffee House. But even if one had no money, it wasn't an obstacle to going there. One could always pay later. The waiters there were trusting. Up until the 1970s, it was possible to live in Allahabad with next to no money at all. I remember that for three of the four years I was at university, I did not have a bicycle but managed to get to the university and back without any difficulty.

Here, people had an abiding faith in poetry. Laxmikant Verma wrote an important book on the subject, which led to other similar books being written. Raghuvansh, Ramswaroop Chaturvedi, Dharmavir Bharati and Jagdish Gupta, the pillars of the New Poetry in Hindi, taught me at university, but left me free to find my own path. Education, then, did not mean mental slavery. The faith which people had in poetry was second only to their faith in the heaven-bestowing properties of the water from the Ganges, which they put into the mouths of the dying. Family worries did not seem to touch these men who, like the commentators of classical times, spent their lives in doctrinal debates.

They kept up an argument that was without end. The best minds of the country did not fail to come to Allahabad.

How is it that a town in which no one gave a thought to the afterlife, even while reading the inscriptions on the headstones in Rajapur cemetery or watching the funeral pyres on the banks of the Ganges, has emptied out so quickly? No one comes to Allahabad to write any more. The literary migration has stopped, and yet the city's population has risen. The longing one associated with Firaq's poetry has gone up in smoke. There is still poetry left in the town, but its creator is the knife or the gun.

I ran away from Allahabad. I travelled to Delhi, Bombay and Calcutta. Walter Benjamin said that there is no face more real than the face of a city. I am hopeful about cities, but not about Allahabad. It's neither a city nor a village, nor anything in between. There is no category in which to put it. It cannot go back to what it was, nor can it strike out a new path.

Translated from the Hindi by Sara Rai

I. ALLAN SEALY

I. Allan Sealy (1951–) was born 'in a thunderstorm' in Allahabad in an Anglo-Indian family which has been in India for almost as many generations as the Trotters of his first novel *The Trotter-Nama* (1988). His other books are *Hero* (1991), *From Yukon to Yucatan* (1994), *The Everest Hotel* (1998), *The Brainfever Bird* (2003), and *Red* (2006). He is widely regarded as one of India's finest living novelists.

'Three Gandhis' was written specially for this book.

∿

Three Gandhis

Last week I almost returned to Allahabad.

Up from Goa, I was stuck in Bombay, trying to get back home to Dehra Dun. It was the holiday season and every train in the country was running full: the one train to Dehra Dun had a waiting list in the hundreds. Delhi, the nearest alternative, had 155 waiting for the August Kranti Express. I saw I must cast my net wider: anywhere up north was better than hanging around Victoria Terminus. As I spread out the map my eye lit on Allahabad. A thick red line of broad-gauge track led invitingly there and the circle at the end of it began to expand with possibilities. Another millisecond and images might have begun to appear, with all their necromancy. But then Lucknow intervened, six hours closer to home, with just six on the waiting list. Allahabad, city of my birth, city of my earliest memories, shrank back to a circle on the *Trains at a Glance* map.

I was born in a thunderstorm. My earliest memory is of Allahabad lightning flashing on the steel tiffin carrier that hung from the handlebars of Nankoo the cook's cycle as he brought my mother's post-parturitional dinner to Kamla Nehru Hospital. It was the month of March when such storms are common enough, but this was a cloudburst (how that word hung over my early childhood) and my mother propitiated the god of war as she lay there curled around me. Tempests beset us in later life and she was always quick to blame Mars. Who could I blame but Allahabad?

But what do I know of that city? I left it before I was two and returned there for a couple of childhood Christmases from the mofussil towns of my father's police career. Once in early teenage I attended a New Year's dance during a holiday from boarding school and witnessed a knife fight over eve-teasing: goons gatecrashed the show and there was Anglo blood on the dance floor. But that was it: nothing after that red stain—someone else's blood—but photographs, black and white, on hard black album paper. Sometimes, just the silver photocorners where some cousin nicked a photo. Allahabad is more slippery than the fine patterned tissue separating those album pages.

Of course the city has an urban profile and an archaeology, a religious and a political history, but these mean nothing to me. Even other fictions won't do. I may glean from say Nayantara Sahgal's *Lesser Breeds*, vivid straws of pre-Independence political life just up the road from the Allahabad of my parents (to whom politics was worse than profanity) but to get close to the city I must rely on older, more primal stories, on family lore. Historical Allahabad is silent; now and again it will awake and mumble something incoherent and unreliable. What do I care? I have only versions of my experience—the sodawater bottle that fell from my small hands and burst like a grenade is an absolute event— and that of my family.

Old photographs, stories, memories. And names. Proper names, nicknames. Bank Road, Clive Road, Albert Road; Girls' High School, Boys' High School; Phaphamau Station (wasn't that what steam engines said on the old railway, *pha-pha-mau pha-pha-mau?*), Naini Jail, Muirabad; Palace Theatre, Barnetts' cakes, Guzder's ice cream: sounds, flavours, textures, not signs. Thing names too: portico, chabutra, cesspit; chinese orange, custard apple, guava cheese; ekka, rickshaw, bogie. I learnt the most primary names in Allahabad. I learnt the word brassiere there, saw my first breast, smothered in Himalaya Bouquet talcum powder.

My father, eighty this year, lives in England on one of surely a hundred English Clive Roads, but he grew up on Clive Road, Allahabad. Three quarters of his life were spent on the Gangetic Plain and this month he's back. Allahabad figured, but not crucially, in his itinerary until Goa displaced it, and now there isn't time for more. And yet to him it is a living thing. To me the city is a board game (as was say Paris to the provincial who ruthlessly redesigned it in the 1850s; he was playing with the future as I play with the past). To my father Allahabad is real, so real he gestures when describing exactly where the house on Albert Road stood, ruling lines in the air. *Here.* I see him seeing it. We are there.

So it's only right that I use my space to chronicle his Allahabad. His Police Lines, his All Saints Cathedral, his courting lanes. Or his Coral Club where a young woman burned to death at another New Year's dance when a teasing admirer flicked cigarette ash on her freshly drycleaned gown. Of course I could just as readily record my mother's Allahabad (she had a horror story too in which another young woman threw her child to safety as she fell from a rickshaw under the wheel of a steamroller). Or Aunty Maureen's bottomless well of Bank Road stories. Or cousin Tony's Allahabad, the city where he was kidnapped and found days later, wandering witless on a bridge over the Ganges. Anybody's Allahabad but my own skimpy version.

My father was born in Cawnpore but Allahabad is the city he remembers best. His father, a superintendent of telegraphs, married one of his trainee telegraphists (she threw a notepad at him when he got fresh) and died of septicemia leaving her to bring up eight children. 'I think,' Dad says quietly, in an all-things-considered voice, his hands folded one over the other after an evening of reminiscence, 'even Mummy would have said it was her home town.' The family moved from house to house, Albert Road, Clive Road, Strachey Road, Colvin Kacchi [the unpaved lane] till at last there was just my father, the youngest. 'Baby', my grandmother called him, until a visiting officer coughed and reminded her the boy was now in uniform. In Allahabad he met and courted his future wife, there they were married.

On the 30 January 1948, my father, not yet four years in the force, was outside the Palace Theatre waiting for the show to start when a group of students came up from the university to protest the manhandling of a fellow student by the owner of the theatre, a certain Ghandhi[1]. This Ghandhi had slapped a loudmouth in the theatre the night before and here was the result. Under the eyes of this young off-duty police sergeant the district magistrate, a certain Mr Crossley, advanced alone to

---

[1] The Palace Theatre Ghandhis spelt their name with two h's.

greet the students to hear their complaint. My father remembers thinking
to himself as he leaned on his bicycle ('a new Phillips', he smiles
bashfully, sixty years later) that here was surely the last of the old guard
ICS at work. But history intervened: just then the news broke of another
Gandhi, one who practised turning the other cheek. The Mahatma had
been shot and shopkeepers began downing shutters on the strength of
a whisper. My father rode straight back to the Police Lines and yes, the
double fall-in had sounded. What triggers my father's story is the
anniversary of that assassination; today is 30 January.

We all have assassination stories, but it's the smaller deaths,
measurable tragedies, that haunt one. My father has another story from
that year. One day that dreadful summer, a boy by the name of Pearse
in one of Mussoorie's boarding schools shot and killed a school bully.
To me this act, judged out of context and with no knowledge of the
facts, remains one of courage; I side instinctively with the killer. My
father took no sides: he simply escorted Pearse to Naini prison. On the
way, at some risk to his career, he removed the boy's handcuffs. The first
time I heard this story I got the impression he escorted the boy by train
all the way from his school to Allahabad; now it turns out he took him
from the jailhouse to the courts. I prefer the train version. I still visit
that carriage and sit in silence beside the escorting officer and the boy.
The train wheels click and grind as I write this, and my father sits in the
next room drinking mulled wine. The bully was another Gandhi. We are
all of us vanishing.

My father's mother, Chloe Beulah Murray, of Clive Road, and my
mother's mother, Millicent Rose Clement, of Bank Road, are both
buried in Allahabad. So are their husbands. All have become one with
that soil: they *are* Allahabad. The men are simply photographs; they
were that even to my parents who hardly knew them, but the women are
to me the very essence of that city. I have only to speak the name, the
city's name, and I touch their dewlaps: one mottled, nicotined, wrinkled
like the skin on coffee, the other honey-coloured and softly bearded, the
throats of hard-worked women in their seventies, white-haired brown-
skinned women in dresses.

Sometimes I'm tempted to go and stand by their graves, but
graveyard nostalgia is always defeated by the encroachments of the
present. The kite-flying boys, the fallen angel, the crouching defecator.

Best leave the geography of the past alone, perhaps even its history. For most of us who don't study or teach the past, the strenuous imagining of another individual is all the history we can manage. That history is a simple mix of experience and memory. Call it phenomenology, call it fancy.

Take the simple name Bamrauli, the village which turned into Allahabad's airport. The sound was evocative to me even as a boy: it booms through my childhood, a word with no content beyond the drone of aeroplanes. When I utter it today I see not the place—I was never there—and certainly not its history, but I see very clearly a blue-uniformed Anglo pilot in his charcoal grey air force cap taking a rickshaw out to the airport—no, *aerodrome* is the word that anchors it in my memory—and I bless him. His plane is going to crash and he doesn't know it. I do, and his single fate weighs more heavily on me than all Bamrauli. A whole village with an ancient if obscure lineage swallowed up first by Allahabad and now once more by my trickster memory.

Every action, I was taught, has an equal and opposite reaction. Does my casual treatment of the objective world tempt fate, setting in motion Newtonic (or is it karmic) law? Will the world now turn and casually erase the presumptuous subject, me? On the brink of erasure I think of this man who is bargaining with the devil. Look, he says, I don't care when I die, I just want to know *where*. But surely when is more important? says Mephistopheles. Sir, says the man, if you'll just tell me *where* I'll sure as hell never set foot there.

Allahabad? I'm not going back in a hurry.

PALASH KRISHNA MEHROTRA

Palash Krishna Mehrotra (1975–) was born in Bombay and grew up in Allahabad. He was educated at St Stephen's College, Delhi, the Delhi School of Economics, and Balliol College, Oxford. He now lives in Dehra Dun, where he teaches English at the Doon School. He is represented in *First Proof: The Penguin Book of New Writing from India* 1 (2005).

'Sex and the Small Town' was written specially for this book.

∾

Sex and the Small Town

On the last day of school there was a fight. No one quite knows what happened. One minute we were standing in neat rows, the next there was pandemonium. The girls huddled together on the stage of the auditorium, like nuns in a besieged convent, while the boys had it out on the floor. The teachers who tried to intervene got beaten up. A group of boys drove around the dusty cricket field in an open jeep, firing shots into the air. It wasn't clear whether this was being done in provocation or celebration. Mayank Luthra, always a loner, stood in a corner of the auditorium, breaking plates. Gingerly he picked up each plate with both hands, then raised it above his head as if offering prayers to the sun god, before finally letting it crash to the floor. He went through two entire stacks, both eyes shut tight, a picture of contemplative aggression in a gallery of flying fists.

By eleven in the morning it was clear that the farewell was not going to last till the afternoon as planned. The plates were all smashed, the cola stolen. I cycled back home to pack in an extra two hours of cable TV. MTV had just come to Allahabad with its drop-your-sideburns ads and all-American programming. The Pearl Jam-obsessed Danny McGill was its star VJ. When I switched on the family's black and white television set, Eddie Vedder was growling 'I am alive' into a microphone. Then, in what looked to be a desperate attempt to drive a point home, Vedder chucked the mike and dived into the crowd. To my seventeen-year-old self, just back from the failed farewell at Boys' High School, this seemed to confirm a growing suspicion—that the world was chaos and anarchy the way forward.

Two years earlier, my school—an all-boys' grind established more than a hundred years ago had turned co-ed. 'I've decided to throw some roses among the thorns,' declared Frederic DeSouza, the principal, at our first co-ed assembly.

I promptly fell in love. Thorny, bespectacled me fell in love with rosy, anorexic Rachna. She had matchsticks for legs and long, very long hair.

I discovered New Kids on the Block and yellow Digene. I bought an Archies card (ten clocks displayed on the front, and inside, the punchline: 'It's time we got together') and gave it to Rachna between the covers of an accounts notebook.

Rachna responded by refusing to acknowledge my presence in class. I was desperate. Then one day she passed me a note: Come for the soccer match today evening.

It's 12C vs 12A. I arrive in a white Smash T-shirt, light blue Wranglers and a rexine belt studded with stars. We say hello and shut up for another hour. Afterwards, she says goodbye and leaves with her girlfriends. Minutes later I am surrounded by three guys. They have country pistols. 'Light-eyed loverboy ('kanja deewana') they tell me, 'get off her trail or else . . .'

In the next few days I discover a thing or two about dating in Allahabad. Want girl? Get 'backing'. Whose backing? Of the Hindi-medium types—the kind who've been flunking Class 9 for the last five years. They carry arms, they have scars, they have the lingo. A typically violent east UP lingo where women are always whores ('chinar') and sex is always about robbing virginity ('seal todna').

The English-medium kids need the Hindi-medium goons. The latter too need the former—they want to be seen with the cooler English-speaking boys. In the evenings, they form groups and hang out outside downtown soft-drink booths.

I want to be able to speak to Rachna freely but can't. After the soccer rendezvous the entire town is out to get me. Rachna and I exchange smiles in class and at the school gate but that's about it. I am shit scared; she is totally confused. I have a vague idea that I shouldn't let on that I am shit scared. Girls like brave men. Besides, what idea could this dainty little girl possibly have about the big bad world, of gangs, motorbikes and bicycle chains?

One morning, just before assembly, Gaurav Arora, the school jock, strolls over to where I am standing. He is reputed to have a way with girls. Gaurav offers some friendly advice: 'Anand Mishra knows about your date. He's really pissed off. Rachna is his *maal*. He's coming at recess to break your bones. At least that's what he told me. Take my advice, buddy. Go home right now, because as far as I can see you have no backing.' I ponder over his suggestion for a minute, then decide against leaving the school campus. If girls like brave men then this is my moment. I will not run away. I will be brave.

Mishra arrives with his gang at the appointed hour. He is twice my size and flaunts a thumb-sized scar on his right cheek. He is in third year BCom. I am summoned to the canteen: 'Mishra wants to see you.' It turns out that's all he wants to do. When face-to-face, he stares at me unsmilingly, then asks me to leave.

The next day, in the library period, Rachna invites me to sit next to her. I hesitate for a moment. I know there are spies in our class. Mishra will get to know immediately. 'Come here, sit with me,' repeats Rachna. Her hair smells of lemon, her hands are tiny and pretty, her eyes are lined with kohl—I allow myself to be seduced. We open a *Sportstar* and have our first proper conversation. 'Why did you have to pass a card? Couldn't you have just said it . . . like with your mouth?'

'If you don't like my card you are most welcome to return it.'

There is a pause in the conversation. She decides to overlook my offer. 'I heard Anand Mishra came to school yesterday,' she giggles. I look up from the *Sportstar*, an expression of surprise on my face. 'What did he say?' I don't reply. 'If you want I will have a word with him,' she offers, and then, without waiting for a reply, she decides the matter for me, 'In fact, I *will* have a word with him. He won't touch you. You don't worry. Call me in the evening.' I dig out the school diary from my bag and write down her number. The bell goes. While we are walking out, Rachna turns to me and says, 'That card. You know what? You bought it from my shop. The stock came in from Delhi on Saturday. I put it on the display rack on Monday morning.'

The librarian is staring at us. She's got a squarish face and an oily nose. One can sense her mind is in turmoil. She feels the world is coming to a premature and violent end. Her gaze latches on to our backs like a fish hook, and refuses to let go even when we are back in our dingy and damp classroom.

I graduate to calling Rachna up every evening at five. I have *her* backing. I never graduate to taking her to the 'tila', which is a desolate mound on the outskirts of town, at the very edge of the cantonment, overlooking mustard fields. Serious couples come here, to plot elopement and discover the sense of touch. There is no place for them on the main drag. They exist on the fringes, away from prying eyes.

I call Rachna every day after my accounts tuition. There is no phone at home so I bicycle down to Kohinoor Chemists in Civil Lines. In the age of the PCO, he is one of the last to have a black, one-rupee slot phone. Drop a one-rupee coin and talk for as long as you like. I usually talk for around three-quarters of an hour, then go home. The Babri Masjid has been brought down in Ayodhya. There have been riots across the country. Allahabad is 'tense but under control'. Like my adolescent dick. My parents want me home before sundown.

Anand Mishra was a regular visitor to school but thankfully I was no longer his centre of attention. He had other enemies to rough up, other battles to fight, other girls to chase. I never asked Rachna about what she'd told him but it certainly had its desired effect. Each time he bumped into me he would insist on a brotherly hug. He would pat me on the back forcefully and offer me his backing: 'Hero, go after any girl in Allahabad, *madar chod koi bhi ladki ho*, I will make sure no one touches you. *Aa jaye koi bhi mai ka lal, uski bahin ke bur mein . . .* You really like Rachna, don't you? Just remember one thing: she's a fucking fireball.'

Once he took me home with him. He and his cronies were watching porn films on video. Black man, white woman, grainy print. After an hour, Mishra seemed to tire of the incessant fucking. '*Abey bas kar, Kaloo, kitna chodega?*' he laughed, switching off the VCR. He said he wanted me to see a bit of his favourite film, a football saga called *Hip Hip Hurray*. Everyone in school had seen it and so had I. It had run to packed houses at Plaza. I had completely forgotten the scene he showed me. Raj Kiran is a teacher, freshly arrived in a small-town college. Some student goons felt that he is getting too fresh too quick with another teacher who is extremely beautiful, and whom they all secretly adore. One night one of the students knocks on his door and delivers a threat: 'Teacher, *yeh Bambai nahi hain, yahaan laundiyabaji nahin chalegi.*' This, Mishra told me, was one of the best scenes in the film. Explaining himself, he said, 'Delivering threats is an art. Your eyes, your tone of voice, your body language, everything has to be just right. One wrong step and the other person will dismiss you as a cunt. And in life, brother, you cannot afford to be called a cunt. Everyone, yes, everyone in Allahabad knows who I am and respects me. No motherfucker dare touch me. There's a reason for this.'

When I was about to leave, Mishra asked me if I could help him out with something. 'How can I ever be of any help to you?' I joked nervously. 'There is this girl,' he said, 'and I want to make her a proposal. I've got this card. You know how these St Mary's girls are: all these English types. I want you to take this card and write some nice poetries in it in your own handwriting. I'll be coming to school tomorrow. That Kamlesh fellow has grown too big for his boots. The bastard was staring me yesterday. No one holds my gaze. Ever. I'll pick up the card from you, then sort him out.'

One year down the line Mishra disappeared. Rumour was that he was in love with a Muslim girl. Both the families were united in their mission: find their wards and murder them. Mishra and his lover, everyone said, had gone underground in Nepal.

Nazneen Khan, who was said to be related to Salman Khan, the film star, was friends with Sameera, the girl who had eloped. One evening, over a vanilla milkshake at Hotstuff, she told me that she had heard from Sameera. The two were in Calcutta but they wouldn't be there for long. They were on the run. Both sets of parents were serious about killing their children. There were rumours in Allahabad that the girl was pregnant and had had an abortion. Nazneen was disconcertingly deadpan and non-judgemental about the whole affair. The couple was doing what they had to do; the parents were doing what they were supposed to do. At the end of the day it was a private matter.

The day after our conversation the vice-principal had a quiet word with Nazneen. 'You have been seen in town, sitting in restaurants, talking to boys. The reputation of the school is at stake. Just don't, OK?'

I was next in line. Jha, the vice-princi, grabbed hold of my tie—which hung loose around my neck in accepted senior-school style—and slid the knot up rather vigorously. 'And you,' he muttered, 'you better concentrate on your studies. OK?'

'OK.'

Almost a year had passed since the Rachna–Archies card–Mishra incident. This was my final year at school. Exactly nine months to the farewell and then I was out of here.

Relationships in Allahabad seldom went beyond phone conversations. I had had my fill of these as far as Rachna was concerned. Things could only go further if your family owned a motor spare parts shop and a Maruti 800. We owned neither. Rachna knew several such characters and had been seen in Jhusi, in an air-conditioned Maruti parked on the banks of the Ganges.

I myself was now besotted with a girl called Divya who had joined school in Class 11. She had silky black hair, which she wore short, and sad brown eyes like a cocker spaniel's. Her face was dotted with pimples. She was a committed NCC cadet. Her walk was a fetching combination of army erectness and girlie bum-swaying. After an afternoon of disciplined marching, she would walk back to the cycle stand, her face the colour of a tomato, the epaulettes on her khaki shirt hanging loose.

This year my backing came from two sources: Nazneen Khan and Karan. Nazneen had invested in six garish rakhis on Raksha Bandhan. She had strategically tied these on the wrists of six school louts who had been making passes at her. Now they were her protectors. And, by proxy, they became my protectors too.

I had also decided to strike out on my own. At a Bollywood-style dance competition called Anubhav '93, organized at the Sangeet Samiti, I met Karan. I was wearing a big, fat gangsta pendant round my neck. I wore it outside my T-shirt, where it hung at around navel-level, glinting proudly in the sun. This caught Karan's eye. He walked over to me and introduced himself. He said he liked my style.

I watched the dance competition sitting with Karan's gang. He was having a squabble with his girlfriend so we didn't get a chance to talk much that afternoon. But each time we met in Civil Lines at Osho's STD booth, he would ask me how things were and if I needed any help.

My self-image had undergone a change in the last year or so. I no longer thought of myself as the self-sufficient introvert who liked doing things on his own. I had realized that if you were in an east UP town, and were mildly ambitious, you certainly needed 'help'. It would be foolish to dismiss the offer. As it turned out, I soon needed help with Divya.

Things were going great with her. She gave me big bar of Cadbury's and a 'best friend' card on my birthday. This was certainly an improvement on Rachna. On the Annual Prize Day in school, we even managed a finger-shake through a slat in the grill. I was standing in the corridor waiting to collect my prizes; she was outside, performing her prefectorial duties: getting the junior prizewinners to stand straight and still. I could not call at her place because, as she told me, her brother had just eloped with a girl and her parents were very upset. If they found out now that a boy was calling their home and asking for her, they might not survive the double shock. My parents still did not have a phone, so I made an arrangement with my classmates, Ravi and Rishi Gupta. They were twins and lived in a neighbourhood not too far from ours.

I would go to their place under the pretext of doing 'joint studies'. We would keep the cordless with us. Divya would call twice; the first time she would let the phone ring a couple of times, then cut the line. The second call would follow exactly a minute later. We never let it go beyond the first ring because Mrs Gupta was a light sleeper and an instinctive slapper. During our conversations, Divya never ceased to remind me of my 'class-topper' status. 'You always do well in exams,' she would say good-naturedly, 'you should concentrate on your books, building a career.'

Divya and I had a friend in common: Sankalp. Sankalp and I were together in middle school. Then he flunked, and kept flunking. But we had been good friends. Our school did not have organized games in the recess, but that didn't mean we did not have team sports. It was a big school; every boy worth his salt was part of a team. There was nothing official about it. Your ability to put a team together and find teams to play with depended on your initiative, persuasive skills and charisma. I had a team of my own: the Allahabad Wings. Our sport was soccer and Sankalp our star goalie. Instead of a proper soccer ball we played with a cricket-sized one made of cork. We played wearing our regular Naughty Boy shoes; needless to say, tackles could be very painful.

It turned out that Divya and Sankalp lived in the same neighbourhood. She had been coaching him every single day and under her tutelage Sankalp had been making progress. He had also fallen for her.

One rainy afternoon after school I found myself surrounded yet again. There was a black Kawasaki Bajaj, a red Ind Suzuki and a silver-grey Hero Honda. The guy on the KB delivered the message: '*Sankalp ka dil Divya par aa gaya hai. Baki to tum jaante hi ho.*' ('Sankalp has got his heart set on Divya; as for the rest, we don't need to elaborate. You know very well how it goes . . .')

I nodded my head but was non-committal. They suggested I nip it in the bud and they promised to return next week. In the evening I went to Osho STD looking for Karan. I hadn't seen him for almost a fortnight now. There was no one at the STD except for Osho, the owner. 'Haven't you heard?' he said, 'Karan's left arm was blown off in a crude bomb attack. Vicky Wadhwa's men. His parents have taken him to Delhi.'

The next morning, before classes for the day had begun, Divya walked up to me and called the whole thing off. 'I won't be able to speak to you any more. Do not try and call me, don't expect any calls from me. In school you will pretend that I don't exist. Goodbye.'

After this incident I was heartbroken. I vowed never to fall in love. I also became a professional go-between. My standard charge was two Pepsis for every card passed. The Pepsis had to be paid for in advance.

This was a market just waiting to be tapped. Allahabad was full of schoolboys who had the requisite backing but possessed neither the courage nor the language skills to get their message across. At Flynn's Coaching Centre I would take on the responsibility—and risk—of passing on other people's cards. The boys would hide behind a bush while I stopped Luna after Luna: 'Aseem has sent this for you. Please accept this. He's a really nice boy.' The message I took back to the boys, nine times out of ten, was: 'I am not that kind of girl. I am not interested in such activities. Will you please stop blocking my way?' I did this with a certain cold-bloodedness. The heartache wasn't mine, and, besides, I had already been paid in calories.

Twelve years later I bump into Gaurav Arora outside El Chico restaurant. He has put on weight, has an air of prosperity. The jock has become a full-fledged businessman. He tells me about his recent Goa trip: *Kya sex ladkiya thi bhai saab.* As for Allahabad, what can he say? It's a village.

It's not so bad, I say, consoling him. Civil Lines has changed. There is a lot more neon, and a lot more street children. I point out the new Sony showroom, the broadband Internet cafes, the restaurant that serves passable Italian food. 'Sure,' he says, 'You're right. It's not that things haven't changed. The spaghetti at that Italian place is not bad.'

He asks me if I am married.

'No.'

'Hey, you know what happened to that *chinar* you were in love with, that Rachna chick? She went to Delhi and settled there. We rarely saw her here. Then, last month, I saw this black and white photograph in a Hindi magazine. The caption read: Six call girls arrested in Delhi. Although the girls were covering their faces with their hands, I could make out that one of them was Rachna. I swear it was Rachna. I am an Allahabadi: I can recognize one when I see one.'

'But if they were covering their faces, you really can't be sure it was her, can you?'

'Sure? What are you talking about yaar, all whores, bhaiya, A-1 whores, take it from me. Everyone knows.'

Arora's cellphone went off somewhere on his body. He dug out a fancy Sony-Ericksson handset.

'Hi, Namrata,' he whispered in English, 'I am with a friend, I'll just call you back.'

'I am getting married next month, Lucknow girl, my bua's choice,' he informs me stuffing the phone back into his front pocket. 'Just enjoying my courtship period.'

Permissions Acknowledgements

Grateful acknowledgement is made to the following for permission to reprint previously published material:

Matilda Spry: 'Our pretty bungalow is now a heap of ruins' by Matilda Spry, copyright © 2006 by Peter Hume-Spry. Reprinted by permission of Peter Hume-Spry.

David Lelyveld: 'Swaraj Bhavan and Sir Sayyid Ahmad Khan' by David Lelyveld from *The Little Magazine*, Vol. IV, no. 4, copyright © 2003 *The Little Magazine*. Reprinted by permission of *The Little Magazine*.

Jawaharlal Nehru: Excerpt from *An Autobiography* by Jawaharlal Nehru, copyright © 2004 by Sonia Gandhi. Reprinted by permission of Penguin Books India, New Delhi.

Harivansh Rai Bachchan: Excerpt from *In the Afternoon of Time* by Harivansh Rai Bachchan, copyright © 1998 by Harivansh Rai Bachchan. Reprinted by permission of Penguin Books India, New Delhi.

Narmadeshwar Upadhyaya: Excerpt from 'Snippets from Memory' by Narmadeshwar Upadhyaya, copyright © 2006 by Govind Saran Upadhyaya. Reprinted by permission of Govind Saran Upadhyaya.

Sudhir Kumar Rudra: Excerpt from 'The Rudra Book' by Sudhir Kumar Rudra, copyright © 2006 by Ritu Rudra. Reprinted by permission of Ritu Rudra.

Rajeshwar Dayal: Excerpt from *A Life of Our Times* by Rajeshwar Dayal, copyright © 1998 by Orient Longman Private Ltd, Hyderabad. Reprinted by permission of Orient Longman Private Ltd.

Nayantara Sahgal: Excerpt from *Prison and Chocolate Cake* by Nayantara Sahgal, copyright © 1954 by Nayantara Sahgal. Reprinted by permission of Nayantara Sahgal.

Kate Chisholm: 'Best Bakery in Town' by Kate Chisholm, copyright © 2005 by Kate Chisholm. Reprinted by permission of Kate Chisholm.

Saeed Jaffrey: Excerpt from *An Actor's Journey* by Saeed Jaffrey, copyright © 1998 by Saeed Jaffrey. Published by Constable and Company Ltd, London.

Esther Mary Lyons: Excerpt from *Unwanted!* and *Bitter Sweet Truth* by Esther Mary Lyons, copyright © 1996 and 2001 by Esther Mary Lyons. Reprinted by permission of Esther Mary Lyons.

Ved Mehta: Excerpt from *Portrait of India* by Ved Mehta, copyright © 1967, 1968, 1969, 1970 by Ved Mehta. Reprinted by permission of Georges Borchardt, Inc., on behalf of the author.

Arvind Krishna Mehrotra: 'Partial Recall' by Arvind Krishna Mehrotra from *Civil Lines* 1, copyright © 1994 by Arvind Krishna Mehrotra. Reprinted by permission of Arvind Krishna Mehrotra. 'The Roys' by Arvind Krishna Mehrotra from *Middle Earth*, copyright © 1984 by Arvind Krishna Mehrotra. Published by Oxford University Press. Reprinted by permission of Arvind Krishna Mehrotra.

Pankaj Mishra: Excerpt from *An End to Suffering* by Pankaj Mishra, copyright © 2004 by Pankaj Mishra. Reprinted by permission of Pankaj Mishra.

Kama Maclean: 'On the Modern Kumbh Mela' by Kama Maclean from *Journal of Asian Studies*, Vol. 62, no. 3, copyright © 2003 Association for Asian Studies. Reprinted by permission of Association for Asian Studies.

Gyanranjan: 'Vagabond Nights' by Gyanranjan, copyright © 2002 by Gyanranjan. Reprinted by permission of Gyanranjan.

I. Allan Sealy: 'Three Gandhis' by I. Allan Sealy, copyright © 2005 by I. Allan Sealy. Reprinted by permission of I. Allan Sealy.

Palash Krishna Mehrotra: 'Sex and the Small Town' by Palash Krishna Mehrotra, copyright © 2005 by Palash Krishna Mehrotra. Reprinted by permission of Palash Krishna Mehrotra.

Every effort has been made to trace the copyright-holders but if any have been inadvertently overlooked the publishers will be pleased to make the necessary arrangement at the first opportunity.